CINEMA
IN
DEMOCRATIZING
GERMANY

CINEMA

IN DEMOCRATIZING GERMANY

RECONSTRUCTING NATIONAL IDENTITY AFTER HITLER

HEIDE FEHRENBACH

The University of North Carolina Press   *Chapel Hill & London*

© 1995 The University of
North Carolina Press
All rights reserved
Manufactured in the United States of America

Library of Congress Cataloging-in-Publication Data
Fehrenbach, Heide.
    Cinema in democratizing Germany : reconstructing national identity after
Hitler / by Heide Fehrenbach.
    p. cm.
    Includes bibliographical references (p. -) and index.
    ISBN 978-0-8078-2204-3 (cloth : alk. paper).—ISBN 978-0-8078-4512-7 (pbk. : alk. paper)
    1. Motion pictures—Political aspects—Germany (West)   2. Motion pictures—
Social aspects—Germany (West)   3. Motion pictures—Germany (West)—History.
I. Title.
PN1993.5.G3F35 1995
791.43'0943'09045—dc20   94-33816
                        CIP

The paper in this book meets the guidelines for permanence and durability of the
Committee on Production Guidelines for Book Longevity of the Council on Library
Resources.

99   98   97   96   95   5   4   3   2   1

Earlier versions of chapters 3, 4, and 5 have appeared in print as *"Die Sünderin* or
Who Killed the German Male?: Early Postwar German Cinema and the Betrayal of
Fatherland," in *Gender and German Cinema: Feminist Interventions*, vol. 2,
German Film History/German History on Film, edited by Sandra Frieden et al.,
135–60 (Providence: Berg, 1993); "The Fight for the 'Christian West': German Film
Control, the Churches, and the Reconstruction of Civil Society in the Early Bonn
Republic," *German Studies Review* 14, no. 1 (February 1991): 39–63; and "Cinema,
Spectatorship, and the Problem of Postwar German Identity," in *The American
Impact on Postwar Germany*, edited by Reiner Pommerin, 165–95 (Providence:
Berghahn Books, 1994).

THIS BOOK WAS DIGITALLY PRINTED.

For my parents,

Gladys Lucia Fehrenbach

and

Herbert Frank Fehrenbach

CONTENTS

ILLUSTRATIONS

ACKNOWLEDGMENTS

I have benefited from the support of many individuals and institutions over the course of this project and am delighted to have reached the point where I can at last thank them in print. The late Harold Poor won me over to the study of modern German history during my undergraduate years with his captivating lectures on the subject; I am grateful for his crucial early influence, wisdom, and support throughout graduate school. Victoria de Grazia first stimulated my interest in the cultural dimensions of Americanization and continues to be both an intellectual inspiration and an invaluable critic. I am also indebted to Robert Moeller, who patiently waded through various drafts of this project and, in a spirit of generosity and good humor, doled out astute insights, helpful criticisms, and large doses of encouragement. My thanks also go to Volker Berghahn and Omer Bartov for raising thought-provoking questions in response to individual chapters; to John Gillis and Miriam Hansen for providing careful readings and helpful comments in the early stages of this project; and to Paul Clemens and Ursula Hardt.

This book would not have been possible without the generous financial assistance of various institutions. A grant from the German Academic Exchange Service in 1987 facilitated my early research in German archives, and fellowships from the Rutgers University Graduate School and the Rutgers Center for the Critical Analysis of Contemporary Culture provided crucial financial and intellectual support. I am grateful to the Colgate University Research Council for a major grant in 1992–93, which allowed me to return to Germany to complete research for the book, and for a second grant in 1993–94, which enabled me to enlist the aid of David Cappillo, who deserves my thanks as a diligent research assistant.

Numerous archivists and librarians have extended indispensable assistance in Germany and the United States. I would like to thank Herr Rüdiger Koschnitzski at the Deutsches Institut für Filmkunde in Frankfurt, Herr Peter Latta at the Stiftung Deutsche Kinemathek in Berlin, Herr Dr. Saupe at the Bayerisches Hauptstaatsarchiv in Munich, Herr Volker Viergut at the Landesarchiv Berlin, Herr Fischer at the Landesbildstelle Berlin, Herr Teutsch at the Stadtarchiv in Mannheim, Herr Hecker at the Stadtarchiv in Munich, Ned Comstock at the Cinema Library of the University of Southern California, Los Angeles, and the research staff at the National Archives in Suitland, Maryland, for their patient responses to my inquiries.

My thanks to John Pommer for generously allowing me access to the personal papers of his father, Erich Pommer, and to both John and Heidi Pommer for welcoming me into their home and sharing their reminiscences about post-war Germany and exiled Germans in Hollywood. Enno Patalas and Fee Vaillant consented to be interviewed about their contributions to the German film club movement in the 1950s and supplied important insights that could not be culled from archival or published sources. I owe a debt of gratitude to Eric Rentschler for offering helpful suggestions, access to his personal film archive, and hospitality in both Berlin and Irvine; and to Richard McCormick for relieving my desperation by graciously sharing his German films on video. At the University of North Carolina Press, I would like to thank Lewis Bateman for his early and ongoing interest in my project, managing editor Ron Maner, and my editor, Paula Wald, for her good judgment and meticulous attention to text and detail.

On a more personal level, I'd like to express my heartfelt thanks to Bob Mensel and Jennifer Ham for their valued friendship and wise input; to my sister, Lori Fehrenbach, for a timely rescue in Berlin; and to Joseph Rotola and my family for patiently supporting me in a myriad of ways during the long life of this project. Finally, special thanks to David Buller for his editorial suggestions and companionship over the past two and a half years.

ABBREVIATIONS

The following abbreviations are used throughout this work. Additional abbreviations used only in the notes are listed at the beginning of the notes section.

BUFA	Bild- und Filmamt
CDU	Christlich-Demokratische Union
CSU	Christlich-Soziale Union
DEFA	Deutsche Film Aktiengesellschaft
DEGETO	Deutsche Gesellschaft für Ton und Bild
EKD	Evangelische Kirche in Deutschland
FBS	Filmbewertungsstelle der Länder
FBW	Filmbewertungsstelle Wiesbaden
FIAPF	Fédération Internationale des Associations de Producteurs de Films
FKB	Filmkreditbank
FSK	Freiwillige Selbstkontrolle der Filmwirtschaft
HICOG	Office of the U.S. High Commissioner for Germany
ICD	Information Control Division (later Information Services Division [ISD])
IMG	Informational Media Guaranty Program
JCS	Joint Chiefs of Staff
MPAA	Motion Picture Association of America
MPB	Motion Picture Branch (of the ICD/ISD)
MPEA	Motion Picture Export Association of America
OMGUS	Office of the Military Government for Germany, United States
OWI	Office of War Information
PWD	Psychological Warfare Division
SPD	Sozialdemokratische Partei Deutschlands
SPIO	Spitzenorganisation der Filmwirtschaft
UFA	Universum-Film-Aktiengesellschaft
UFI	Ufa-Film GmbH

CINEMA
IN
DEMOCRATIZING
GERMANY

INTRODUCTION
CINEMA AND
NATIONAL IDENTITY,
1945–1962

Entertainment offers the image of "something better" to escape into, . . . something we want deeply that our day-to-day lives don't provide.—Richard Dyer, "Entertainment and Utopia"

On 9 May 1945, the day of unconditional surrender, few in Germany were preoccupied with thoughts of cinema. By all accounts, most Germans were intent on one thing, *das Überleben*, or mere survival, and Allied armies were grappling to impose a victor's order on the wartime chaos. Over a dozen major cities had been badly damaged: the former Reich capital—which U.S. general Lucius Clay declared "the city of the dead"—had 75 percent of its buildings destroyed, Düsseldorf was more than 90 percent uninhabitable, and a British observer was trying to ascertain just how many "catacomb people" were living in the underground labyrinths below the rubble of what had been Cologne. The Allies needed to establish order, locate and arrest Nazi officials, contain the spread of disease, insure public hygiene, and organize the basic requirements of life for the conquered population and its newly liberated victims. There were serious shortages of housing, clothing, food, and soap; cities were without water, gas, or electricity; transportation and communication lines were damaged or destroyed; roads were impassible; and mountains of rubble had to be cleared. Moreover, the Allies were faced with the historically unprecedented dislocation and migration of millions. Forced laborers, concentration and death-camp prisoners, and prisoners of war had to be fed, housed, provided medical treatment, and, in some cases, repatriated. Over the course of the next year, nearly 10 million refugees entering from the eastern reaches of the former Reich needed to be absorbed and integrated. Day-to-day life remained precarious through 1948, when deaths from malnutrition, disease, and exposure to the cold finally fell off. Until then, survival depended on a combination of stamina, skill, and resourcefulness, as official rations (only 800 calories per day in the fall of 1945) were supplemented by black market bartering, gardening, scavenging, and pilfering.[1]

Organized cultural life had been suspended in the last weeks of the war. Theaters and cinemas were closed; film collections had been scattered in the days before defeat or seized by Allied soldiers. Within two months, however, regular screenings of films began. Germans lined up to pay their worthless Reichmarks for a couple of hours of entertainment and, by autumn, the comfort of a heated hall. Even after residential utilities were reconnected, viewers kept coming; by the early 1950s, postwar West Germany boasted more cinemas and higher attendance rates than the prewar Third Reich.

Not everyone considered this grounds for celebration, however. As cinema rapidly reemerged as an object of fascination in early postwar West Germany, it also became a focus of heightened social and cultural concern. Since the first decade of the twentieth century, cinema had startled observers by its unmatched power to draw unprecedented numbers of people into darkened public theaters and its fictional world. The experience appeared to be at once communal and individual, for it welded "an audience" out of socially diverse human throngs by operating in a complex manner on individual perceptions and desires. Surely, but inexplicably, viewers seemed forged into a unified whole, temporarily joined by similar emotional reactions to the projections on the screen. What so astonished observers was cinema's apparently overwhelming influence on the viewer's psyche—especially as suspicions grew that illusions of lightplay could condition both social behavior and perception.

From its inception, German cinema was embedded in the politics of culture and identity. Initially marketed as lower-class entertainment, cinema drew the attention and ire of groups interested in the regulation and moral elevation of the unruly working classes, be they political conservatives, bourgeois reformers, or socialist leaders seeking to lead their pupils to disciplined self-emancipation. Thus, criticisms of the medium were always also criticisms of the social and cultural impact of economic modernization, industrialization, and urbanization. Cinematic control was a form of social control: cultural reform was expected to counteract the undisciplined immorality of the working classes and their leisure pursuits. As the medium increasingly attracted women and youth as avid film consumers, film control expanded beyond class considerations to embrace issues of gender and generation.

Cinema, moreover, provoked heightened cultural anxiety once its popularity began to extend up the social ladder. The very fact of a "mass" entertainment that both transgressed class lines and displayed artistic ambitions threatened the undisputed superiority of a lofty "high" culture based upon the self-proclaimed taste and cultivation of a social elite. Commercialized culture disrupted the hierarchy of class-cultural forms in Germany and undermined the distinctions of the high-low cultural divide. Its opponents fought back by proclaiming its consumers a herd of undiscerning philistines, a response that would color discussions of cinema as a mass medium throughout the century but would do nothing to dampen its appeal.

Cinema also attracted state intervention. On the eve of World War I, government and military leaders became alarmed that their domestic market was dominated by foreign film products—not because of economic or even cultural considerations but because of the potentially pejorative political impact of such an imbalance. Recognizing the popularity of moving pictures, these officials were determined to assure public support for state policy by marshaling the medium's potency for political persuasion. Thus, political sovereignty was linked to cultural sovereignty. Cinema became the premier cultural tool to achieve both, precisely because of its transclass, transgender, and transnational appeal. Due to its ready marketability and exportability, cinematic culture was enlisted as a helpmate to further the interests of the state.

Despite its merits for fostering citizen loyalty and national identity, cinema never became a mere political pawn of the state. Throughout the twentieth century, cinema has also remained a commercial enterprise, run by profit-oriented businesspeople interested in enhancing and expanding the audience appeal of their products. To do so, they have played to the public's erotic and consumer fantasies and through camera, editing, and narrational strategies, have encouraged viewer identification with leading performers. By the 1920s, contemporaries commented on the trend among young urbanites to mimic their favorite film star's manner of dress, behavior, or bearing; and those with a nose for business shrewdly developed and expanded a related consumer market for magazines, fashion, and beauty by playing (in particular) on women's fascination with film. These ventures to expand the commercial potential of the market were so successful that many thought they altered social reality by creating a uniquely modern and liberated female type, which they dubbed, appropriately enough, the "new woman."[2]

More rattling, however, was the application of marketing practices and mass cultural techniques to politics. This was the exclusive domain of neither the political right nor left, but the fascists of Central Europe seemed to have had a special knack for it. Hitler spent his months in Landsberg prison ruminating about the best ways to influence and control "the masses." His formula was based upon such a low opinion of the anonymous public that he would have done the most elite intellectual snob proud. "The receptive powers of the masses," he claimed, "are very restricted, and their understanding is feeble."[3] The technique that was expected to work, then, was something akin to a toothpaste commercial: a barrage of simple messages drawn from a morally Manichaean *Weltanschauung*, incessant repetition, and the promise of an improved social status if you bought the product. The deadly difference was that in this case the product was only available to those deemed racially superior.

If Hitler's opinion of the susceptible nature of "the masses" was carried over into the immediate postwar period—by occupation officials, educators, and German political and religious elites—it was probably the result of a longer intellectual tradition (reaching back to the late nineteenth century) of elite disdain for the industrial masses and mass behavior that was confined neither to Germany nor to the political right. Even members of the intellectual left shared a similar conceit. By the 1920s, they theorized a process by which authentic (popular) urban entertainments were expropriated by profit-oriented businesspeople and transformed into leisure-time "distractions" offering vicarious—rather than material—compensations and masking the "real" power relations of capitalist society. Like critics to the right of the political spectrum, these commentators assumed the psychological susceptibility of the working classes. They feared that love of leisure lured them away from radical politics and revolution and made them willing participants in their own oppression. For cultural critics associated with the Institute for Social Research in Frankfurt (the so-called Frankfurt School), mass culture—and cinema in particular—became an important prop for a strikingly resilient capitalism-in-crisis.

Although the leftist slant of this analysis was rejected by most, by the post–World War II period alarmed contemporaries increasingly focused on the psychosocial role of film and its putative effect on impressionable German masses, who had now only recently been released from the totalitarian grasp of Hitler and Goebbels—those self-proclaimed masters of mass persuasion. The commitment of Western Allies to reeducating Germans to Western-style democracy raised questions about the psychological state of their pupils. Initially, the American occupiers operated with a similar low opinion of the critical faculties of the German public and dismissed signs of resistance to reeducation programs as evidence of the Nazis' success at shaping their subjects' psyches.

Recent studies, however, have called into question the effectiveness of Nazi propaganda and suggested that resistance and argument during the occupation did not necessarily indicate loyalty to Nazi precepts—or nostalgia for the Third Reich. German reconstruction was not, after all, an easy or uncontested process, nor was it confined to the political sphere. Political liberalization was, indeed, the focus of the Western Allies; and German elites also exhibited a tendency to think of democratization strictly in political terms and as a necessary, though foreign, imposition. But although they understood the need to dismantle the authoritarian political structures erected under Hitler, they exhibited a marked ambivalence regarding the reformulation of other areas of public life within a new, liberal context.

Some of the most fervent clashes over postwar reconstruction occurred in the putatively "apolitical" realm of culture—where politics could run rampant precisely because hard-nosed economists and political scientists considered it a tertiary sphere. In an atmosphere of often acrid and bitter debate, cinematic representation attracted attention as a powerful participant in ideology construction and dissemination.

I was drawn to investigate West German reconstruction through the cultural lens of cinema precisely because of its highly politicized status in the postwar period. After Hitler, as after German defeat in 1918, the social role of cinema again became the center of a vortex of public debate. In both postwar periods, contemporaries scrutinized cinema's potential as mass persuasion, mass entertainment, and commercial practice with an eye toward exploiting or controlling its impact. With the opening of the German market to foreign—and especially American—films and capital in the 1920s, cinema also came to be defined as a constituent part of national culture and identity, of Germany's integrity as a nation.

After 1945, national identity reemerged as the definitive problem for Germany's military occupiers and native elites alike. This time around, the focus was on national and cultural *redefinition*: on creating a new political and cultural heritage untainted by associations with the Nazi past. In the aftermath of a war whose weaponry was as much psychological as technological, cinematic representation, reorganization, and control constituted a crucial cultural component of both the victors' postwar plans to denazify and democratize Germany *and* German elites' attempts to construct a new, uniquely "German" identity cleansed of fascist traces.

Initially, of course, this process was dominated by the ideologically grounded visions supplied by the American and Soviet occupiers, who paid special attention to the mass media in their denazification and reeducation efforts. By 1948, American styles of organization triumphed in the Western zones, while the Soviets countered with their state-managed alternative in the East. These became the reigning foreign models of organization projected for the reconstruction of German society.

Although many Germans resisted adopting one or another of these models wholesale, they were initially forced to work within the confines of such policies. Within two years of defeat, however, German civilians in the Western zones were increasingly resuming administrative responsibilities due to strains in the budgets of the occupation powers and the developing Cold War. West German elites fiercely rejected the socialist alternative presented by the Soviets in the East, but they also harbored little affection for the American liberal democratic model. Eschewing both as foreign intrusions into domestic affairs, German conservatives pushed for a "third way," based on native forms of organization developed during the Weimar Republic, which favored state and church influence in social and cultural matters. The passionate and unrelenting nature of their quest revealed the fact that these elites considered the regulation of culture to be crucial to the reestablishment of a healthy, stable German nation. In effect, native elites recast the dilemma of German reconstruction in cultural terms and implicitly focused on the question of national identity: what it would mean to be "German" after national socialism. Given the fact of military occupation, territorial division, and the radically altered political geography of the Cold War world, this quest to define an "acceptable" postfascist identity went hand-in-hand with the larger project of native elites to reestablish national integrity (both territorial and cultural) and political sovereignty.

In rehabilitating Germans as historical agents in the reconstruction of their own identity, this study is intended as a partial corrective to scenarios alleging the uncontested "Americanization" of the culture and consciousness of postwar Germans. Specifically, I focus on the various ways that postwar Germans articulated national identity in relation to three issues: the challenges of occupation policy and open markets, particularly the reintroduction of American consumer culture; native debates over the content of a democratic German culture and the agents of its control; and the redefinition of social (and gender) identities and the role cinematic representation and film spectatorship were assumed to play in this process.

By setting the study of postwar German film culture within this broader historical problematic, this project questions the conventional characterization of the late 1940s and 1950s as a period in which American commercial forms were quietly instituted and investigates the extent to which Germans adopted, adapted, or rejected American forms of organization—and the meanings they attributed to them. It also provides a manageable context within which to explore the degree of resistance of interest groups and institutions who fought to reinstate "historical rights" denied them under Hitler and within which to assess the complex role historical memory—and forgetfulness—has played in the reconstruction of national identity and German public life.

After 1945, cultural integrity struck many Germans as a crucial prerequisite for regaining national sovereignty. Autonomy appeared all the more pressing as foreign occupation, political liberalization, and American insistence on abolishing state regulation of the economy opened the German market to international products and influences. Hollywood film companies, in particular, eagerly sought to establish a strong foothold in the unrestricted German market. This they accomplished with the initial support of American occupation officials, who expected American films to instill democratic values in the German population and counteract the powerful impact of the Nazi media machine.

The Hollywood rush into the German market was perceived by native elites as an economic, as well as cultural, challenge. In the prewar years, the film industry was the fourth largest industry in Germany. Commanding a substantial economic and cultural presence on the world market, the German film industry represented Hollywood's only serious competitor. After 1945, German film industry members, recently purged of their Nazi pasts, suspected that American film interests would monopolize the domestic and international markets, given official American insistence on decartelization, unrestricted markets, and free competition. They feared extinction.

Social conservatives, on the other hand, feared the cultural effects of an open market. Early in the occupation period, local state and church leaders began to indicate their nervousness—and often antagonism—concerning the free market orientation of American policy. When American occupation policies reintroduced foreign-style mass culture to West Germany, conservatives in church and state denounced it as a grave threat to the cultural integrity of the German nation. The United States was condemned as the producer of Wild West and gangster films, the insidious propagator of a secularized commercial culture that addressed itself directly to the viewer, bypassing the mediation of traditional cultural and religious elites. The offending products need not even issue from Hollywood. German filmmakers and their wares were attacked with equal vehemence if they seemed too cosmopolitan.

Given their strong desire to encourage "normalized" gender and family relations after the disruptions of the war, these cultural critics also denounced the anticipated social ramifications of unconstrained cultural exchange. In response to the new Cold War paradigm, they constructed the notion of a "moral nation" based upon the patriarchal family as a counterweight to the influence of both American-style mass culture, which operated through the market, and the cultural seepage from the despised "godless" socialist system to the east. After 1945, the threat was no longer identified as issuing from ethnic or religious groups alien to a racially superior *Volksgemeinschaft*, as during the Third Reich. Rather, it appeared in a form more difficult to control: the unmediated influence of cultural products that touted the merits of secular materialism—whether consumerist or communist in nature. The issue at stake for German state and religious leaders was who would exercise cultural sovereignty within Germany's borders, who would define the nature of the new German nation.

Conservative interference in film matters inhibited the recovery of the German film industry by influencing the look and content of its products, adversely affecting its ability to market them abroad. Church and state leaders were more concerned with controlling the social and cultural effects of cosmopolitan products than with resurrecting a viable industry. Yet the industry eventually complied with moral regulation for a number of reasons. The most significant was industry members' decision to again appeal to the state for funding to bolster their weakened position, as they had during critical periods in the late 1920s and

A scene from Helmut Käutner's controversial film parody of the Adam and Eve story, *Der Apfel ist ab* (1948), which chronicles Adam's postwar "rebirth." Before the apple is plucked, Adam and Eve amuse themselves with an American CARE package. (Courtesy of the Deutsches Institut für Filmkunde, Frankfurt)

mid-1930s. In return, the industry "coordinated" its products to reflect (or at least not transgress) Christian Democratic values.

The moviegoing public, however, was not as easily intimidated by the authoritarian posturing of state and church leaders. Attempts by these groups to regulate film production and exhibition provoked substantial local resistance. Angry citizens, who had not forgotten the lessons of the recent German past, compared the actions of these new elites to those of their Nazi precursors and demanded the full range of rights accorded them in the new democracy. This meant not only freedom of speech but also freedom of choice and access to international culture, which had been denied them under Hitler.

While demanding consumer freedoms, the German filmgoing public nonetheless avidly consumed the domestic fare provided them by native filmmakers. In what appears to be an ironic twist, the most successful film genre of the early postwar period became the critically disdained West German *Heimatfilm*, which seemed to relegate the viewer to the cultural provinces. But while *Heimatfilme* drew upon popular interwar genres—such as the musical revue, the operetta, and the comedy—it reassured postwar viewers by releasing them from a problematic past and orienting them to an optimistic future. Far from marking a simple reversion to Nazi filmmaking, the postwar *Heimatfilm* was very much a product of the early postwar period and, for a while at least, gave Hollywood products a run for their money.

Not everyone, however, was enamored of *Heimatfilme*. Educators, cinephiles, and film critics with higher artistic aspirations busied themselves with attempts to stimulate a cultural renewal in Germany by educating the filmgoing "masses." They paid no attention to the putative social dangers of the medium identified by conservative officials, nor did they address the ideological role of film in German society—a curious omission in the aftermath of national socialism. Instead, they founded film clubs in the late 1940s, based upon French precedents, and concentrated on fostering an appreciation among the German public for aesthetically sophisticated products. Most of the films screened in the clubs were of European origin: the products of French or Italian art cinema or expressionist films from Weimar Germany. Heralded as "quality" cinematic culture, such films were implicitly contrasted to the standardized commercial products of Hollywood and the output of their native West German industry, as well as the tainted issues of Goebbels's Film Chamber. Club leaders attempted to build a nation of film aesthetes, nurtured on the European traditions of filmmaking. By winning the mass of film viewers to their side, they hoped to pressure the domestic film industry to create a more responsible and polished product, attractive for foreign export. The new film type, then, was to project a new cultural identity for Germany. Admired cinematic products would enable Germany to reenter the international order as a proud but peaceable *Kulturnation*. In this scenario, the insidious *völkisch* elements of Nazi culture would be eradicated by means of a civilized cosmopolitan style.

This approach was challenged by the emergence of a small but vocal contingent of left-leaning students in the film club movement who began to denounce their club leaders' studied apolitical approach to film by the mid-1950s. These young radicals were the first organized group to clamor publicly for a clean break with the German cultural past. Pointing to continuities in film personnel, film style, genres, and ideology from the Nazi era, these "angry young men" demanded a thorough housecleaning. They maintained that political democratization was incomplete without cultural renewal. Their vision of cultural renewal, however, necessitated a dispassionate investigation of "authoritarian" elements in postwar West German films. Informed by the writings of Siegfried Kracauer, Walter Benjamin, and Theodor Adorno, they argued that ideology and culture were inextricably linked. Genuine democratic cultural renewal, therefore, would result only when old filmmaking forms were discarded.

Some educators and local German officials, on the other hand, looked precisely to old German filmmaking forms to counter the increasing influence of the Hollywood-style product that was beginning to dominate German theaters. The mayor of Mannheim, for example, attempted to resurrect and revitalize the old German interwar specialty, the *Kulturfilm*, in the early 1950s in order to spark a cultural renaissance. In this case, renewal was linked to German economic and cultural might, since this genre represented a significant German export during the 1920s and early 1930s.

Cultural renewal, when it finally came, issued from the cultural politics of the left and the efforts of young independent filmmakers outside of the dominant industry structure. These independents studied the creative impulses of both Eastern and Western European films and transformed the nationalist *Kulturfilm* into short documentaries informed by political or social consciousness. The result was an avant-garde alternative, "Young German Cinema," which occupied the narrow sector of the film market devoted to art cinema. Young German Cinema succeeded in reviving international interest in German cultural production but ultimately failed to break the spell that Hollywood-style products cast on the broad public. These young independent filmmakers eventually received financial support from the state and came to represent "New German Culture" abroad at film festivals and art cinemas. Yet on the domestic market, its appeal was limited to cinema aficionados; it had little perceptible effect on the film-viewing habits of the average moviegoer.

The popular appeal of American-style cinematic culture was, in fact, expertly exploited by West German officials for purposes of Cold War politicking throughout the 1950s. The best-known German festival of the decade was founded in 1951 in the geopolitically sensitive Berlin, where images of plenty and popular film stars were used to sell the Western way of life (as well as the Federal Republic's political sovereignty and economic superiority) to German compatriots in the East. Clearly, the Christian Democrats in Bonn were not averse to employing the popularity of American-style culture to make a political point among "peripheral" German populations. What emerges from this investigation of the film festivals, the film clubs, and their dissenting minority, then, is a surprisingly complex picture of the political uses of film culture in early postwar West Germany.

My approach to this study has been self-consciously interdisciplinary and is indebted to recent developments in the fields of cultural and social history, cultural studies, and film studies. Since I have been trained as a historian, my decision to incorporate analysis of film texts posed theoretical problems and demanded a foray into the challenging world of film theory as well as a familiarity with current debates concerning cultural representation and gender construction. If it turns out to have been an ill-advised endeavor, it was nonetheless terribly stimulating. As I hope it has become clear, I do not consider my focus on cultural products—in this case, gender-sensitive analysis of film content and reception—a "supplement" to a more traditional discussion of the problems posed by German reconstruction. Cultural and film studies have taught us that culture is not a discrete category, separated from and supplementing the more weighty discussions of politics and economics. Rather, it is inextricably bound up with political, social, and economic debates and forms of organization, and my use of sources and evidence is intended to underscore that vision. This study delineates reconstruction debates along sociocultural lines in an attempt to explore the links between national identity and cultural production, consumption, and control. In the process, I hope it provides a richer picture of what that reconstruction entailed—for both women and men.

1

CINEMA AND GERMAN SOCIETY BEFORE 1945

In the movies
On five continents simultaneously
Is my homeland.
—Claire Goll, poet, 1922
(translated by Sabine Hake)

By the interwar years, filmgoing had become a habit, and sometimes an obsession, for millions in the industrialized West. Contemporary
thinking attributed to cinema the power to shape perception, to somehow render the unreal more "real"—or at least more attractive and compelling—than
lived actuality. In a wonderfully evocative reminiscence of the period, Italo
Calvino recalled that "the cinema, for me, was the world, a different world from
the one that surrounded me, but as far as I was concerned only [that which] I
saw on screen possessed the properties of the world: the fullness, the necessity,
the coherence. Outside of the screen, meanwhile, heterogeneous elements were
shuffling together as if by chance, materials of my life that seemed to be devoid
of form." For Calvino and millions of other moviegoers, cinema offered an
"imaginary" that could compete with experience and win—largely because it
presented an aesthetic unity that appealed to the desire for meaning and order,
particularly in a period of political and social upheaval.[1]

In the first decades of the twentieth century in Germany—at a time when
cinemas were proliferating and film was doing a brisk business attracting mass
audiences—police, educators, clergy, and cultural elites began commenting, in
strong and critical language, on the powerful "immediacy" and impact of the
new medium. Film, they argued, drew the viewer into its fictional world by
barraging the psyche with its visual specificity, photographic realism, and naturalistic locations. One energetic middle-class crusader for film censorship even
warned in 1913 that film's "profound impact upon its viewers would ultimately

12

undermine their sense of reality."[2] The unprecedented popularity of film provoked sustained concern and public debate regarding the psychological, emotional, and moral effects—or *Wirkung*—of movies on viewers. In addition, *Filmwirkung* was assumed to represent a potentially serious challenge to the social order, and many argued that film viewing caused, or at least contributed to, an explosion of crime, asocial behavior, and juvenile delinquency in imperial Germany. All assumed that its technological nature and mass appeal represented a marked departure from earlier forms of popular culture and thus presented new challenges to German society that could not be contained by traditional resort to the local police.[3]

Midway through World War I, a second approach to film developed. Recognizing the massive popularity and cross-class appeal of the medium, the German high command and imperial government attempted to employ film for purposes of "enlightenment and education." By 1917, cinema's potential as a "state-supporting medium" was officially endorsed,[4] and *Filmwirkung* was redeemed as a positive force for social and political integration, a function that was further and most notoriously refined under the National Socialist regime.

State intervention also represented a push for national cultural sovereignty. Until World War I, the German market had been dominated by the film products of other (mostly European) nations. Native productions, in fact, constituted a minuscule number of the total films screened in German cinemas through 1914. No one seemed particularly alarmed by this situation until the outbreak of war, when the imperial government banned enemies' products for reasons of state security. Shortly thereafter, General Erich Ludendorff proposed that the state exploit the propagandistic potential of film as a means to rally domestic support for the war effort. Thus, the state began to buttress domestic cinematic production to gain unimpeded access to the German viewer's psyche. Moreover, official recognition established the fact that cultural sovereignty was a crucial dimension of a nation's political sovereignty.

State interest also highlighted the tension that would develop between cinema as national culture on the one hand and as an object of commerce on the other. Cinema at the time was only the most technologically advanced form of commercialized culture to emerge from Germany's ongoing process of modernization. Large-scale industrialization and urbanization initiated a period of long-term social disruption and political adjustment that extended into the second postwar period. Increased immigration and overall mobility began to alter the traditional ethnic and religious composition of localities, particularly in heavy industry and mining areas like the Ruhr and Berlin; and the repeal of anti-Socialist legislation in 1890 led to an explosion of Socialist Party membership and influence, which the terrorized propertied classes feared would destabilize the political and social system. World War I, the Depression, and the intensive economic rationalization and cartel building of the 1920s and 1930s increased an already pervasive sense of social disruption.

During this period, cinema and film-viewing practices acted as both an agent and indicator of social change. Moreover, the general understanding of cinema's role in German society evolved as well. In the early years of the century, bourgeois society decried cinema as a force of social and cultural destabilization, and aspects of this response persisted throughout the period covered by this study. But film was concurrently embraced, at the highest levels of the German state and military, as a tool of social and political integration. This trend was amplified under Nazi rule, when Propaganda Minister Joseph Goebbels shrewdly supervised the cultivation of heroic and inspiring images of Hitler that, although "for the most part at crass variance with reality," were designed to win legitimacy for the newly installed fascist leader and build consensus for his policies.[5] Hitler entered the political sphere promising to "restore the disrupted 'normality' of life," which had been disturbed by German military defeat, civil war, political factionalism, class tensions, economic restructuring, economic crisis, and cultural modernism. As Detlev Peukert has argued, this was a "utopian normality, to be sure, with a social hierarchy which was somehow 'just' and in which everyone had a niche where he could feel secure and respected: in short, a true 'national community' (*Volksgemeinschaft*) from which all sources of friction and unease had been removed . . . all abnormality, all that could jeopardize the ultimate 'ideal order.' "[6] Goebbels's emphasis on "image" served the function of disguising the gaps between the promises of Nazi ideology and the actualities of life, including the social-psychological dissonances caused by economic and technological modernization in the Third Reich. Thus, although "National Socialism was unable to abolish the reality of industrial society, . . . it did, through propaganda, impede the clear perception of this reality."[7] Given fascist preoccupation with visual self-representation and its reliance on "appearances, histrionics, and simulation," film acquired a critical political role in the Third Reich.[8]

In order to gain a more differentiated understanding of the role of film under national socialism, one must examine the broader historical context of German film reception—both official and popular. The Nazi period did not, after all, represent a complete break with the imperial and republican past but rather continued and intensified trends that had developed earlier in the century.

Cinema's Early Years

By the outbreak of World War I, cultural critics, intellectuals, and educators had dubbed motion pictures the quintessential "mass" medium, precisely because—unlike earlier cultural forms—their appeal and popularity transcended class, gender, and generational divisions. From cinema's inception, its power to attract and fascinate claimed the attention of its mostly middle-class critics. Due to the socioeconomic background of cinema's early customers and milieu and the foreign origins of most of its products, cinematic power appeared threatening and as a result provoked a great deal of anxiety among bourgeois Germans. Indeed, between 1895—when the first films were screened at the Wintergarten, a popular vaudeville theater in Berlin—and the outbreak of World War I, many in the upper and middle classes considered cinema to be a force of social and cultural destabilization.

Film historian Anton Kaes reminds us that the emergence of commercialized mass culture in the late nineteenth century was accompanied by a corresponding shift from the "word" to the "image." This shift occurred slightly earlier in the print media with the popularization of the pictorial "yellow press" but also affected the theater, which revived mime and gestural acting styles (banished for years from the serious stage) under the influence of silent film. Yet unlike the theater, illustrated dailies, American-style dime novels (Groschenhefte), and film became big business and were marketed predominantly to the lower social and economic classes in the first decades of their existence. The serialized adventures of Buffalo Bill and Nick Carter, for example, sold up to 80,000 copies a week among the prewar German reading public. Given the size of that market, filmmakers were quick to appreciate the potential benefits of cross fertilization and freely borrowed the characters and plots of the most popular "trash literature" to translate the appeal of these Westerns and crime stories to the screen.[9]

Once the back rooms of pubs and small, poorly appointed shops were converted into exhibition rooms by enterprising local businesspeople around 1904, film evolved quickly from its early status as a traveling sideshow curiosity—displayed at fairs and circuses in cities, towns, and rural villages at the turn of the century—to popular entertainment for the working classes. Over the next few years, cinema became an increasingly urban entertainment, gradually moving from hastily constructed and inadequate accommodations to larger theaters designed specifically for film screenings, which began to be constructed in Berlin and other large- and medium-sized German cities. By 1910, cinema had attained the status of big business and mass entertainment, with 500 new cinemas founded each year. Four years later, Berlin had nearly 350 cinemas—over 10 percent of the estimated 2,500 to 3,000 German cinemas.[10]

Rapid commercial expansion meant that unprecedented numbers of people were seeing each cinematic product. On the eve of World War I in Mannheim, one-third of the population visited the cinema each week. Underscoring both its commercial significance and social impact, one industry report boasted that "every film is shown in ca. 20 theaters. . . . Every theater has an average of 550 guests per day . . . which adds up to 3,850 per week; so when a film has made it through its 20 theaters, it has been seen by 77,000 people. The same film idea has been copied a total of 45 times and offered into the public domain, so that a single film idea has been brought to the attention of 3,465,000 people."[11] The largest German cinemas seated 1,000 people, and film programs were attracting over a million customers a day. Moreover, statistics indicated that the lower social classes (and especially industrial laborers and residents of densely populated working-class districts in larger cities and ports like Berlin and Hamburg) had a "higher than average" attendance rate.[12]

By the early 1910s, film came to be considered the quintessential urban entertainment, in part due to its massive popularity in urban areas. Indeed, film struck contemporaries as particularly well suited to the urban psyche. One early commentator, perhaps taking his cue from Berlin sociologist Georg Simmel's essays on the psychological impact of city life, noted that the "psychology of the cinematographic triumph is metropolitan psychology . . . because the metropolitan soul, that ever-harried soul, curious and unanchored, tumbling from fleeting impression to fleeting impression, is quite rightly the cinematographic soul."[13] The identification of cinema with the city became a recurrent theme in literary and legal reflections on the new medium into the Weimar period. Often, unsurprisingly, cultural commentary slipped easily into social and moral critique. Kaes notes that "insofar as cinema [was] a part of metropolitan mass culture, the critique of cinema adopt[ed] some elements of the critique of the big city."[14]

Cinema was also linked to the city by its very content. Representations of urban life—and particularly its underside—figured prominently in early silent films. Whereas the first nonnarrative films may have depicted mundane urban scenes like strollers on the famous Berlin promenade, Unter den Linden, by the early 1900s, the most popular pictures focused on "urban exoticism." These featured sensational stories involving gangsters, detectives, robberies, murders, seduction, poison, arson, adultery, and prostitution, with titles like *Robbers' Revenge*, *Lost in the Metropolis*, *Hell of Death*, *Sinful Love*, *White Slave Woman*, *Death in the Nude*, and *Queen of the Night*.[15]

Prewar critics of the cinema were not reticent to draw parallels between the sensational presentation of the stories on the screen and the behavior of cinemagoers. Admittedly, the unchaperoned darkness was conducive to sexual experimentation, particularly among working-class adolescents, and the atmosphere has been described as "raucous" and "uninhibited" when compared to early twentieth-century bourgeois conventions of behavior. Local police seemed to suspect cinemas as sites of potential criminal activity when they declared them "centers of immorality" and cast a suspicious eye on the clientele, which they characterized as composed of "all types of disreputable characters." Perhaps as telling, those moviegoing members of the lower middle class (such as salespeople and clerical workers) who aspired to middle-class status were more concerned with the reputation and respectability of the theater than with what was showing on the program.[16]

The cinema was also visited by young intellectuals who attempted to quench their curiosity by going "slumming." Given the accounts they left behind, it seems that these observers—almost exclusively young men—were often fascinated as much by what went on in front of the screen as by what was projected onto it. Writer Alfred Döblin's comments from 1909 provide a colorful example of this fascination: "[The] screen glares over a monster of an audience, a white eye fixating the mass with a monotonous gaze. Couples making out . . . are carried away and withdraw their undisciplined fingers . . . children wheezing with consumption . . . badly smelling workers with bulging eyes, women in musty clothes, heavily made-up prostitutes. . . . Here you see 'panem et circenses' fulfilled; spectacle as essential as bread."[17] Miriam Hansen has argued in an analysis of early German cinema that the hindrance to cinema's respectability "was sexual and gender-related, rather than primarily class-related." Male intellectuals focused their descriptions on the women in the audience, who in fact constituted a large proportion of film viewers. According to Hansen, "It is no coincidence that literary intellectuals fascinated by the whiff of Otherness that emanated from the movies hardly ever failed to mention the presence of prostitutes in the audience. The image of the prostitute was actually used as an epithet for the cinema as a whole."[18]

Thus, cinema came to be understood as a force of moral and national corruption, the irresistible seductress responsible for luring the susceptible (uneducated, undisciplined, undiscerning, and often youthful) masses away from a loftier national culture. Couched in gendered language intended to underscore the urgency of the threat, criticism of the medium sprang from national-cultural and class biases. Pointing to both its popular appeal and its overwhelmingly foreign (and particularly French) origins, prominent detractors denounced cinema as an "orgy of tastelessness" that would result in the "wholesale spiritual poisoning of the Volk." Many also targeted the film entrepreneurs, who, they claimed, sprang from the "dregs" of society, had no education, artistic taste, or ideals, and lacked "the scruples of even a schnapps stall owner." According to early cinema reformers, these people possessed neither the cultivation nor the moral uprightness necessary to lead the lower social orders in matters cultural. As a result, they contended, filmmakers and cinema owners failed to employ the medium to elevate or educate the masses and instead offered an endless supply of fictional dramas that highlighted crime, sex, and violence and played to the "basest instinct of the broadest masses . . . by shamelessly and *commercially* exploiting the public's lust for sensation."[19]

It was film's vigorous commercialization of culture as much as its perceived negative moral impact that caused many to fear for the future of German culture.[20] The Prussian minister of culture derided film as comparable to "trashy pulp fiction and pornography" and accused its lowly commercial appeal of "perverting" the aesthetic sensibilities of the young and "eroding . . . their ability to contemplate great works of art."[21] Pre–World War I cinema rattled intellectuals, educators, and state officials because it "seemed to offer an un-checked, unstandardized, and un-mediated entertainment, which, unlike bourgeois art [and serious literature in particular], did *not* have to legitimize its practical and pleasurable character with a claim to some everlasting, eternal value." One film historian has even speculated that cinema "became the haven to which lower social classes could *escape* from culture."[22] If this is so, then the very act of moviegoing challenged the role of the educated middle classes or *Bildungsbürgertum* as the producers and purveyors of aesthetic taste and artistic heritage—indeed, of national culture itself.

Highbrow culture appeared to be under attack by lowbrow entertainment and was thought to be losing ground quickly. The panic felt by cultural elites is perhaps best illustrated by the reaction of stage actors and theater professionals, who organized to lobby against the proliferation of movie theaters, which they dubbed a "cinema epidemic." Declaring the "cinema and the legitimate dramatic arts . . . born enemies," theater organizations attempted to counter the commercial success of cinemas by petitioning the state to require them to follow the same licensing procedures governing theater operations. In addition, many groups banned members from participating in any activity related to film production.[23]

That this campaign ultimately proved unsuccessful cannot be attributed to official disinterest. In fact, in February 1914, the imperial government submitted a draft bill to the Reichstag to revise the commercial code and create more stringent laws to regulate the establishment and operation of film theaters. The text of the bill argued that by charging only pennies for admission, cinema owners "preyed" upon "that segment of the population which lacks the [cultivation and] education to resist the evil influences of popular films. . . . The attraction of the cinema for youth and for the undereducated classes . . . represents a moral threat to the nation that must absolutely be resisted." The bill had widespread support across the political spectrum and would likely have been passed had World War I not preempted the voting in the summer of 1914.[24]

Prior to World War I, then, cinema drew ire from bourgeois circles because it "represented a plebeian counter-culture which, without invitation, had established itself beside mainstream culture." Cinema offended because it "challenged traditionally held notions of poetry and culture" and appeared to be directly responsible for the declining cultural cachet and flagging market for "serious" literature and theater. In 1910 the conventional theater in Hildesheim, for example, reported a 50 percent decrease in subscriptions to its three cheapest categories of seats—a drop assumed to be attributable to a corresponding increase in film attendance. Yet local businesspeople also blamed cinema for the demise of establishments such as taverns, music halls, and circuses, which had been the loci of working-class politics, sociability, and leisure since the foundation of the Second Reich. As it won a mass audience and hence cultural "power," cinema challenged the nineteenth-century class-based geography and moral Manichaeanism of the "high-low" cultural split and thereby managed to "destabilize the contemporary cultural system."[25]

Socialists also fretted about the social effects of cinema and the inroads film viewing was making among the working classes. Socialism too had a strong moral component; workers, after all, were expected to constitute the revolutionary troops responsible for securing the socialist future. Its leaders therefore encouraged worker education and self-discipline and sought to wean their charges from the vices of drink, ignorance, and excessively indulgent frivolity. For these reasons, they tended to support calls for cinematic control (but rejected the censorship of "serious" literature and art on the grounds that such action compromised civil liberties). In contrast to middle-class moral reformers, Socialists came to consider cinema the product of bourgeois society, "targeted to render the working class passive." They feared that the growing popularity of cinema—indeed, all commercial entertainments—would culminate in the erosion of their political base.[26]

Calls for the medium's regulation, however, issued from the ranks of middle-class morality leagues, which, beginning in 1905, helped to launch a nationwide cinema reform movement. These self-appointed defenders of German culture and respectability marshaled their forces to undertake a "defensive" strike against film as a form of public corruption. The push for cinema reform was part of an older tradition of middle-class attention to workers' physical and spiritual welfare, which intensified with the repeal of anti-Socialist legislation in 1890. Reformers sought to entice workers from both party membership and their extracurricular "course, sensuous enjoyments" by providing them with alternative "unadulterated, spiritual pleasures."[27]

Early reform activities included attempts to squelch the new medium, which, along with lowbrow literature, was considered a breeding ground for "trash and smut [Schund und Schmutz]" and hence working-class degeneracy and juvenile delinquency. By 1910, with the increased commercialization of the medium and the realization of its potential as an entertainment industry, most resigned themselves to lessening its perceived negative social and psychological impact and lobbied instead for its containment and control. At this stage, reformers concentrated on broadening legal definitions to include prohibition of material that, while not pornographic, could be considered harmful or offensive. Furthermore, they introduced the idea of protecting youth from such material without denying access to adults. Finally, reformers also undertook a positive program of sponsoring "good" or "acceptable" forms of film and other entertainment for youth and workers. This involved exhortations to the film industry to produce educational films on nature, science, and geography as well as broader efforts to found public libraries and parks that, it was hoped, would provide attractive, healthy, and "morally uplifting" alternatives to the "dark and stuffy" movie houses (and meetings of the Social Democratic Party). It bears noting that while the morality leagues tended to have a middle-class constituency with a heavy representation by educators, the concern about the impact of mass culture transcended party lines and received support from Socialists who, by the way, established their own reading rooms for the working classes, stocked with carefully screened literature.[28]

During this time, the German courts determined that film should be subject to the same controls as theater and live performances. Film censorship was therefore mostly a local issue, entailing the mandatory review of films by the local police before public screening in their jurisdiction. This arrangement satisfied no one. Local control resulted in duplication of effort by overburdened police, who too often had neither adequate personnel nor training to render reasonable and timely decisions regarding upcoming cinema programs. Further, any initial confidence in the ability of local police to distinguish acceptable films from trash rapidly eroded when neighboring jurisdictions reached contradictory decisions. The arbitrary and unpredictable nature of the censorship process infuriated filmmakers, distributors, and theater owners, who lost money every time (and everywhere) a negative decision was reached.

To address these criticisms, the German states, which retained responsibility for cultural matters at the creation of the Second Reich, attempted to standardize film censorship within their boundaries by establishing film control offices in their state capitals. Prussia led the way in July 1912 when Karl Brunner, a history teacher and avid opponent of trashy literature and film, was installed to head the film control office in Berlin. Brunner's office banned films or required editing of material containing "brutalizing scenes" involving crime or violence, immoral scenes (including seduction, adultery, prostitution, and abduction), as well as "politically-, socially-, and religiously inflammatory material"—all of which clearly left plenty of latitude for the censors' discretion. Furthermore, the appropriateness of the film for viewing by children and adolescents was to be determined and publicized. This centralization of censorship within state bodies reduced some of the stresses and confusions of purely local initiatives, but the decisions of states continued to vary. Catholic Bavaria, for example, often banned films that the more liberal Berlin censors allowed and demanded that all films shown in Bavarian cinemas be suitable for viewing by both adults and children. Other states dealt with the youth issue by requiring that juveniles be accompanied by adults or that they be allowed to attend only special children's matinees with appropriate film programs.[29]

It was no coincidence that cultural and moral outrage against the cinema reached its peak in the prewar years, right around the time that film began to shake off its exclusively working-class associations. This was the result of a conscious marketing strategy on the part of film producers, distributors, and cinema owners to follow the example of Hollywood businessman, Adolph Zukor, and "kill the slum tradition of the movies." The idea was to expand the market potential of the movies—and thereby maximize profits—by appealing to more cultivated, wealthier customers. Movie palaces were built to create a more "hygienic" and aesthetic forum for film viewing—one that rivaled traditional bourgeois theater in its magnificent scale, dazzling design, and luxurious appointments. The form and length of films were altered from the three- to four-minute fictional *Tonbilder* set to gramophone music, which dominated the screen around 1904–5, to longer features based upon adaptations of dramatic plays, novels, and fairy tales that would be familiar to the newly targeted middle classes. To lend added respectability, film companies recruited admired literary figures (for example, Gerhart Hauptmann and Hugo von Hofmannsthal) and stage professionals (such as Berlin theater producer Max Reinhardt and actor Paul Wegener) to write, direct, and act in film productions. Producers quickly learned to cultivate "stars" by repeatedly employing actors with proven broad box-office appeal. Large salaries were effective in quelling lingering doubts such artists might have had about allying professionally with such a "low" form of entertainment. Finally, large state-of-the-art film studios were constructed on the outskirts of Berlin at Tempelhof and Neubabelsberg, and a great deal of effort was expended on developing and improving filming, editing, and storytelling techniques. What gradually emerged—in Germany and elsewhere—was a cinema that "positioned viewers" in a way that encouraged "intense specularity, constructing narratives (through a straightforward flow of events, seamless editing, identification with stars, and closure) that permit[ted] total immersion."[30] All of this enhanced the illusory quality of the film-viewing experience and, in effect, insured "the complete absorption of the spectator into the fictional world of the film and the imaginary flow of linear narrative."[31]

The bid by the emerging film industry to win the broadest possible audience was wildly successful. By 1914, cinema had become a fad among many in the urban middle classes, prized as a reliable and enjoyable source of up-to-date information on the latest international fashions and consumer trends. Despite the substantial efforts of native filmmakers, however, imported movies continued to dominate the German market, in part because banks were still reticent to put up capital for lowbrow entertainment ventures, a situation that would change only during the war years.

In sum, the push to make movies respectable had a critically important three-fold effect. First, cinema was brought out of its working-class ghetto and into mainstream culture. Second, the very nature of that culture was transformed, liberated from its restricted, class-based exhibition space to forge a "universalized, homogenized mass culture." This universalization was marked, nonetheless, by bourgeois cultural traces. The new film products tended to validate the nineteenth-century (bourgeois) literary device of the heroic, autonomous subject and encouraged viewer identification "on the basis of individual character traits," at the expense of more diverse, and perhaps divisive, class, ethnic, and gender identities. Yet this influence was decidedly reciprocal.[32] The works of many pre- and interwar artists, writers, and dramatists were profoundly changed by film; one need only mention the fragmented, "cinematic" structure of Döblin's expansive novel, *Berlin Alexanderplatz*, or Bertolt Brecht's ready comparison of the acting demands of his epic theater with the films of Charlie Chaplin.[33] This reciprocity is indicative of the gradual but steady "blurring" of boundaries between "high" and "low" culture. In pursuing respectability, filmmakers positioned themselves and their products in a way that facilitated their later, ultimate claim for cultural status: the concept of film as a serious art form.[34]

Building a National Cinema: World War I and the Propagation of German Interests

Just how far cinema had succeeded in conquering the German cultural mainstream was made plain by the intervention of influential nationalist businessmen, the German military, and the imperial government in film matters between 1916 and 1917. Unconcerned with film's cultural or moral worth, these interests sought to exploit its propagandistic, psychological, and commercial potential for purposes of profit and national prestige. First, Alfred Hugenberg, the director of Krupp industries, and shipping magnate Ludwig Klitzsch joined forces in a private initiative to create the Deutsche Lichtbildgesellschaft (Deulig) in order "to mobilize visual means for economic expansion," particularly in the Balkans, and "publicize the fatherland at home and abroad." A primarily commercial enterprise, Deulig was observed warily by a suspicious German high command and Reich government, who found its activities "too little focused on wartime propaganda [zu wenig kriegspropagandistisch]."[35]

In response, General Ludendorff, in a secret memo, urged the War Ministry to expand its current battlefield to include a psychological barrage on the "minds of men" at home and abroad. Ludendorff was especially sensitive to the effective use Germany's enemies were making of film to propagandize their cause and undermine Germany's reputation internationally. In 1917, for example, the U.S. government began to work closely with its domestic commercial film interests through the Creel Committee to disseminate "America's plans and purposes" within and outside of the United States. Not incidentally, this cooperative arrangement greatly expanded the distribution of American educational, industrial, and commercial films worldwide—and in some areas, like Scandinavia, it nearly succeeded in closing German films out of a once secure market.[36]

Ludendorff was doubtless deeply concerned about the increasingly precarious domestic order, which was being tested by war weariness and growing frustration over severe food shortages and unequal distribution of wartime privations, all of which was dramatically expressed in frequent public demonstrations in the German capital beginning in 1916. Employing the language of calculated overstatement, he warned that the fate of Germany could turn on the question of official support for the visual medium and demanded a wholesale onslaught on public opinion: "Our victory absolutely depends on our using films to exert the greatest possible persuasion wherever people can still be won over to the German cause."[37]

As a result, the Photo and Film Office (Bild- und Filmamt [BUFA]) was created in early 1917 to organize the production of newsreels and documentaries about the war effort and to supply the necessary footage by arranging for the filming of military battles (and, in some cases, their subsequent restaging). In addition, BUFA established a "foreign service" for the spread of German propaganda abroad and developed programs for the 900 German "soldiers' cinemas" established along the eastern and western fronts. These activities indicate official recognition of cinema's powers of persuasion in German society as well as an eagerness to employ it as a means of education and, not incidentally, of counterpropaganda against the Entente on the national and international level.[38]

Yet the goals of the Reich government and military in film matters appear to have been still more ambitious. Officials saw themselves as laying the groundwork for enhanced political, economic, and cultural influence of the German state in the postwar period. In this regard, World War I was also a determined fight for markets and cultural prestige and was genuinely perceived as a defensive battle, at that. Ludendorff warned of the strong position Scandinavian firms, especially the Danish Nordisk Film Company, had developed in large sections of the European market. And toward the end of the war, it became clear that American productions were conquering markets in Western Europe (especially Britain, France, Italy, and Spain) and South America (including Brazil and Argentina) that had previously been supplied by European films.[39]

An overview of the weakness of German film interests and their market position was laid out in detail in an official report written in 1917. The report began by noting the prewar domination of the German market by French and American films, which led the way in developing and perfecting popular film genres and, in effect, shaped public taste. The report alleged that the sophisticated products of France, "the land of pantomime and expressive gesture," charmed the viewer with "cultivated and elegant Parisian theater culture" and "alluring women," while the "stunning packaging and presentation of Yankee films" from "the land of sensation" fascinated with "carefree . . . fantasy" and "physically fit figures." German filmmakers, in comparison, were criticized as unimaginative, even stodgy, laggards whose creations were unable to compete for national-cultural reasons.[40]

In fact, before 1914, domestic productions claimed only 15 percent of the screentime in German cinemas. The market was dominated by foreign productions, including French (30 percent), American (25 percent), Italian (20 percent), Danish, and English imports. This point was not lost on one member of the Prussian War Ministry, who complained that the German film industry of that period was "split, retrogressive, and dependent on large, foreign firms. . . . Home production was limited and . . . of poor quality" and therefore unattractive for export. German officials feared that if this trend continued, the blow to national cultural prestige would be irreparable, and Germany would be "not only economically but also politically shut out" of the international order.[41]

Thus, the absence of a viable national film industry was expected to have a debilitating effect on the German present and future. At stake was not only the power of the imperial government to shape domestic public opinion and secure its influence and image abroad, as weighty as those concerns were, but also, according to some, the cultural integrity and spiritual health of the German nation. In 1916 one staunch nationalist continued the prewar trend of blaming the "substandard" quality of film on its foreign origins and urged officials to take more aggressive action against such films as a matter of national cultural survival. In a flurry of mixed metaphors and exclamation points, film reformer Konrad Lange thundered: "Down with this cheap and artless trash! Away with this disgusting potion that poisons the soul of the German *Volk*! Let us impose severe economic sanctions against the foreign and international film capital, the canker that blights the tree of German culture."[42]

In order to meet this range of threats to the national interest, military commanders regulated film more strictly during the war years, using emergency powers to act against movies they found offensive or objectionable. Indeed, some squelched any form of frivolous film entertainment they deemed incompatible with the "gravity of the times." At the beginning of the war, the German War Ministry had banned all films that dealt with espionage and treason for fear that they would provoke emulation of those activities! By 1915, the ban was extended to all foreign films, regardless of content. And as the war dragged on, some local commanders acted to prohibit children from attending the movies, especially when sustained mobilization left many without parental supervision, given the dramatic increase in employment for women whose husbands were at the front.[43] Thus, official interest in cultivating a national cinema did not translate into a simple retreat from moral concerns regarding the medium's impact; it did, however, implicitly affirm and legitimize "responsible" use of the medium for the purposes of social integration and political unity.

Moreover, the resolve among military and state officials to "mobilize the German cinema" involved more than simply freeing the domestic market of foreign competitors so that native firms could work their magic. Mobilization was not envisioned as a process of winning over the existing commercial industry to the goals of the state. Rather, the military leadership planned to intervene directly in the private sphere of the commercial film industry. BUFA officials argued in 1917 that the present structure of the film industry discouraged the production, distribution, and exhibition of effective propaganda films. Their analysis centered on three points: that German production firms lacked the interest, resources, and training to make propaganda films that were effective, attractive, and entertaining; that German film firms were relatively small and scattered, and some were co-owned by foreign interests; and that the structure of the industry discouraged easy cooperation between film companies and the state. For example, BUFA officials complained that distribution companies controlled consumer taste by their influence on cinema programming; as a result, BUFA had found it nearly impossible to get cinema owners to screen government films because they booked features with distributors months in advance. The best they could expect was to supply short films free of charge to cinema owners and arrange for these to be shown before the main commercial feature.[44]

The military leadership's understanding of film appeal appears to have been surprisingly sophisticated, given its rather late conversion to the efficacy of the medium. Officials consistently insisted that propaganda films, whether features or shorts, be well written, technically competent, and attractively packaged. Film programmers for soldiers' cinemas were instructed to dispense "enlightenment" in moderate doses; every half hour of propaganda was carefully sweetened by an hour and a half of accompanying "harmless entertainment" to avoid "propaganda overkill." For civilian propaganda, a BUFA report stressed the importance of winning the participation of successful German directors and popular actors and made special mention of the overwhelmingly enthusiastic response one film received due to the star presence of Henny Porten. Officials appreciated the importance of adopting commercial marketing strategies to win audiences for their messages. And one suspects that, even absent hard psychological proof, the BUFA staff instinctively appreciated the positive effect of diversionary entertainment in a stressful wartime setting.[45]

To accomplish their goals, German military and government officials maneuvered to establish a large film company that would function as a centralized organization for the manufacture and dissemination of German propaganda and culture. The enterprise was to be vertically organized to encompass every aspect of film activity, including production, distribution, and exhibition. The Reichschancellor rejected out-and-out state ownership in order to avoid the rigidity in business and production operations that he anticipated would accompany bureaucratic control. Additionally, many felt that the organization would be more effective if it were not perceived at home and abroad as a German propaganda factory. For all of these reasons, there was official consensus that state participation and control would remain a strict secret.

Initially, the German high command proposed to accomplish this task by buying up the shares of existing private film companies and the majority of shares of the successful Nordisk Film Company. When the Treasury Department declared this plan "unviable," the high command consulted the Office of Foreign Affairs, the Office of the Interior, and the Treasury for advice. What resulted was the creation of a large new company, Universum-Film-Aktiengesellschaft (UFA), in December 1917, which was purportedly privately owned (capital from private industry, shipping, and banking was involved) but was in fact designed to follow government directives. The banks funding the deal were, in the words of an official from the Prussian War Ministry, "act[ing] as a front" on the government's behalf, and the government indirectly held one-third of UFA shares.[46]

Weimar Cinema and the Emergence of a "German Style"

This impressive achievement was cut short by German capitulation in November 1918, at which time UFA was sold to Krupp, Deutsche Bank (which was involved in the original deal), and IG Farben and became a private company. In 1921 UFA absorbed the German film companies Decla and Bioscop. As a result, UFA strengthened its hold on the German market, especially in the areas of production and exhibition. Beginning in the 1920s, it controlled the largest studio in Germany (and interwar Europe) as well as the largest chain of domestic first-run cinemas. Moreover, the deal secured for UFA the considerable talents of Erich Pommer, who established his reputation as a film producer with *Das Kabinett des Dr. Caligari*. Over the next decade, Pommer excelled at developing both popular domestic genres (like the film operetta *Der Kongreß tanzt* [*The Congress Dances*]) and highly exportable UFA products (such as *Der blaue Engel* [*The Blue Angel*]).[47]

The stimulus to German film production derived from the experience of World War I, which represented a "cultural caesura in German cultural relations." The war isolated Germany from the West and resulted in a notable period of cinematic "self-sufficiency," which initiated the rapid expansion of German film production—indeed, mass production.[48] The number of German film production companies rose dramatically from 11 in 1911 to 131 in 1918. Sparked by inflation and the devalued Reichsmark, this trend continued into the next decade: by 1920 the number stood at 230, in 1922 it rose to 360, and by 1929, with the beginnings of the worldwide economic crisis, the number topped out at 424. Most, it should be said, were small- to medium-sized firms that released only two or three films a year. Distribution companies proliferated at a steady, but less astounding, rate (from 19 in 1911 to 135 in 1922, with a drop off to 118 in 1929); and cinemas flourished, increasing from nearly 2,300 in 1918 to 5,078 in 1929. Perhaps the most telling figure is the status Germany achieved in worldwide feature film production. By 1927, Germany ranked third, with 241 productions, after the United States (743) and Japan (407), with fourth and fifth places going to Russia (141) and France (74). Moreover, technological innovation played a role in strengthening the position of the German film industry. In 1928 the Ton-Bild-Syndikat (Tobis) bought up all existing patents for German sound film processes and led an initiative to create a monopoly on sound technology in all of Europe, designed to disadvantage American firms operating there. By the early 1930s, German talkies would drown out the universal language of silent film, thereby erecting a language barrier behind which a national cinema could be cultivated.[49]

The growth of German cinema was assisted by the country's economic difficulties in the immediate postwar period. The tottering Reichsmark boosted German exports and created a competitive international market for German films while shutting Hollywood films out of Germany for a while. Perhaps more importantly, the German government protected its native industry by pioneering a national quota system for imports that would become the model for other European countries over the course of the decade. The wartime embargo against Allied film imports (essentially extended to all foreign films through 1921 by the German Finance Ministry in an attempt to reserve German currency for critical imports of food and other essentials) was replaced in January 1921 by a quota system, which limited film imports to 15 percent of the total number of German films produced. American distributors complained that their German counterparts block-booked German theaters for a year immediately before the quota went into effect, thereby severely limiting American access into 1922. Moreover, the quota system was revised twice over the course of the 1920s. In 1925 one film could be imported for each film produced in Germany; three years later, the German government abolished the 1:1 rule and instituted a system by which they would designate an annual, fixed number of import certificates to be issued. While some loopholes could be found, import restrictions did have the effect of rendering the German market "undependable" for American film distributors and discouraged them from establishing permanent offices in Berlin. Thus, the war, and a combination of state and private initiatives, helped keep American competition at bay and set the stage for the development of a national film industry in Germany.[50]

For a short time in the early 1920s, the German film industry seems to have created a highly exportable national film style as well. During this decade, first Decla, then UFA, managed to become Hollywood's only serious competitor in the international market by offering what was billed as a unique aesthetic alternative to American-style productions—the expressionist film. Beginning in 1920, this visually striking "German style" stirred audiences in New York, Paris, and London with its fantastic plots and gothic characters, chiaroscuro lighting, and claustrophobic, highly stylized sets. One American exporter shuddered to see the high quality work of the German historical epic, *Veritas Vincit*, while in Copenhagen in 1919, and by 1920, the Hollywood press was warning of a "German invasion," which, however, never materialized thanks to American protectionism (and Adolph Zukor's creative solution of buying up at least two dozen German films to keep them off the U.S. market).[51]

While some sat transfixed by Robert Wiene's *Das Kabinett des Dr. Caligari* (1919), F. W. Murnau's *Nosferatu* (1922), and, somewhat later, Fritz Lang's *Metropolis* (1927)—the earliest examples of the horror, vampire, and science fiction film genres—others found them overwrought or worse. One detractor described his viewing experience in vivid gustatory terms: "It had the odor of tainted food. It leaves the taste of cinders in the mouth." Yet most agreed that their fascination was fueled by the films' "macabre, sinister, morbid" feel, which seemed somehow to express the darker aspects of a creative, specifically German, soul.[52]

Indeed, German films did differ from their American counterparts in a number of ways. To begin with, German film professionals like director Ernst Lubitsch and producer Erich Pommer insisted that their films could compete on the world market only if they did so on the basis of *difference*—by offering something that American films could not. Thus, German films earmarked for export were conceived as *Kunstfilme* or *Stilfilme*—artistic or highly stylized films. Moreover, since the German film companies, unlike American firms, were not controlled by a management intent on planned production and rationalization, German films were not fettered by strict budgets, timetables, and release dates. As a result, film directors and technicians—particularly those working in Pommer's productions—were permitted a great deal of creative latitude by Hollywood standards. German expressionist film, then, achieved its distinctive look and international reputation precisely due to an export strategy and nonrationalized management style that encouraged artistic experimentation and improvisation with technical effects, camera work and movement, editing, lighting, costuming, and acting. Also, unlike American films, which emphasized viewer identification with stars and a logical, linear narrative based upon continuity editing, German films of the period employed less economical storytelling techniques that allowed for visual excess, narrational circumlocutions, and costumes and sets that competed with the actors for attention. As a result, German films were praised for their "psychological depth and emotional interiority" and received enthusiastic critical reception internationally.[53]

Germany's growing filmmaking reputation abroad was built on the distinctiveness of the expressionist product, yet its home audience was exposed to a much more varied range of genres and cinematic styles. In addition to thrillers (like Lang's *Dr. Mabuse, der Spieler* [*Dr. Mabuse, the Gambler*, 1922]), Weimar cinema offered historical biographies and costume films (like Lubitsch's drama, *Madame Dubarry* [1919]) and adaptations of classical literature, myths, and legends (such as Lang's *Der müde Tod* [*Destiny*, 1921], Gerhard Lamprecht's version of Thomas Mann's *Die Buddenbrooks* [1923], G. W. Pabst's silent version of Frank Wedekind's *Die Büchse der Pandora* [*Pandora's Box*, 1929], and Josef von Sternberg's *Der blaue Engel* [1930], drawn from Heinrich Mann's novel, *Professor Unrat*). Light musical comedies like Lubitsch's *Meine Frau die Filmschauspielerin, Die Austernprinzessin* (*The Oyster Princess*, 1919) received a huge domestic—and, in this case, international—following. In contrast, German filmmakers also developed a film genre based upon "intimate screenplays" (*Kammerspiele*), whose plots often focused on characters from the lower social orders and incidents from daily life. F. W. Murnau's *Der letzte Mann* (*The Last Laugh*, 1924), for example, highlighted the experiences of a washroom attendant; while films like Karl Grune's *Die Strasse* (*The Street*, 1923) and Pabst's *Die freudlose Gasse* (*The Joyless Street*, 1925) focused on the unfulfilled desires and discouragements of urban life.

German films of this period also succeeded in creating domestic and international stars, such as Pola Negri, Emil Jannings, Greta Garbo, Marlene Dietrich, and Peter Lorre, many of whom—along with Germany's most successful directors and producers—were recruited by Hollywood over the course of the decade. This phenomenon attests to Hollywood businessmen's recognition of (and confidence in) the international appeal and marketability of the products and performances of German talent and confirms the competitive edge that German film had achieved worldwide. At the same time, however, it indicates the relative economic power of American film companies vis-à-vis their less centrally organized German competitors and was one component of an ambitious—and ultimately successful—American business strategy to attract talent that would help to build markets abroad.

Through the mid-1920s, the cultivation of a distinct German cinematic style was intended primarily to capture international markets. It took German film companies another several years, on the other hand, to locate a loyal domestic market for their films. Thus, the "German cinema" and "German style" that emerged during the 1920s is more a reflection of a national variant of film production strategies and business management than a reflection of the psychological-social state of the German public (as Siegfried Kracauer argued in his famous "Caligari to Hitler" thesis). In building a dependable domestic cinematic audience, the film industry borrowed modern advertising and marketing strategies that tended to segment the national market with their specialized pitches to female consumers, in particular. Thus, one should not draw hasty conclusions about the attitudes, desires, or notions of political or national identity of interwar Germans from a scrutiny of the content of these particular films alone. The German market in this period cannot by any stretch of the imagination be considered monolithic; it is not possible to locate a single (representative) "German" audience that can stand as a model for the nation as a whole. Film spectatorship, like any form of modern consumption, is conditioned by factors of gender, class, education, generation, and ethnicity, and any discussion of the meanings of film consumption must take these identities into account.[54]

Film Control after World War I

The commercialization of culture and the expansion of native leisure industries had continued apace during the war years. At the conclusion of hostilities, Germans faced imperial collapse, civil disorder, and wholesale social disintegration. The republican constitution insured full freedom of expression and the abolition of censorship, which was used to advantage by entrepreneurs of all types, who produced and disseminated literature and films that claimed to deal with the pressing social problems of the period. Printed advertisements hawking condoms and abortion aids (and guaranteeing to "ensure every wife's happiness") appeared in nationally distributed publications as well as local newspapers in rural Catholic villages.[55] Aside from advertisements, much of this material was little more than pornography that attempted to trade on the titillation to be found in the postwar spread of venereal diseases or the rising incidence of prostitution. "Enlightenment films" (Aufklärungsfilme) appeared at this time, sporting titles like Opium, The Girl and the Men, Lost Daughters, Hyenas of Lust, Wedding Night in the Woods, Love That Gives Itself for Free, and even Vow of Chastity, which detailed the sexual exploits of a Catholic priest.[56] The balance of such films, however, were genuine attempts to aid public enlightenment, generate public understanding and sympathy, or spur official assistance and intervention. As such, they could be considered polemical pieces, usually in dramatic form, which were sponsored by a variety of interest groups such as life-reform movements or sex researchers active since the turn of the century.

One well-known and well-intentioned film of this type was *Anders als die Andern* (*Different from the Others*, 1919), which featured the up-and-coming star Conrad Veidt as well as an appearance by the Berlin sexologist and advocate for homosexual rights, Magnus Hirschfeld. In keeping with the genre, *Anders als die Andern* cast its sexual issue, homosexuality, as a social problem, openly lobbying for the repeal of §175 of the German penal code, which declared male homosexual sexual relations "a vice against nature" punishable by imprisonment. This feature-length melodrama premiered in the mainstream Berlin Apollo Theater, received serious reviews in the press, and promptly became a cause célèbre due to both the disruptions of its screenings by uniformed soldiers in Berlin and decisions by local officials to ban it in the Catholic cities of Vienna, Munich, and Stuttgart. Needless to say, the film was a box-office smash.[57]

Nonetheless, such public displays of openness regarding alternate forms of sexuality and identity shocked broad sectors of German society and fed fears that defeat had precipitated a period of national degeneration, marked by social drift and moral decline. This "moral panic" spanned the political spectrum, seizing the nationalist parties of the right and the Catholic Center Party and extending leftward to the Socialists. While the Social Democratic Party (Sozialdemokratische Partei Deutschlands [SPD]) blamed the brutalizing nature of the war and postwar unemployment for the moral slippage, members of the right medicalized the threat, claiming that socialist revolution acted like a "bacillus" and exposed the body politic to further disease. Some even suspected this situation had been exacerbated by the reduction of the length of the workday in 1918 to eight hours, which was thought to encourage workers and others to seek immoral—or at best "frivolous"—pursuits. Frequent reports appeared in the press that urban areas like Berlin, Hamburg, and Munich were plagued by a "mass psychosis of pleasure-seeking after four years of war-time deprivation." In Düsseldorf, for example, local authorities and Christian trade union officials cast a concerned eye on the ever-intensifying *Tanzwut* or "dance craze," which lured young men and women into newly reestablished dance halls, nightclubs, and cabarets in early 1920. In part, they feared the resumption of prewar behavior, with young unmarried couples drinking and dancing until closing time, when they would search for inconspicuous places like parks and fields to release their pent-up passion. But their condemnation of such behavior had a political basis as well. Indeed, "it was a commonly held view that any outward sign of public enjoyment and gaiety would give both foreign governments and the occupying powers a false impression of the condition of the German people and the economy." City-dwellers, young working women, and especially youth of both sexes from the working and middle classes were beginning to behave like modern consumers, demanding the right to leisure as well as their choice of "specialized entertainments" in commercial enterprises, and were paying little heed to the exigencies of the national situation.[58]

The unrestrained freedoms of the young republic were short-lived, and in May 1920 a film censorship law (Reichslichtspielgesetz) was easily passed by the Reichstag due to the weak lobbying power of the German film industry and a general consensus among the major political parties that some form of national control was urgently needed to counter the nationally distributed, unwholesome products of commercialized culture. This law mandated that every film scheduled for exhibition in Germany be examined prior to its release by one of two German film boards, which sat in Berlin and Munich. The censorship boards were comprised of representatives from education, the arts, and the film industry and were chaired by state officials who had some experience or background in pedagogical and artistic matters. Films determined by the boards to "endanger the public order, injure religious sensibility, function in a brutal or demoralizing manner, endanger Germany's reputation or [its] relations with foreign countries" would be required to undergo a further round of editing or would be banned outright. Films could not, however, be rejected for "political, social, religious, or philosophical tendencies, as such [or] . . . for reasons external to the content of films." In addition, the law addressed ongoing concerns regarding the susceptibility of youth to negative cinematic influences by barring children under the age of twelve from movie theaters and restricting adolescents between twelve and eighteen to specially designated performances.[59]

Democratization and the American Challenge

The year after the national film censorship law was passed, the German market was again opened to foreign films. Over the course of the 1920s, Hollywood films came to constitute one-third to two-fifths of all feature films screened in Germany and nearly all of the entertainment shorts. Through 1924, American films were the rage and were praised by cultural critics and intellectuals as the breath of fresh air that would at last dispel the stifling stench of the long-lingering imperial system, steeped in an outdated aristocratic culture. American culture, in the form of Hollywood films, jazz music, boxing, and the Charleston, would update German culture and orient it toward the future. Kurt Tucholsky, for example, credited American films with providing a way to escape the deadening sense of isolation, provincialism, and even claustrophobia that pervaded early postwar Germany; he stated in 1923 that, while watching Charlie Chaplin, "one is removed from this country, far, far away to be with real people. . . . We are grateful to you, Charlie Chaplin, for you show us that the world is not German and not Bavarian, but very, very different."[60]

Enthusiasm for American culture was at once a challenge to German political, cultural, and social traditions. Anton Kaes has argued that in the aftermath of the failed leftist revolution in 1918–19, some Germans embraced American mass culture as a "substitute revolution" that represented a "vehicle for radical modernization and democratization." The United States seemed to offer a future of social harmony based upon "humanized technology" in marked contrast to the recent technological bloodbaths of World War I and the German civil war.[61] American culture was admired for its "naturalness," "playfulness," and unreflected self-confidence, which made Wilhelminian culture appear effete, idealistic, and bankrupt, especially given the recent military humiliation. Bertolt Brecht and other well-known German intellectuals of the left, in fact, admired the boxer as the corporification of American cultural vitality and the quintessential expression of a new American-style masculinity.[62]

Thus, American culture offered a modern model of male subjectivity as well as the basis for cultural modernization in its "unpretentious . . . rejection of high culture" and its "affirmation of a new, tough, 'realistic' set of cultural values." By mid-decade, artists and intellectuals developed a style of representation dubbed "the New Objectivity [*Die neue Sachlichkeit*]," which was thought to embody this new perspective. According to contemporary Kurt Pinthus, "It is matter-of-fact, it is male; it is the very expression of the male, if one understands by male not the swaggering boastfulness of the *völkisch* notion of maleness, which precisely in its insincere heroicizing is sentimental, exaggerated, i.e. unmanly. No, the language of *Neue Sachlichkeit*—minus any poetic fat, minus any mentally tired blood; hard, tough, trained to the core—can only be compared to the body of the boxer."[63] For a short while at least, "America" promised self- and cultural renewal for some influential male intellectuals.

American culture held out a model for social renewal as well, due to its astonishing effectiveness in combining technological expertise and humor to produce a cinematic social lubricant called slapstick. This American comedic form, and especially Charlie Chaplin films, gained the devotion of a wide viewing public, and by 1922 (a relatively late date by Western European standards) whole programs of slapstick shorts were offered at leading Berlin cinemas. German journalists, cultural critics, and intellectuals indulged in utopian fantasies in which slapstick, and Hollywood films in general, would become the "folk art (*Volkskunst*) of a future, united world."[64]

These highbrow devotees were encouraged in this view by their own experiences of watching Chaplin's films. Initially skeptical intellectuals testified that

Chaplin's antics on the screen eroded their self-consciously critical perspectives, which had the result of uniting them with the filmgoing "masses" through shared laughter. Slapstick comedy, said one critic, "reduces us brain snobs to human beings" by effacing the divisions of class, education, and social position—or so the argument went.[65] An artist told the tale of a chance meeting with his housemaid outside of the cinema after a Chaplin film: "Though not able to converse, [we] experienced . . . a momentary sense of comradeship."[66] Thus, the merry film-viewing audience offered the key to a new society based upon consensus and consumption. Some went even further and argued that the utopia could span the world, since the international appeal of Hollywood-style silent films "undermined the ethnic-cultural concept of the nation-state [and] . . . was seen by German intellectuals as an antidote to the belligerent patriotism of World War I."[67]

Finally, Chaplin drew both hearty praise and vehement condemnation for his role as a revolutionary who "consistently challenged the established order," and his rumored communist leanings no doubt only reinforced this interpretation.[68] The film antics of Chaplin's marginalized "Little Tramp" were described as subverting nineteenth-century standards of plot structure, narrative coherence, and heroic individuality. In addition, they transgressed accepted distinctions between reality and unreality as well as scientifically determined natural laws in their "uninhibited disregard for usual notions of probability and logic." Moreover, it was generally agreed that Chaplin's tramp ran amok in ways that ridiculed authority and conventional bourgeois values "and exposed the hypocrisy and inconsistencies of the bourgeois social order."[69] By the mid-1920s, then, slapstick was applauded by leftist intellectuals as a tool that (perhaps unwittingly) served to foster social enlightenment and cultural criticism among the masses.

And yet, as historian Thomas Saunders has noted, slapstick's "dialectic of realism and surrealism both generated more profound understanding of everyday reality *and* offered . . . welcome relief from it."[70] By the late 1920s, cultural critics like Siegfried Kracauer began to emphasize the illusory nature of cinematic liberation, a perspective that would be adopted and developed by Frankfurt School critics Theodor Adorno and Max Horkheimer in the 1930s and 1940s. Perhaps the most telling detail in the chance encounter at the movies between the artist and his maid is that his sense of "comradeship" based on their shared enjoyment of Chaplin was, like the flicker of images on the screen, merely "momentary." Thus, the only common ground between them was that they were both Chaplin fans, which to the artist was shocking enough. Still, for some reason, they were "unable to converse" at that meeting of souls, and presumably she showed up to clean his house the next day.

The point is that left-leaning cultural critics like Kracauer soon backed away from their initial optimism regarding the transformative effects of commercial cinema. Kracauer explored the way that the radical potential of the medium was subdued by capitalist business practices, "festooned with drapes and forced back into a unity" that was both deceptive and (therefore) bourgeois. The result was the emergence of "a new idealist culture." In contrast, early cinema, he claimed, was a form of entertainment that appealed to the urban masses precisely *because* of its incoherence, fragmentation, and "pure externality," which manifested itself in "the surface glamour of stars, films, revues and production values":

> Indeed the very fact that the shows which aim at distraction are composed of the same mixture of externalities as the world of the urban masses; the fact that these shows lack any authentic and materially motivated coherence, except possibly the glue of sentimentality which covers up this lack but only in order to make it all the more visible; the fact that these shows convey in a precise and undisguised manner to thousands of eyes and ears the *disorder* of society—this is precisely what enables such shows to evoke and maintain that tension which must precede the inevitable and radical change. In the streets of Berlin one is not seldom struck by the momentary insight that one day all this will suddenly burst apart. The entertainment to which the general public throngs ought to produce the same effect.[71]

According to Kracauer, cinema was transformed into a prop for the capitalist order precisely when filmmakers and businesspeople conspired to make it respectable by giving it artistic weight. After this, the only function it served was to mask social anarchy, not expose it. It became a "distraction" that served to make life more bearable for the working and lower middle classes. Even Charlie Chaplin's antiauthority escapades in an illogical universe became little more than a temporary "antidote to a highly-mechanical assembly-line world,"[72] while social, economic, and power relations remained intact. Thus, according to this line of analysis, commercial cinema worked to reinforce the capitalist system.

Communists expressed skepticism about the status of cinema as popular culture and its prospects as a tool of revolution from the beginning of the Weimar period. Their cultural criticism was directed less against American cinema per se than against commercial cinema as a whole, regardless of national origin. At the founding of the German Communist Party in 1919—even before American films had reentered the German market—the problem was posed concerning "how the proletariat masses can be ripped away from the influence of the bourgeois cinema, an advanced means by which the bourgeoisie spreads its ideology."[73] Yet not much attention was paid to cultural matters until the mid-1920s, when the first communist film company, Prometheus Films, was founded by Willi Münzenberg, head of International Workers' Aid (Internationale Arbeiterhilfe), in order to distribute Soviet films in Germany. By 1926, Prometheus had made sufficient profits from the distribution of Soviet director Sergei Eisenstein's *Potemkin* to begin producing its own films, which, through their social realism, were designed as aesthetic and ideological alternatives to the commercial "cinema of illusion." Yet only a few feature films were made, including the first sound film of the German left, *Kuhle Wampe*, before Prometheus was dissolved in February 1932. This production was notable for the range of talent it enlisted—including composer Hanns Eisler, director Slatan Dudow, and writer Bertolt Brecht—as well as for its commitment to communal production methods. It represented an attempt to draw upon Eisenstein's theory of film montage to create a radical, proletarian art form that would counter the Hollywood style by subverting viewer complacency and encouraging audience involvement, analysis, and revolutionary action.[74]

By 1925, Germany's honeymoon with Hollywood was over. The market had been saturated by American films and Hollywood formulae. In fact, many of the films had been disappointing—of inferior quality and outdated, since American distributors made the most of the opportunity to screen older films that had been shut out of Germany during the war. One German trade paper suggested that the Hollywood product might suffice "to feed the hillbillies in Arizona" but was indigestible gruel for the more cultivated German audience. Thus, as the old adage goes, familiarity bred contempt—and allowed German commentators to theorize national difference based upon taste.[75]

Moreover, Hollywood's active campaign to recruit successful German producers, directors, screenwriters, and actors away from native cultural production offended many. But perhaps even more importantly, the international and economic situation had changed. The Dawes Plan temporarily relieved Germany's reparation payment burdens in 1924. After this and the ensuing currency stabilization, German exports dipped as their prices rose. Simultaneously, Germany became a much more attractive and secure place for foreign business ventures.

By mid-decade, then, American investors invaded the German market, and the film industry was not immune to this trend. As the American journal *Photoplay* boasted: "We're getting a throttle-hold on the old world; it's all to the jazz and the celluloid right now."[76] Beginning in 1921, a number of Hollywood companies maneuvered to expand into Eastern European markets through Germany. They began negotiating agreements with financially strapped German film companies to realize that goal and in the process control the "German danger" to their expanding market interests. German executives, on the other hand, sought to forge a profitable working arrangement with Hollywood while discouraging lucrative deals between the Americans and Germany's European competitors; the anticipated payoff would be increased visibility for German films abroad and a larger share of the international market. This business strategy, however, was riddled with risks for German interests, who struggled—often unsuccessfully—to fend off "junior partner" status when concluding and executing agreements.[77]

One of the larger deals of this kind occurred in 1926, when Metro-Goldwyn-Mayer and Paramount concluded a deal with UFA, which worked to the disadvantage of the ailing German firm. UFA received 17 million Reichmarks and the promise that ten of its films would be distributed in the United States annually, but in return it was compelled to distribute four times as many American films and assign them long-running terms at its theaters. In fact, Metro-Goldwyn-Mayer and Paramount envisioned their bailout of UFA as a sure way of circumventing frustrating German import barriers since their products would be guaranteed access to UFA theaters, which were considered to be the "cream of the German amusement world." Similar deals were cut by Universal (with Terra in 1925) and Metro-Goldwyn-Mayer (with Phoebus in 1927) in the hopes of conquering this singularly resistant European market.[78]

This trend, along with Hollywood's overall dominant position in the international market, provoked widespread alarm about the integrity of Germany's national culture and initiated a period of cultural anti-Americanism. By the late 1920s, "America" was no longer synonymous with openness, democracy, and freedom but instead came to be identified with dehumanizing rationalization and the technical efficiency and rigid discipline of Henry Ford's auto plants. According to theater critic Herbert Ihering, "an ardent proponent of mass culture and cultural modernity" and, not incidentally, an admirer of Charlie Chaplin: "The number of people who watch movies and do not read books is in the millions. They are all subjugated by the American taste, they become standardized and uniform. . . . The American film is the new world militarism. It marches on. It is more dangerous than the Prussian military. It does not devour individuals but whole countries." Thus, after mid-decade and an altered historical context, the metaphors of national culture reversed, rendering German culture the menaced victim of an uncontrollable all-consuming American culture.[79]

Hollywood's high profile on the German market sparked an "identity crisis" for Weimar cinema along with an increasing rhetoric of national cultural protectionism by German filmmakers, who, at this precise historical moment, were looking to Hollywood for know-how and financial assistance to sharpen their competitive edge vis-à-vis both European and domestic rivals. Thus, a tension developed as German film firms positioned themselves as ready protégés of Hollywood benefactors only to chafe—in oedipal distress—at their continued junior status.[80]

Fearing irremediable economic and cultural subordination, the trade organization for the German film industry identified Hollywood as a threat to German interests and identity, claiming that Hollywood peddled propaganda whose power lay in the fact that it "slips unnoticed into the unconscious of the masses." American films were accused of bombarding German viewers with images of automobiles, appliances, and the like, thus stimulating the viewer's desire to possess such products. Hollywood developed a potent—and highly exportable—vehicle for self-advertisement, in which visual pleasure was inseparable from fantasies of consumption. The problem for German business interests, one assumes, is that Germany was not yet fitted with Ford-style plants that could produce sufficient quantities of inexpensive, mass-produced goods to satisfy these desires. As a result, film industry leaders argued, Hollywood films, with their depictions of American technology and consumer goods, convinced the world of the higher quality of American products and therefore of the economic and technological superiority of the United States.[81] It appears, by the way, that this analysis accurately reflected American assumptions that "trade follows film." In fact, Hollywood won the sustained support of the American government, as well as the establishment of a film division in the U.S. Department of Commerce in 1926, by arguing that its films were more effective than "100,000 salesmen" in selling American products, ideals, customs, and culture and "undermining those of other countries"![82]

America's growing economic and cultural influence on the German market did not go unchallenged. Again, as in World War I, the German military and nationalist businessmen rallied their forces to resist the American offensive. The War Ministry, in a repeat attempt to influence national film production, secretly sunk millions of Reichmarks into a new company, Phoebus Films. Contemporaries were stunned by the mercurial growth of Phoebus, which seemingly emerged out of nowhere to assume an impressive position in film production and distribution as well as the control of a chain of movie theaters. The money invested in Phoebus never appeared in the federal budget, and the Reichstag was left in the dark about the venture. When the investment information finally leaked in 1927, the resulting scandal forced the sale of Phoebus's assets. Alfred Hugenberg, however, stepped in to rescue its director, E. H. Correll, by appointing him board member and head of production at UFA.[83]

Hugenberg, by now a media magnate and leader of the German National People's Party, repatriated UFA in 1927 by paying off Paramount and Metro-Goldwyn-Mayer, thereby initiating a period of impressive expansion and cartelization. By 1931, UFA controlled 6 production companies, 5 distribution companies, 37 theater chains, and 19 foreign companies, among other holdings. In addition, UFA led the way in reclaiming the Austrian and French markets for German films. In 1923–24 with Austrian currency stabilization, Germany had lost its overwhelming postwar advantage (90 percent of the market) to the Americans. From a dismal proportion of 5 German for every 40 American films on the Austrian market in 1924, Germany came back in 1927 to hold a 37 percent share (to the United States' 48 percent). By the end of the decade, the introduction of sound helped bump Germany to the 50 percent mark, and in 1933 the German share stood at 60 percent (with the United States down to 30 percent). In France, the German share of its former enemy's market went from less than 3 percent in 1924 (the United States held 85 percent) to nearly 30 percent just five years later (when the American share declined to 48.4 percent). This jump is remarkable, given the hostile atmosphere that dominated even business relationships after the war.[84]

The increase in German exports must be credited to the efforts of German producer Erich Pommer, who in 1924 succeeded in concluding an important bilateral agreement between UFA and the major French film distributor, Etablissements Aubert, that served to reopen the French market to German films in earnest. By 1928, a flurry of similar bilateral agreements were made by various film firms across Western and Central Europe, thus increasing the overall circulation of European films throughout Europe and securing a prominent place for UFA by chipping away at American competition.[85] By this time, UFA had become the self-appointed ringleader of a cooperative venture that came to be dubbed "Film Europe." Beginning in 1924, Pommer lobbied European film interests in a campaign to create a large European market, comparable to that of the United States. Pommer recognized that European film companies could not hope to compete in the long run with the more expensive productions of Hollywood companies (whose investments were covered by domestic receipts alone) without a "system of regular trade which will enable the producers to amortise their films rapidly." German companies at that time could recoup only 30–40 percent of production costs on the domestic market. His goal, then, was to find a way to allow producers to increase their production budgets—and hence create more lavish and visually compelling pictures—and still turn a healthy profit. Although he argued on behalf of a European-style film "which will no longer be French, English, Italian, or German,"[86] the result would have been a boost in revenues for UFA, which was one of the only European companies that would have been in a position, due to its size, assets, and facilities, to take advantage of the expanded market. Thus, the creation of a healthy national cinema in Germany was linked to a kind of market imperialism, which would reach its brutal climax under Hitler.

So despite Hugenberg's nationalist-conservative propensities, his leadership of UFA seems to have struck a balance between the desire to propagandize his right-wing views and the overtly commercial pursuit of profit. The UFA newsreel *Wochenschau* disseminated the only consistently nationalist messages, although Hugenberg-controlled newspapers periodically entered the fray to denounce the screening of controversial American films like *All Quiet on the Western Front*, which was deemed insulting and injurious to German national pride and masculinity.[87]

Perhaps Hugenberg's greatest "nationalist" achievement was his success in reclaiming and consolidating a significant portion of the German film industry under UFA control and the management of Ludwig Klitzsch. Drawing on Hollywood business techniques, Klitzsch by 1928 embarked on a course of vigorous centralization and rationalization that, for the first time in German history, insured that a major domestic film firm would be run according to "strict economic principles"—something that went a long way toward building a viable national cinema. Moreover, Klitzsch founded a German film trade association, Spitzenorganisation der Filmwirtschaft (SPIO), modeled after the American Motion Picture Producers' and Distributors' Association, in the hope of building a central body that could be as effective as its American counterpart in lobbying for industry interests at the national level.[88]

Hugenberg's restraint from intervening in feature film production ultimately allowed producers like Pommer to locate a loyal audience for German films as well as create a recognizable look: the highly polished UFA style. Here too, ironically, Hollywood provided the model. Pommer returned from a two-year professional stint in California in 1928, having learned the lesson of how to manufacture "mass appeal." Abandoning an export strategy based upon avant-garde aesthetics and "difference" from Hollywood, Pommer maintained that art film (*Kunstfilm*) could neither elevate the taste of the masses nor do good business: "What is most peculiar is that it is precisely the simplicity, naïveté, and happy-go-lucky attitude [*Problemlosigkeit*] of American film that is criticized Europe . . . that constitute its principle strength" at home and abroad. The challenge for German filmmakers, then, was to cultivate "entertainment value" by following Hollywood's example. "While there is no recipe" for guaranteeing international success, he argued, "at least a financial flop can be avoided by eliminating all of the elements that annoy the foreign mentality."[89] For Pommer, this meant developing simple stories that had both well-defined conflict and emotional immediacy—products with universal appeal that would captivate both "demanding and less demanding" viewers. Thus, Pommer advocated tried-and-true Hollywood techniques: product standardization, narrational economy, the cultivation of stars, and camera work and editing that situate viewers in such a way that they identify with the action and the actors on screen. The point was to broaden the film's form of address in order to transcend the barriers of nationality, education, class, and sex in order to reach the largest possible international and domestic audience. Thus, this strategy was intended to enhance the attractiveness of German films for export and, as importantly, to secure a larger loyal domestic viewership for German films.[90]

To some extent, however, a distinction remained between those films produced mainly for export and those intended for domestic consumption. German producers experimented with German themes to win over native audiences and developed feature films based upon national history, biography, legends, and fairy tales (like *Fridericus Rex* and *Die Nibelungen*). With the introduction of sound, Pommer and others perfected and popularized operettas (such as *Die Drei von der Tankstelle* and *Die Kongreß tanzt*) featuring up-and-coming favorites like Willy Fritsch and Lilian Harvey and relying on stars like Hans Albers and, later, Marika Rökk (who modeled herself on her Hollywood idol, Eleanor Powell) to build a loyal following for the native product. The German film industry had gone a long way toward modernizing itself by mimicking the capitalist techniques (such as centralized management and rationalized and standardized production) pioneered by Hollywood over the previous decade and a half. By 1933, German films dominated the domestic market—a national cinema had finally been born.[91]

Film and the Fascist Response

It was once a historical truism that Joseph Goebbels was a propaganda genius who expertly dazzled the German public with Nazi visions of nationalist grandeur and then led it down the bloody road of war and extermination. More recently, scholars have begun to deemphasize Goebbels's role as evil pied piper in order to consider the nature of Nazi propaganda (its formal elements, its appeal, and the extent of its effectiveness) as well as the place and meanings that it—and other cultural products—had in the social and cultural "economy" of the Third Reich.[92]

Such studies have taught us to stop taking the Nazis at their word when assessing the effectiveness of their public relations efforts. Nazi propaganda, it seems, was most effective when it confirmed what people already believed to be true.[93] Furthermore, it has been suggested that we be more critical both in our analysis of what constituted propaganda and in our use of images that appeared in German feature films and documentaries under Hitler. Most, after all, were some form of fantasy construction. Eric Rentschler has argued that the classification "Nazi film" implies a semiotic unity that is difficult to locate in the "highly popular" German cinema of the 1930s and early 1940s. Far from being straightforward "ideological containers," films produced during the Nazi period were "replete with popular stars, upbeat scores, and alluring production values"; as a result, they resemble pre-Hitler *and* Hollywood-style productions in their film-formal strategies and modes of address. In sum, scholars are beginning to suggest that in gauging the way ideology functions in films of the period, what should be "emphasized is less the peculiarity of National Socialist films than what they have in common with the entertainment films of other countries and periods."[94]

Films from the Nazi period are now understood to be "ambiguous and complex entities" whose ideological potency and processes reside "in the details of form and structure" more than mere content or story line. What needs explaining is the way in which the many overtly nonpolitical films of the period nonetheless served a crucial ideological function during the Third Reich. What needs explaining is *how* ideology is grounded in entertainment, how it works on the needs and wishes of the psyche, and whether and how its appeal differs according to sex, class, or ethnicity. Answering these questions will help us ascertain the extent of its social and broadly political impact and may well account for its past and even current appeal—for "Nazi films" continue to be recycled (and more frequently than one would wish, historical documentaries on the Third Reich uncritically employ footage from Nazi-sponsored docu-spectaculars, like Leni Riefenstahl's *Triumph of the Will*, to represent the "realities" of that period).[95]

The best studies of film and culture under Hitler have renounced the geographical and temporal isolation of Nazi Germany—thus bridging the historiographical divide that closed it off from the imperial and republican pasts—to investigate an extended period of German economic, social, and cultural modernization and explore the fit between Nazi hypernationalist politics and the realities of an increasingly American-dominated world market. The problem, then, is to determine the ways in which cinematic production, control, and spectatorship during the Third Reich departed from earlier German developments and to situate Nazi cinema in the context of the international trends of the time.[96]

National Socialist attention to the broadly political uses of cinema initially lagged behind even that of the Communists, and it was not until 1930 that Joseph Goebbels was assigned the task of exploiting the possibilities of the medium for advertisement, recruitment, and electioneering. Once Hitler assumed the chancellorship in January 1933, Goebbels became head of the newly established Ministry for Public Enlightenment and Propaganda and moved quickly to extend party control over the media and accelerate trends, begun during World War I, to centralize and later nationalize the cinema.

To this end, Goebbels founded the Reich Film Chamber in July 1933, which became responsible for prescreening film treatments and approving the consequent film scripts and personnel for each planned production. In addition, this body reviewed and censored each finished product before release. The Film Chamber included a special department for "political guidance," which exerted ideological control. This function became an official criterion for film control in 1934 as a result of a revised film censorship law. The new legislation mandated that each film be graded according to a system of distinctions, or *Prädikate*, which were designed to encourage the production of politically and artistically valuable commercial films as well as instructional films for use in the classroom. Thus, Goebbels proclaimed that Nazi film control would have a "positive" effect on film quality. Films awarded high grades benefited from reduced local entertainment taxes, a promise of material advantage that gave the Nazi Party some real leverage over film content and presentation.[97]

The Nazi drive to consolidate and "nationalize" the German film industry was not finally realized until 1942. But the future of domestic film production was secured early on by the Reich-controlled Filmkreditbank (FKB), which was created in June 1933 to provide much-needed credit to German producers. The Nazi regime thereby won the loyalty of many in the film industry who were quick to recognize that cooperation with the state could protect their interests and increase profits. By 1935, 70 percent of all German films were financed through the FKB. This financing mechanism helped to consolidate the film industry, since the receipt of film credit was tied to membership in the SPIO (which joined Goebbels's Film Chamber in June 1933). Over the next year, the film industry and state settled into a "harmonic" working relationship as it became clear that there were no necessary conflicts between the political-ideological goals of the Nazis and the profits goals of industry members. In fact, Goebbels bolstered industry health by lowering entertainment taxes for films and generally alleviating some of the most chronic and debilitating annoyances of the home market.[98]

The government intervened again in 1936–37 to bolster the domestic market for UFA's films at a time when exports were falling off. What emerged was a revived UFA, transformed into a "state protected oligopoly." Then, in January 1942, UFA, Tobis, Terra, Berlin Film, and Bavaria-Filmkunst were merged (along with Vienna Film and Prague Film) to form a centralized holding company, Ufa-Film (UFI), under state authority. The Austrian *Anschluß* and Germany's military pursuits multiplied outlets for German films, so by 1942, the Nazi government lorded over 8,400 cinemas across Europe, which screened German films for an estimated 1 billion viewers.[99]

In his first speech to German film industry members in March 1933, Goebbels called upon the audience to "reform" German film by making works of art imprinted with the "power of conviction"; only then would German films realize their full potential to influence the public's beliefs and behavior. And only when the ideological "conviction" of German films surpassed the best products of the Soviet Union (such as *Potemkin*), and the quality exceeded that of Hollywood films, would it be proclaimed that "Germany leads the world."[100]

Goebbels's quest for a cinematic alternative to the American and Soviet styles was the cultural accompaniment to Hitler's plan to construct a Germanized "Mitteleuropa" to counterbalance the political and economic influence and ideologies of the territorially expansive United States and Soviet Union. In 1935 Goebbels pushed this plan one step further by resurrecting Pommer's project of establishing a "Film Europe." This time around, the organizing body was the German-led International Film Chamber, which, by 1942, enforced European unity through strong-arm techniques like military censorship and the confiscation of (particularly Jewish) property. "Its real aim," wrote one contemporary, "was to bring the European cinema under Nazi supremacy."[101]

Like the German high command in World War I, Goebbels emphasized the importance of aesthetics, technical competence, and entertainment value in creating effective propaganda and tended to favor the "soft sell" of dramatic features over the more aggressive devices of overt propaganda pieces. As a result, only one in every six feature films produced during the Third Reich was a recognizable vehicle for disseminating Nazi racial or nationalist ideology.[102] Moreover, Goebbels exhorted native filmmakers to learn from their international competition and continued to screen Hollywood films in private showings—both for his own enjoyment and as instruction to industry members. As late as 1942, however, he was struck by moments of doubt about whether native filmmakers were up to the task. After a private screening of *Swaney River*, Goebbels marveled at the boldness of the American effort but reflected sadly that German film artists, in comparison, were "too burdened with tradition and reverence" in cultural matters; they lacked the vision and courage to repackage their "museum pieces" for the modern age—hardly the sort of cultural vitality required to lead a Reich into its 1,000-year future! What was needed was an infusion of the sort of cultural boldness and feel for the modern that characterized Hollywood productions. Thus, what Victoria de Grazia has argued for fascist Italy applies equally to Nazi Germany: "exceptional familiarity with Americanism, even outright imitation, was not considered antithetical to forming a self-consciously nationalist mass culture."[103]

Goebbels and Hitler understood after all that viewers were discerning customers who had to be coaxed into the cinema by tempting advertisements and promises of adventure and romance. Anyone who has seen the Agfa-color fantasy extravaganza, *Baron Münchhausen*, which was designed to rival Hollywood's *Thief of Baghdad* and Disney productions, knows that there is plenty of visual pleasure still to be had in the best German films from the Nazi period, in spite of the dubious gender and racial ideologies that can be read out of them.[104]

And one might add that Goebbels appears, on at least one occasion, to have been willing to sacrifice Nazi racial ideology in favor of commercial appeal—when he sought to retain the Jewish Erich Pommer and his golden marketing touch in Germany, despite the official push in 1933 to "nationalize" German culture by purging some 5,000 "non-Aryans" from the mass media.[105]

In fact, the appeal of national socialism may well have been enhanced by Hitler's immersion in and internalization of commercialized mass culture. Robin Lenman has noted that "Hitler himself could be described as a product of *Schund*," which was expressed in his particular style of "political self-represen-tation [and] gave him much of the allure of a pulp-book savior: a kind of Captain America for the lower middle classes." Hans Dieter Schäfer has broadened the argument, suggesting that the Nazi regime won the loyalty of the majority of Germans by playing on consumer desires while exhibiting the savvy of com-mercial advertisers in formulating political packaging and its content. As Schä-fer put it, national socialism benefited from the "unabashed display of con-sumer and entertainment values"—something that, along with a more general appeal to national identity, may help account for its cross-class appeal.[106]

Like a good advertising executive, Hitler was sensitive to the cognitive disso-nance accompanying social trauma and, following the New York stock market crash of 1929, diagnosed the renewed crisis in Germany to be as much psycho-logical as economic. His solution involved bolstering the public's confidence with election slogans like "Think optimistically!" and "Raise the standard of living!" Over the course of the 1930s, his government encouraged workers' longing for a comfortable life-style by organizing vacations, theater and concert visits, and lessons in horseback riding, sailing, tennis, and skiing—leisure pas-times previously limited to the higher social classes.[107]

Hitler consolidated support for his regime through a determined drive to build a consumer society that would rival that of the United States. Proclaiming in 1936 that the "German *Volk* has exactly the same needs and desires as the American!," Hitler called for the production of affordable German automobiles. His much-publicized goal to "motorize Germany" must have seemed within reach, given the fact that the regime recently had fought unemployment by putting Germans back to work building the *Autobahnen*. The reality, however, never lived up to the hype, and by the end of the decade, there were only 1.5 million automobiles in Germany, compared to the 23 million that Americans were driving almost ten years earlier.[108]

Up until the war years, Germans were promised access to all that the inter-national market had to offer, and American products were prized above all. Coca-Cola bottling plants and distributors multiplied under Hitler, making that soft drink so popular that in 1947, even after a five-year absence from the market during the war, it was placed at the top of Germans' list of best-known brands of nonalcoholic beverages. The 1949 ad campaign proudly proclaimed, "Coca-Cola ist wieder da! [Coca-Cola is back!]." German banks offered savings plans for purchasing single-family homes, German electrical firms advertised household appliances and technologies pioneered in the United States, and German women read magazines to get the latest makeup, fashion, and diet tips and to compare their body measurements with those of Hollywood starlets.[109]

American culture remained accessible to the German public through 1940. And although German filmmakers continued to refine the popular genres they launched during the Weimar Republic, the hottest Hollywood films bested prewar domestic features at the box office. Nonetheless, perceptions of a Hollywood "threat" to German cultural identity and economic sovereignty, articulated by business and cultural elites in the mid-1920s, seem to have dissipated to a great extent. This was probably due to Hollywood's declining share of the German market, which slipped from 44.5 percent in 1926 to 21 percent in 1933 (following the introduction of sound movies), while the German share of its own market rose during this same period from 39.2 percent to 65 percent. Moreover, the Nazi regime's concerted efforts on behalf of its native industries no doubt also quelled anxieties.[110]

Over the course of the 1930s, Berlin cinemas ran special week-long programs focusing on the films of stars like Clark Gable, Joan Crawford, and Greta Garbo. According to one critic, the German public responded with feelings of "primitive joy" when watching the comedies of Buster Keaton or Laurel and Hardy, which impressed with their aura of "robust self-confidence." Betty Boop and Popeye (or "Pop der Seemann") had enthusiastic followings, and a film reviewer in the *Berliner Tagesblatt* wrote in November 1936 that an "evening of Disney films—no matter when it occurs—means the gift of a Christmas present." Irving Berlin's music in *Broadway Melody* was praised in the press for its "lightness and effortlessness," while the movie's tempo and character treatment were described as conveying a sense of "powerful vitality." This dazzling array of cinematic virtuosity caused one critic, in 1937, to call upon German filmmakers to undertake a systematic study of Hollywood's artistic specimens, "not in order to surpass America" but to produce in Germany "to the extent it is possible, similarly consummately crafted films."[111]

Film magazines and illustrated weeklies featured stars' biographies and interviews with such stars as Katharine Hepburn, Myrna Loy, Claudette Colbert, and Gary Cooper, along with Clark Gable, Joan Crawford, and Greta Garbo. Special attention was lavished on former hometown girl, Marlene Dietrich, whose film *The Scarlet Empress* was a smash hit in 1934 Berlin. Her singing performances in *The Devil Is a Woman* drew audience applause in 1935, and her popularity was such that her last new release in Germany in 1936, *Desire*, was followed by reprises of her older films, like *Blonde Venus* and *Shanghai Ex-*

press. Dietrich's Hollywood stardom provoked both sycophantic praise and scornful rebukes from some in the press who accused her of spurning "the ideal of [German?] womanhood" in favor of an "undisguised [American?] eroticism" (a characterization that, interestingly enough, reversed the American reception of Dietrich as the sophisticated *European* vamp, whose sex appeal derived from her exotic origins and husky accented voice). Detractors were not, however, permitted the final word, and the popular *Das Magazine*, which often featured news on Hollywood stars and American fashions, issued a passionate defense of Dietrich.[112]

Thus, national socialism won popular support by keeping its population integrated into the international leisure and information circuit. It promised access to the best products and the most modern technology on the world market and insured Germans that national renewal would not entail confinement to the cultural provinces. Moreover, it seemed to suggest that it would be possible to enjoy the security of membership in the German *Volksgemeinschaft* and to cultivate modern social and individual identities as well. By 1937, for example, a "camping trailer movement" was well under way, and its advertisements and advice books emphasized the freedom gained from mobility: "We live where and how we want, and no one tells us what to do. Truly a paradise!"[113] Thus, consumption became the focus for fantasies of a life of autonomy and independence apart from the national community and Nazi politics.

Nonetheless, one would not want to argue that Nazi culture was built on the same forms of address and fantasy as those generated by Hollywood. An appraisal of Nazi cinema and film aesthetics yields a number of crucial differences. Unlike Hollywood, Nazi cinema attempted to counteract the "disorienting" impact of modern life by providing "a sense of belonging and ritual continuity." This, according to Saul Friedländer, was achieved through "a return to a debased romantic inspiration, to an aesthetic stripped of the force and novelty it had 150 years ago at the dawn of modernity." Expanding on Friedländer's analysis, Eric Rentschler has emphasized that this "reflects National Socialism's penchant for the premodern world as the source of all values, the recourse to prior notions of unspoiled nature, organic communities, and primal directness as antidotes to the ills of the modern world. For Nazi ideology, argues Friedländer, 'the model of future society is only a reflection of the past.' And this past harbors a romantic fatalism, one dreaming of *Götterdämmerung*, the heroic death, surrender to destiny."[114] According to Rentschler, this "dissolution of alienation in ecstatic feelings of community" takes a profoundly misogynist and male form in films of the Third Reich. The result, he argues, is a "triumph of male fantasy production" that forsakes heterosexual romantic attachments in favor of a more intense—and eroticized—male bond, which is ultimately safely sublimated through struggle in the service of a greater cause—the German nation and *Volk*:

"Crucially and consistently, the projected weak images of women form the basis of signification for many Nazi films, reflecting a vulnerable and ultimately paranoid order. Put in other terms: women act as a negative image without which no positive one can exist. . . . Nazi cinema goes far beyond the institutionalized sexism of Hollywood movies and the way in which the classical narrative recuperates even the strongest women in the male discourse. Nazi cinema does not leave it at simple recuperation, though; women are to be overcome, indeed sacrificed."

Yet not only women had to be "overcome." Films of the Third Reich also externalized qualities undesirable for the new *Volksgemeinschaft* by projecting these onto racial or cultural "others." Thus, while the German hero attained his heroic masculinity through the sacrifice or subjugation of German women, he achieved his Aryan purity and cultural superiority through the containment or destruction of the Jew, Gypsy, or Communist.[115]

Rentschler suggests that Nazi cinema also differed from Hollywood in terms of its mode of address. He speculates that while the commercial industries (of democracies?) "centered on the single viewer's narcissism," the "state run apparatus" of Nazi cinema focused on the "collective response" of the larger community. "Quite consistently," he continues, "Nazi film narratives—and not just the shrilly propagandistic ones—forsake visual pleasure, voyeurism, and female sexuality, the sources of fascination in the classical [Hollywood] narrative text, in the name of more compelling categories."[116] Thus, it seems, films of the Nazi period praised seriousness of purpose, self-discipline, and female self-abnegation and held out the hope that such individual sacrifice would be rewarded by the revitalization of a (masculine) German community.

Rentschler's interpretation is useful in providing insight into the nature of the "fascist imaginary" and in locating more precisely where and how it overlapped with or differed from its Hollywood counterpart. Moreover, it provides a starting point for analyzing male film-viewing pleasure under Hitler. On the other hand, reading Nazi cinema as representing the "triumph of male fantasy production" raises significant issues for female film spectatorship during the Third Reich. One wonders what pleasures or "compensations" (emotional or other) these films offered women, who, after all, constituted a significant percentage of moviegoers. For, as feminist film theory has taught us, films are often riddled with textual ambiguity, and their reception and mode of appeal can vary according to the social positioning and personal desires of their historical audience and the political-historical context in which they occur.[117]

The same question might be posed for youth, for there is some evidence from the 1940s that suggests that not all young Germans accepted "National Socialism's promise that private and public happiness are one and the same."[118] By the war years, and especially after 1941, when Nazi mobilization of the population involved compulsory service and membership in organizations like the Labor Service and Hitler Youth and when the civilian population began to feel the effects of the war through Allied bombings, the meaning of consumption—and especially consumption of Western products—appeared to shift once more. American and British culture became the basis for fantasies of escape and nonconformist identity, particularly among teenagers. Middle-class teens in Hamburg, Frankfurt, and Karlsruhe flouted Nazi prohibitions against "Nigger and Jew music" by forming their own "Harlem," "OK-Gang," and "Cic-cac" clubs, where they listened to the latest jazz, sported British and American fashions, and called each other "old-hot-boy." Urban working-class youths gathered in renegade groups called the Edelweiss Pirates, Navajos, and Roving Dudes and set out on hiking or camping trips to flee the supervision of school and state. While on such trips, they shed their received identities and transformed themselves into rugged individuals modeled on their favorite cowboy or gangster hero; thus Hans would become "Texas Jack," Dieter "Alaska Bill," and Klaus "Whiskey-Jonny." Although this behavior is best documented among teenage boys, there is some evidence to suggest that girls sometimes went along and sexual experimentation was often the result. It is not clear, however, if girls were admitted to the fantasy play—if they were assigned or chose temporary new identities—but their presence at least suggests that they too were engaged in a quest for freedom and autonomy.[119]

Although such behavior might be dismissed as a generational (and working-class) revolt against authority, which happened in this case to be represented by the Nazi state, the content of both the rebellion and the official response suggests that something more was afoot. Hitler's attempt to maintain the sense of a peacetime economy into the early 1940s, with its accompanying access to consumer goods, created expectations that could not be met—and behaviors that could not be controlled—once wartime sacrifices were demanded by a regime that could no longer guarantee consumer plenty or permit access to international culture. Nazi officials did, on a number of occasions, attempt to soften the stick with a carrot. During the late war years, for example, German troops on the Eastern front were permitted to enjoy American jazz both to keep up morale and to prevent them from tuning in to the BBC. By then, it had become clear that Goebbels's efforts to wean German jazz fans away from popular American recordings to a more "wholesome" native imitation, German dance music, had failed miserably because the latter was not hot enough (due to the replacement of brass horns by strings!) to satisfy discriminating consumer tastes.[120]

Yet the official ban on foreign—and especially American—imports altered the cultural meanings of these goods; consequently, their continued enjoyment or imitation became an avenue of resistance to the ever-increasing "stage management of public life" by the Nazi regime. Sometimes this cultural nonconformity turned political and evolved into active resistance to the state. But this occurred only in rare cases. More frequently, illicit consumption was a form of symbolic revolt and was used to construct an alternate ego, which thrived outside of the public eye in an "isolated, depoliticized privacy," peopled only by the individual and some like-minded friends.[121]

All of this raises fascinating questions about the relationship between consumer expectations and identities on the one hand and the creation of political legitimacy and national identity on the other. This problem did not end with the Third Reich but continued across the divide of military defeat at "zero hour" in 1945 to complicate the work of postwar reconstruction by Allied officials and native elites alike.

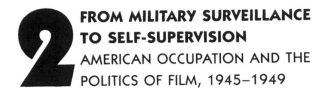

FROM MILITARY SURVEILLANCE TO SELF-SUPERVISION
AMERICAN OCCUPATION AND THE POLITICS OF FILM, 1945–1949

The Allied victors understood their military success over Germany in May 1945 as merely the crucial first step in eradicating national socialism. After defeat, Germany was to be occupied, demilitarized, and politically decentralized; moreover, all agreed some months before at Yalta that defeated Germany would be denazified and democratized. Although the general principles upon which German reconstruction would be based were mutually established, the Allies' interpretations of these principles, and of the specifics of implementation, differed considerably.

Despite dissonant ideological agendas, all four powers recognized the centrality of the mass media in facilitating the democratization process. During the first days following German defeat, military personnel seized German presses, radio stations, and film studios, along with their support industries, effectively suspending German media production and control. Allied officers closely regulated the media in their zones and initially forbade German use of these critical tools of communication and popular reeducation. All four powers embarked on a process of denazifying media personnel and reorganizing the media industries. Initially, the media were regulated strictly on a zonal basis, since issues involving national reconstruction and political and economic centralization were hotly contested among the Allies. By 1948, it was clear that ideological differences between the Western Allies and the Soviets would result in the creation of two separate German states, each marked by the dominant victor's vision of political, economic, and cultural organization.

This chapter focuses on postwar negotiations concerning the revival of German film production and control in the Western zones, and in particular on the triumph of the American model for industry organization and censorship. The U.S. Military Government advocated a reconstructed German film industry based upon the principles of free competition, open markets, decartelization, and the abolition of state control. Thus, democratization was linked to structural changes in the industry. State control of the cinema was condemned as a totalitarian practice, an ideological weapon employed against domestic (and conquered) populations. As one contemporary argued, "Hitler's Fourth Army after the Army, Navy, and Air Force was Propaganda, of which the psychological 'atom bomb' was the film."[1] In a democratically reconstructed Germany, film would be subject only to the putatively nonideological dictates of the market economy. American film officers were therefore mandated to abolish film cartels, which could be easily controlled by state authorities. The Nazi model of the state-sponsored, state-regulated film monopoly, which found its culmination in the creation of UFI in 1942, was to be extirpated.

Although the American vision ultimately prevailed in the Western zones of Germany, it was not realized without a protracted period of negotiation. American authorities first had to convince their British and French counterparts that their vision would serve the process of democratization without threatening the political and economic interests of these Allies. They then had to appeal to members of the German film industry for cooperation, dangling the promise of official assistance and protection against the threat of local moral censorship by renascent native authorities. Finally, American officials were confronted with substantial resistance from state and church leaders. Local authorities had a long history of cultural influence in Germany and were often vocal opponents of the American vision. American officials needed to quiet the rumblings of these native elites, who sought to regain the voice in matters of film control that they had lost under Hitler.

Critics of American film policy in postwar West Germany have argued that the American principles of decartelization and open markets weakened the native film industry, rendering it incapable of competing with Hollywood for domestic or international markets. At stake was the revival of national culture and the recovery of an important industrial sector of the German domestic and export economy. American officials were accused of cynically engaging in a project of economic and cultural imperialism in the U.S. zone, assisted by the major Hollywood companies.

In this chapter, I will argue that the U.S. government and Hollywood did not share the same agenda and only rarely presented a united front. Although American officials saw a political purpose in keeping the German market open to the "free flow" of American cultural products, they resisted wholesale American domination of German markets in the interests of a stable German reconstruction. American officials acted decisively to organize native film interests in order to tie cultural production and control to a market mechanism. They genuinely believed that by importing American forms of film censorship and industry organization (the American film industry had been forcibly decartelized in the 1940s), they were laying the foundation for a viable German cinema. German industry members complained sorely about decartelization; nonetheless, they were quite willing to cooperate with their new masters, particularly since the American plan seemed to offer a solution to the distressing cultural meddling of local state and religious leaders.

Although the West German film industry ultimately found itself confined to the ghetto of the domestic market, the causes of this cultural and economic plight are tied to more than the incursions of Hollywood, abetted at times by the American government. As we shall see in the next two chapters, domestic German interest groups, and the industry itself, must also share the responsibility.

Military Occupation and Cinematic Reorientation, 1945–1946

Shortly after German defeat, the American victors began to dismantle their wartime organizations to prepare to meet the demands of governing occupied Germany. In mid-July 1945, the Anglo-American Supreme Headquarters Allied Expeditionary Forces was disbanded and with it went the Psychological Warfare Division (PWD), which had been responsible for the "planning and organization of psychological warfare against the Germans." In the U.S. zone, the PWD was replaced by the Information Control Division (ICD). There were continuities in personnel, as might be expected. General Robert McClure, who had led the PWD during the war, became the director of the ICD; and the ICD received a new commission, as befitting the switch from a wartime propaganda mission to civil reconstruction, "to assist in the reestablishment of a free German media on a sound basis and reorient the German spirit."[2] On a practical level, the ICD published U.S. Military Government directives, attempted to foster German understanding of the American occupation program, and monitored and oversaw the various media, each of which had a separate branch within the ICD.[3]

During the first months of occupation, American authorities in Germany were bound by Joint Chiefs of Staff (JCS) directive 1067, which called for German demilitarization, denazification, and deindustrialization. A punitive directive, JCS 1067 was based upon a thoroughgoing mistrust of the German people, whom it declared collectively guilty for the slaughter of the war and the Nazi death camps and whose history putatively proved that they were, as a group, fundamentally militaristic and antiliberal. Because of the perceived virulency of the German contagion, JCS 1067 strictly forbade fraternization between the occupation forces and German nationals. Shamelessly engaging in tourist-variety national stereotyping, the official instructional film for U.S. soldiers, *Your Job in Germany*, counseled wariness and extreme caution when confronting the natives, "no matter how charming and clean and blond and music-loving they seem, no matter how prettily and innocently they execute peasant dances in the village square."[4] It even "specifically warn[ed] soldiers to ignore children, all steeped in Nazi propaganda."[5] Given official assumptions regarding the spiritual state of the German population, ICD officers had their work cut out for them.

At the end of the war, the German film industry was at a standstill. Allied bombing in the last months of the war had interrupted production, disrupted screenings, and made the reliable distribution of films impossible due to impassible roads and damaged railways. Once military occupation began, all German film activities were forbidden, and German mayors were mandated to collect and surrender to the ICD any German films in their localities. Such early and forceful control of film in the U.S. zone reflected ICD assumptions regarding the power and potential virulency of the moving image. As an official at the U.S. Office of War Information (OWI) commented the previous year while preparing for peace, films "have an obvious propaganda potency. They have a longer life than the spoken word and . . . more authenticity."[6] For both ideological and practical reasons, then, the Motion Picture Branch (MPB) of the ICD initially looked to Hollywood to supply films for its reeducation efforts.[7]

Films began to be screened regularly in the U.S. zone in late July 1945, when film officers permitted twenty theaters to open. Within two months, thirty more cinemas were licensed to show American films. Shortly thereafter, the order was given to open up to 250 cinemas a month in the U.S. zone in order to facilitate reorientation and to provide Germans with "some form of entertainment and . . . warm shelter during the impending winter months." Within the year, the MPB reported 730 functioning cinemas.[8]

In order to fill screentime and initiate the reeducation process, ICD officials "urgently requested" that Hollywood donate quality feature films, which they expected would assist "in conveying to the people of the occupied areas an understanding of American life and democratic institutions."[9] The eight major American film companies promised full cooperation and then took their time sending old, fully amortized films that had not yet been screened on the German market. By late 1946, only thirty-two films had been designated by the ICD as suitable for showing. These ranged from *The Maltese Falcon* (Warner Brothers, 1941), *Young Tom Edison* (Metro-Goldwyn-Mayer, 1940), and *Going My Way* (Paramount, 1944), to *Remember the Day* (Twentieth Century-Fox, 1942), *One Hundred Men and a Girl* (Universal, 1937), and *I Married a Witch* (United Artists, 1942). Some were subsequently pulled from exhibition. *Action in the North Atlantic* (Warner Brothers, 1943) was withdrawn because it provoked "unrest" among viewers in Bavaria and Bremen, who "refused to accept . . . that a [German] U-boat commander would willfully run down a lifeboat, even though the occupants were Allied seamen." *Air Force* (Warner Brothers, 1943) and *The Sullivans* (Twentieth Century-Fox, 1944) were canceled because they "extolled the martial spirit"; and *Hold Back the Dawn* (Paramount, 1941) was banned because it showed refugees denied access to the United States, which made the nation of immigrants appear "unduly harsh." Other popular American films, like *Grapes of Wrath* and *Gone with the Wind*, were rejected out-of-hand by the ICD and the OWI due to their subject matter and, in the case of the latter, the portrayal of "objectionable . . . Negro incidents." Finally, a number of approved films were withdrawn from cinemas in the U.S. zone when the Hollywood companies demanded "parity" in the distribution and exhibition of their films. Thus, when the ICD withdrew objectionable films by Warner Brothers, Twentieth Century-Fox, Metro-Goldwyn-Mayer, Universal, and Paramount, they had to balance the offerings by pulling Columbia and RKO films as well. Despite such difficulties, the number of American feature films circulating in the U.S. zone rose to 112 by September 1948 (see appendixes A–B).[10]

Although American occupation authorities realized that liberal democracy would be easier to swallow as entertainment, they lacked a well-formulated positive program that detailed the sorts of feature films required to reeducate former subjects of a totalitarian state. Like their Nazi counterpart, Joseph Goebbels, these democratic masters realized that propaganda was only as good as its "aesthetic and technical quality."[11] Thus, the efficacy of the message was understood as inextricably linked to its entertainment value and the attractiveness of its packaging. Hollywood interests had argued in 1943, in fact, that the "unimpaired entertainment power of the American motion picture . . . constitutes its great strength." They demanded that U.S. officials stop trying to *"write things into* scripts," lest they ruin the international appeal of the Hollywood product. As Eric Johnston, head of the Motion Picture Association of America (MPAA), put it to a Senate committee a few years later, "Our pictures . . . are completely free pictures, and they reflect the freedom under which they are made and the freedom under which they are shown." The U.S. film industry therefore advocated a sort of "free market" approach to propaganda—based upon the success of the American model—and apparently succeeded in convincing many in Congress and the War and State departments that their products "already conveyed the American point of view and that no further positive steps" were needed to enhance it.[12]

Ironically, given such initial optimism, the ICD film program was hampered by the delaying tactics of Hollywood firms bent on reserving their finest wares for a more profitable future, when the German mark would be convertible to hard currency. The ICD resorted to concentrating on the "negative" censorship of American films, for if they could not clearly articulate the desirable, they nonetheless could identify the unacceptable. Domestic problems plaguing the

world's greatest democracy—like racial tensions, civil inequities, and poverty—
were taboo subjects. Despite what appears to have been honest efforts under
difficult circumstances, however, the U.S. film officers in Germany were subject
to criticism and derision, particularly from industry sources at home. "Screwy
Choice of Pix for O'Seas Paints U.S. as Race of Gangsters, Jitterbugs" screamed
one *Variety* headline. Hollywood was crestfallen about the unanticipated delay,
caused by ICD policies, in opening the German market to the free enterprise of
foreign commercial interests like itself.[13] Its criticisms, however, reverberated
beyond the confines of trade papers (like *Variety*) to influential dailies (like the
New York Times), and even received a hearing by the State Department, as we
shall see.

If the thinking of American officials was somewhat murky regarding the
role feature films were to play in the reeducation effort, their expectations for
documentaries and newsreels were clearer. Over the course of late June through
July 1945, ICD officials tested the OWI atrocity film, *KZ (Death Camp)*, and the
American newsreel *Welt im Film* (produced with British cooperation by the
OWI in London) on audiences in Erlangen. Attendance was high in the 400-seat
cinema—recorded at 90 percent capacity for the first week's screenings of the
film, with standing room only at some shows—even though Germans were
charged nominal admission fees and had been led to believe that a feature film
called *Cowboy* would be shown. Audience reaction to *KZ* was described as
"respectful, but scarcely enthusiastic," and an attending American official noted
that "a palpable feeling of incredulity ran through the audience when the
narrator said that the wife of the commandant at Belsen had made lamp shades
from tattooed human skin." At the end of the program, audience members were
"extremely anxious" to express their opinions in questionnaires distributed by
the Americans—if only to point out the "inferior" quality of American documentaries and newsreels when compared to their German equivalents, the
Kulturfilm and *Wochenschau*.[14]

During the first year of the occupation, the newsreel was intended to convince Germans of the criminal nature of national socialism, the "extent of the
allied [military] might," and the strength of Allied cooperation and unity; it
also served as a conduit for information regarding the Anglo-American administration of Germany. Thus, early installments of *Welt im Film* contained reports by eyewitnesses of Nazi atrocities and covered the punishment of Nazi
criminals—with special attention given to the Nuremberg Trials. Scenes involving the Allies' detonation of a gunpowder factory served to symbolize the
destruction of German militarism; and German "actions of absolution," like the
laying of a memorial stone at the former site of a Frankfurt synagogue, were
highlighted and held up for emulation.

By 1946, *Welt im Film* shifted its focus to the tasks of German reconstruction, in both the material and political-democratic sense, and began to emphasize the mentoring role of the American and British occupiers. The production of the newsreel had been transferred to Munich in September 1945, and about 40 percent of its material was shot by film crews operating in Munich, Berlin, Frankfurt, and Stuttgart. The balance was extracted from American newsreels supplied by News of the Day, Paramount News, Universal News, and Pathé and offered German viewers international news as well as sports and entertainment clips. The reason for the change in emphasis was both political and practical. *Welt im Film* had to compete with the Soviet and French newsreels, the latter of which was merely the domestic *Actualités* dubbed into German. In terms of audience appeal, the "softer" approach seems to have worked. In late February 1946, a random survey showed that 78 percent of all cinemagoers had seen *Welt im Film*, and of these, 61 percent considered it "good" or "interesting"—mostly because it brought them news from the "outside."[15]

Early American documentaries produced for release in Germany relied more on the stick than the carrot. These engaged in a kind of "evangelical propaganda" that began by reminding German audiences of their recent collective sins under Hitler and ended by pointing the way to personal and social redemption through a process of submission and contrition. Needless to say, German response was markedly negative. In the first years of military occupation, most Germans were unprepared to undertake a thorough soul-searching at the command of an alien victor; and many were so consumed by their own (admittedly substantial) physical needs that they preferred to consider themselves the true victims of the war.

This point was brought home in January 1946 when the U.S. Military Government released a documentary on the death camps entitled *Todesmühlen* (*Mills of Death*). The film was an overt piece of reeducation propaganda, based upon footage taken during the liberation of the death camps and delivered in a "hammer-and-tongs assault." After twenty minutes dominated by heartrending scenes of suffering and death, the film concluded with verbal finger-pointing that placed the responsibility for this grisly program of murder unequivocally at the feet of the German people:

> "The farmers received tons of human bones as fertilizer . . . but apparently never suspected it came from human beings. . . . Manufacturers received tons of human hair . . . but apparently never dreamed it came from the heads of murdered women. . . . No nightmares ever haunted those who lived near concentration camps. . . . The cries and moans of the tortured were no doubt believed the wailing of the wind." The film cuts to crowd scenes from Leni Riefenstahl's *Triumph of the Will*, as we are told that Germans . . . still "bear heavy crosses now . . . the crosses of the millions crucified in Nazi death mills!"[16]

Unremarkably, the film was a flop. While some American officials reported that German "audiences received the film with attention and solemnity," others encountered disbelief in the veracity of the film and expressions of resentment, especially by youth and ex-POWs.[17] Rather than stimulate a much-needed wave of introspection among German viewers, it drew their scorn. "For the next propaganda performance . . . take Dr. Goebbels as advisor," one sixteen-year-old girl suggested.[18] Officials in the U.S. Office of the Military Government for Germany (OMGUS) reported that in the small town of Eichstätt, as in the rest of Bavaria, "the local population . . . stayed away in droves."[19] Moviegoing declined throughout the zone about this time, and official surveyors suspected that the film precipitated the dip. This occurred despite the fact that attendance at such films was mandatory and Germans were required to have their ration cards stamped at the cinema to certify that they had gone to the screenings.[20] Clearly, if the reeducation program was to succeed, American film officers would need to be more responsive to the tastes of their pupils.

The Reconstruction of German Cinema in the U.S. Zone, 1946–1947

Despite such mishaps, American ICD officials were initially reluctant to recommend the renewal of native film production. This was due in part to American skepticism regarding the potential value of German contributions to the democratization effort. In addition, ICD officials were responding to the enormity of the practical task of denazifying the film community, which had so obediently capitulated to Goebbels's orders to eject its Jewish members and submit to state control. Well before any actions were taken to reestablish German production, one U.S. film officer articulated the ICD position: "Film production is inextricably wound up with the future regeneration of the German people. . . . It is important not only what future possible German pictures say on the screen: it is also important to be circumspect about who made them."[21] The ICD proceeded in an extremely grudging manner in allowing the reintroduction of German film production. In an ICD memo dated 24 November 1945, discussing the establishment of policy regarding renewed German film production in the U.S. zone, the following principles were set:

Licensed producers should not only be politically white or at least bright gray, but should be as professionally competent as possible. Most important of all they should be men who instinctively think or respond to ideas along the lines of Allied policy in Germany, i.e., freedom and dignity [sic] of the individual, civic courage, the general democratic principle of the right and responsibility of the individual to think and act for himself in terms of the common good, anti-militaristic, anti-Prussianism [sic], the responsibility of a citizen for the policies and actions of his Government, freer family and parent-child relationships, etc.[22]

In short, German filmmakers, to be licensed by the U.S. ICD, were to both internalize and project through their films those values and intangibles publicly praised as "the American way of life."

The licensing process got off to a slow start due to the U.S. Military Government's insistence on thoroughness in examining filmmakers' pasts and their present loyalties. Prospective German film producers, directors, actors, and technicians were required to complete lengthy questionnaires regarding their political past, especially membership and activity in the Nazi Party. Before a film project was begun, the script and list of individuals involved in the project had to be submitted to the ICD for investigation and approval. Denazification was attempted by a rigorous questioning and "vetting" process, the effect of which, at least in retrospect and in the area of German film, appears to have caused mostly paperwork and delay in production and little long-term success in denazification. Notorious Nazi filmmakers were denied licenses under the occupation, only to resume activity in the 1950s. The proscription against Communist filmmakers, however, would continue throughout the Adenauer era in the West.[23]

By April 1946, however, American film officers were feeling increasingly pressured to initiate film production in their zone. Most of this pressure stemmed from the Soviets' early and avid attention to the film medium. Within one month of German defeat, the Soviets had begun to synchronize their films at the Tobis studios in Berlin for German release. In August 1945, shortly after the Americans started screening their films to German audiences, without adding German subtitles or dubbing, the Soviet Military Administration established a Filmaktiv in its sector of Berlin to facilitate German film production. Three months later, it sponsored a meeting at the Hotel Adlon, officially opening German film production in the East. Film producers, directors, actors, and technicians attended from all zones of Germany.[24] German film production actually began in the Soviet zone in early 1946, with the filming of Wolfgang Staudte's *Die Mörder sind unter uns* (*The Murderers Are among Us*).[25] Staudte had attempted to gain permission to make his film in the West, but due to the foot-dragging of American and British officials, he finally appealed to the Soviets, who lent their support to his project.

It was around this time that American officials began to reassess their overly cautious approach to renewed German filmmaking. Clearly, the political situation was changing, and the ideological threat of national socialism was being displaced in the minds of American officials by the ideological threat of communism. The fight was on to influence the postwar order, and the ICD did not want

Wolfgang Staudte's *Die Mörder sind unter uns*, the first postwar German film, was made in the rubble of Berlin under Soviet license. (Courtesy of the Stiftung Deutsche Kinemathek, Berlin)

to be caught napping. Already, American officials had received reports that twelve films were currently in production in the Soviet zone, two of which were said to deal with overtly political subject matter. In addition, the Soviets were reportedly luring well-known German filmmakers from the Western zones by promising to allow artists "to start their work within ten days after acceptance of the offer."[26] An intelligence officer noted that "numerous film artists have turned down repeated offers made by [the Soviet-sponsored German film monopoly, Deutsche Film Aktiengesellschaft] DEFA and are still waiting to be given a chance to work in collaboration with U.S. authorities. Therefore our reluctance in licensing individuals or companies is regretted in Film circles."[27]

The competition for German film talent had begun, and American officials feared that their hesitation in stimulating German production would provoke increasing dissatisfaction, culminating in the defection of German filmmakers to the East. American intelligence reported that film personnel complained about the severity of American political and artistic standards in the licensing process: "Whoever earned more than 30,000 marks during the Nazi era is considered a Nazi sympathizer," groused one filmmaker.[28] Other complaints were directed against the American refusal to license film groups (rather than individuals, whom they could more easily control), the absence of raw material, and the failure to establish a German-run distribution agency. The report ended by urging ICD officials to step up momentum in the licensing process in order to avoid finding themselves at a disadvantage in relation to the Soviets in the future.[29] Although the author of this account was overly optimistic about production in the Soviet zone (only three feature films were actually produced there in the calendar year 1946),[30] the memo did signal a changing awareness among ICD personnel in the U.S. zone. It was symptomatic of the changing political situation in the face of Allied division over issues involving the management of the German economy and the dismantling of German industry.

In part, American officials shifted to a "positive program" of encouraging German film production as a competitive response to a more dynamic Soviet film production policy. But another reason for the change in policy was financial: American officials needed to trim the fat from the Military Government budget. At an ICD meeting at the end of October 1946, General McClure, director of the ICD, reminded attendees that "Congress is still our master and today we are on a rigid Congressional budget, which President Truman has cut further." Although the meticulous investigation of licensees was to continue through 1949, based on McClure's insistence that the ICD "must have the right to maintain political competence," the budget cuts took a serious toll on ICD programs. McClure was well aware of the effect of the cuts: "If we are to cut personnel we must cut functions. . . . We are passing from the negative control side of our operation to the positive reorientation of the German people."[31]

Finally, American film officers could no longer justify bombarding German audiences with Hollywood products when it became clear that American films were not the most effective means of instilling democratic values in the population. Although some American films, like Mervyn LeRoy's *Madame Curie*, won popularity with German audiences, others were "severely criticized." Moreover, American film officers detected a "general suspicion" that Germany was being treated as a "dumping ground for old and inferior films by all Allies." Soviet films, for example, were considered politically tendentious by many Germans, and French imports were criticized for their low quality in comparison to those screened in Germany before the war. Moreover, the British and Soviets were relying on old German features to fill screentime in their zones, and it appeared that "German films of any merit" were better attended than "even the best imported films." *Die Große Freiheit #7* (1944), starring the wildly popular Hans Albers, and the Austrian-made Paula Wessely vehicle, *Episode* (1935), both made during the Third Reich, were runaway box-office hits. OMGUS surveys reported that German audiences were clamoring for reprises of other old German favorites—particularly the nonfiction, educational *Kulturfilm*, escapist "glamor" films, and musicals.[32]

The interwar fascination with American culture faded once it became associated with the unilateral policies of military occupation. Harkening back to their prewar habits, Germans in the U.S. zone demanded freedom in the form of consumer choice and scorned the exclusive presence of Hollywood films in their theaters. An intelligence report submitted to the MPB noted increased resistance to the American monopoly in a small German community:

> There is a steadily mounting criticism by the local population of the American . . . films being shown here. In the first place, Germans are more or less homesick to hear their own language in films rather than have a language they don't understand dinned into their ears. Secondly, they want backgrounds and themes as well as . . . actors, which are familiar to them and somehow indigenous, rather than foreign backgrounds with which they have no associations. Thirdly, the carefree and superficial escapism of many pre-war American films irritates the Germans who are now faced with bitter realities. Also, there is a purely local condition which exists probably only in rural communities rather than in larger towns. It is the inability of the simple, str[a]ightforward farmers in this *Kreis* to understand the subtleties, or ironies, of many films. Thus such relatively good films as "All That Money Can Buy" and "Here Comes Mr. Jordan" were not appreciated, and the whimsical "Tom, Dick and Harry" was a catastrophe for [the] local theater owner who said that it kept the audience away from the movies for three or four weeks afterward.[33]

Ironically, from its inception the ICD envisioned using American feature films to reach just such an audience—of farmers, youth, housewives, shopkeepers, and workers—which it identified as "distinctly different from the one covered by books or theaters."[34] Yet now Hollywood products were failing to peddle the American agenda to a presumed lowbrow audience. American officials reading this report were faced with a difficult situation to remedy: the existence of cultural differences and resentments, which created obstacles to understanding and internalizing the victor's implicit values. How could film officers "sell" the American message of democracy, individualism, and free enterprise, when the German audience was not "buying" the package in which these messages were delivered?

A decisive shift in U.S. film policy to a positive program of encouraging native film production did not occur until July 1946, when the former UFA producer Erich Pommer, now German émigré-turned-American-citizen, was named chief of the MPB. Pommer's appointment to this position caused quite a stir among German and Hollywood film interests alike, for he had built a successful career and a notable national film industry in interwar Germany based on his broad range of international experience, business acumen, and finely tuned artistic sensibilities.[35]

Pommer abandoned his career and his homeland in 1933, when Goebbels institutionalized his anti-Semitic politics, only to reappear on German soil thirteen years later in the uniform of the victor. His former countrymen interpreted Pommer's return as a sure sign of American intentions to reactivate German filmmaking; initially, then, he was greeted as the "Miracle Doctor," come to restore an ailing industry to health. As Erich Kästner put it in 1946: "When Pommer comes, it's time to roll up your shirtsleeves!"[36]

Hollywood interests, on the whole, were much less enthusiastic; they suspected Pommer and his presumed mission as a potential threat to their unimpeded access to the German market. Worse, they feared that Pommer, given his professional history, might again construct an industry that could mount a challenge to Hollywood interests on the world market, and particularly in Latin America, which promised "vast new audience possibilities."[37]

Such fears of German commercial and cultural dominance were laughably unfounded in the early postwar years. German filmmakers in the West suffered from sustained shortages of film rawstock, since the IG Farben cartel's Agfa film production facility wound up in Soviet-controlled territory and smaller film plants in Munich and Frankfurt were inadequate to meet the needs of even a nascent native production. Of the UFI studios, the Soviets held Babelsberg and Johannisthal near Berlin, while the Americans controlled the war-damaged Tempelhof in the former capital and Geiselgasteig in Munich (which was almost completely intact but was being used as a displaced person's camp at the beginning of the occupation). Furthermore, the Western Allies' policy of decartelization prohibited vertical integration and would insure the creation of small, independent firms without the resources to compete with the Hollywood majors.[38]

Pommer apparently hoped to assist his former colleagues in creating a viable industrial structure in Germany and expressed frustration at times with American prohibitions on monopoly formation. He was, however, forced to follow policy guidelines dictated from above, a situation that provoked irritation among German filmmakers and caused them to consider him a turncoat or Hollywood pawn.[39] A 1952 article in the *Oberbayerisches Volksblatt*, for example, lambasted Pommer for reentering Germany in 1946 as an Americanized "*Eric* Pommer . . . all powerful US film officer and—as he called himself proudly —'father of decartelization,'" intent on destroying "the Ufa system which he once helped build."[40]

Pommer did, however, sincerely lobby for German film interests, often running afoul of American film interests in the process. After several months as film officer, Pommer was forced to respond to a *New York Times* article alleging that the ICD was reviving German film production "too quickly and on too broad a scale." The article criticized American film policy in an indirect way by pointing out that liberal measures would prove insufficient against the "Nazi poison . . . [that had] so deeply pervaded the whole German mentality." Re-education, to be thorough, would require "extreme measures" and a good deal of time: "The German industry should be rebuilt more slowly. People now should be fed heavy doses of all pictures, except those of their own making, in order to counteract the long years of Nazi-propaganda" and stimulate "the necessary mental catharsis."[41]

ICD investigations revealed that the "U.S. Aide" quoted in the *New York Times* article was none other than Irving Maas, the vice president of the Motion Picture Export Association of America (MPEA), a trade association that represented the eight largest film production companies in Hollywood. Public attack at home elicited a strong response from Pommer, who defended his efforts on behalf of German film interests to ICD director Robert McClure.

Privy to the recent change of heart among ICD officials, Pommer stressed the value of a native film product for the reeducation effort: "There is no better way to counteract the long years of Nazi-propaganda than to have carefully selected independent German film producers present to German audiences . . . documentaries and feature films dealing in entertainment form with their own problems, and striving in the future to imbue the German mind with new and better ideas and ideals. It has long been Mil[itary] Gov[ernment] belief and policy that Germans of sincere intent can do more than can foreigners."[42] After carefully noting that the "political and spiritual reorientation of the German people is, of course, our primary object," Pommer highlighted the economic benefits to be derived from a renewed German film production whose exports could generate much-needed foreign currency funds to pay for reparations and imports of scarce raw materials and food. Reminding McClure that film was "one of the permitted industries under the Potsdam agreement," Pommer declared that ICD initiatives to revive "the German film industry along democratic lines in independent decartelized form" were in line with both Allied agreements regarding the German future and the overall American reconstruction program for Germany. Pommer concluded by reassuring McClure of his support for the American film product, remarking that "it is of great importance to show a maximum number of good U.S. produced features" to acquaint German audiences with "American ideals and the American way of life." Nonetheless, he tempered this with the observation that, as "experience in the last 18 months has proven, feeding the German people with foreign produced pictures alone would produce results exactly opposite to the intended purposes."[43]

Pommer's response pacified his boss at the ICD, but the public smear campaign launched by the MPEA continued. In existence for only a month when Pommer assumed his duties in Berlin, the MPEA was founded as the export branch of the MPAA and aspired to handling the marketing of all U.S. motion pictures to Europe and Asia. The enduring goal of this organization was the commercial penetration and domination of open, unregulated markets abroad. This "little State Department," as it has sometimes been called, fought fiercely to defend its unimpeded access to postwar European markets, and Germany was no exception.[44]

The amount of MPEA vitriol directed against Pommer may have been due in part to shattered expectations. It appears some American industry members initially thought Pommer might harbor ambitions to assist Hollywood, presumably because of his sporadic employment there in the mid-1920s and 1930s. Soon after Pommer's arrival in Berlin, an American trade paper optimistically headlined a story applauding Pommer's assignment to "integrate the German and Austrian film industries, . . . purge both pro-Nazi and pro-Communist personnel, . . . build strong pro-American sentiment . . . and open up the German market, potentially Europe's greatest, to American products." In addition, the article suggested that in "two or three years" American studios could be built there, and Hollywood would finally have a strong presence in a once intractable market. A month after that report, the ICD found it necessary to assure the War Department, the Civil Affairs Division, and the Reorientation Branch that, contrary to reports in the American trade papers, the Military Government was not "preparing the way for . . . MPEA take-over" in the U.S. zone.[45]

By the spring of 1947, however, the MPEA was hearing rumors that Pommer was facilitating German production and, perhaps worse, that the ICD was considering permitting the export of old German—and even Nazi—films. In early May 1947, American industry papers indicated that Pommer masterminded the change in policy, with *Variety* reporting that

> behind the move to export German films to the U.S. and other countries . . . is considerable personal feeling. . . . The charge in American film circles is that Pommer volunteered to take on the task of revitalizing the German industry in a mixture of personal ambition and spleen—mostly spleen. It's been said in Hollywood that Pommer took something of a kicking around during his years there—a kicking around that some admit may have been unfair—and that he's now out to prove that almost single-handed he can make the German industry a further threat to Hollywood's world preeminence.[46]

Hollywood's public attacks on Erich Pommer rapidly intensified. During the first two weeks in May, a flurry of articles appeared in prominent American newspapers misrepresenting Pommer's authority over film matters in Germany. Most of these reports drew liberally upon material contained in a letter from MPEA representative Robert Vining to his boss, Irving Maas, describing a fictitious interview with Erich Pommer in Berlin, or at least a highly distorted rendition. Vining has Pommer committing one shocking verbal indiscretion after another, which culminates in the revelation that he returned to Berlin for "sentimental reasons" and to pursue unfulfilled personal ambitions:

> I am not a young man anymore and this is taking a lot out of me, but I loved the German film business and I want to see it back on its feet once more. I am 57 and am only getting ten thousand [dollars] and working like a dog. . . . I built up the German industry once and would like to do it again because if I don't the Russians will take what should be German markets away. Doesn't Hollywood recognize this fact? At my secret meetings [with German film interests] I hear all my old friends . . . say [that] . . . if there is one thing they are united on it is a determination that the old days and conditions when . . . all the [Hollywood] boys rode roughshod over this German market are gone forever, they will never come back, even if I have to lick them again as I did once. I am a famous producer, but production is not what I really enjoy, it is getting into foreign markets. . . . The smart boys back in New York . . . know that my Ufa turned out an average of 40 good titles every year and that Germany had the best studios and facilities in all Europe and must again. . . . [I] would enjoy being the foreign sales manager for [the] German product. In South America alone the German settlements are crying for my pictures from Germany.

American newspaper articles reporting congressional inquiries into Anglo-American film policy in Germany curiously contained rough approximations of the more damning sections of Vining's letter and in at least one case falsely attributed the quotes to statements Pommer made in the context of a meeting of the official Joint Film Policy Working Body. Another article repeated a scenario in which Pommer orchestrated late-night secret meetings at his home between German film industry moguls and American "decartelization boys," "economic boys," and "other key people of the Military Government." Yet another had Pommer boast of having "the German film business right in my pocket and there it is going to remain"; this article expanded Pommer's export aspirations to the Middle East, Near East, and Scandinavia. Another gave a parting shot of Pommer proclaiming: "Hollywood can take care of itself. I am not going to stick my neck out for it anymore."[47] The MPEA appealed to the State Department for support and apparently went so far as to conspire to have Pommer recalled to the United States.[48]

The MPEA's press campaign resulted neither in Pommer's dismissal as film officer nor in a change in ICD policy regarding the reconstruction of film production in Germany. Pommer retained the support of the War Department and the Military Government, and American occupational authorities stood firm in their objective to create a German film industry that was "not necessarily large, but . . . competitive and adequate to meet German needs." In the end, the export of "acceptable" German films was permitted in order to secure foreign credits and currency to aid domestic production; but the ban against German films of Nazi vintage remained.[49]

Frustrated in their machinations and determined to protect their commercial interests in Germany, MPEA representatives met with War Department officials in Washington, D.C., and ICD officials in Berlin to voice their opposition to Military Government policy. ICD officials informed the War and State departments that MPEA demands were "directly opposed to Military Government's established policies and . . . indicative of the MPEA's striving for a monopoly position."[50] In addition, they explained the need to avoid the "charge of unfair treatment of German industry or preference for U.S. industry . . . if our ideas and enactments are ever to be adopted by German industry and German people at a later date."[51] The ICD refused to support the wholesale monopoly of the German market by Hollywood interests.

Although committed to creating a viable film industry in Western Germany, ICD officials simultaneously reassured the MPEA, the War Department, and the American public that their project would leave plenty of latitude for the advancement of American economic and political interests. They stressed the impossibility of a German challenge to Hollywood on the international market in the foreseeable future and rebutted the inflated figures for German film production provided the press by MPEA vice president Irving Maas. ICD officials countered Maas's assertion that 50 to 60 German films would be produced in 1947 with a description of the shortage of studio space, film rawstock, and technical resources. They emphasized that top priority had been given to the synchronization of MPEA films and concluded by adjusting down to 8 to 10 the number of feature films that "independent German producers" would be able to complete in 1947. While acknowledging that the number of German feature films produced under Anglo-American licenses would increase during the following year, the ICD director added that MPEA products would still outnumber native productions by a ratio of at least 5:1.[52] The ICD was careful to stress the importance of the American product to the reeducation effort in Germany and to reassure the American film companies that their access to the German market would not be compromised completely.

Still, MPB efforts to step up the licensing of German film producers and discussions regarding the potential export of German films dispersed any Hollywood fantasy of uncontrolled access to German markets. The MPEA attempted to illustrate its importance to the American reeducation effort—and thereby win concessions from the ICD—by slowing the release of its films to the Military Government.[53] But to no avail. The situation did not improve over the course of the year, and in December 1947, the ICD proposed a plan to increase the use of French, English, Italian, Scandinavian, and even acceptable old German films to offset the decrease in available American films.[54]

It was evident that the ICD intended to walk the thin line of encouraging the re-creation of a viable commercial film industry in Western Germany while at the same time insuring that it did not become too strong to challenge the commercial and cultural supremacy of the MPEA abroad. ICD officials clearly saw that it was in American interests to maintain a strong position for the American film product in Western Germany, yet these same officials often became exasperated at unreasonable attempts by MPEA representatives to monopolize German markets and suffocate early signs of the revival of an indigenous film industry.

Nonetheless, the MPEA was able, in the long run, to secure a strong position in the German market. In February 1948, the MPEA was granted the exclusive right to the commercial distribution of member companies' films in Germany, although its earnings there remained inconvertible to dollars. This situation changed within the year, when the MPEA was able to benefit from the Informational Media Guaranty Program (IMG), in which the U.S. government promised dollars "at attractive rates, for certain soft currencies earned by American media exporters, provided the communications material earning the money reflected the best elements of American life." Although the IMG was designed to assist in America's Cold War cultural offensive abroad, along the way it became a "gravy train" for the MPEA, as one congressional representative pointed out. The lure of IMG money boosted the number of U.S. films sent to Germany from 64 in 1948–49 to 226 in 1951–52, which remained the annual average throughout the decade. And by 1955, when the program ended, MPEA companies received over $7 million for their "cooperation" in Germany alone. Finally, although Hollywood companies were frustrated in their attempts to buy up chunks of the former UFI empire, by the early 1950s their overall position in the German market far surpassed that of the previous two decades. With the abolition of the ICD and the end of the Military Government in 1949, the MPEA had an easier time convincing the newly instated watchdog of West Germany, the Allied High Commission, to reject the German government's bid to reinstate film quotas on imports similar to those imposed in the interwar period to protect domestic production. In the midst of the painful postwar shift to a bipolar world, American officials and the high commissioners did not require convincing that Germany was "the focal point in the current battle of ideologies," and they permitted MPEA companies to determine the number of films to send to that country.[55]

From Zonal to National Organization:
Film Control and the American Agenda

From the beginning of the occupation, film policy had been organized on a zonal basis, with each occupation authority exercising sovereignty within its zonal boundaries. Yet by 1946 the changing political situation and American plans for economic union with the British zone stimulated ICD attention to the future control of German film. The Americans opened negotiations with the other Allies in an attempt to convince them to disavow state control of culture, prohibit film monopolies, and affirm the principles of open markets, free competition, and censorship by industry interests.

In the months following the creation of Bizonia in January 1947, American ICD officials moved to insure that the economic merger would not result in an imposition of British forms of film organization on Bizonia. American ICD officers worked to create a structure that could be merged with, yet subvert, the existing British associations. The effort on the part of the ICD was twofold. First, the ICD set up German organizations within the U.S. zone with functions identical to those already existing in the British zone. Concurrently, the ICD initiated talks with its British counterpart agency in an effort to formulate a common film policy, including the establishment of principles upon which control could be exercised jointly.

In early 1947, initial conferences were held with British authorities regarding the impact of economic fusion on film policy. A committee for joint film matters was established but was reportedly "making slow progress." "Major difficulties" were anticipated by the Americans in overcoming "diverging ideological policies." While the U.S. Military Government insisted on decartelization, the British were committed to nationalizing the German film industry and favored the principle of centralization in film matters, with censorship and licensing powers concentrated in the hands of the future German government.[56]

Despite these projected difficulties, British-American cooperation proceeded quite smoothly. During the first meeting of the Joint Film Policy Working Body on 2 April, participants agreed to license German film distributors jointly and to establish a cooperatively owned, nonprofit forwarding company for interzonal film transport. In addition, they created organizations to "facilitate" the export of German films in order to raise money to import rawstock and equipment needed by the German film industry—a move that drew the wrath of Hollywood. Moreover, it was decided that an Anglo-American Joint Film Production Control Board would license German filmmakers, review scripts, allocate rawstock, and advise the German film industry on material procurement and production facilities. This concerted effort was to culminate in the establishment of the German motion picture industry in the U.S. and British zones "on an independent competitive basis as a German activity, subject to Military Government regulation."[57]

The creation of Bizonia was a result of the American and British desire to rationalize the German economy, increase industrial productivity, and generate more revenues. It was also a sign of increasing discord between the Americans and the British on the one hand and the Soviets and the French on the other regarding reparations and industrial dismantling. This discord carried over into negotiations concerning the reconstruction of the mass media in Germany and the appropriate form of cultural control.

As early as 1946 American ICD officials identified a serious divergence between their plans for a German cinema based on free competition and an open market and the Soviet-sponsored film monopoly, DEFA, which had been founded in the Eastern zone. American officials considered DEFA a continuation of state control of culture, similar to that constructed under the Nazi regime. They feared that such control would threaten their efforts at postwar democratization should a peace settlement be concluded and the zones reunified. Pommer articulated American fears in a 1947 memo:

[The Soviets] have assembled every branch of the film industry in one interlocking organization. Raw stock manufacture, film production and distribution are monopolies, and film theaters have had to sign 5 year contracts with a Russian-owned distribution company. They have built a powerful industry along the lines of the old UFA, and if the zonal boundaries are ever dropped, they will be in perfect position to absorb the weak, decentralized industry in the U.S. Zone. The final result may well be a Russian-dominated industry releasing the same kind of films they approve throughout at least the Russian and U.S. Zones.[58]

In addition, American officials were worried by the continued stiff competition with the East for German filmmakers' loyalties. At the beginning of April 1947, an ICD informant outlined the attractive packages offered to film employees by the Russians:

The Russian Authorities . . . have offered very favorable contracts to some of our most important employees, such as fixed contracts with [a] very high salary and an extraordinary premium at the completion of the feature. Furthermore, guarantees . . . [of] a sizable supply of additional food (potatoes, fat, meat, etc.) and 20 hdwht of coal were given. We know that those guarantees are not just promises, and that food and cigarettes have been supplied every month to directors, production managers and actors, even if they have no permanent contracts. Immediately after completion of a feature the members of the staff get tax-free premiums up to 3,000 RM for each picture.[59]

Similar payments-in-kind were given to employees of a new Institute of Cinematography founded by the Soviets at Babelsberg. In existence for nearly a year, this institute was created to centralize all available experience in the film field and to facilitate the development of new technologies by German talent. The institute was given an excellent prognosis for success owing to a very knowledgeable German manager. A U.S. intelligence source warned that the institute could "make Babelsberg a center of motion picture technique, such as never previously existed in Germany; for many former employees of industrial firms [as well as many university professors and other specialists] will now be giving their experience to this institute."[60]

American ICD officials sought to counter Soviet influence in film matters by securing affirmation of American principles in quadripartite negotiations.[61] The struggle for dominance in cultural production and control was evident from the early days of the occupation, yet by early 1947 the American vision of the desired organization and control of the German film industry, as well as strategies to achieve it, had begun to assume a definite shape.

In March 1947, at a quadripartite meeting on film policy, American officials presented a proposal to repeal all censorship legislation of the German Reich and explore the possibility of substituting self-censorship by the German film industry for censorship by the state. This proposal represented the American attempt to seize the initiative in shaping new German censorship legislation based upon the homegrown Hays Code, which was established in the United States by the Motion Picture Distributors' Association of America as a self-regulating mechanism to preempt the bothersome intervention of local American officials, educators, and clergy who sought to censor films on the basis of political or moral considerations.[62]

The Soviets, who were still participating in Allied meetings at that time, raised no objections, but the French resisted the proposal. In an informal meeting, the chief of the French Film Section informed Erich Pommer that he had received authorization in a policy letter from Paris to agree to the repeal of the old German film censorship laws but could not support the establishment of an industry-controlled production code. The French objected to self-censorship by the film industry because it would create a "unified and central body of censorship for the whole of Germany."[63] There is some indication that French officials feared industry self-censorship would result in hostility to the French product (since imported films would also be subject to review by the censorship board) and that the historical competition between the two countries would be carried over to the sphere of economics and culture in a way that would disadvantage

French interests. French officials disliked the idea of German competitors censoring French products. Since German defeat, French policy in Germany was dictated by interests of national security and economic recovery. The French had therefore consistently maintained an "absolute ban on any form of centralization in Germany."[64]

Due to their concerns for postwar military security, the French endorsed a federal structure for German political reconstruction and rejected central institutions in favor of state (*Land*) prerogative. They therefore criticized the American proposal for film censorship on the grounds that it would "prevent the German states [*Länder*] from exercising film censorship," a situation they deemed dangerous. Arguing that censorship exercised directly by state authorities existed in democratic countries and should not be considered an "exclusive creation of fascist regimes," they predicted that the elimination of such film censorship "would unavoidably lead to a complete anarchy and expose . . . young German film production to very great dangers." Furthermore, they alleged that the American solution to transfer the control of censorship to the film industry "would favor the formation of trusts" and hence contradict "the allied policy of the democratization of the German people." Industry control, they claimed, would "endanger especially the small independent producers which often represent the artistic avant-garde," which in turn would eliminate aesthetic and ideological diversity and homogenize German cultural production. In its place, the French proposed the creation of censorship committees at the *Land* level, to be comprised of minority representation by the German film industry and representatives from churches, cultural and youth organizations, labor unions, and universities. Thus, the French countered the American model for film censorship with one of their own, based upon regional participatory committees that would include representation of various public interest groups and deflate the presumed advantage German films would enjoy under a system based upon industry self-censorship.[65]

Pommer rejected the French proposal out of hand, insisting that *Land*-level censorship would prevent the reconstruction of the German film industry on a sound basis. Such a plan would, according to Pommer, further weaken the German film industry by subjecting films to local codes of morality and religious belief, which was apparently precisely the French goal. Since films can only be amortized on national markets due to their high production costs, regional variations in censorship decisions would undermine the base of profitability that the film industry required in order to survive and prosper. The French representative finally acceded to Pommer's position, after receiving assurances that a national "production code would for some time to come take place under present quadripartite Military Government censorship" and that such a code would be implemented only with "the support or at least the consent" of the state governments—something he knew would be difficult to secure.[66]

At a Quadripartite Information Committee meeting in May, the tide turned completely against the American initiative. The Soviets not only joined the French in objecting to the self-censorship code, but the British representative voiced strong reservations as well. He opposed giving any right of political censorship to the Germans, but he maintained, with shocking naïveté, that "censorship on moral grounds" could be surrendered to them "at an early date"—a position that "didn't make any sense at all," according to one American film officer. Due to the impasse, the Information Committee decided to bounce the censorship issue back to the Quadripartite Film Policy Working Party with the proviso that it should "study the possibility of unification of censorship throughout Germany . . . [and] of setting up a German advisory body to assist the Allies in censoring films either in each zone or centrally."[67]

Although the four Allies were far from reaching an agreement on the future form of German film censorship, the Americans and the British concluded a common program for their film activities, prodded by the economic union of their zones. Cooperation between the American and the British in film matters was sealed by the creation of Bizonia, but the agreement of the French continued to be withheld.[68]

Progress was not made on this front until early 1948, during the Anglo-American push to resolve the remaining issues concerning the postwar order in Germany. In response to the inability of the quadripartite council of foreign ministers to conclude a peace settlement at the end of 1947, the Americans and the British agreed to address the issue of German reconstruction without consulting the Soviets. They called a conference in London in the spring of 1948, where it was decided that the Marshall Plan should be extended to the Western occupation zones of Germany. This act marked the beginning of the economic and political unification of Bizonia with the French zone, which was sealed in June by the tripartite currency reform and the creation of a new monetary system in Western Germany.[69]

The French were gradually integrated into the Western system organized by the Americans. Their resistance to American organizational forms subsided as the international situation changed. Furthermore, they recognized that they were heavily dependent on American capital, since their economy too was being reinvigorated by Marshall Plan funds. With the impending creation of the North Atlantic Treaty Organization (NATO) to provide assurances of security that were formerly lacking, the French had fewer reasons to resist. The clear emergence of two blocs competing for European dominance and the resulting Cold War left the French little room to maneuver. Their fate was sealed, and they reluctantly fell in step with American policy.

Acquiescence was not, however, immediate. Negotiations continued throughout most of 1948 before an agreement could be reached on a trizonal basis. American and British officials made French access to Bizonia dependent on their acceptance of the Anglo-American principles of free trade, open competition, decartelization, prohibition of monopolies, and state noninvolvement in film matters. In February 1948, French officials confirmed their support of these principles during tripartite talks, but disagreement flared some months later regarding substantial French investment in German film companies. Carl Winston, by then chief of the U.S. Film Section in Berlin, contended that "the French are stalling, trying to squeeze everything possible out of the situation."[70] In particular, he criticized movements by French film interests to control the German market in the French zone, arguing that "the French have an even tighter monopoly in film at the moment than the Russians." U.S. officials asserted that film studios in that zone were being used for French productions, that Union Française Cinematographique (a French firm headquartered in Paris) held 51 percent of the German distribution company, Internationale Film, and that such "monopolistic film practices" were being "condoned"—if not actively encouraged—by the French government. American officials feared that Reich-owned film properties would be sold to "individuals or firms . . . directly or indirectly under French or Russian influence" and that Bizonia could soon be "flanked" by French and Soviet monopolies.[71]

The French, however, were unable to maintain their solitary stance in the face of the united British and American front.[72] At a meeting on 31 August 1948, George Dessauer, the representative of the British Film Section, French film officer Marcel Colin-Reval, and Erich Pommer drafted a list of conditions that would become the basis for cooperation in film matters by the three Western Allies. These included the adoption of all film legislation from the U.S. and British zones in the French zone and the subjection of the French film industry to the decisions of the Joint Import/Export Agency. The agreement also stipulated that the French would adhere to the moratorium on foreign investments existing in Bizonia, the principle of free competition between German and foreign film interests, and full reciprocity among the three zones—including the mutual recognition of production and distribution licenses granted prior to 1 August 1948. Furthermore, all three Allies would have equal access to German audiences in the French-held Saar. An Allied coordination and advisory board was created on a trizonal basis to deal with licensing, censorship, production, distribution, and exhibition. In November, the Tripartite Film Committee was formally constituted.[73]

By late fall 1948, the structure for Allied cooperation on film matters was in place in the West.[74] The French were finally assimilated into the economic and ideological framework favored by the Americans. This conclusion was a tribute less to American negotiating skills than to American economic might, which ultimately convinced British and French authorities that their national recoveries depended on the maintenance of American goodwill.

Implementing the American Model of Film Control: American-Industry Negotiations

In early 1947, concurrent with the creation of Bizonia, officials at the MPB established a German Film Producers' Association (Verband deutscher Filmproduzenten) in their zone, which was fashioned after a similar organization in the British zone. The goal was not simply to provide an institution to represent producers' interests during the impending economic merger. Rather, American officials hoped to transfer agreements made between the U.S. ICD and the Film Producers' Association in the U.S. zone to all of Bizonia. The creation of the association was therefore an important step in the process of imposing the American style of film control on Bizonia, and later all of West Germany. Moreover, Pommer had been committed to creating a German Film Producers' Association since his arrival in Germany, for he saw it as a way to head off "unwarranted cultural and political influence of the states, magistrates, church[es], political associations [and] trade unions."[75]

Licensed German film producers in the U.S. zone were summoned to a meeting with the MPB in Berlin at the end of March 1947. Erich Pommer directed much of the discussion and oversaw the official founding of the German Film Producers' Association for the U.S. zone, although producers had informally agreed to the creation of such an organization upon receiving U.S. licenses. Pommer sought to convince attending producers that the association would be a German construction, "independent" of the U.S. Military Government, and emphasized that the Americans were there "to help" but would not finance the association.[76]

Pommer's promise of producer "independence" was belied, however, by the ensuing discussion. When several producers protested that the foundation of the association was "premature," Eberhard Klagemann (who would be appointed vice president of the association) replied that all doubts should be set aside since it would be easier for them to protect their interests if they dealt with the authorities and the individual German states as a group. Indeed, ICD officials had convinced Klagemann and two other influential producers, Josef von Baky and Richard Koenig, of the necessity of establishing such an organization in a preliminary meeting in January on the basis of such an argument. Klagemann's role at this meeting was to push the project through to its agreed-upon conclusion.[77]

Much of the March meeting was devoted to a topic dear to the hearts of

American officials: the creation of a voluntary censorship code by the film industry. The centrality of the censorship question for American officials is suggested by the fact that Pommer introduced it and General McClure closed the meeting by congratulating the producers on drafting such a code. In fact, Pommer's presentation of the censorship issue surprised many attendees, who claimed to be "confronted with . . . problems hitherto unknown to them." They need not have fretted: the American officials had a censorship plan drafted for their consideration.[78]

Pommer introduced the plan by explaining that it was based on the American model of film censorship, which was controlled by the film industry rather than state interests. He described the functioning of the Hollywood Hays Office in the United States and stated that the producers should create a similar organization. Every film firm would be required to agree, in writing, to abide by the voluntary censorship code; distributors and theater owners would also be bound to comply with the censorship code, so that a three-fold guarantee could be given to the state.[79]

Klagemann raised the concern that, although the system functioned well in the United States, it was not suited to the German situation. He expected interference by the state ministers of culture and the individual *Land* governments, which traditionally had rights in the area of cultural control. Pommer answered that the Military Government would not tolerate these "old attempts at censorship suddenly becom[ing] a cultural trend [*Kulturrichtung*]." American officials intended to subdue state meddling in favor of a self-enforced industry code. On the issue of film censorship in relation to German youth, Pommer noted that church and other representatives from the public sector "must sit only as advisers" in the new censorship body. When reminded of the strong influence of the schools, Pommer responded that the state and local communities would retain their traditional moral authority to decide what constituted "trash and smut," a task that, as later events demonstrated, could provide a good deal of latitude for maneuvering.

Klagemann pointed out that the future German constitution would affirm the right of freedom of opinion and that organized opposition to certain films could arise on that basis, constituting a great threat to the film industry. Pommer replied that in order to avoid such problems, representatives of those sections of society must be invited to participate in an advisory capacity. He affirmed that the future German constitution would have "full freedom of movement" but promised that the German film producers still had at least two years of Military Government protection.[80]

The threat of government and church interference in film matters undoubtedly aided in the quick mobilization of producer support for the American model of film censorship. Erich Pommer reminded the producers that an uncertain future awaited the film industry once the occupation was over. On the other hand, German film producers were guaranteed preeminence in censorship decisions under the American plan. The message was clear: German filmmakers should present the new German government with an institutional fait accompli.

Although the Americans dictated the principles and policies the association would adopt, ICD officials hoped the film producers would perceive the newly created body and its resolutions as the product of German initiative. The creation of a producers' association assured individual producers' conformity to ICD policies and thereby defused potential resistance to the American variety of industry organization. Furthermore—and perhaps more importantly, since intransigent individual producers could still be weeded out through the licensing process—the producers' association would act as a counterweight to the traditional authority of the local governments and churches in German society. Members of the newly constituted German Film Producers' Association understood the dangers that state intervention in censorship could pose to the economic viability of the German film industry as a whole and to their individual enterprises in particular. Criticism by state and public interests would be defused by their representation in the censorship process in an advisory capacity. Conflict would then be contained institutionally and relegated to a debating chamber where dissenters' opinions would be politely listened to and then voted against. The principle of industry self-censorship was readily accepted by German film producers. The support of state officials was, predictably, much more difficult to secure.

The Contest for Cultural Control:
The Resurgence and Containment of State Authority

Walter Keim, *Regierungsdirektor* of the Bavarian Ministry of Education and Culture and head of the Standing Conference of Cultural Ministers of the German States, commented in 1949 that the administration of film censorship by Allied authorities during the occupation had not "satisfied the German public. The official posts and organizations as well as the broad public urgently demanded that the exhibition of films be controlled in some form." He stressed that this situation was only exacerbated in 1947, with the formal repeal of the Nazi film censorship law (Reichslichtspielgesetz) of 1934.[81] The Allies, of course, thought they had been rigorously censoring films throughout the occupation. Indeed they were, but they were evaluating the films on the basis of their political or ideological content, determined to screen out any traces of national socialism. Keim and like-minded state officials exhibited little concern for such political considerations. They demanded instead that censorship be responsive to local cultural norms and religious values and pushed, in effect, to have control over such cultural matters returned to officials at the *Land* level. Such a move would reverse the legislation of the Weimar and Nazi periods that nationalized cultural control and return to state officials the authority they enjoyed in this area during the Second Reich. In addition, there were indications that some officials had loftier ambitions and were maneuvering to extend state control over film production and distribution as well.[82]

Local official attention to questions of film censorship was especially sharp in Bavaria during the occupation period. The overwhelmingly rural nature and Catholic composition of the state—along with the staunch Catholic loyalties of the Bavarian minister of culture, Alois Hundhammer—were crucial factors in accounting for Bavaria's socially conservative cultural policies. What is more, concerns articulated in the state buildings of Munich periodically achieved a broader resonance when Bavarian officials, not content to limit their activities to the regional level, overstepped state borders to assume a leadership role in nationwide cultural initiatives during the late 1940s and early 1950s.

The ICD began receiving troubling reports from Bavaria early in the occupation. In January 1946, ICD officials were informed that "minors [were being] banned from attending film performances" in several Bavarian communities on the orders of mayors or regional officials. In the village of Bruckmühl, for example, the school administration requested that the theater owner "bar minors from the cinema in the future" after many local youths had seen the American film *Young Tom Edison* there. This ban was eventually backed up by an order from a local Landrat representative. The theater owner reported that both the local teacher and priest had corporeally punished children for watching American films, and that "the minister of Bruckmühl . . . went so far as to 'teach' the children at school that the days of Hitler and going to the movies are passed [*sic*]," indicating that film viewing was forbidden. The theater owner continued to admit children to her theater, but the report noted that "the attendance of minors . . . is . . . rapidly dropping since the children are fearing punishment."[83]

Local attempts to limit and regulate the film attendance of minors commanded the attention of the American film officers, who initially perceived them as isolated actions directed against American policies of reeducation and denazification. But the Bruckmühl minister's striking association of "moviegoing" with "the days of Hitler" indicates that something more was afoot. Under Hitler, party officials arranged special performances of handpicked feature films for youth in order to indoctrinate them with National Socialist "ideas and patterns of behavior" and encourage the habit of regular cinema attendance. Cinema owners who held special youth screenings were rewarded with tax exemptions, and extra effort was made to reach rural areas, small villages, and locales without cinemas, where traveling shows were sent to entertain the young. In 1936 attendance at youth performances was made compulsory; and by 1942–43 annual visits exceeded 11 million, with nearly 72 percent of Germans between the ages of 10 and 17 making monthly visits and an additional 22 percent attending weekly.[84] The problem was that local religious and political leaders, like those in Bruckmühl, tended to interpret such Nazi policies as wreaking "catastrophic changes" in the "traditional pattern" of communal life and culture, which was perceived as leading to "alienation" from Christian practices. Moreover, some characterized Nazi intrusions into the culturally cohesive community as an unwanted urban impulse that destroyed the "inner unity" of village life by accelerating the spread of the "corrupting influence of the town."[85] Presumably, then, Nazi defeat was expected to herald the end of encroaching secular materialism in the outlying villages and initiate a period of "normalization"—in the sense of a return to earlier religious practices and cultural traditions—for Christian believers throughout Bavaria.

American officials had a rather inchoate notion of life in the provinces under Hitler and were privy to neither local longings for a revitalized village idyll nor resentments felt toward policies (Nazi or other) regarded as disruptive to that goal. ICD policy was predicated on the assumption that all Germans required reorientation, and film officers therefore deemed it "highly desirable" for minors to attend its cinema programs since "all such exhibitions, besides showing a feature film, consist of a carefully angled newsreel and an American documentary film considered educationally valuable." The German *Länder* were notified by the ICD that "no censorship or audience limitation will be exercised by German civil authorities."[86] During the first year of the occupation, the U.S. Military Government treated such actions as individual examples of local intransigence or the outgrowth of misunderstandings of American policy, which would be readily squelched by dictate.

Yet by late 1946, film officers began to suspect that these incidents were not unrelated but expressions of a more organized, state-sponsored attempt to influence the nature and form of postwar German film censorship. In a confidential memo in October 1946, Erich Pommer reported meeting several times with the Bavarian ministers of economics and of culture and the mayor of Munich to discuss cultural and economic questions. Throughout the talks, Pommer warned state officials to cease their efforts to introduce a new film censorship, since it "would not be compatible with the democratic principles of U.S. Military Government."[87] It appears that the Bavarian government was trying to extend to film control the mandate given to the Council of German Minister-Presidents (Länderrat) by U.S. military governor Lucius Clay to draft legislation regulating information control. This legislation apparently was intended to apply only to the press, but the U.S. request sent German state officials mixed signals regarding the desirability of state control of the media. Indeed, by mid-1947, OMGUS realized the dilemma and retreated from sponsoring German legislation for press controls. It came to fear that any state intervention in the media would be "essentially undemocratic" and stepped up its vigilance regarding attempts by German officials to "control or dominate" this area.[88]

Even after the American position had been made plain, *Land* officials continued their campaign to determine the future form of film censorship. At the end of 1947, an ICD memo noted that the "tendency toward the establishment of *Land* government or local German film censorship . . . is growing rapidly and is being fostered particularly by cultural and religious organizations."[89] In order to defuse this situation, U.S. officials decided in mid-1947 to institute a German Advisory Film Committee of their own.[90] At this time, talks with the French were not progressing satisfactorily, and ICD officials apparently felt some action was needed to coopt the support of disgruntled local groups while Allied negotiations regarding the permanent form of film censorship continued. The committee was to be composed of three representatives from each of the following interests: youth groups, government, the churches (no more than one per denomination), labor, press, political parties (one per party), trade and commerce, women's clubs, theater and the arts, and, last but not least, the film industry (in order to "represent the showmanship angle and . . . counterbalance biased, prejudiced and bigoted attitudes," which would presumably be expressed by the others!). In addition, it was mandated that at least one representative from each group be female. Officials did not comment explicitly on the reason behind the stipulation of sex but did indicate that they wanted the group to "represent a cross section of all walks of life."[91] One can speculate that female input was considered desirable since issues regarding youthful spectatorship figured heavily in calls for stricter censorship controls, and unquestioned assumptions regarding women's special maternal and moral roles continued into the postwar period among Germans and Americans alike.

The German Advisory Film Committee was never instituted in the U.S. zone, perhaps due to strenuous objection by MPEA representatives, who feared that their films would fall victim to German censorship wrath. Yet ICD officials crafted the proposal in the hope of soliciting German cooperation and tempering the influence of church and state interests in film matters. American officials were more comfortable working with members of the German film industry, whom they apparently considered to be free of ideology, perhaps purged by their participation in the market. The establishment of the committee was proposed as a stopgap alternative to subdue criticism from influential sectors of German society, especially when talks with the Allies regarding the same matters were not progressing according to American design.

Much of the motivation for *Land* and church officials' involvement in censorship issues grew out of concern for the "spiritual welfare" of German youth; and contemporaries resurrected earlier claims that juveniles had to be protected from the "danger of film [*Filmgefahr*]."[92] An article in the state-funded Munich newsletter, *Jugendnachrichten* (*Youth News*), explained that "in the matter of film censorship there is not only the question of keeping . . . erotic scenes [away] from youths. . . . [Many] foreign as well as German films paint quite the wrong picture of life, and by their unreal sphere—no matter if films show a gangster or adventurer life or . . . [one of] luxury and far from troubles— . . . stir up wishes in youths that are especially misplaced nowadays."[93] Such wishes were "especially misplaced," it seems, because material luxuries were inaccessible, apart from the illegal black market, and could only be obtained through some sort of criminal activity. Convinced of the argument linking uncontrolled film viewing with juvenile crime and delinquency, the Bavarian State Committee for Youth Affairs (Bayerischer Landesjugendausschuß) announced its intentions to push for the reestablishment of film censorship for youth.

Land governments readily extended their assistance, since educational and cultural affairs fell under their jurisdiction. In late 1947, the Committee for Cultural Politics (Kulturpolitischer Ausschuß) and the Public Welfare Committee (Wohlfahrtsausschuß) of the Länderrat prepared a petition concerning the control of cinematic threats to German youth. Within two months, the Länderrat constituted a commission made up of the various state ministers to study the problem.[94] This commission, "after many hours of discussion" with representatives of the German Film Producers' Association, agreed to forego legislative solutions in favor of voluntary cooperation by public officials and interest groups with the film industry. Furthermore, they prepared the ground for negotiations between the film industry and state representatives.[95]

Despite the assurances given the film industry regarding their willingness to forego state control of culture, Bavarian state and religious leaders continued to explore options for strengthening regional censorship. Such initiatives should not be underestimated; the largest film production facilities in Germany were located in Munich, and any local Bavarian censorship legislation would impact the entire national film industry. In early April 1948, Bavarian cultural official Walter Keim called a meeting on film censorship, at the request of Jesuit leader Max Gritschneder, to which representatives from the Bavarian Catholic and Protestant churches, the Workers Welfare Organization, the provincial court, and municipal and state youth organizations were invited. Gritschneder assembled "a total of fourteen persons," according to an ICD source, "selected in such a way that they were largely representatives of the Catholic faith, to which Dr. Keim also freely acknowledged his adherence." The purpose of the meeting was to create a Bavarian film committee responsible for preproduction censorship to counter the industry censorship the Americans had planned. In particular, Gritschneder was seeking a guarantee that films which violated "the principles of natural law" and whose plots "include . . . divorce and remarriage" would be banned; furthermore, he demanded a retraction of the stipulation that required the identification of groups sponsoring "propaganda films or films of a tendentious nature." It was later learned that he feared this clause would prejudice the marketing of films the Christian Lodges were planning to sponsor secretly. Although the Protestants present balked at Gritschneder's demands, he received a sympathetic hearing from his Catholic colleagues, and in the end his persistence paid off. The age for unregulated cinema attendance in Bavaria was raised from sixteen to eighteen years. Also, a Bavarian film committee emerged from the proceedings, on which the film industry was granted only three seats —half the seats awarded state and church representatives. The ICD informant in attendance commented that she "had the impression that the Catholic Church [was] . . . principally interested in controlling the majority of the votes."[96]

Word of the closed meeting drew a radio protest by the Bavarian Union of Intellectual and Cultural Workers, whose leader denounced as undemocratic the tendency of the Bavarian Cultural Ministry to handle "cultural questions which concern the people as a whole" in a backroom manner.[97] It also disturbed American authorities, who were eager to head off local solutions to the censorship issue. To this end, they summoned state officials to the negotiating table with industry representatives in early May 1948. The basic form worked out between the U.S. film officers and the German Film Producers' Association would emerge intact from the May 1948 meeting; after all, state representatives had already agreed to forego state censorship.[98] Although this represented a major concession, presumably they could see the futility of fighting against a principle about which the American occupiers had remained adamant since 1945.

Debate centered on the administrative and operational aspects of film censorship, not the content of control—an approach that would characterize discussions during the next year, until the formal implementation of voluntary self-control by the film industry in July 1949. The major point of contention between the film industry and the state representatives became the composition of the film review board. The Film Producers' Association first suggested a ten-member board, with three of the seats occupied by representatives of the *Länder* and the remainder by representatives of the industry. As Johanne Noltenius has pointed out, this was almost purely a "branch censorship" since the film industry, up to this point, was represented only by members of the Film Producers' Association, and no agreements had as yet been reached with the distribution or exhibition branches.[99] The *Länder* representatives rejected this proposal. They had no intention of surrendering all influence over film censorship to U.S.-licensed producers.

The proposal for the constitution of the Freiwillige Selbstkontrolle der Filmwirtschaft (FSK) that emerged from the May 1948 meeting balanced the representation of the "public sector" more equitably but still retained an absolute majority for the film producers: out of a fifteen-member Kontrollkommission, eight seats were to be filled by representatives of the film industry and the remaining seven were to be divided among representatives from the state ministries of culture, the churches, and youth offices.[100] From this committee, a Vorkommisson was to be elected, comprised of two representatives from the "public sector" and three from the film industry. As Noltenius correctly noted, the inclusion of representatives from the churches and youth offices was as important as it was "conspicuous." When they recognized that branch censorship would not be possible, the film producers rapidly amended their proposal to include and thereby coopt their "sharpest critics," in order to dull any later attacks against the FSK. After the May meeting, the German Film Producers' Association's business manager sought to emphasize the conciliatory nature of the agreement:

> We are of the opinion that by this arrangement the best possible result has been reached for the time being. Government representatives . . . will cooperate with the new control commission and thus this autonomous film censorship will be deprived—in contrast to the USA—of its character as an *exclusive* institution of the producers' association. The cooperation of government representatives is, however, a prerequisite in the present state of Germany in order for the different states to forego the enactment of special laws of censorship, of which some have already been prepared. We are also of the opinion that cooperation of government representatives, representatives of the public, the churches etc. will enhance the effect, authority and significance of film censorship more than a film censorship practiced by one association only ever could.[101]

A compromise had finally been reached, but only after the arduous negotiations "collapsed totally three times."[102] The most divisive issue centered on determining which group would receive the majority of votes in the working committee of the FSK. Government officials eventually conceded to the film industry, "but only after offering strong resistance."[103] Afterward, Bavarian Cultural Ministry official Walter Keim credited the results of the meeting to the "consent" of the public sector (*öffentlicher Hand*) but emphasized that it represented a "temporary expedient." Moreover, his insistence on the "provisional" nature of the agreement hinted at the tenuousness of the truce.[104]

Adam and Eve in the Garden of Eden, from Helmut Käutner's *Der Apfel ist ab*. (Courtesy of the Deutsches Institut für Filmkunde, Frankfurt)

Indeed, despite the agreement, Bavarian state and religious interests stepped up their challenge to American-style industry self-censorship by undertaking their own censorship crusade against "unacceptable" native film production. Just two weeks after the May meeting, Bavarian leaders launched a campaign—in the press and the pulpit—against director Helmut Käutner's film parody of the Adam and Eve story, *Der Apfel ist ab* (*The Apple Has Fallen*, 1948). The protest was provoked by the tireless Max Gritschneder (a member of the Munich Catholic Film Office), who infiltrated Camera Film studios in Munich and secured a script of the unfinished film. Gritschneder convinced a number of influential Catholics that Käutner's film contained offensive depictions of Adam and Eve (clothed only in fig leaves) and distasteful portrayals of Heaven, Hell, and angels. He called for a public boycott.[105]

Gritschneder's campaign soon received the support of Bavarian cultural minister Alois Hundhammer, who publicly and ominously asserted that the state "would not tolerate instances of moral poisoning [*sittliche Vergiftung*]." Munich bishop Johann Neuhäusler publicized his opposition to the film first in a sermon and then in a press conference. At the latter, he stressed Catholic leaders' determination to prevent the completion of the film; failing that, he threatened to create a "League of Decency" throughout Germany that would be mobilized along with the Catholic Young Men's Associations to lead a "lasting boycott against all cinemas that exhibit such . . . undesirable films." When a person at the press conference could be heard whispering that the Nazis had once launched such a campaign against *All Quiet on the Western Front* (in 1931), Bishop Neuhäusler responded that "even if the church was silent on matters of decency during the Nazi period, it would be guilty of a violation of duties if it did not speak up now."[106]

Neuhäusler blasted the film for its "irreligious cabaret-style presentation of the biblical creation and fall from grace" and its "portrayal of repulsive perversities." Later, the Episcopal Information Office in Cologne (Bischöfliche Informationsstelle Köln) would advise Catholics to avoid the film because it "ridicules sin, guilt, responsibility, the seriousness of personal decisions, divorce, marriage, [and] family." The Protestant Bishop Hans Meiser of Bavaria accused the film of appealing to "erotic instincts . . . and poisoning the minds of youth," adding that national regeneration would be impossible "unless moral libertinism is stopped, and the holiness of wedlock protected again." At the national level, the Protestant leadership issued a more general condemnation, criticizing the "political satire [because it] caricatures and distorts essential teachings of the Christian church."[107]

Käutner did indeed create a celluloid satire beholden to his early experiences in Berlin cabaret. The biblical story attracted Käutner because of its appeal as a "naive folktale"; but its cinematic resurrection was anything but simple and was praised by reviewers for its sophisticated—even "avant-garde"—treatment, accomplished technique, and "masterly" cinematography. In France, where it did a good business, critics applauded it as an updated example of German expressionist film.[108] Käutner was an experienced director, active during the Third Reich, with popular entertainment films like *Die Große Freiheit #7, Wir machen Musik* (*We Make Music*, 1942), and *Romanze in Moll* (*Romance in a Minor Key*, 1943) to his credit. Because of his clean political background, Käutner was one of the first filmmakers licensed in the U.S. zone and directed *In jenen Tagen* (*In Those Days*, 1947) and *Film ohne Titel* (*Film without a Title*, 1947) before beginning this more controversial film.

Käutner wrote the script for *Der Apfel ist ab* together with Bobby Todd, who also played the leading part of Adam Schmidt, the apple juice manufacturer, in the film.[109] Todd's Adam is a physically diminutive, unsubstantial "Everyman," who, according to the authors, "stands in the middle of encircling postwar ruins on the rubble of his personal life." The obvious problem that confronts Adam is which of two women to marry. But the larger dilemma is one of personal choice and individual responsibility; the biblical story of human creation—which is played out in a "surrealistic dream revue"—becomes an allegory of these themes. Thus, the film follows Adam from the German ruins, which symbolize the result of a sustained period of "unreflective . . . animalistic irresponsibility," through a couple of halfhearted attempts at suicide, which are frustrated by his dog's firm grip on his pant leg as he prepares to jump off a bridge and by the flimsiness of the venetian blind cord with which he tries to hang himself. While stumbling along through the ruins in this humorous fit of botched acts, he sees a sign that reads: "Why despair? Come out of the ruins, away with the rubble! Get cured at the White Heights [Weissenhöhe]." Thus, Adam is lured to the spa, where Dr. Petrus (played by Käutner) listens to his romantic woes and dubs him "OdZ" or "victim of the times [Opfer der Zeit]." Adam's cure begins, in effect, only when he is re-created in the Adam and Eve dream sequence. There he ultimately learns that he must, as an individual, think, decide, and act for himself and that he must accept the consequences and responsibilities of those actions rather than attribute blame to rules, laws, or higher authority. Thus, the political and ethical lesson for postwar Germans was manifest. And all who claimed to have merely "gone along" with national socialism in order to weather the fascist storm, or would complain of victimization by Allied bombing or occupation policies, were prescribed a dose of honest self-scrutiny.

A summary of the film's moral, however, does little to convey its sociocultural richness. Adam's arrival at the spa initiates an extended dream-like sequence. The action now takes place in closed, highly stylized sets, and we can never be entirely sure whether we are observing an elaborate treatment by the omnipotent Dr. Petrus at the "White Heights" or the character's troubled fantasies. For Adam has been sent to Paradise to await the creation of Earth and is accompanied by Eve (Bettina Moissi) and his dog. Eve is lovely and chaste, despite her diaphanous dress; Adam looks comically immature in his plastic schoolboy's knickers, which expose his twig-thin legs. The couple amuse themselves for a while watching angel-tourists, but soon boredom sets in, for there is little to do in Paradise and only manna to eat. They are enticed to the apple tree and reach out to touch a lone, forbidden fruit—but suffer an electric shock. Fortunately, they encounter a Care package and a white baby grand piano and divert themselves with song. But along comes Lucifer, who, after indulging in a musical number, orchestrates a limousine trip for Adam and Eve to Hell.

Hell is a nightclub where the dress is formal and temptations abound. The food is rich and plentiful, and the entertainment is, well, American. Eve orders a dish of whipped cream, while Adam enjoys a chorus line, followed by a boxing match. As the show turns into a grisly revue of martial arts and torture, the Devil grins malevolently, for he knows full well that indulgence does not come cheap. Yet the Fall occurs back in Paradise, when sexy Lilith (Joana Maria Gorvin), the Devil's agent, slithers like a snake to tempt Adam way from the sleeping Eve. The flesh has proved weak: the apple is plucked, and Adam abandons Eve to accompany Lilith to Earth. The game appears up. Adam seems to

"Evenings in Hell" with a tuxedoed Devil, from *Der Apfel ist ab*. (Courtesy of the Stiftung Deutsche Kinemathek, Berlin)

have solved the problem of his unstable subjectivity, which fluctuated between attraction to a spiritual, though admittedly boring, ideal (Eve) and a much more sensually satisfying (and American-style) materialism (Lilith). But the fantastic voyage continues, and soon we are in the present, where Eve reappears as a secretary in Adam's office. The indecision returns, and a (heavenly?) conference is arranged at which Adam at last is to announce his selection. He rejects both Eve and Lilith. But as he makes this "manly choice" (as the movie program described it), divine technology intercedes; the women are encapsulated in glass tubes and merged into one perfect bride. Thus, Adam discovers that decisive acts result in happiness—or perhaps not, for at that moment Adam awakens from his sweetly concluded dream. As he leaves the clinic to return to the world, he crosses the street to catch the train and there meets his perfect composite woman.

So self-knowledge and courageous action *do* make the man and secure his happiness after all. Or was the fantastic—though happy—ending the product of the backstage machinations and techno-factory of some divine being? The matter was muddy, and some viewers were not convinced that Adam was not a passive pawn of greater powers—and one without a manifestly masculine will at that. In the opinion of one engineer who saw the film, Adam should have been "much more manly." Otherwise, how could it be possible that "his son later killed his brother Abel—from whom did he inherit this energetic robustness?" As we shall see in chapter 3, unflattering cinematic representations of German masculinity would become a significant sore spot for many in church and state offices in the early Adenauer years. But in 1948, little attention was devoted to these matters by Catholic critics; and apparently Bishop Neuhäusler was the only one to complain that the scripted Eve was "that type of well-mannered woman who possesses no sex appeal"![110]

Käutner admitted a number of years later that the film might have been "served up in too intellectual" a fashion and that allusions and gags came too fast and furious for most viewers. Indeed, critical response was likely more favorable than popular assessments, since reviewers often mentioned Käutner's highbrow approach to story treatment and film aesthetics. Moreover, many seemed unconvinced by the arguments of state and church officials in Bavaria regarding the hurtful impact of the film. One incredulous viewer from Munich, for example, wrote to a newspaper complaining that the controversy was "a lot of noise about nothing," noting that *Der Apfel* was neither more nor less "moral" than many other films. A Berlin journalist questioned how the film could harm religious sensibilities when no one was being forced to see it; he suggested that its significance might lie instead in its test of intellectual freedom in postwar Germany.[111]

This was precisely the angle that Käutner took. In late spring 1948, in the face of intensifying controversy, Käutner alerted the American ICD and held a press conference to answer the mounting criticism of his (as yet) unreleased film. Comparing the tactics used against him to those practiced during the "Nazizeit," he threatened to emigrate. Käutner questioned whether democracy could be successfully introduced in a country in which such attempts at public intimidation were tolerated.[112]

U.S. authorities had an obvious stake in defusing the situation: their authority in this case was being implicitly questioned and explicitly ignored. The ICD called a meeting four days after Käutner's press conference and invited representatives from the Catholic archdiocese and the Evangelical Lutheran Church Council of Bavaria; Walter Keim of the Bavarian Cultural Ministry; Curt Oertel, president of the German Film Producers' Association in the U.S. zone; a representative of the motion picture press; and Helmut Käutner.[113] All present were requested to affirm the principle of industry self-censorship and renounce control by the state—and all complied. Although these issues had already been formally agreed upon by German cultural ministers the previous fall and again just a few weeks earlier, this renewed pledge represented a pointed demand for Bavarian cooperation by American film officials and was issued to defuse any further problems during the resolution of film censorship questions.

Yet the acquiescence of state and religious authorities to ICD demands was certainly not wholehearted, and an element of coercion existed—perhaps not in word or deed, but by implication. The Military Government was, after all, still an authoritarian power. As General Clay's successor, John McCloy, once pointed out, his powers were comparable to that of a Roman proconsul's.[114] And Walter Keim had acknowledged German subordination to the Military Government's wishes when he commented that his "government had in principle approved" industry self-censorship when it became clear that the ICD was "not interested in any other solution."[115]

A Temporary Peace: The FSK Begins Operation

By February 1949 a proposed industry self-censorship code was agreed upon by the German producers, the U.S. MPB, the British and French military governments, and the state ministers of culture in the three Western zones. The final agreement gave a majority voice to industry interests. Industry representatives occupied four out of six seats on the Working Committee (Arbeitsausschuß), which would review all films before their release in Germany, and eight out of fifteen seats on the Main Committee (Hauptausschuß), which was responsible for settling contested decisions. In addition, U.S. film officers stipulated that an Appeals Committee composed of German jurists be added to the FSK, to be constituted at some future date.[116] For the interim, the Americans,

British, and French created a temporary Tripartite Board of Appeal, which was commissioned to act upon protested FSK decisions.[117]

The FSK began operation on 15 July 1949 in Wiesbaden, which was also the seat of the industry's umbrella trade organization, the SPIO.[118] Arthur Mayer, who had succeeded Erich Pommer as head of the MPB eight months earlier, announced both his resignation and the cessation of censorship activities by his branch as of mid-July. He added that "this announcement was motivated by our desire to bring to an end the interminable procrastination of the Germans and get self control at length in operation."[119]

The debates surrounding the creation of the FSK lasted over two years, and although an agreement was hammered out between the Allies, the German film industry, and the representatives of the *Länder* and the churches, the censorship solution was not accepted by all groups as immutable. The British voiced doubts that would later be picked up by liberal jurists in West Germany in the late 1950s. British officials considered the final FSK proposal "much too far reaching and restrictive to be in line with principles of the Basic Law and the Occupation Statute." They feared that the FSK would expose the film industry to "undue influence by pressure groups" and insisted that tripartite agreements should "guarantee the independence of the German press, radio and film industry from the control of government and administrative authorities, and political, economic, denominational and other groups." In spite of these "considerable doubts," the British gave the FSK their authorization, in part because of all of the work that had gone into the proposal but also because "the Germans worked it out for themselves," a surprising assertion that ignores strong American input.[120]

Keim termed the founding of the FSK an "experiment" in the "democratic self-administration of a great cultural area." He explained that *Land* representatives agreed that the principle of industry self-censorship should be instituted "on a trial basis"[121] and then proceeded to embark on an agenda that foreshadowed future directions in which *Land* governments would move concerning film issues.

Most important for bolstering state influence was *Länder* involvement in film financing. According to ICD intelligence, the currency reform in the Western zones in 1948 initiated a decline in bank credit for film production: "Soon, however, with Bavaria leading the way, the *Land* economics ministries put up guarantees for productions approved by the *Land* governmental agencies. While it is impossible to prove this, there seemed to be a connection between the stopping of credits by the . . . banks and the opening of these offices." Needless to say, state officials demanded the right to review scripts and casts and monitor all stages of production for films they helped fund. Given the fact that Munich film studios had the capacity to produce over half of the total domestic output in the Western zones, American officials feared a "Bavarian stranglehold" on German production. Although many producers "opposed this as best they could," Bavaria and Hamburg eventually funded "immense" projects, some of which enlisted the experience of recent Nazis like Ludwig Klitzsch, formerly of UFI, and Fritz Hippler and Max Winkler, Goebbels's influential assistants at the Reich Film Chamber.[122]

In addition, Keim called for the *Länder* to resurrect state distribution of prizes and corresponding tax incentives for films they deemed worthy. He further encouraged sustained *Länder* interest in issues involving morality and particularly the protection of youth—areas in which the state and church representatives would remain active throughout the Adenauer era.

Finally, we must return to the churches, which obtained representation in the FSK and were thereby bound to uphold the principles of self-censorship. Military Government authority insured the cooperation of church officials at pivotal points during the occupation, as, for example, in Munich in June 1948 during the *Apfel ist ab* controversy as well as later in negotiations involving the creation of the FSK. During these talks, church representatives were especially careful to emphasize that they did not want their participation in the FSK to be misconstrued as church endorsement of every picture released. They therefore were interested in guaranteeing generous appeal rights to keep open the possibility of representing their dissenting opinions before the next highest committee in order to win a favorable decision there.[123]

With the creation of the Federal Republic and the withdrawal of Military Government authority, certain issues could again be subjected to question and review. The precedent had been set of presenting issues directly to the public over the heads of competent authorities; this tactic would again be invoked when the normal institutional channels yielded no results.

3

DIE SÜNDERIN OR WHO KILLED THE GERMAN MAN?
EARLY POSTWAR CINEMA AND THE BETRAYAL OF FATHERLAND

The big world rests upon this small world! The big world cannot survive if the small world is not secure!—Adolf Hitler, address to the National Socialist Women's Organization at the Nuremberg Party Rally, 8 September 1934

In January 1951, director Willi Forst's film *Die Sünderin* (*The Sinner*)—the story of a woman's resort to prostitution, redemption through love, and eventual suicide—premiered at the Turmpalast in Frankfurt. Within days of its release, Protestant film commissioner Werner Hess lambasted it for "call-[ing] into question the last vital forces of morality during a time of distress for our Volk,"[1] and the Protestant and Catholic churches set in motion a series of public demonstrations against the film's exhibition. Clergy initiated protests in Koblenz and Bielefeld, as well as in Aschaffenburg, Düsseldorf, and Regensburg, where street scuffles broke out and stink bombs were thrown into theaters. Screenings were interrupted by tear gas in Frankfurt and Mannheim and by the release of white mice in Duisburg. Priests led schoolboys in street marches in Lüneburg, Munich, Regensburg, Karlsruhe, Ulm, and elsewhere. In Lüneburg, Catholic minors fired off a letter to the local theater owner charging that *Die Sünderin* exacerbated the spiritual crisis of postwar youth; while in Erlangen, confessional students disseminated leaflets demanding local censorship and condemning the film's "glorification of the new heathendom."

In the midst of the uproar, Cardinal Josef Frings declared that "this public vexation cannot remain unchallenged" and issued a pastoral statement from his archbishopric in Cologne calling on all Christians to boycott the film. Catholic and Protestant clergy in Füssen/Allgäu went one step further and refused to hold Sunday church services, perform weddings and funerals, or allow the ringing of church bells for the duration of *Die Sünderin*'s run in local theaters. By spring, the film was banned in dozens of small- and medium-sized towns across West Germany—including the new capital, Bonn, where the local press refused to print either ads or descriptions of the film.[2]

What was it about *Die Sünderin* that stirred such immediate and passionate response by German clergymen? The dramatic nature of the language employed against the film suggests that these clergymen were motivated by more than a predictable moral squeamishness concerning the depiction of female nudity and prostitution on the big screen. The stakes, they argued, were much higher. They considered their mobilization an act of "self-defense" against a grave cultural threat. In a remarkable film review that established both the tone and the agenda for the ensuing campaign, Protestant film commissioner Werner Hess "cried out from a plagued heart" with the near-hysterical plea, "Who will help hinder such spiritual murder of our young people and women, tested by suffering, and our broken-bodied men?"[3]

The question was rhetorical; the churches would obviously lead the campaign. After 1945, the German churches rapidly assumed the leadership of social and ideological reconstruction and in fact became the "great normalizers" of postwar West Germany. The Catholic church in particular served as both an important messenger of alarm and a sounding board for conservative attitudes. No other group had a comparable institutional base or exhibited such unity of action and conviction of purpose. Church influence was further strengthened by the avid support of coreligionists in state and governmental offices, who were able to translate church concerns into new legislation. By the beginning of the Bonn Republic, these well-entrenched interests dominated the process of social and cultural reconstruction.[4]

Yet Hess's images of violence and ruin, of gender and generation, are inexplicable without further scrutiny of the film and the social-sexual context in which it was produced and distributed. As one film historian has argued: "Reading a film is not simply a matter of 'drinking the meaning off the screen' . . . but of investigating the film's mode of address and its relationship to the specific historical conjecture, the context of its conception."[5] It is also, however, a matter of investigating the context of its *reception*. The anti-*Sünderin* campaign can be read as a story of the struggles involved in the post-Hitler reconstruction of cultural representation and social ideology in West Germany. An analysis of the discourse surrounding the release and exhibition of *Die Sünderin* exposes the ideological justifications for conservative social policy toward women and the family promulgated in the early 1950s.[6]

The film itself is artistically unexceptional, and its message strikes the modern viewer as hopelessly romantic and socially conservative. Marina, the female protagonist, after a brief period of prostitution, finds love and redemption with one man and ultimately affirms her fidelity to him by surrendering her own life

A protest in Cologne against Willi Forst's *Die Sünderin*. The signs covering the *Sünderin* marquee read: "The health of the *Volk* comes before profit!" and "Sünderin without us!" (Courtesy of the Deutsches Institut für Filmkunde, Frankfurt)

to join him in death. The death scene frames and structures the narrative; it provides the dramatic ending of the film but also, more significantly, the enigmatic first scene. *Die Sünderin* opens just before Marina commits suicide in the arms of her dying lover, Alexander. Exclaiming "Oh my God, I've killed you!," she initiates a series of flashbacks that answers the question of why she killed the man she loved. Her answer indicates that her actions grew out of despair over Alexander's increasing incapacitation, which their love was unable to cure. But some influential Germans thought she answered the question badly. They did not seek an answer to the broad question of what killed "the German man." In fact, there is reason to believe that they resented the question posed in that fashion. They did not want the particular answer offered by the film; indeed, they did not want the answer left to the movies at all.

Die Sünderin aroused extraordinarily strong passions for two reasons. First, it challenged German leaders to confront what they had preferred to suppress: the fact that traditional social ideologies and gender relations, which had been exalted and exaggerated under Hitler, had been profoundly disrupted and perhaps destroyed. Second, the film highlighted the ability of mass culture to disseminate this devastating message. For these reasons, the film provoked intense anxiety and a sharp public response from conservative elites.

The fact was that "the German man" was a real social problem in the postwar period. German women outnumbered men by 7.3 million in 1945, leading contemporaries to speak of a "Frauenüberschuß" or surplus of women, which was particularly marked among women in their childbearing years (ages 20–40). Nearly 4 million German men had been killed in the war, and at the end of hostilities, 11.7 million German soldiers were held in prison camps.[7] By 1950, even with the return of most of the German prisoners of war, almost one-third of West German households were headed by divorced women or widows. In those households in which a man was present, he was "often physically or psychologically scarred, unwilling or unable to work, or disqualified from some jobs because of [his] National Socialist loyalties." He could not, therefore, easily resume his traditionally defined social role as husband or father.[8]

Postwar Germany seemed plagued by a crisis of masculinity. And since this crisis coincided with military defeat and occupation, it was intimately bound up with notions of national identity. Postwar memoirs that discuss the behavior of German men in Berlin after the arrival of Russian soldiers—and the beginning of widespread raping of German women—testify to this. In his book, *The Russians in Berlin, 1945*, Erich Kuby recalled: "We know of some half-dozen Berliners (among hundreds of thousands) who stood up for their wives and paid for it with their lives. We know of a couple dozen (it may have even totaled a few hundred) who were smart and kept their senses and, without getting killed, protected their own wives or women in their immediate vicinity from rape. . . . Otherwise, we know that the great majority of men crawled behind their women, were frightened and cowardly—unimaginably cowardly. The women too were afraid, but they were courageous—unimaginably courageous."[9] Looking back on those times, women tend to explain their responses as not a matter of choice—or elected bravery—but of necessity. Helga Born, for example, noted that "time and again, whenever the door opened, the 'heroes' hid behind our skirts. Then they became little boys, who were scared of the bogey man and needed mother's protection. When the women objected, they argued, 'They won't do anything to you, if you just hold still. But they'll ship us to Siberia.' "[10]

Another Berlin woman recorded in her personal journal that her friend, a widow, agreed during this period to house a former male tenant, who "from the day he returned [to Berlin] . . . put himself to bed with a 'neuralgia,' allowing himself to be cared for, fed, and protected. . . . Only after the Russians withdrew did he get out of bed, healthy and fully recovered." The same diarist noted a similar change among Berlin men in public on 8 May 1945, the day the Russian troops pulled out of the city: "For the first time in weeks . . . I've heard German men talking in loud voices, seen them move with any sign of energy. They were acting in a practically masculine way—or in a way that used to be called 'masculine.' Now we're going to be on the lookout for a better word, one that can still be used even in bad conditions."[11] Such displays of male inactivity occurred in response to the presence of enemy soldiers and so carried with it associations of submission and national humiliation—especially since, in the eyes of German commentators of both sexes, these Berlin men actively infantilized themselves and opted to behave in a passive, nonheroic manner.

The infantilization of physically and emotionally disabled veterans was a common phenomenon following the German defeat in World War I. After World War II, chilling parallels would not have been difficult to draw. "What the war victims need . . . is not only the hand of fatherly justice, but the soft hand of the mother. After all, they are really sick children, not so much because of the medical problems they have, but because of the terrible shock they have endured," read one article in the German press in 1921.[12] Several years earlier, Catholic bishop Michael von Faulhaber, who would later become cardinal of Bavaria, complained of the "lack of emotional vigor, a frightening paralysis of will, a perverse kind of homesickness and an endless grubbing for pensions" among disabled veterans. Critical of this marked lack of volition and productivity, Faulhaber insisted that those "who have been touched by death must not be allowed to wander around with their peg-legs and music boxes as they did after previous wars. . . . Even the blind cannot be permitted to become drones. Self-pity is like being buried alive."[13]

This failure of masculine "will" was regretted as much after World War II as after World War I. Yet in the post-1945 world, the situation was further exacerbated by the missing (or consciously withheld) "soft hand of the mother," which was necessary in earlier times to nurse the fatigued and prostrated former warrior.[14] After 1945, women were depicted as repudiating, in great numbers, their traditional roles as wife and helpmate.

Husbands returning home after years away in the war or prison camps often experienced disappointment and disorientation following their long-awaited reunion. Men described their shock at finding not the young, amiable, and soft-spoken wives who inhabited their fond memories but women rendered haggard, hardened, and self-reliant as a result of the war on the home front. In order to survive, women learned to provide for themselves and their children despite food rationing, nightly bombing raids, evacuations, epidemics, and even brutalization and rape. As one returning soldier recalled: "The women completely emancipated themselves during the time we weren't at home—although they had no knowledge of this expression. They had to do everything on their own. I found it extremely difficult to deal with. We [he and his wife] both had the impression that we had changed completely."[15]

Moreover, while many women reported gaining a sense of confidence and self-sufficiency for surviving harrowing times, men's experiences of military defeat and imprisonment frequently resulted in physical and mental debilitation and feelings of profound dishonor and despair. Homecoming did nothing to boost men's severely flagging self-esteem, for German veterans entered a baffling new world in which unemployment was rife and military pensions were outlawed by the victors as a remnant of Germany's militarist tradition.[16] As a result, survival depended on ration cards, illegal black market deals, long hours of waiting in line, scavenging, gardening, and the efforts of women and children. In oral histories, women described the contributions of children as young as ten years old as "indispensable" to the household economy during the starvation years of the occupation, when minors were often sent to outlying rural areas or the black market to barter and steal, since they would be subject to lesser penalties if caught in an illegal act. Thus, women, assisted by their children, continued the exhausting work of subsistence into the postwar period and became the primary providers of the family household.[17]

It seemed, then, that the war had emasculated men and masculinized women. In a telling article, publicist Walther von Hollander, a frequent contributor to women's magazines, blamed women for the increasing number of broken marriages in postwar Germany, noting with regret that not all women were willing to submit to their husbands and surrender their newfound freedom:

Women have proven themselves during the war to be capable of enduring life-threatening situations and work normally befitting men. They have often led a sexually active life that until now—justifiably or not—was reserved only for men; only those who shut their eyes can deny it. Now there are innumerable women, perhaps they are the majority, who would be only too happy to give the burden of a masculine life back to the man; however, not all are so ready to surrender the pleasure of masculine life [and] its relative liberty. . . . Women have learned to bear responsibility. They can be relieved of this responsibility only if someone [else] actually has the strength to lead. Only then will women again happily and mildly extend their trust.[18]

In order to contribute to "normalization," women were again being asked to join the family in the roles of wife and mother and to defer to male authority.

Yet gender roles are relational; in order for women to (re)assume their traditional roles, men needed to summon the will to reassert their authority. It is not surprising, then, that when men in Berlin "crawled out of their beds and hiding places," they felt the need to reestablish their gender identities and the national identity so intimately bound up with them. They attempted to rescue their self-image and social position by reestablishing their sexual dominance. Shortly after the withdrawal of Soviet troops, Berlin men began to proposition German women in public by inquiring, in an expression that rapidly gained common currency, whether they could "offer [them] a little abuse." German women were not blind to the violence and grim irony of gender and international relations; many who suffered through the raping raids "suspected that they were doing time in Berlin for the crimes committed by German men in Russia."[19]

Annemarie Tröger has observed, based upon her research in Berlin, that the war and defeat demolished the myth of German masculinity and undid "the ideological fetters of traditional femininity," allowing German women to "experience a certain sexual and social emancipation" during the first years of the military occupation.[20] Often, of course, this sexual "emancipation" was forced and brutal, with "the rights of the victor nations . . . acted out on [women's] bodies."[21] Estimates of the number of women raped after the fall of Berlin range from 20,000 to half a million, and thousands of Berlin women resorted to prostitution in order to survive.[22]

Despite the predominantly coercive and violent quality of German women's emancipation, it was not uncommon for German men to vilify them publicly for having had sexual relations with enemy soldiers. Often these commentators did not distinguish between rape and prostitution, nor did they, in order to carry their arguments, dwell upon the miserable material circumstances that drove women into prostitution:

Another very bitter symptom, which is difficult to articulate, would be senseless to suppress. It is not only the case that the German man returned home defeated. The victors marched in with him, and he had to observe that a small, and not very valuable, number of women fell prey to the[se] victors. It is almost impossible to pronounce objectively on this. Nevertheless, the German soldier must admit, based upon his experiences during the war, that such things did and still do happen throughout the world. Does he wish revenge by their countrymen on the women who gave him pleasure abroad? Surely not. But for the sake of the dignity of the defeated, he naturally wishes that all German women would maintain the morally necessary distance. And for those who trespass against this he feels a thoroughly understandable disdain, mixed with hate, for women who give themselves to the victors for meager material advantages.[23]

Public rhetoric such as this, which condemned women for their sexual intercourse with (and often victimization by) victorious soldiers, was symptomatic of the drive to reestablish the "myth of masculinity" in occupied Germany. More precisely, it advocated a specific brand of German masculinity that linked gender roles and sexuality in a complex way with nationality and national pride. Wartime raping raids by conquering German soldiers were cloaked in euphemism by the above commentator and excused as the expected corollaries of war—and pleasurable diversions to boot. German women, however, were assigned full responsibility for their involvement in such incidents on home territory. A metalworker from the Ruhr, for example, recalled a "Negro" American soldier saying that "German soldiers fought for six years, German women for only five minutes!" The German added, "He was absolutely right. I was ashamed." And the fact that this metalworker thought it significant to emphasize the American soldier's race suggests that racist attitudes and fears regarding the national effects of "miscegenation" had not died with the Nazi defeat.[24]

Moreover, by portraying women as selling themselves for "meager material advantages," male commentators resurrected the putative connection between consumption and femininity, an assumption that would inform postwar government policy toward women, the family, and mass culture. Such rhetoric insinuated that German women were unfaithful partners and egotistical materialists. From here it was a short step to shifting responsibility for national humiliation onto these women, thereby creating a generalized public amnesia regarding men's contribution to the military defeat that preceded this painful foreign occupation.[25] In 1946, for example, the Protestant High Consistory (Oberkirchenrat) in Stuttgart denounced the implications of German women's postwar behavior by declaring:

> Germany is destroyed and dismembered. We have become completely destitute. Sorrow, desperation, despair oppress many. But in the midst of all of this trouble and affliction, a sinister craze of pleasure-seeking runs through the *Volk*. Numerous German women and girls degrade themselves through licentious behavior. They disregard the Sixth Commandment, which tells us to live chastely and modestly in word and deed. Such women and girls forget their honor and dignity; they forget the thousands of graves that surround them. They forget the frightful plague of starvation and dying in the East. They forget their husbands, brothers, sons, boyfriends, who are still imprisoned or missing. They forget the many thousands of war-wounded. They forget the entire plight and affliction of the Fatherland. Their conduct is an affront to the returning men and a vexation for the entire public.[26]

If the rhetoric of gender in the immediate postwar period was to be believed, then, the National Socialist war of aggression was a mere prelude to a more devastating national catastrophe brought on by the betrayal of German women. Moreover, this betrayal was understood to extend beyond the sexual. Journalist Walther von Hollander, for example, quoted the "bitter" response of a "bright female doctor" to illustrate the critical—and morally superior—attitude of German women toward their male countrymen: " 'The women,' so says the doctor, 'entrusted the men with their lives, they followed them trustfully into this war, which they inwardly objected to. The women have known for a long time that the war was lost. But the men reassured them that they would still win. Now, since the defeat, they cannot demand that we once again submit to their leadership.' "[27] The men may have lost the war, but women were represented as sabotaging the reconstruction through their unsympathetic demeanor and unsubmissive behavior.

The answer to this postwar dilemma seemed to lie in the redomestication of German women, who were expected to "obey their husband[s] and bear [them] children, thereby securing the existence of the *Volk*."[28] The success of German reconstruction was linked by social conservatives to the renewal of the "small world" of the normative family structure. This vision of the patriarchal family righted the skewed universe of postwar German society by reestablishing a reassuring, orderly domestic hierarchy with the father at the pinnacle.[29] The mother retained her traditional role as socializer and nurturer of the children but was sexually and socially redomesticated. The process was one of ideological repatriation: women could reclaim their influence as mothers of Germany's future only by submitting to patriarchal authority and bourgeois morality.

The overarching problem with this solution was that the postwar experience of many Germans contradicted the ideal. Just over half of all West Germans lived in "intact families," the divorce rate was high, and it would continue to rise for several more years.[30] Magazine articles regularly bemoaned the prevalence of "wilden Familien" headed by unmarried parents as well as "half families" comprised of mothers and their "illegitimate" children. This situation, which one author erroneously claimed "has never been the case up until now," was expected to have devastating results: "One cannot remove the men from the family for ten years and think that the organization of the family [*Familiengestalt*] would remain untouched and be easily reassembled. . . . The overall shape of the family is changed, and somehow destroyed."[31]

In the midst of increasing rhetoric of family dysfunction and collapse, Catholic politicians in the Christian Democratic Union (Christlich-Demokratische Union [CDU]), supported by Cardinal Frings, demanded that the family become the building block of the new German political order since its "living space is holy." Advocating a political renewal based upon God's "natural law," the CDU, in a successful bid to become the governing party of postwar Germany, advertised its support for the family as the reversal of the Nazi perversion of nature, which attempted to subordinate the family to the state. Although liberals and socialists rejected such explicitly Christian rhetoric, they agreed that the new West German state should strengthen and protect the German family, which had been so recently ravaged by Nazi policies of intervention and aggression. Thus, the commitment to family renewal transcended partisan politics precisely because it marked one's rejection of, and difference from, national socialism.[32]

This broad political consensus soon received the endorsement of science. By the early 1950s, empirical sociologist Helmut Schelsky acquired an influential voice in postwar social policy by heralding the family as "society's last bastion, the ultimate place of safety" in West Germany.[33] Schelsky's emphasis on the normative family served an important cultural function. As Robert Moeller has suggested, the "reconstitution of a private family sphere . . . embodied a critique of the ideological alternatives presented by Germany's recent past and by a Communist East Germany in the present. In the confused categories of totalitarian theory, it was possible to reject both at the same time; the family could serve as a vehicle for anti-Nazi *and* anti-communist rhetoric."[34]

West German social policy makers were indeed careful to distinguish family-oriented programs, on ideological grounds, from both their Nazi precursors and their counterparts in the Democratic Republic.[35] Yet an examination of the discourse accompanying film matters reveals that German social and political leaders also sought to protect their revived nation from the cultural and moral implications of another kind of "materialism"—commercial culture, which they identified with democratization and Americanization. The normative family, then, was to provide a bulwark against three ideologically unappealing alternatives—the Nazi, the "Commie," and the so-called "Ami"—an expectation that was succinctly captured in the sociological catchword "*Fluchtburg Familie*" or the family fortress.[36]

Conservative ambitions to reconstruct the family as a national bulwark against cultural threats were problematic, given the current crisis besetting it. As noted, the German family suffered from both an internal structural weakness caused by absent or enfeebled fathers and the same external challenges against which it was supposed to provide protection. As one contemporary noted: "Our family has . . . become helpless. It has become dependent to an alarming degree; not only dependent in terms of its social security, but dependent in its spiritual alignment. The *Meinungsraum* of the family is no longer closed; ideas from the outside muscle their way in, so that the child's sense of security, the sense of the family as a place of safety, no longer exists. The independence of the family is gravely threatened by this."[37]

Indeed, the very fact that an individual film could be denounced as a threat to reconstruction illustrates just how vulnerable the social order was thought to be. Such areas of vulnerability were associated with the challenges posed to German identity by military defeat, democratization, and the cultural and social forms pressed upon West German society from both the East and the West. Given these larger international forces at work, social conservatives considered it a matter of national life and death to insure the maintenance of a separate cultural identity. Although over the course of the early 1950s, Konrad Adenauer steered the Federal Republic firmly along the path of political integration with the West, German elites displayed a pronounced ambivalence toward cultural integration. They pushed, instead, in the direction of a cultural *Sonderweg* or special path.

The fear that godless, materialist culture would accompany democratization and spell the death of a culturally discrete, capitalist West Germany was widespread among churchmen and conservative state leaders. One Catholic bulletin praised the absence of erotic decadence in the Soviet media, commenting pointedly that one should not be surprised if those "unbroken youths someday become masters of the lustful boys" in the West.[38] Church leaders were particularly active in asserting that "the time had come, after years of dissolute living and lawlessness, to once again make decency and morality felt."[39]

In the midst of this atmosphere of social disruption and moral crisis, activist priests led armies of schoolboys onto the streets across West Germany in protest against *Die Sünderin*, demanding a new public morality and the "protection of our women's honor."[40] In order to understand more fully why this specific film was targeted by social conservatives, and to identify the themes that touched an exposed nerve in the early years of the Bonn Republic, we must examine the film in some detail. We must then explore the way the film organized the sociological data and how some contemporaries interpreted this organization.

Die Sünderin was released to much fanfare in the popular press. It was the young German actress Hildegard Knef's first feature film since her return from the United States, to which she had immigrated with her American husband in 1948 after starring in a number of successful postwar German films.[41] The film opens just before Knef's character, Marina, commits suicide in the arms of her dying lover, Alexander (Gustav Fröhlich). It then launches into a series of flashbacks, slowly building layers of meaning, which ultimately culminate in a fuller, and now comprehensible, encore of the opening scene.

The first flashback occurs in a small house on the Italian coast, where Marina and Alexander are vacationing. Alexander, an aspiring artist, is at work on a painting. Suddenly, he clutches his head in pain and vents his rage by smashing the canvas. Shaken, Marina inexplicably resolves to help her lover by selling one of his paintings. After failing to interest numerous gallery owners, she finally makes the sale by bartering herself, thinking of Alexander and his pain as she agrees to submit to the proprietor's sexual advances. On reflection, she calls this a "step into filth, nothing more."

Marina was a high-class call girl in a posh Munich nightspot when she first encountered Alexander, drunk and staggering, as he was being forcibly bounced from the bar. Bristling at his mistreatment and overwhelmed with pity, she hires a taxi and takes him to her apartment to sleep off the alcohol. The next day, when Alexander awakens, Marina realizes that although he is unkempt and unemployed he is from a "good family," and she wonders if she is really any better than he is. This thought prompts another flashback to her own family life.

The year is 1939; Marina is a teenager. After her father's death and her mother's remarriage, Marina's family relocates to Hamburg from Danzig. She describes how her stepfather (Robert Meyn), an anti-Nazi, lost his job as the head of a firm, forcing the family to move to a more modest house. With the onset of austerity, her mother (Änne Bruck) deserts the family every evening to rendezvous with a wealthy male friend, who announces his arrival during dinner with the sound of a car horn. Draped in jewels and evening wear, Marina's mother springs from the table, throws on her fur wrap, and whisks out the door. Her infidelity is portrayed as the outgrowth of a marked lack of maternal devotion and an excessive inclination for self-indulgent materialism.

Thus, the film is concerned with the private rather than the public past. National socialism, the war, and the occupation provide the dramatic backdrop for the story of Marina's fall and redemption. Her voice-over narration lends the film the character of an inner monologue: a personal reminiscence and taking-of-stock. The Nazi and postwar periods assume the form of domestic melodrama, in which the moral dilemma is relegated to the personal and sexual rather than the public and national.

Marina's decline, then, is spurred by her mother's promiscuous example and the rapid disintegration of her family. One evening after the mother has left, the Gestapo come and arrest the stepfather. Left to her own devices, Marina amuses herself by trying on her mother's clothing and is in the process of admiring the reflection of her adult femininity when her stepbrother (Jochen-Wolfgang Meyn) stumbles upon the scene. Stunned by his sister's newly sexualized look, the stepbrother seduces Marina by offering her money for sexual favors. Marina delights in her sexual precociousness; it bestows knowledge, satisfies her curiosity (she would at last experience "the unknown!"), and teaches her a newfound "power over men." She quickly learns the material rewards to be gained from perfunctorily satisfying her stepbrother's passion. With her stepfather's return, Marina's family life continues to erode. The dramatic culmination occurs when her stepfather strikes his wife and storms from the house, returning some days later to find Marina and his son in bed together. He ejects Marina from the house and beats his son, perhaps fatally; the family is irrevocably destroyed.

Marina begins a profitable life of prostitution in Munich, fraternizing with Nazi and later American soldiers. She explains that this "was the way it went until Alexander," when she realized that "love means giving . . . never taking." Life with Alexander is not without problems, however. Marina learns that he was an officer in World War II and that his personal and professional decline began with the German defeat. His wife has left him, and he suffers from a malignant brain tumor, which is causing a gradual loss of sight. He carries sleeping pills so he can choose the time of his death.

Marina and Alexander travel to Italy on vacation, and after several happy days, Alexander suffers the head pains that caused Marina to resolve to sell his painting, as we saw earlier. Only now do we understand Marina's sexual surrender to the gallery owner: she needs to raise money to pay for an operation for Alexander and will barter even herself. "My whole existence has only one purpose," she gushes, "to help you, to keep you alive." Yet their return trip to Munich consumes much of the profit from Marina's transaction, and she desperately tries to earn more money by resorting, once more, to her former profession at her old hangout. As luck would have it, she hooks up with a man who turns out to be the medical doctor (Andreas Wolf) who diagnosed Alexander's condition. In the hotel room, the doctor realizes that Marina is prostituting herself on Alexander's behalf, declines the encounter, and orders the operation.

Recovered, Alexander moves with Marina to Vienna to escape the inquiries of his estranged wife, whose interest in Alexander has been rekindled due to his renewed health and artistic success. The days in Vienna are happy ones. Alexander is now a prosperous artist, painting "as [if] possessed," until one day he is blinded by a sudden relapse and convinces Marina to administer a fatal dose of pills to him. After drinking champagne before the fireplace, Alexander slowly dies, unaware that Marina has also taken the pills and is dying in his arms. She whispers: "I love you. I'm coming darling."

Although the film has since become renowned for containing the first postwar nude scene, church officials offered no objections to the exposed flesh.[42] Instead, they denounced the high degree of sexual independence exhibited by the character Marina, who engaged in sexual relations unsanctified by marriage. Predictably, objections centered around the film's presentation of prostitution as the answer to Marina's financial worries. What most offended protesting priests was that prostitution brought no decline in Maria's economic status. Her early sexual encounters first intensify, then satisfy, her desires for clothing and jewelry. One symptomatic example of the protests was the review in the *Katholischer Film-Dienst*, which denounced the film's portrayal of prostitution as a highly lucrative profession for fear that it would tempt young women into emulation: "We see this danger . . . as a positive romanticization of prostitution. . . . Who can make us believe that a prostitute can earn the 4,000 DM required for an operation in the course of a few hours?"[43] Churchmen were gravely concerned about the possible social effects of the film, which elevated an unrepentant prostitute to a melodramatic heroine.[44]

By portraying prostitution as an avenue of economic independence and matter of individual choice, the film may actually have served to allow contemporaries to draw uncomfortable—and inaccurate—parallels with the experience of German women, who bartered their bodies for food and cigarettes during the early years of the occupation in order to support themselves and their families. Social workers in the city of Aachen reported on the "grievous confusion of notions of morality" among women who "sexually submit" themselves to improve their standards of living: "Mothers excuse their behavior by arguing that they must provide bread for their children." The same report bemoaned the behavior and moral judgment of young girls, stating that "it has almost become a truism, that a girl will proposition a 'foreigner' in order to secure the enjoyment of coveted food or consumer goods."[45] Such reports minimized the real conditions of want and the overwhelming incidence of *Hungerprostitution* in the early postwar period and instead identified materialism (and a corresponding moral degradation) as the cause of prostitution.

The free use, by an independent woman, of her own sexuality was clearly a theme that caused deep disturbance among conservative political and religious leaders, and one that was not peculiar to *Die Sünderin*. Officials at the Bavarian Youth Office were outraged by a report they received from the office of the *Regierungspräsident* of Upper Bavaria that quoted an advertisement making the rounds in local newspapers for the Italian film *Bitter Rice*: "17-year-old Silvano Mangano [*sic*], discovered for this film, the overnight sensation, the nubile Roman girl! A young woman, without inhibitions, totally natural, without shame! Silvano Mangano, the erotic superatomic bomb—in a stormy, passionate, tumultuous film. Everybody wants to see her—Silvano Mangano!"[46] The author of the report questioned how the office's social programs could successfully "place a 17-year-old girl in a home or under protective supervision for moral degeneracy, while 'girls without inhibitions and . . . shame' are at the same time being publicly prized." The problem that faced the churches was how to make mothers and daughters once again out of war-shattered women, how to corral German women back into the newly reconstructed home. Films like *Bitter Rice* and *Die Sünderin*, which openly celebrated sexuality, were perceived as grave dangers to this effort.

Clearly any depiction of prostitution reveals a great deal about male-female relationships and the socially constructed definitions of masculinity and femininity. What was so disturbing about *Die Sünderin* was that Marina did not fit the role of victim; Alexander, however, did. Throughout the film, the figure of Alexander emphasizes the instability of German masculinity, and his death hints at the futility—or even failure—of a reconstruction based on old, familiar terms. Since definitions of masculinity and femininity are necessarily interdependent, a confident and energetic Marina, who can set a goal and achieve it through the use of her sexuality, threatens the normative social and sexual order. One striking aspect of *Die Sünderin* is that it inverts the traditional characterization of male as active and female as passive. In the film, Marina embodies autonomy and is the agent of change. Alexander cannot help himself; he is a cinematic incarnation of Werner Hess's "broken-bodied man"—set off by a self-reliant woman. Marina literally pulls him from the gutter and provides him with the means and self-respect to resume his career as an artist. His survival and success, throughout most of the film, result only from Marina's efforts and volition.

The film, then, portrayed an ideological world turned on its head and, most frighteningly, one that had obvious parallels in recent experience. In the years following the war, at least some German women were reluctant to surrender their responsibility for their individual fates to men and reaffirm too quickly the principle of social patriarchy, especially when the projected patriarchs were not up to the challenge. One woman in Berlin told of her husband's returning from war physically and emotionally drained:

> We had absolutely nothing. It was so bad between us, especially since he didn't want to, or couldn't, do anything. . . . I went to work and did the work at home that I had to do as a housewife and a mother, but my husband didn't want to do his work—for example to find wood. . . . And so I can well observe, if I place myself back in those difficult times and attempt to make a meal out of nothing, to collect herbs just so the food has a little flavor, stand on line for hours, keep the apartment clean, keep myself clean, keep him clean, wash his filthy underwear, that I also expect him to do his men's work! And so I'd rather be alone. I got myself a divorce. . . .
>
> I was fed up with marriage. . . . I am not the type of person who likes so terribly to subordinate herself to others. The men of my generation are still used to having their wives submit to them unquestioningly. I know many women . . . whose husbands can't pour their own coffee. The men bray, "Butter me a piece of bread." Then the bread will be buttered for them. But I don't consider myself to be a *Dienstmädchen*. . . .
>
> You know, the things one used to need a man to get can be had without one; you don't need to marry.[47]

Another Berliner remembered how she felt, at the age of fourteen, when her father returned home after seven years in a prison camp. She considered his reappearance an unwelcome intrusion and burden on the "women's household," comprised of herself, her mother, her grandmother, her aunts, and her sister:

> I hardly knew him. And I was totally uninterested in him; he could have just as well stayed away. He was, at that time . . . superfluous for us; we did fine

on our own. He was just one more [to care for]. . . . And the men all came back sick from being imprisoned. Most of them didn't work. My father, for example, lost an arm and had stomach ulcers. Yes, he was ill and he couldn't work, he was absolutely incapable of it. . . . It is difficult for one to say, but we were totally independent because of the war. He was an encumbrance for us, so to speak, adults. We were again subjected to patriarchal authority [*väterliche Erziehung*], which was and is totally senseless, because it is always the mother who raises the children.[48]

A third woman described a husband who insisted that it was solely her responsibility to manage the household and care for their children while he sat in the corner, read the paper, and complained. Unhappy with the inequitable division of labor, the woman queried: "Haven't these men had enough of giving orders yet? He says he's entitled to a comfortable home, but to my way of thinking he's not 'entitled' to anything."[49] It was clear, then, that many women quickly tired of caring for husbands and fathers who returned from the war to assume a dependent, unproductive status in the household—especially when these same men ignored the changed circumstances and attempted to reassert themselves as domestic decision makers and disciplinarians.[50]

While such signs of female independence were common in the immediate postwar period, other German women eagerly expressed their support and desire for marriage, especially at a time when the loss of male life in the war made this option highly improbable for many women. Doris Schubert has suggested that women's willingness to revert to traditional roles may have been due, in part, to the stiff competition for available men. In July 1949, for example, the popular women's magazine *Constanze* printed an article entitled "A Kingdom for a Man" that referred to "panicked women" and "pasha men."[51] This postwar problem received a good deal of press coverage, which might have encouraged some women to surrender romantic fantasies in order to avoid single life. Not all women, then, rejected the return to traditional sexual and gender relations. Many willingly traded the responsibilities of heading a household for the more familiar role of wife and mother and the hope of a more equitable distribution of productive labor.[52] Nonetheless, the eagerness with which many German women embraced marriage and domesticity did not relieve male apprehension of permanently altered gender relations.

The historical push for the redomestication of German women was echoed in the film *Die Sünderin* and found its parallel in the parameters of Marina's powers. Marina's efforts, although considerable, are circumscribed and ultimately thwarted by Alexander's fatal physical flaw. What is striking in this connection, however, is not Alexander's loss of will to live and determination to die but his relegation of that task to Marina and her willingness to administer a

Marina (Hildegard Knef) and Alexander (Gustav Fröhlich) in the double death scene of
Die Sünderin. The painting highlighted above the mantel in the background, Alexander's
last grand artistic gesture, portrays "The Sinner" herself. (Courtesy of the Stiftung Deutsche
Kinemathek, Berlin)

fatal dose of pills to him. She indicates by her action that she too recognizes the
physical, psychological, and social implications of Alexander's loss of sight and
accepts the necessity of his death as well as her own, since it was only through
her devotion to him that her life had gained meaning and happiness.

Within the context of the film, then, Marina's actions may be understood as
supporting "normalization," or the reversion to traditional gender and sex
roles. Marina is spurred into action only in the face of dire situations, and tilted
camera angles visually underscore the abnormality of such scenes. During periods depicted as "happy," the camera is righted, and Marina becomes passive and
ornamental, deferring to Alexander, who, recovered and strong, takes command
of both the relationship and his career. Thus, the film presents such times as
"normal," implying the exceptionality of those scenes in which Marina embodies agency.

Alexander's successful surgery and restored eyesight, moreover, initiate a
striking montage of images, blending medium close-ups of Alexander overlaid
with double exposures of nude sketches of Marina—all of which prominently

feature her bared breasts. As the sketches flash before our—and Alexander's—eyes, we hear Marina's voice-over addressing her lover. "You had to paint nudes. You had to start from the beginning; to see with other eyes"—eyes, that is, of a man in control, whose reassertion of self fixes Marina as an object of visual enjoyment and sexual fantasy.

Thus, Alexander must die when he permanently loses his sight, for loss of sight means more than loss of livelihood—it means loss of aesthetic and sexual control. It heralds the end of both the artist and the man. This point is illustrated in a scene near the end of the film. Alexander and Marina have moved to Vienna, where Alexander's career has flourished. Since his operation, happiness and normalcy have been reinstated, if temporarily. Alexander has taken to painting "only Marina," thereby containing her on his canvas. He emphasizes her femininity in languorous, reclining, nude poses that highlight her passivity and ornamentality. At the same time that Marina is contained and objectified by Alexander's gaze, she is also the object of our gaze and, in one garden scene in which she poses nude for Alexander, the gaze of two male intruders who have eagerly climbed the garden wall for some visual titillation. Alexander's loss of sight means that he can no longer control and domesticate Marina and, more seriously, that he cannot protect his proprietary interest in her by aggressively chasing away other encroaching gazers. Loss of sight signifies loss of power, loss of control—in effect, impotence and the negation of masculinity.[53]

Tellingly, *Die Sünderin*, like many films of the Nazi period, presents the image of "a vulnerable and ultimately paranoid male order" in which women must "be overcome, indeed sacrificed." Although Alexander, like Nazi-era protagonists, exhibits "deficient ego-strength" and attempts to "develop his identity" by asserting himself over a woman, the postwar film differs from its predecessors in that he ultimately fails at this enterprise.[54]

Indeed, in its treatment of masculine and feminine roles, *Die Sünderin* can be read as an allegory of postwar German gender relations. "That was the collapse of my whole world . . . this feeling that no one could help me," recalled one woman who was raped by Soviet soldiers in 1945 at the age of sixteen; "this feeling . . . that there isn't a safe place in the whole world." A female representative of the SPD argued in the Parliamentary Council in 1949 that the claim of male authority was extinguished at Stalingrad, because since then there had been "no aspect of life in which the actions of German men have protected German women."[55] The film echoed these accusations and illustrated that German masculinity had lost its potency, that "neither collective protection nor individual heroic deeds [could be] expected," as the convalescent and passive behavior of German men in the face of Russian raping raids had made painfully clear to Berlin women.[56]

Ultimately, however, gender identity in the film is permitted to remain neither ambiguous nor problematic. *Die Sünderin* exposes gender instability only to resolve it in a way that reinforces conservative social ideology. The aesthetic death scene at the end serves to "right" the skewed world of male impotence and gender inversion. The healing properties of heterosexual love have transformed Marina, causing her to renounce her solitary existence and self-centered materialism to devote herself fully to her man. If this autonomous woman is ultimately "overcome," it is because she sacrifices herself willingly for Alexander and without his knowledge—a convention employed frequently in films of the Nazi period.[57] Thus, female martyrdom brings gender redemption and the containment of once-threatening female sexuality, as the camera pans, for the closing shot, to the wall above the fireplace and the framed portrait of the nude "sinner," now safely dead.

Remarkably, critics of the film disregarded this transformation and attacked Marina's role as prostitute and murderess. The film was read strictly in terms of its challenge to the traditional morality and normative relationships that members of the clergy and their political counterparts wished to reestablish. Moreover, critics posited the film as a dangerous and disruptive cultural agent, accusing it of working directly on the mind of the viewer by influencing individual desire and social behavior. A police officer (*Landpolizeibeamter*) from the small Bavarian town of Lenggries, for example, betrayed his fear of the effects of *Die Sünderin* in a letter to the Cultural Committee of the Bavarian State Parliament:

> This film is . . . no entertainment film, and it is not a matter of whether more or less white flesh will be set before the viewer. No, *this film is an unmistakably grave assault on the foundation of our morality with regard to love—* all but the basest elements have recognized that. Because the innocent viewer, who seeks entertainment and a little excitement, sits in the theater and allows himself to be gradually lulled by the racy and dazzling poison, so that he finally accepts without resistance that a woman who, according to the film is supposed to truly love deeply, occasionally walks the streets in order to improve the household finances—something, however, that does no damage to her "great love." . . .
>
> *The loving woman can . . . calmly walk the streets [and] the purity of a true love does not suffer from it*—or at least that is what it's trying to say.[58]

The author of this letter gendered his portrayal in interesting ways. The viewer he describes is male (a consequence of his use of the masculine German word, "Besucher"), innocent, and passive. Out for "a little excitement," he finds himself defenseless against the slow, cinematic poisoning of his psyche. The author, moreover, blurs the distinction between the female protagonist in the film and the film itself, thereby feminizing the latter. The film thus becomes a seductive ("racy and dazzling") agent, lulling the viewer into complacency so he cannot recognize the ideological threat it represents. As a result, the male viewer takes on the status of victim, like the war-torn Alexander. But whereas Marina poisons her lover at his request and with his knowledge, she surreptitiously dispatches his alter ego in the audience, who is caught unawares. This act grievously offended precisely because it echoed the perceived postwar betrayal of uncaring wives and disrespectful daughters, who abandoned their filial devotion in a time of extreme masculine need. Thus, patriarchy did not die a natural death, nor was it killed on the battlefield in World War II. It was murdered by strong and autonomous women who dominated a sexually charged and dangerously feminized home front.

Critics were therefore disturbed as much by the effects of the medium as its message. Officials in the Bavarian town of Rosenheim, for example, objected to the film's "subtlety and cleverness," for technical sophistication was identified as a treacherous tool that could provide direct access to the viewer's psyche. The Evangelical Men's Club in Feuchtwangen worried that the purportedly realistic style of *Die Sünderin* would make the portrayal of the characters more convincing and encourage the audience to surrender to despair:

> We also have in our city many mothers who have mastered an extremely difficult life, similar to that which the girl Marina had to lead, in a thoroughly respectable manner. We also know from firsthand experience of disabled ex-servicemen, who, with quiet valor, accept and bear their fate given by God.
>   When a film . . . portrays social misery with its muddled relationships in a totally realistic way, one would at least expect that it lead . . . to a way out and not to hopeless dead ends.[59]

Thus, the film itself and Marina's behavior in the film were represented as a challenge to traditional notions of morality, monogamy, and the socially constructed and fiercely protected ideological coupling of love and monogamous sex. Church-sponsored protests against *Die Sünderin* only served to endorse this assessment, fostering a heightened sense of crisis. In this case, film was not mere entertainment but a powerful tool for "inappropriate" socialization.

The dreaded malady of despair and loss of will, which social conservatives feared would overtake and undermine the nation, found its victims only among the male sector of the German population—or so conservative rhetoric would have us believe. Women were thought to be susceptible to other contagions. Given the important role women were to play as mothers in the German reconstruction, any outside influence that interfered with their vocation was considered a threat to normalization. Employment outside of the home was one such threat; mass culture was another.

An examination of the rhetoric of conservative cultural critics in both church and state strikingly reveals that they ultimately considered women and youth— more than the "broken-bodied," debilitated German men—to be most suscepti- ble to the attractions and influences of cinema and commercial culture. This can be read from the fears, expressed in a Catholic bulletin, that "the lustful boys in the West" would fall prey to the uncorrupted, "unbroken boys in the East."[60] It appears also in the comments of some local leaders that mothers could not be trusted with the regulation of their own children's film attendance. This state of affairs was used as justification for moral intervention by an outside authority, be it church or state. A letter from the office of the *Regierungspräsident* of Upper Bavaria to the Bavarian Ministry of Education and Culture maintained that "as much as one, at this time, may greatly dread . . . that which smacks of censorship, a means and a way must be found to redress this deplorable state of affairs, which exposes the already greatly endangered youth to further dangers. This is not served by appealing to the reason of parents . . . because experience shows that parents oftentimes lack the necessary understanding. . . . Otherwise it would not happen that mothers appear at film screenings with small children in their arms."[61]

How could one expect mothers to be responsible for the moral development of their charges when they themselves were seduced by the very source of the corruption? Instead, women were urged to embrace motherhood and "serve with self-evident self-sacrifice . . . to defend the Christian world order from the *Zeitgeist* suffused with 'bolshevik collectivism in the East' and the 'Hollywood- ideal in the West.' "[62] Women who forsook their calling threatened German regeneration and were thus implicated in the postwar moral decline perceived by conservative elites.

Given male distrust of women's ability to withstand the seductive powers of the mass media and consumer culture, *Die Sünderin* was considered a direct threat to traditional religious and community values because it allegedly fos- tered a desire for consumer goods and a cosmopolitan life-style.[63] It was Marina, then, as a symbol of unregulated female sexuality and rampant con- sumerism, who killed the German man. Conservative criticism focused almost exclusively on the representation of Marina, who moves from one urban set- ting to another, acquiring material finery and in effect achieving economic mobility by using her body as a medium of exchange. Marina's consumption was construed as an expression of excessive materialism and dangerous individ- ualism. She was not the postwar consumer condoned by conservatives, who was expected to save her pfennigs to purchase a family refrigerator. Rather, she represented the single city-dweller who threatened to sabotage German recon-struction by renouncing motherhood in favor of selfish pleasure seeking.[64]

By the early 1950s, the bishop of Würzburg, alarmed by widespread rural depopulation, rapid urbanization, and an ensuing increase in secular behavior and belief, demanded legal means be adopted to ban films such as *Die Sünderin*, which were "meant to enervate the body of the *Volk* and, particularly in the villages, to encourage flight from the land."[65] The rural exodus was particularly unsettling for social conservatives, who, since the empire, consistently praised the peasantry for yielding "a bountiful harvest of crops, children, and moral values." They feared that postwar demographic and cultural trends were erod-ing the basis for a spiritually healthy and populous nation.[66]

Urban origin, after all, had been popularly associated since the 1920s with secularization, economic independence, sexual emancipation, and consump-tion.[67] This polyglot of meaning continued into the postwar period. One Berlin woman, for example, transplanted to a small town in West Germany for profes-sional reasons, noticed that "it was not at all easy to be a single woman in a small city in West Germany. That was much more difficult than in Berlin. That was because the men above all thought that if you were a Berliner, you would also be Parisian in part. . . . And men imagine that a woman who is alone is fair game, that they can do with her what they want. But they were mistaken. . . . And it also wasn't so easy with the married women. . . . They were constantly jealous, even though one wanted nothing to do with their husbands, just worked with them."[68]

Bavarian Cardinal Faulhaber faulted democratization for giving rise to a pluralism of values and behaviors that intensified the trend of secularization and spawned widely divergent opinions regarding immorality and obscenity. The alarming result, according to Faulhaber, was the loss of a universally recog-nized moral compass: God's law. He cautioned that if left untended, the situa-tion would continue to worsen, "increasingly confounding more values until it destroys the basis of our entire moral order and national community."[69] This reasoning, in conjunction with the belief that women and children were suscep-tible to the pernicious influences of film and materialism, resulted in the call for state regulation of film, a kind of "discriminatory paternalism" of male supervi-sion through state agencies.

The same year that churchmen led public protests against *Die Sünderin*, the federal government passed a law (Jugendschutzgesetz) intended to protect mi-nors from the insidious influences of the mass media. This legislation hear-kened back to the 1926 "trash and smut" law, sponsored by the Catholic Center–Nationalist coalition government in response to both the German dis-tribution of the Soviet film *Potemkin* and the perceived "sexual anarchy" of the times. The Weimar legislation permitted *Land* ministries and youth offices to proscribe the distribution or display of certain films and printed material (apart from newspapers) to children under the age of eighteen.[70] As during Weimar, the timing of the second postwar law was not fortuitous. The 1949 film censorship legislation had lowered the age of unrestricted film viewing to sixteen years from eighteen, which had been the legal limit established by the Reichslichtspielgesetz in 1920 and retained under the Nazis. Over the course of 1950, state ministries of culture were bombarded with letters from angry parents, clergy, and educators demanding the further restriction of youthful film attendance.

One school administrator attempted to underline the gravity of the situation by providing empirical proof—in the shape of an infrared picture of children engaged in "inappropriate" viewing—of the deleterious impact of film on "growing youth as well as the young democracy." Dubbing the photo, which had been featured in the Catholic *Filmdienst*, "one of the most disturbing pictorial documents in pedagogical history," the educator quoted its accompanying text without further comment: "Grimacing . . . children who have clasped their hands in front of their faces in alarm, fear, and horror; eyes wide open, the stare of fright, faces of the ruins, such as those photographed during the war among soldiers, who staggered into the trenches during an attack." The published commentary both inflated and sensationalized the gravity of unrestricted youthful film viewing, and the bald analogy to the frontline experience of soldiers further propelled the point by calling forth fears of irremediable psychological damage and behavioral problems. This type of hyperbole was not uncommon, at least in Bavaria, where a letter from the Unified Citizens Committee of the city of Schwabach requested state action and financial subsidies for the production of "worthwhile" films and literature, contending that "all the money that one would wish to spare [in addressing these problems] today, will have to go toward prisons in the future."[71]

Unsurprisingly, then, the most vocal opponents of *Die Sünderin's* exhibition constituted the most active proponents for stricter federal regulation of the media. The Catholic hierarchy in Bavaria, for example, played a crucial role in lobbying for the legislation.[72] In an "Appeal of the Bavarian Bishops for the Protection of Youth and the Security of the People [*Volkssicherheit*]," directed to the office of the minister president, Cardinal Faulhaber called for the expedient enactment of a "far-reaching law for the protection of youth and public morals [*Volkssittlichkeit*]." Arguing that there was an empirically proven relationship between the increasing circulation of "trash and smut" and the "moral brutalization" of the young, Faulhaber warned that the somber social effects of unregulated consumption and a free market were daily becoming more "evident in the increase in youth criminality, the growing number of crimes against morality, and the climbing curve of illnesses resulting from immoral acts."

Although Cardinal Faulhaber's rhetoric was directly aimed at printed matter, this law was understood to apply equally to films.[73]

Although federal legislation for the protection of youth was enacted in 1951, Adenauer's family minister, the Catholic Franz-Josef Wuermeling, extended conservative cultural lobbying well into the 1950s. In 1954, for example, he bemoaned the negative effects of film on older teenagers (aged sixteen to twenty), whose cinematic attendance remained unregulated. In particular, he decried postwar film's tendency to undermine marriage and the family—"the life-foundation of our democratic order"—through a celebration of the "erotic." By mid-decade, the state youth welfare offices had pressured the film industry to agree to expanded influence on the film censorship board for youth psychologists (appointed by both the federal and state governments) as well as a more generous appeal procedure in decisions regarding film ratings for viewing by minors.[74]

The problem of juvenile film attendance remained a hot topic for research and lobbying by state youth offices through the late 1950s, when sustained public pressure from educational and religious leaders finally resulted in an increase in the age of unrestricted film attendance to eighteen.[75] Yet periodic anguished cries regarding the prevalence of youth criminality continued. In an article at the end of the decade, the head of the Munich-based Aktion Jugendschutz reaffirmed the need for public commitment to the regulation of film and its increasingly popular domestic rival, television. The author asserted that such regulation

> concerns something fundamental: the totally elementary task of self-defense, the protection of the human against profit-hungry production and the managerial dominance of economics. . . .
>
> And now we hear, from both adults and youth, an energetic boast about their own accountability, on the one hand about the right of parents (which is occasionally adroitly exploited . . . by the film industry), and in the case of youth as aversion to any type of "tutelage."
>
> In this climate, it has completely disappeared from view that our freedom is no longer markedly threatened by restrictions and encroachments by the state, but rather by the predominance of misused freedom. We only need to think about the cunning ways that consumer coercion through sex appeal . . . is pushed by the film industry.[76]

The danger was not identified as the long arm of the state but the cultural effects of democratization and unrestrained commercial culture. The state was appealed to as the great protector of moral order.

State paternalism extended to the social reproducers as well. In 1952 German mothers were the subject of legislation introduced in the workplace for their "protection." Although the law may in fact have had a beneficial effect in preventing the firing of pregnant women, it required women workers to bare their private lives to the scrutiny of the Labor Ministry and factory inspectors. Moreover, its formulation rested on the conviction of social policy makers that women's primary social task was motherhood. Women's employment was viewed not as a matter of individual choice but as the result of economic hardship. Thus, women workers were treated as a "disadvantaged group, forced out to work while fulfilling their natural obligations as mothers."[77]

Furthermore, the law's enforcement was based upon a "consensus" among factory inspectors and the courts "that pregnant women needed protection *because their physical and psychological capacities were diminished.*"[78] Factory inspectors went so far as to attribute unruly behavior in the workplace—for example boisterousness or theft—to "pregnancy psychosis" and maintained that pregnant women suffered from an inability "to control themselves from pursuing irrational resolutions and desires once formulated." Kleptomania was considered a particular problem, but in this case materialist pursuit was excused as emanating from the mother's "desire" to provide for her offspring.[79] The Mutterschutzgesetz went into effect in 1952, at the height of concern for cultural retrenchment of women's roles.

Demands for "discriminatory paternalism," buttressed by state power, were made at a time when paternal standing and authority within the family was diminished or absent. The protective legislation for youth and women was in fact an attempt to restore an impotent patriarchy with an infusion of state power.

The reconstruction process in West Germany was clearly not dominated merely by the straightforward, though arduous, task of material and institutional restructuring. Reconstruction also demanded a process of redefinition. Local elites needed to address the question of national identity: What would it mean to be "German" after national socialism? This process of national redefinition was complicated by the fact of foreign occupation, and German political and religious leaders struggled to constitute a "new" Germany that would depart from the communist and capitalist ideologies of the dominant victors.

After 1945, it was generally agreed that national regeneration would have its foundation in the family. Yet conservatives in church and state went a step further and maintained that this required the resurrection of traditional gender relations. Self-sufficient wives and disrespectful, precocious children had to be tamed in order for German men to achieve a stable, uncontested "masculine" identity and reemerge as self-assured patriarchs. The assumptions underlying protective legislation were based on a generalized desire—among men and women—to remake autonomous and productive women and children into wayward or vulnerable victims, who needed the protection of revitalized German men. Indeed, the great surprise of the postwar period was that the conservative social agenda (to provide state protection for the family and insure that women be freed from paid employment outside of the home to devote themselves to motherhood) received support across the political spectrum and was written into the West German Basic Law (Grundgesetz).[80]

Thus, the redomestication of German women became a political necessity; they were to be purged of their wartime adventurousness and convinced that the apron was their natural uniform. Resuming their duties as wives and mothers was billed as a service to themselves, their families, and their country; it would insure normalization. Most women willingly complied, provided they were part of intact families or had the opportunity to remarry. Yet German women did exact a price for redomestication—constitutionally guaranteed equality with men.

By the early 1950s, then, the "normalization" of gender and generational relations and the reestablishment of the patriarchal family and the ideology of motherhood were considered a matter of national survival—a bulwark against the materialism of national socialism, communism, and Americanism. Cultural representations that questioned the efficacy or implications of this agenda were therefore harshly condemned by church and state leaders. Culture was feared as a corrupter of national morals at the same time that it was embraced as a means—in a new bipolar world—to promote a particular vision of a distinctly German identity. In the postwar period, as in the Third Reich, the cinema again became a crucial focus for constructing social ideology in Germany. And despite official protestations to the contrary, this was an ideology that, minus theological rhetoric, would have seemed comfortably familiar to Adolf Hitler.

4 THE FIGHT FOR THE "CHRISTIAN WEST" FILM CONTROL AND THE RECONSTRUCTION OF CIVIL SOCIETY

The postwar normalization of German public life was a contested process, with heated debates over the limits—as well as the social and moral implications—of the new democratic order frequently played out in the cultural arena. Catholic and Protestant church leaders became prominent players in this process, in an attempt to reclaim the social and cultural power denied them under Hitler, and devoted special energy to the area of cinematic control. After all, the political status of cinema as the mass medium of propaganda and public education had been confirmed by the Nazi and occupation governments alike, and its social importance was reflected in the medium's immense postwar popularity. Film attendance figures soared between 1945 and 1956, during which time box-office sales jumped from 150 to over 817 million tickets, which translated into nearly 16 visits per year for every man, woman, and child living in the Federal Republic and West Berlin.[1]

Apart from its popularity as entertainment, German film was again looked to as an important product for export and international prestige. As we saw in chapter 2, Hollywood interests fought to retain their international commercial advantage after World War II and attempted to secure a privileged place in the German market. This strategy had limited success in winning the support of U.S. Information Control officials and was not sufficient in itself to insure the international demise of the German film industry. That result was sealed by the intervention of the German churches in the area of film control and censorship. Their initiatives, in conjunction with the American principles for industry reorganization, forced the German film industry into provinciality and, ultimately, commercial failure by directly affecting the aesthetic, moral, and narrative qualities of German films.

During the occupation, the German clergy began to challenge the competing ideological models for cultural organization supplied by the United States and the Soviet Union by pushing for a third alternative based upon aspects of the Weimar experience. While shunning the artistic experimentation and leftist social criticism associated with that period, these individuals sought to salvage earlier native forms of cultural management and censorship in a self-proclaimed "Fight for the Christian West" designed to battle perceived postwar threats to their renascent national community and cultural traditions.

This struggle for social and cultural influence was not exhausted by resistance to the imposition of foreign forms of organization and ideology. Catholic and Protestant churchmen and lay leaders responded to perceived domestic threats to their cultural authority as well. With the demise of the Nazi state monopoly on cultural production, the specter of a reemergent German film industry regulated solely by market imperatives began to haunt German social conservatives. Confessional leaders resolved to defend their remembered pre-Nazi roles as cultural arbiters by selectively reaffirming strategies from their own institutional pasts to ward off—or at least control—the forces of secularization and commercialization inherent in both "foreign" American and homegrown cultural practices. In particular, they targeted the secular materialism they believed was embodied in both the National Socialist organization of culture of the recent past and newly introduced liberalizing policies of the social market economy advanced by West German economics minister Ludwig Erhard. Thus, struggles over cultural reconstruction were highly politicized and waged as a form of ideological warfare against an unacceptable national past and an unacceptable internationalizing present.

In challenging commercial films released in West Germany, church leaders typically employed the old argument that films that exercised a "religious or morally endangering influence upon the viewer"[2] should be banned. This idea of *Filmwirkung*—which emphasized the presumed spiritual, moral, and psychological response of a viewer rather than a film's measurable effect on behavior—emerged during the Weimar Republic, was utilized under the Third Reich, and continued to serve as justification for the expurgation of various films throughout the Adenauer period. During Weimar, film censorship shifted away from an earlier reliance on police action against concrete threats to security and the public order and by 1931—at a time when nationalist veterans and Nazis were barraging cinemas with stink bombs and mice in protest against the pacifist film, *All Quiet on the Western Front*—was expanded to apply not only to films that disturbed the public order but to those that "intended to." Thus, censorship became justified on the basis of *potential* degradation of the viewer, even in the absence of "illegal or otherwise disapproved of actions of the viewer under the influence of the film."[3]

This interpretation of cinema's certain, though intangible, puissance was rooted in the widely accepted assumption that the masses were malleable. Although this judgment had a long historical currency, reaching back to the period of intensified industrialization and urbanization in the late nineteenth century, it reemerged with a vengeance after 1945. Early postwar appraisals of national socialism in Germany—in both political discourse and the media—tended to suggest that the hapless masses fell victim to more cunning National Socialist masters and lacked the cognizance (more than the courage) to stop Hitler's murderous policies. Thus, older elitist prejudices regarding the lower social and economic orders merged with more recent self-serving disavowals of wartime responsibility to produce a nearly unquestioned vision of an intellectually and politically immature public. As we shall see, the postwar German "masses" disproved their complacency by exhibiting signs of analytical and activist vigor in the face of conservative attempts at cultural leadership. Yet this resistance was not enough to contain the cultural effects of the conservative challenge to the newly constructed national cinema.

In the early years of the Bonn Republic, film politics were characterized by skirmishes between economics and ideology, and astonishingly ideology won. This chapter investigates both the impact of church intervention in the regulation of cinema and the role of the state in this area of cultural reconstruction. It explores the question of why the capitalist industry could not defend itself better from ideological attacks and provides an assessment of the cultural implications of this triumph of ideology for German reconstruction in the West.

Churches under the Occupation: The Voice of German Interests

During the military occupation, church officials eagerly engaged in the pressing issues of reconstruction. As leaders of the only German institutions to emerge from the war intact, Catholic and Protestant bishops immediately assumed the role of German ambassadors to the occupying powers, dispensing often unwelcome advice and criticism and intervening in political affairs over which they had no jurisdiction. In May 1945, the future Protestant bishop of Holstein urged the churches "to be the advocate, and intercessor, and voice of our Volk,"[4] while Catholic Cardinal Josef Frings unremittingly offered his opinions on "legitimate" German concerns, such as the postwar "famine" and the housing shortage, the return of German prisoners of war, and the Allied dismantling of German industry. Church leaders were the only group permitted to criticize occupation policies, and although such criticism was certainly not encouraged by American officials, it was not decisively squelched either. As Frederic Spotts has argued, at least initially, "churches were tacitly recognized as the sole institutions above direct military control, as national bodies . . . exempt from 'reorientation' into directions determined in Washington, London, or Paris."[5]

By mid-1946, however, American and British officials began to fear the churches' "nationalistic" and "potentially subversive" influence on German society. The activities of the Bavarian Catholic church—particularly its dubious role in the denazification process—appeared threatening enough to American goals for democratization to merit scrutiny in an extensive intelligence report. U.S. officials became increasingly cautious as they began to register the number of implicated Nazis declared "good Christians," denazified by letter of a bishop or priest, and even proposed for government office. Consequently, they initiated the surveillance of clergy to insure that church meetings were not used as a pretext to resurrect viciously nationalist activity. The concern was whether church leaders would surrender their old-style nationalism for American-style democracy. And the prospects did not look good, given the Christian clergy's lack of reticence when it came to opposing Allied policies perceived as neglecting or injuring their congregations. After all, as an American intelligence report put it, "the Church well knows she will outlast the Military Government."[6] As a result, criticism of Allied policies by the church hierarchies—be they Catholic or Protestant—was increasingly met by impatience, and the Western Allies attempted to limit church involvement in public affairs to spiritual, moral, and educational matters.

Precisely because of their unwillingness to assume a passive public stance during the occupation—especially in the face of Allied resistance and irritation—church leaders acquired local recognition as both interpreters of military government policy and lobbyists for German interests. Consequently, church leaders possessed a large degree of de facto public authority immediately following German capitulation. Moreover, since internal church affairs were not interfered with by military governments, church officials used the opportunity to gather and reorganize. The Catholic episcopate, in particular, worked to strengthen and institutionalize its informal public authority during the occupation and more intensely during the first years of the Adenauer era by organizing lay movements, professional associations, and a Catholic press, radio station, trade union, and university.[7]

Indeed, the Catholic church readily emerged as the institution most capable of assuming a leadership position in discussions of social and cultural issues in the Western zones. In territorial terms, much of the heartland of Protestantism was surrendered to the Soviets, while Catholicism predominated in the remaining southwestern territory.[8] Additionally, the church benefited from a highly organized structure and unified voice on issues of national interest. Unlike their Protestant counterparts, members of the German Catholic hierarchy suffered

from little dissension in their assessment of their church's relation to the immediate German past. Indeed, the chairman of the Fulda Bishops' Conference,
Josef Frings, declared that guilt was an issue to be taken up "between man and
God," thus relegating it to the personal and spiritual, rather than the public,
sphere.[9]

Protestant leaders emerged from the war more deeply divided, and "cleavages among the provincial churches and political divisions among the clergy
threatened ecclesiastical disintegration on a nationwide basis." Much of this
tension developed under Hitler, when Protestantism splintered as its leaders
clashed over the church's relationship to national socialism. After 1945, numerous members of the Protestant clergy and episcopate were compromised
due to their cooperation with the Nazi regime. Unlike their Catholic counterparts, Protestant leaders advertised their rifts, airing their lingering animosities
and differences in front of the laity, which tended to "focus attention on matters
dividing Protestants rather than those elements that united them."[10]

Moreover, this fragmentation was reflected institutionally, since each provincial church was autonomous and sovereign. Although the disunity was par-
tially addressed in July 1948 with the establishment of the Evangelical Church
of Germany (Evangelische Kirche in Deutschland [EKD]), a loose confederation
of provincial churches, German Protestantism remained marked by "territorial
particularism and confessional division," a condition that impeded effective
organization around social or moral issues. As a result, Protestant activity in
film matters was much less coordinated than that of the Catholics, whose unified voice and "outward serenity" would not be compromised publicly until the
end of the 1950s.[11]

Official Catholic efforts benefited from a highly organized institutional
structure and adherence to papal principles. Although members of the German
Catholic episcopate disavowed direct political activity among the clergy after
1945, they were committed to reassuming a leading voice in social and cultural
issues and became a formidable lobbying power.[12] As Ian Connor has noted, the
Catholic church in the immediate postwar years "adopted a policy of *Menschenführung*," whereby priests were encouraged to establish "close contact
with refugees at a local level" in order to "gain control over the new groups of
population."[13] While Connor's work focuses on the fears provoked by the flood
of refugees and expellees into the Western sectors of occupied Germany and
Catholic attempts to prevent the political radicalization of these distressed
groups, his broader theme is the Catholic quest for social control of the malleable, confused, and perhaps willful masses. Thus, the concept of *Menschenführung* can be applied equally to postwar Catholic film activity, where similar
assumptions were at work and similar goals—like social normalization and
national regeneration—were at stake.

The Renewal of Confessional Film Work after Hitler: A New Course

Catholic attention to film predated the German defeat in World War II, but the organized character of its film activity after 1945 was unprecedented.[14] German bishops took their cue from an encyclical issued by Pope Pius XI in 1936, which articulated the principles for Catholic film policy worldwide and lavished praise on the efforts of American bishops, who had successfully waged a battle against cinematic immorality by founding the American Legion of Decency. The encyclical reiterated an understanding of cinema's influence and propagandistic potential that, by the late 1930s, had already been implicitly accepted by Western political leaders.[15] While the negative immoral influences of film were condemned, the medium was generally affirmed as an important tool of instruction and education, particularly in relation to youth. The encyclical advocated active religious involvement in the production of "the good film" based upon Christian ethics and an optimistic *Weltanschauung*: "The essential purpose of art," of which film was an example, "its raison d'être, is to assist in the perfecting of the moral personality. . . . For this reason it must itself be moral."[16] This was to be effected by the dynamic expansion of organized Catholic film activity worldwide.

Pius XI envisioned a two-pronged attack against immoral films, based on the experience of the American Legion of Decency. Catholic bishops were to lead the campaign by rallying their dioceses and forging a grass roots movement. The goal was to stimulate "all faithful Catholics and decent men, . . . solicitous for the decorum and moral health of the family, the nation and human society," to combat individual films that functioned as "school[s] of corruption."[17] Additionally, the church was to appeal for film industry cooperation in expunging immoral influences from the commercial product.

The papal letter conveyed a sense of urgency, of fighting for a Christian future in a world of technological and moral change. The actions of the American Legion of Decency were heralded as a "holy crusade" undertaken during a "crisis" in which vice and crime were glorified for mass consumption.[18] The Pope underscored the importance of his concern by tying it to the welfare of the state: "A people, who in their leisure hours devote themselves to amusements that offend one's healthy sense of propriety, honor, and morality, that provide the opportunity for sinfulness, especially among the young, find themselves in great danger of losing their greatness and national strength."[19]

This position, linking immoral pursuits and the loss of national greatness, found a deep resonance in postwar Western Germany. Furthermore, although the German Catholic clergy enthusiastically embraced the encyclical, postwar Catholic film activity reflected more than mere obedience to papal prescriptions. The actions of Catholic leaders and laity were grounded in the peculiar political and social climate of defeated Germany, and public appeals to congregations were made with as much regard for their national as for their religious identities.[20]

Catholic film activity in postwar Germany distinguished itself from its earlier initiatives by its broad scope, passionate lobbying, and occasionally flamboyant tactics. Prior to 1933, Catholic film groups had sought to reshape the market and produced Catholic films intended to compete with the commercial industry. However, by 1934 even the largest Catholic film companies—like the impressive Leo-Film Gesellschaft, with branches in Switzerland, Spain, and Austria—collapsed due to financial difficulties unrelated to Hitler's rise to power. What little confessional film activity remained was sharply regulated, and by 1943 all such activity had ceased.[21]

Protestant film work was historically less organized. Prior to World War II, the Protestant clergy tended to view film as antithetical to the mission of the church. Film activity was confined to lay organizations, which produced and distributed films chronicling the accomplishments of missionaries or church social workers. After the devastation wrought by the war, however, Protestant leaders increasingly recognized the need to assist "the homeless, uprooted and neglected" German youth.[22] Thereafter, Protestant leaders, like their Catholic counterparts, shifted their emphasis to concentrate on influencing the nature of the products released by the commercial film industry.

Sharing a common goal and philosophy for the social role of film in postwar Germany, these confessional groups modeled new strategies for influencing commercial film production and policy. Early in the postwar period, both Catholic and Protestant churches created organizations to deal with film questions. In 1946, at the Fulda Bishops' Conference, Catholic bishops founded the Kirchliche Hauptstelle für Bild und Filmarbeit in den deutschen Diözesen, a central office for film matters in Cologne. By the following year, two publications, *Filmdienst der Jugend* and Max Gritschneder's *Filmüberschau*, appeared to provide moral guidance to the Catholic community regarding films released in the Western German sectors. The Protestant churches took somewhat longer to organize. A Protestant film journal was not issued until late in 1948, when *Evangelischer Film-Beobachter* appeared in Munich to advise Protestants on the moral and narrative content of films; the EKD appointed Pastor Werner Hess as special commissioner for film matters some months later in the spring of 1949.[23]

Recognizing a convergence of purpose with respect to the film industry, the churches initiated an informal policy of interconfessional cooperation in film affairs. This move grew out of the domestic political atmosphere and paralleled the tone of confessional conciliation best symbolized by the creation of the Christian Democratic Union and the Bavarian Christian Socialist Union

(Christlich-Soziale Union [CSU]).[24] Cooperation had already been initiated in 1948 with the production of *Nachtwache* (*Nightwatch*), a movie based upon an idea conceived by Hess, who, along with Catholic film commissioner Anton Kochs, was appointed adviser during its filming. The plot centered on a Catholic priest and a Protestant pastor who share the only remaining church building in their community at the end of the war. The film stressed interconfessional cooperation and understanding as well as the cathartic effects of religious faith for those faced with the grim task of surviving and overcoming personal loss. Heartily endorsed in both the Protestant and Catholic press, the film quickly became a success with the public: millions saw it, and actor Dieter Borsche, who played the Catholic priest, achieved overnight stardom.[25]

Although the confessional press and film offices readily promoted *Nachtwache* as a positive example of postwar German film, the project was an anomaly and did not signal the development of a working alliance between the churches and the commercial film industry. Lacking the resources to produce Christian films designed to compete with the commercial product, church film commissioners instead fought to modify the values of commercial film production and, if possible, hammer out an understanding with sympathetic filmmakers.[26] This goal was illustrated during the 1950 Schwalbacher film conference, which was sponsored by the Protestant church and attended by representatives from both churches, the film industry, the censorship board (the FSK), and the state and federal governments. Although the closing statement at the meeting announced the churches' determination to oppose "the deformation of Christianity . . . as well as its falsification under the pretense of humanitarianism,"[27] it introduced an agenda intended to appeal to commercial filmmakers. Church representatives recognized that the production of "quality" films in Germany was linked to the health of the native film industry and therefore advocated a plan to bolster the industry's precarious economic position through a range of financial incentives for domestic production and a program of education intended to provide technical and critical training of younger generations in filmmaking and film appraisal.[28] Although the meeting resulted in no formal agreement, its primary significance was to open lines of communication on film matters outside the confines of the FSK and elicit an expression of the desire by all parties to continue cultivating such contacts. It is quite clear, however, that church leaders took such expressions of cooperation much more seriously than did industry representatives.[29]

Although critical of the commercial film industry's general and long-standing unwillingness to assist in fostering a Christian film culture, Catholic film commissioner Anton Kochs understood that this response was grounded in the economics of film practice, which is dictated by technological and profit considerations and "thrives on extraordinary and psychologically laden material." He admitted that cinema would "lose much of its audience if it treated a Christian or merely religious theme," conceding that audiences would not seek out such films as long as their more popular competition existed. Kochs had experienced these difficulties firsthand during the Third Reich when he headed the Katholischer Lichtspielverband, which coordinated the distribution of films to the Catholic parish cinemas—whose ghettoization was insured by Nazi state film policies and programs for youth.[30] The postwar task was not, therefore, the eradication of the commercial competition but a reform of the film product itself.

Initially, the Protestant and Catholic film commissioners attacked the indiscriminate use of religious motifs, settings, and ceremony in feature films—a practice they charged was becoming particularly widespread in the early years of renewed German film production. According to Hess, there was "hardly a comedy, a crime thriller," or any other type of film in which "a church scene wasn't inserted, [or] somewhere a pastor or monk cropped up. The church has become the most acceptable and obvious accessory when it is deemed necessary to appear serious or to take on the tinge of great art. . . . Only . . . the opposite effect is usually achieved: they appear untruthful, inappropriately posited and . . . distressing, because one notices they are not affirmations of Christ but of mammon."[31] Kochs seconded Hess's objections to Christian kitsch, false sentimentality, and the "decorative" uses of sacred objects, complaining that "clouds of incense smoke and burning candles, friendly monks, and almond-eyed acolytes" did not insure that a film was religious.[32] Hess and Kochs objected to the commercial exploitation and cooptation of religiosity by the film industry. Yet their statements can also be read as metaphors for their opposition to the peripheralization and trivialization of religion in a period marked by both the abrupt release of culture from Nazi state control and the influx of American cultural forms. Struck by the rapid commercialization and ongoing secularization of German society, churchmen feared the loss of their traditional cultural authority. They needed to strike back.

For a New, Moral Film Control

The most obvious place to start was with a modification of the postwar film censorship apparatus, the FSK, which German churchmen generally viewed as a foreign imposition and the outgrowth of an Allied policy unresponsive to their cultural and social concerns. Although church and state officials won inclusion of the "public voice" in FSK deliberations—in the form of minority representation by the state ministries of culture, the churches, and youth offices—the industry retained an absolute majority of votes on the Working Committee, which reviewed films for release, as well as on the Main Committee, to which contested decisions were brought.

The new postwar film censorship legislation actually represented a blending of old and new principles. The American model of exclusive censorship by film producers was merged with the principle of representation by social welfare and religious groups, which had its roots in the Weimar film control legislation (Reichslichtspielgesetz) of 1920. Similarly, the actual censorship criteria were largely carried over from the Weimar legislation. Both codes prohibited the release of films that offended religious or moral sentiment or endangered German relations with other states. Although the 1949 criteria dropped the stipulation banning films that threatened the public order, it added post-Hitler clauses outlawing films that exhibited "National Socialist, militarist, imperialist, or nationalist tendencies or encouraged racial hatred; that endangered the constitutional and civil rights of the German population; or that falsified historical fact by means of propagandistic or tendentious devices." Moreover, the new legislation lowered the age of unrestricted film attendance to sixteen years from eighteen (where it had been fixed during the republic and retained under the Nazis).[33]

From the beginning, church and state representatives considered this an unsatisfactory compromise imposed by foreign dictate. They had been compelled to accept the American principle of industry self-censorship, but they refused to consider the situation permanent or irremediable—a position articulated by Walter Keim, whose influence transcended Bavaria due to his leadership of the Standing Conference of Cultural Ministers of the German States.[34] In a characteristic show of alliance with Catholic interests, he published a piece in the *Münchner Katholische Kirchenzeitung* exploring the desired role of the church vis-à-vis commercial culture in a democratic state. Entitled "Do We Catholics Enjoy Constitutionally Based Freedom of Opinion in the Area of Film?," Keim's article targeted "the decisive and fundamental question of our cultural and constitutional life: if and to what extent Catholics—who after all make up a quite considerable percentage of filmgoers and therefore are not unimportant to the business interests of film producers—should satisfy themselves with the decisions enunciated by the Self-Control Board in Wiesbaden."[35] Rather than betray nervousness regarding the new political order, he carefully justified increased church influence in film censorship, grounding it in a firmly "democratic tradition" by pointing to analogous developments, such as the creation of the American Legion of Decency, in the "unarguably" democratic United States.

Thus, the censorship board—despite Christian representation—rapidly became, in the words of Werner Hess, the "target of passionate ecclesiastical criticism," with Catholics and Protestants alike expressing grave misgivings about the "laxity" of the film review process and the enforcement of the code. The cause of this "laxity" was, according to the churchmen, the voting strength of the secular commercial interests in that body and the corresponding weakness of the churches.[36]

In the months before the FSK began operation, the Catholic church consolidated its film activity, founding a Catholic Film Commission for the purpose of reviewing and rating all films—domestic and imported—shown in Germany and awarding prizes to the "year's best" products. Shortly thereafter, the Catholic Film Commission united *Filmdienst der Jugend* and *Filmüberschau* to create a single official organ, *Filmdienst*, which printed the commission's opinions on all films exhibited in Western Germany. The judgments of the commission were posted "on almost all church doors and in many public showcases."[37] Although such activity obviously paralleled in part the functions of the new censorship board, industry and American officials did not object immediately to this organization. Presumably the Americans considered it an internal church affair instituted to advise congregations on the moral content of films and not a body that sought to usurp or subvert the work of the FSK. Members of the German commercial film industry learned by bitter experience that the work of these organizations would have broader repercussions.[38]

From the beginning, state officials were kept abreast of complaints regarding the operation and decisions of the FSK. The Bavarian Ministry of Culture, for example, continued to receive letters, typically routed through higher church authorities, from concerned parents, teachers, and local officials complaining about the inadequacy of film censorship, particularly in relation to youth.[39] Although officials at the Cultural Ministry were sympathetic to their complaints, they could not intervene against FSK decisions; their hands were bound by the new legislation.

The Catholic church's official position was announced in Cardinal Faulhaber's "Appeal of the Bavarian Bishops for the Protection of Youth and the Security of the People" in early 1950, which denounced the circulation of "trash and smut" and demanded its regulation. Intending to pressure the political authorities, Faulhaber addressed his appeal to the Bavarian minister president and warned that social decay was the necessary corollary of a democracy that knew no limits:

> In view of these undeniable facts, it is inconceivable and irresponsible to underestimate so great a threat to and corruption of public morality and conceal it with the cloak of democracy. . . .
>
> We are well acquainted with the voices, which perceive in a law against trash and smut a threat to democratic freedom. But freedom may not survive in unrestraint and cannot be freedom for any ungodly action.

Alarmed at signs of increasing secularization in postwar German society, Faulhaber cautioned that disregard for law and morality would intensify "until it destroys the basis of our entire moral order and national community."[40] Faulhaber's impassioned plea echoed the earlier apocalyptic imagery of Protestant Bishop Otto Dibelius, who thundered in 1947 that "either this secularization must be brought to an end, and a countermovement be cultivated with seriousness, purpose, and strength; or if a moral order cannot be constructed . . . what was once a *Volk* will become an instinctual, agitated mass . . . that will one day perish in a battle of all against the others. The destruction of our *Volk* is then upon us."[41] Protestant and Catholic leaders agreed that the fight was for God and nation, and the high stakes sealed interconfessional cooperation.

Writing for an international Catholic journal, Catholic film commissioner Anton Kochs summarized the issues and attempted to cast the debate in terms congenial to the Catholic position by asking a series of questions that were indicative of the demands to be made on film and the industry. The responses were to be worked out over the course of the Adenauer era: "Does film . . . assist in the reconstruction of the Christian West? Does it counter the destructive powers of the present with something positive? Does it provide something that actually helps people? or does it undermine and corrupt that which responsible people wish to construct—since the destruction of the war—in the home, in public, and in the church?"[42]

The Case of *Die Sünderin*

In early 1951, then, members of both the Catholic and Protestant churches took up arms to protect Christian morality and, with it, the "Christian West" in their battle against Willi Forst's film, *Die Sünderin*. Initiated in the chambers of the censorship body, the debate about the film quickly transcended narrow bureaucratic confines and exploded into the public arena, resulting in a mobilization of civil society. The film became a cause célèbre, around which debates concerning the reorganization of social roles and relationships, and issues of cultural authority, were played out.

Willi Forst very self-consciously heralded his film as an innovation, both in terms of his own personal style of filmmaking and within the tradition of German cinema. Best known for the musicals he had made in the 1930s and 1940s, Forst claimed to have reconsidered his career since he "took shelter" by making apolitical films during the war and decided to forsake the "dream factory" school of filmmaking in favor of a German realism: films "the public could identify with." He advocated a new cinematic style for postwar Germany and called for the creation of a film drama based on "real" experience, a vision that evokes associations with Italian neorealism but contrasts greatly with the popular film genres of interwar and wartime Germany.[43] Implicit in his campaign for cultural renewal was his rejection of the hegemony of the "UFA style" of escapist filmmaking that flourished under Hitler. Forst intended to break away from this stylistic hegemony.[44]

Criticism of the film arose during an evaluative screening before the Working Committee of the FSK, on which Protestant film commissioner Werner Hess and an unidentified Bavarian Catholic representative sat. Although no firm decision was made about the advisability of the film's release, the committee did agree that it contained objectionable scenes, including Marina's resort to prostitution and the portrayal of mercy killing and suicide. There were indications, however, that if appropriate editorial cuts were made, the committee would provide a license for its release.

Willi Forst adamantly refused to make cuts and considered the summons to appear before the committee "a personal insult." Forst's response reveals his confidence that he commanded a strong position vis-à-vis the FSK, particularly when backed by his production and distribution companies, Junge Film Union and Herzog Film. Furthermore, his statement that the censorship board "should not make itself look ridiculous" and his threat to "take the issue public" indicate how little legitimacy he accorded the body when he thought it would endanger the commercial and critical success of his film.[45] Reportedly, the film's producer, distributor, and exhibitor decided to premiere the film even without proper FSK authorization if necessary. Such action would threaten the very function of the FSK and further erode the trust of church representatives in both the purpose of the institution and its effectiveness in curbing renegade behavior by industry members.[46]

The contested action was assigned to the Main Committee of the FSK, which was composed of four representatives named by the film industry, three named by the public institutions (one representative each from the Catholic and Protestant churches and a confessional youth group), and three representatives of the state governments. Although the film was criticized on several counts, the committee ultimately authorized its release by a vote of nine to four but warned that it pressed "hard on the limits of the permissible." The film was approved for viewing by audiences "over the age of sixteen years" but was prohibited from screenings on religious holidays.[47]

The day after the decision was reached and the film premiered in Frankfurt, Werner Hess resigned from the FSK; Anton Kochs followed shortly thereafter. Each acted at the request of his superior (respectively, Protestant Bishop Hans Lilje and Catholic Archbishop Wilhelm Berning), and the resignations were designed both to illustrate interconfessional solidarity in issues of film control and to pressure a revision of the FSK bylaws in favor of church and state representation.[48]

The Catholic church moved to the forefront of the organized fight against the film on the local level. It became the subject of church sermons and protest activity, often by "believers" who had not viewed the film but relied on the reports of their local priest or film journal to supply details. This was certainly the case for the packs of schoolchildren paraded around numerous German towns by pious superiors, since the film was banned for youth.[49] Although it is unclear exactly how local priests and religious teachers throughout West Germany decided to take to the streets using identical tactics and whether this action was directly encouraged or even orchestrated by the Catholic hierarchy, it is clear that the calls of Catholic bishops for the defense of "Christian humanity" were considered justification for their actions.[50] Furthermore, neither Catholic leaders nor the religious press ever publicly criticized anti-*Sünderin* protests, even when they resulted in violence and, in one case, the sensational trial of a Catholic priest.[51] Instead, they stuck with the strategy of blaming the film itself for domestic unrest, charging that it, not the protesters, posed a "threat to democracy" and the German nation.[52]

The rallying point for this campaign became "Christian morality," and generalized rhetoric centered on the "good," "true humanity," and "honor"—all values with unimpeachable appeal. Yet in the heat of the Cold War, concepts like "Christian morality" and the "Christian West" had more than an ethical appeal —they had a political thrust. Such pronouncements played upon the anticommunist sentiments prevalent among Catholics, creating an atmosphere of moral and political crisis. The belief in the overwhelming power of film was peculiar neither to concerned religious and educational leaders in West Germany nor to the postwar period. Yet its currency in debates and research papers on the medium reflected and fed an anxiety intensified by the consequences of war and military defeat, including unprecedented material destruction, the immigration of millions of refugees, the influx of foreign forms of political and cultural organization and values, and, it was feared, an ensuing lack of moral resoluteness among the German population. Hess and his like-minded colleagues feared that films like *Die Sünderin* would influence individual desire and social behavior, thus corrupting the "spiritual" health of the fatigued and susceptible national community and shredding the last, weak moral fibers that held it together.

Die Sünderin: Counterprotests and the Threat to the Public Order

Germans flocked to the cinema to watch *Die Sünderin* despite, or perhaps because of, widespread clerical campaigning against the film and the difficulty of viewing it in many localities. Some 6.5 million people ignored the churches' proscription, making it the most popular German film in the Federal Republic in

1951.[53] Simple curiosity spurred by church sermons and reports in the press may account for its overwhelming popularity, yet film viewing as a method of resistance to the circumscription of civil liberties surfaced in various locations. What was being tested was the strength—and limits—of the new democracy.

Perhaps the most dramatic show of disapproval occurred in Regensburg, where thousands of citizens gathered in front of the town hall for two consecutive evenings to protest the actions of local priests against *Die Sünderin* and the mayor's belated decision to ban the film.[54] On the morning of 22 February 1951, an announcement was made during church services that Catholic associations were planning to demonstrate against the film, which had already been screened in the city in six peaceful performances. That evening, 4,000 to 5,000 people gathered in front of the town hall, most of whom, curiously, favored the film's screening. The shouts of protest against the film by a group of thirteen-to-fifteen-year-olds led by their religion teacher were answered by profilm protesters who yelled, "Freedom of press and film" and "We want to see *Die Sünderin!*" Although urged by local clergy to ban the film, the mayor of Regensburg refused to move against it unless and until it "disturbed and endangered the public peace and safety, life and property." However, upon receiving reports of brawls and injuries caused by the stink bombing of a cinema, and after conversing with a ministerial adviser in Munich, Mayor Zitzler instituted the ban. Upon hearing the news, the pro-*Sünderin* protesters booed the decision, chanting "What about democracy?," and broke up.

Meanwhile, the local cinema continued to show the film until a written order to suspend the screening was delivered by city authorities. The audience initially refused to leave but finally relented and joined the profilm demonstrators leaving town hall in search of the mayor. Unable to find him in any of the local pubs, some 3,000 demonstrators assembled in front of the bishop's residence but were dispersed by police, who used pressurized water and rubber nightsticks against the crowd.

The next evening, several thousand demonstrators gathered in front of the town hall and began to yell: "We demand our rights. Zitzler is a servant of the clergy! [Wir fordern unser Recht, der Zitzler ist ein Pfaffenknecht!]" and "The clergy have seen the film, the dumb people should go without! [Die Pfaffen haben den Film gesehen, das dumme Volk soll leer ausgehn!]". The profilm demonstrators milled around peacefully until the police, equipped with steel helmets and rifles, started pushing into the crowd with their nightsticks. Radicalized by the violence, the indignant citizens chanted, "Down with the Black dictatorship!," and marched to the film theater to protest the mayor's ban. On the way through town, demonstrators broke the windows of the Catholic bishop's house. The strength of the new democracy was being tested, and in this case, it was found to be sadly lacking.

The mayor, having secured support for his actions from the Bavarian Ministry of the Interior, issued a written statement to the town population urging the preservation of peace and order. Astonishingly, the statement also asserted that authorities had proof that "these disturbances of the public order have been exploited by unscrupulous and Bolshevist-disposed elements for the purposes of incitement, the employment of force, and the undermining of the democracy."[55] The mayor assembled the city council to elicit its agreement to continue the ban. At the meeting, the director of police reported that another demonstration was scheduled for that evening and that protesters were expected from Munich and Nuremberg. He predicted that the demonstration would be marked by violence by "elements of the most extreme left,"[56] who would force a struggle for power. Other council members characterized the demonstrators as the "mob of the street" and students "who study with our money" and who, in effect, were "marching for the East zone."

SPD members countered by criticizing police violence and the "misuse" of minors and schoolchildren by the clergy, suggesting that Bavarian Cardinal Faulhaber and other "eminences" were implicated. Enraged Christian Democrats denied that the demonstrations originated with their party. To end the debate, a vote was taken to confirm the film's prohibition. The vote, 16 to 15, yielded no decisive majority, and Zitzler requested a revote, with the same results. When he suggested a third vote, the SPD members "demonstratively left the hall," fed up with the charade.

The following day, the theater was permitted to resume showing *Die Sünderin* due to both the "massive public protests" and the city council's failure to reach a consensus on the issue. There had been one last disturbance following the town council meeting, when armed police again intervened against demonstrators who aggressively demanded to see the mayor; yet public unrest ceased once the ban was lifted.

The abrupt halt to public demonstrations in Regensburg once the screening of the film resumed disproves the allegations by the mayor and police that they represented an insurgent and destructive "leftist threat" to German democracy. Yet the readiness with which those fears surfaced and were articulated, and the characterization of the counterdemonstration as insidious and disruptive of the social order, indicates the local authorities' interpretation of the limits of democratic public protest. Their position, in fact, closely resembled that of the churches. When *Die Sünderin* was banned in Koblenz after two days of unrest, a Catholic newspaper in Cologne applauded the action: "In fact, the film is disturbing our communal life, and it has impinged on the structure of our public and governmental [*staatliche*] order. . . . The state has not broken into the free preserves of art, but art, to which film also belongs, has broken into the area of the state, and by doing so has shaken the foundations of the *staatliche* order."[57]

What is striking about the events in Regensburg is the intensity and scale of counterprotest, of public resistance to the strong voice of religious and municipal leaders in film censorship. This sentiment was underscored in a 1952 survey regarding film control. Many respondents exhibited marked unease and disquiet at the very mention of the words "control" and "censorship," which, according to one academic commentator, appeared to resurrect "personal or political resentments" from the recent Nazi past. All told, one-quarter of those polled rejected any form of film control and justified their response by arguing that they wanted neither to be patronized nor subjected to tutelage: "We want to make our own decisions!"[58] Rather than paint a picture of postwar political quietude, both this response and the demonstrations in favor of the film suggest that sectors of the German public took the promise of democratization seriously and were willing to fight against infractions—by any authority—against freedom of expression and consumption.

Moreover, public behavior demonstrates that the churches' power was by no means consolidated and unquestioned by the early 1950s, even in Bavarian towns known for their robust Catholicism. Attempts to limit the range of viewing choice of local populations were resisted in other Bavarian Catholic strongholds as well. In Weissenburg, protests forced the theater owner to show the film against his will; and in Freising, where the film was banned, a group of people took a bus to Munich to see it. Told there that it had been sold out, they continued on to Garmisch-Partenkirchen, where they fulfilled their mission, and where, by the way, half of the population had seen the film.[59]

The role of the churches in the new democracy remained an object of intense debate. Certain sectors of the German public demonstrated both a rejection of the churches as cultural arbiters and an unwillingness to conform to the moral dictates of local religious and governmental authorities regarding leisure activity and cultural consumption. Although the level of political organization remained neophyte, one can assume on the basis of these examples that the churches did not express the voice of the "masses." In fact, the strong voice of the informal, socially conservative church-state coalition in cultural matters was challenged as an infringement on the population's new constitutional rights.

The dramatic tactics of the confessional campaign against the film were criticized as undemocratic in the more liberal press as well as film trade papers. Perhaps one can question the impartiality of the German cinema owners' trade paper that condemned the "mob-like practices" of Catholic groups by charging that their effort to "disrupt the guarantees of constitutional law is a crime against the *Volk* and against our young democratic state."[60] But criticisms in nontrade papers of Hess's and Kochs's walkout from the FSK called into question the political loyalties of church leaders and their vision of where they fit in the new democracy: "[The FSK] is supposed to be a democratic forum, a true parliament; but today who sits in a democratic parliament if he believes he has to resign his seat as soon as his view has not prevailed?"[61] The implication was that the churches had to adjust to the democratic system, to the condition of being just one interest group among many.

Protestant response to this type of criticism was not to deny the charges but to subvert them. Agreeing that the FSK was a democratic institution, a Protestant commentator and pastor queried whether it was proper that the Christian churches possessed only one vote out of fifteen (on the Main Committee), given the fact that the body dealt with issues crucial to "the foundation of Christian belief." He went further, suggesting that the matter went beyond democratic politics; it did not concern an attempt by the church to secure power but rather "the understanding that the Ten Commandments, which the church must preach, can never be subjugated to a democratic vote."[62]

Industry Reaction and the Threat of Cultural Provincialism

Ecclesiastical attacks on the film's content, based on the concept of *Filmwirkung*, were interpreted by members of the film industry as threatening to the very existence of a national cinema. From the beginning of the controversy, Willi Forst defined the issue for German filmmakers when he asked: "Will there ever again be a German film?" The economic strength of the German film industry had been severely weakened as a result of the war and the regulation by Western Allies. Even when these political and material hindrances were alleviated, German film companies continued to have great difficulty securing funding for production.

The situation was even bleaker with regard to the international marketing of German films. The export of German films outside of Central Europe had declined drastically over the course of the 1930s. Economic autarky and ideological considerations under Hitler dictated that the German market be cut off to foreign productions during the war years, and affected countries responded in kind by closing their markets to German films. The industry suffered a further blow in the aftermath of the war when American officials insisted on the breakup of the powerful UFI film trust, which limited film companies to one area of film activity (production, distribution, or exhibition) and resulted in the proliferation of small, often economically inviable production companies. Postwar German film companies engaged in a life-and-death struggle to win back a portion of the international market. In order to accomplish this goal, they needed a stronger economic base and a new cosmopolitan look. The issue here was not merely the intellectual and moral content of future German film production but industry survival and international competitiveness as well.[63]

Industry representatives correctly expected that the churches' fight for a narrowly defined Christian culture, with its limitations on film content and form, would produce "provincial" pictures that would be difficult to peddle on anything other than the domestic market. Industry spokespeople attacked church initiatives as interventionist and unconstitutional, charging that they infringed upon freedom of opinion, the press, and artistic expression. The industry had much to lose if the vision of a church-mediated culture triumphed.

After the premiere of his film in Frankfurt, Forst asked the press not to create more chaos by opposing the release of his film, for fear that future filmmaking would beget only "The Third Black Forest Girl from the Right [Das dritte Schwarzwaldmädel von Rechts],"[64] a new hybrid combining the worst of the old UFA film genres. Forst's pejorative comment was a play on words that merged the titles of two popular, current German films: Schwarzwaldmädel (Black Forest Girl, a sentimental Heimatfilm of the previous year, which celebrated the unspoiled beauty of the Black Forest and of young German womanhood) and Dritte von Rechts (Third from the Right, which was part detective film, part musical revue).

Comparing his film to those on the international market and to Italian, French, and American films released in West Germany, Forst pronounced it "suitable for showing at a children's matinee."[65] This bit of hyperbole conveyed the conviction of filmmakers that moral censorship by West German churches was excessive and potentially fatal to the reestablishment of an internationally competitive national film culture.

Forst and his production company, Junge Film Union, held firm in their refusal to allow editorial cuts to be dictated to them by the churches. Yet they emphasized their earlier receptiveness to Christian film commissioners' advice during the film's production. Because Die Sünderin was one of the first postwar German films to benefit from a newly created system of state and federal film credits (Bürgschaften), the script had been made available to church and state representatives prior to filming. The use of public funds for the project brought with it the inconvenience of formal preproduction review. In this case, Forst and company had been bound to entertain the suggestions of church representatives after receiving state funds but in the end refused to be coerced.[66]

Curiously, filmmakers and industry officials never launched a major effort to refute the theory of Filmwirkung but typically sought to establish the reasons a particular film could not be considered dangerous to an average viewer. They did, however, question the motives and mentalities of moral critics. In a handwritten note in the confidential files of the FSK, industry representative Fritz Podehl rhetorically asked: "How tainted must those [critics] be who assume that the viewers of such a film—also the younger ones among them—could be induced either to become a prostitute, kill a suffering relative, or commit suicide? The morally healthy could not possibly react with the wish to imitate."[67]

Nevertheless, this was exactly the argument of ecclesiastical critics. The churches did not need to address the issue of film's effect on a society that was healthy, morally or otherwise. In a postwar Germany inhabited by victims of material want, physical weakness, psychical despondency, and moral decay, the vulnerability of the population was assumed. By stressing the exceptionality of social and moral conditions in West Germany, they sought to foster a sense of a social order so precarious and tenuous that even a single film could jeopardize it.

The *Sünderin* Aftermath: Industry Capitulation
and the Triumph of the Christian (Democratic) West

Although the content and artistic value of *Die Sünderin* continued to be criticized in the press and in angry letters to state ministries, public debates rapidly transcended the disputed film and focused on the validity of the current form of film censorship and funding. Additionally, since *Die Sünderin* had been one of the early recipients of officially sponsored film credits, the controversy helped facilitate the resumption of state involvement in cultural production and regulation—a situation the Americans had been determined to block. At stake ultimately, then, was the issue of who should control the resurgent national culture and the principles upon which such control should be based.

Film credit programs had been initiated between 1949 and 1950, when a number of state governments—including Bavaria, Hesse, Hamburg, and West Berlin—attempted to address the film industry's financial problems through a system of state guarantees designed to bolster both the production of German films and the local economies. By 1950, the federal government created its own program of film guarantees, or *Bürgschaften*, intended to produce films that could compete on the international market. This was part of a larger program of federal assistance (provided for in the Gesetz über Sicherheitsleistungen zur Förderung der deutschen Wirtschaft) enacted to stimulate national economic growth and increase export revenues. The federal government earmarked 20 million marks for the first *Bürgschaft* plan, which ran from mid-1950 to the end of 1953. On average, the credits covered 25–35 percent of a film's production costs, which were estimated at 800,000 marks for black-and-white features and 1.25 million for color. In the first year, 1950–51, 75 percent of all German feature films were supported by state and/or federal funds; Willi Forst's film was one of them. This fact fueled the controversy surrounding the film, rapidly broadening both its cultural-political significance and the amount of publicity it received. Indeed, the day after Werner Hess withdrew from the FSK, journalists and parliamentary representatives walked out of a special screening of the film in Bonn to protest the use of public funds for its production. The press quickly took up this line of argument and demanded that stricter moral criteria be instituted for films made with public money.[68]

Hess's resignation from the board was designed to advertise his strong dissatisfaction with its methods of operation and the tendency of licensing decisions to favor the position of the industry. He complained that the "public voice" in the decision-making process was disproportionately small and that church participation on the board was being exploited by the industry to serve "propagandistic purposes." When joined by Kochs, Hess's action challenged the ability of the FSK to claim the exercise of censorship activity as an outgrowth of public consensus. This situation was further exacerbated when at least one state representative withdrew from the FSK in a show of solidarity with the Christian film commissioners' criticisms and demands.[69]

In spite of the support Hess received from his Catholic and government counterparts, his superior, Bishop Lilje, chairman of the Media Board of the EKD, while seeking reform did not abjure Protestant involvement in the FSK. The week following Hess's resignation, Lilje told him to sustain contact with the organization, and several days later Protestant and Catholic representatives met with the film industry to affirm their willingness to work with the FSK, provided certain modifications were made.

This gesture of reconciliation caused industry representatives to declare that there would be "no Kulturkampf . . . neither now nor later." Film trade papers pointedly reminded readers that the resignation of church representatives had not disrupted the operation of the censorship board; film screenings and evaluations continued.[70] This likely accounted for the clerics's sudden moderation. The churches had apparently reached the limits of their subversion of the FSK.

Despite the triumphant tone of the film trade press, the industry was ultimately forced to capitulate to demands for a stronger "public voice" in the censorship process due to pressure applied by the German states. When church officials met with representatives of the trade association of the German film industry (the SPIO) in late January 1951, representatives of the state cultural ministries were also present. State involvement in the negotiations lent weight to the churches' demands and, although these were not met in toto, the industry was pressed to accept important modifications.[71] The final settlement established a parity between industry and public representatives on the Working Committee by increasing the number of members to eight—four of whom now came from the "public sector." These four seats were distributed to representatives of the Catholic and Evangelical churches and the Jewish religious community (in alternation); state ministries of culture; the federal youth office; and, for the first time, the federal government.[72] The SPD made a separate—though futile—bid for inclusion in order to introduce "socialist cultural and moral ideals" but was rejected out of hand by the SPIO, which wanted to insure that the FSK did not become "a platform of party-political confrontation."[73] Indeed, due to these modifications, the "public voice" at the time was essentially represented by one party: the Christian Democrats.

Criticism did not end, however, with the churches' successful negotiations to modify the censorship apparatus. Ecclesiastical complaints regarding film industry business practices continued, and throughout the spring, the Bavarian Ministry of Education and Culture received numerous letters from religious organizations appealing for state intervention against industry business practices.[74] Such demands received the support of government officials nationwide. The chairman of the Parliamentary Committee for Press, Radio, and Film publicly condemned the operating methods of the film industry and announced that the Sünderin matter had thoroughly destroyed the trust of wide circles of the population, and particularly that of "the entire Christian camp."[75]

Specifically, critics attacked the industry marketing practice of blind- and block-booking, whereby film distribution firms required exhibitors to contract groups of films (rather than individual titles), including, in the case of blind-booking, some that were unnamed in the contract. This was considered to be a coercive practice by industry outsiders and some theater owners, since the latter could secure desired films only by agreeing to take others they did not want or knew nothing about. Frequently during the Sünderin controversy, local theater owners blamed blind- and block-booking for the film's appearance in their program—a charge that encouraged public scrutiny of the practice.

Church groups and parents furthermore expressed their vehement opposition to the moral quality of film posters displayed in theater lobbies and showcases, as well as film advertisements in the press. The Rosenheim Catholic Girls School administration in Upper Bavaria, for example, lashed out against theater owners who publicly displayed "offensive, seductive, and often vulgar" film posters and sexually "provocative" pictures. Terming such displays "potent poison for our youth," they demanded strict prohibition.[76]

Although the new FSK bylaws did provide for the review of film advertisements, this provision apparently did not go far enough for some. The Bavarian Ministry of Culture requested that clergy, youth group leaders, and parents keep it apprised of local infractions. On the national level, industry members were publicly humiliated and thoroughly incensed when, in late 1951, film posters they lent Ernst Thiele, head of the Emergency League for German Art (Notgemeinschaft der deutschen Kunst), became the center of an exhibit in Bonn. Thiele invited representatives of the federal and state governments, the churches, and youth organizations to his display in the hope of spurring action against the "flood" of film posters "that defile good taste, brutalize, or have an

In its coverage of the October 1951 Film Poster Exhibit in Bonn, the West German news magazine, *Der Spiegel*, ran this photo and the following text: "Even Federal President [Theodor] Heuss visited the chamber of horrors at the Parliament Building. While at the exhibit, he shook his head; and the disagreement over why he shook his head still hasn't been resolved. The sponsor of the exhibit in Bonn claims it was in disgust over the quality of German film advertising. Representatives of the FSK in Wiesbaden maintain, however, that Theodor Heuss was mocking the selection of posters" (19 December 1951, p. 26). (Courtesy of *Der Spiegel*)

immoral effect." This action was heartily endorsed by Rudolf Vogel of the Parliamentary Committee for Press, Radio, and Film, who, standing amid the pictorial prevalence of décolleté and exposed flesh, regretted the "overly Italian influence of many atomic-bomb-like" female representations. A delegate from the Protestant church counseled the film industry to outgrow its extended "state of puberty." Furious film distributors demanded the return of their donations. Anticipating such a reaction, Thiele moved his show to the Bundeshaus (Federal House) in Bonn, where the posters would be immune from confiscation.

Meanwhile, the film industry launched a counterexhibit in Wiesbaden, highlighting forty-four of the previous four years' best posters. Furthermore, industry spokespeople answered critics by attributing the use of titillating material to consumer taste, pointing to their advertising experience with the film *Sündige Grenzen* (*Sinful Boundaries*), which did five times the business when posters at the box office depicting a train roaring through a tunnel were replaced with ones featuring a collage of character close-ups, including the requisite display of plunging necklines and brandished pistols. As the industry member of the FSK argued: "We can't function without eroticism—we might as well call it quits. But the limit lies where the sexual begins."[77]

Thiele's show drew press interest, and the popular national news magazine, *Der Spiegel*, ran a two-page article along with a photo of West German president Theodor Heuss attending the exhibit. Strikingly, *Der Spiegel* gave the episode serious coverage but hinted at its assessment of the proceedings by concluding with a quote from an SPD representative from the FSK, Max Lippmann, who noted that "if I consider what was presented to the children in the Third Reich, then I'm for this democratic freedom and not for '*Hitlerjunge Quex*.'"[78]

Lippmann was responding to renewed calls for the state regulation of film posters, which found an official spokesperson in Rudolf Vogel, who warned that if the FSK did not do its job, the state would have to intervene.[79] The SPD had, in a 1950 memo, supported the introduction of a federal credit program for film production in order to both resurrect a national cinematic culture based upon democratic principles and stimulate economic growth through the export of German films. Although SPD representatives in the West German Parliament (Bundestag) joined their colleagues in the CDU/CSU in urging the industry to produce "responsible" films, they objected to attempts by the Interior Ministry—and later, Wuermeling's Ministry of Family Affairs—to dictate morality and a specific conservative social agenda by intervening inappropriately in matters of film censorship or funding. As one SPD member of the Bundestag argued: "The distribution of state credits according to state-political criteria must be rejected" since their origin could be traced to the Nazi period.[80] This position was seconded by Horst von Hartlieb of the Film Distributors' Association, who maintained that "there are only two alternatives: either a free economy defined by matter-of-fact box-office taste or the [domination of] state censors."[81] Thus, democratic freedoms were linked to economic liberalism, and a retreat from either signified the return to fascist policies.

In the end, this argument must have been convincing, for no legislative action resulted. Yet the FSK stepped up its vigilance concerning film advertisements—at least temporarily.[82] Thus, the exhibit was significant both for keeping the issue before the public's eyes and for indicating a general party-political split between the CDU and the SPD on the issue of revived state cultural authority.

The *Sünderin* controversy also set off a wave of demands on the federal government to tighten up the criteria for granting public credit for film projects. Federal credits were awarded by an interministerial committee comprised of representatives from the economics, finance, and interior ministries. This committee was assisted by an advisory board whose members were drawn from the Bundestag, the Parliamentary Committee for Press, Radio, and Film, the film industry, and the press. For a judgment on the commercial potential of a project and the supervision of productions awarded credit, the *Bürgschaft* committee enlisted the talents of Robert Liebig and others from the Deutsche Revisions und Treuhand Aktiengesellschaft, which between 1933 and 1937 had been commissioned by Goebbels to oversee the production of films funded by the Nazis' Reich Credit Association. These bodies evaluated the professional and financial credentials of applicant producers and scrutinized their scripts, casts, and technical personnel. Frequently, projects were approved for credit contingent on the participation of particular stars, scripts were sent back to be reworked, or editing cuts were ordered for completed films. Thus, the committees could influence the commercial appeal, style, and content of approved films. Moreover, there was no appeal procedure—either for a denial of funding or for mandated changes. As a result, since most production companies lacked adequate sources of funding for German filmmaking, credit programs strengthened the voice of the state regarding the types of films realized.

This voice, however, was not to be one of moral authority. Since the film credit programs were designed as economic stimulus packages, the state and federal economics ministries sought to circumvent cultural-political concerns— a situation that often led to interministry squabbling. In Bavaria, for example, Cultural Ministry officials fought for inclusion in the decision-making process but were rebuffed by Economics Ministry officials, who indicated that credit decisions would be based strictly on financial and profit considerations. Also, over the course of the summer and fall of 1951, when the federal Ministry of the Interior attempted to secure the right to veto the funding of any productions that threatened the West German "free democratic state" by employing the talents of directors, stars, or technicians who had also worked on East German films, the federal Economics Ministry squelched the bid. Issues of political or moral concern would not be entertained.[83]

It is probable that the emphasis on economic viability led to the funding of *Die Sünderin*. Willi Forst was a well-known filmmaker during the Nazi period, and the credit commissions screened for both professional experience and the likelihood of a film's commercial success. This method of assessment favored "sure bets" like Forst, a situation that reinforced the continuation of the same worn-out genres and technically polished but artistically disappointing films that were produced by UFA.[84]

Moreover, the availability of state and federal credits encouraged heightened self-censorship by the industry, which directly affected the nature of postwar production. Production companies justified their interference with directors' "artistic control" by appealing to the need for financial assistance. Director Josef von Baky, for example, considered taking legal action against Fama Film Company for surreptitiously replacing his tragic ending in the film *Der träumende Mund* (*The Dreaming Mouth*) with a happy one before release. While Baky excoriated the substituted scenes as "clumsy" and "thoroughly cheap," company officials defended their action as necessary since "Bonn subsidies would only be received under the proviso that the film closes with a happy ending." Whether this was the case is uncertain, but such examples of intervention were frequent. Even dismissing auteurist theories regarding the centrality of the director's artistic vision to the cinematic process, it appears that the quest for financing did affect the decisions West German film companies made regarding film style and content.[85] As one commentator suggested, federal credit indeed succeeded in stimulating production but flooded the market with homegrown mediocrity. "The few good films" were made without federal assistance.[86]

Consequently, credit was not extended to innovative or experimental films but to films featuring the comfortably familiar. Chairman Vogel of the Parliamentary Committee for Press, Radio, and Film in Bonn insisted that the "German film, as in earlier times, . . . possesses a great possibility for the future if it once again returns to . . . musicals, landscape films, and *Kulturfilme* and thereby achieves that which is rightfully expected of it by foreigners based on its earlier tradition."[87] Government representatives never embraced a *Stunde Null* in terms of film style and genre but assumed that the industry should resume production based upon the historical specialization of the German film industry in the world market and in line with "the old UFA tradition"—a strategy that would fail them this time around.

Stymied by the economic ministries' application of purely economic criteria to credit decisions, the state cultural ministries created another type of economic incentive and dispensed it according to ideological criteria. In 1951 the German *Länder* created a Film Rating Board of the German States (Filmbewertungsstelle der Länder [FBS], later Filmbewertungsstelle Wiesbaden [FBW]).[88] This body possessed no mandatory authority over film content but was authorized to grant significant tax breaks to films awarded with the designation of either "valuable [*wertvoll*]" or "especially valuable [*besonders wertvolle*]." Government officials dominated the rating board, which included minority representation by film journalists, the film industry, and the churches.[89] In practice, the credit commissions and rating board encouraged the production of technically competent, putatively apolitical feature films. This helped shape an "acceptable," if provincial, style of filmmaking that might have satisfied some political and social conservatives but reinforced the scorn of serious film critics and the indifference, indeed disinterest, of international distributors and audiences.

The final stroke was administered at the Fulda Bishops' Conference in late 1951 when Catholic bishops attempted to buttress their cultural authority by calling for the creation of *Filmliga*, or film leagues, in every West German diocese. The first leagues had been founded some months earlier in the Rhineland, Baden-Württemberg, and Bavarian Nuremberg, and by late fall—after a pastoral letter was read from every Catholic pulpit on 14 October 1951—the movement spread throughout the Federal Republic. Membership in the *Filmliga* was voluntary but required one to take an oath promising not to attend films that were rejected by the Catholic Film Commission and to support those it endorsed.[90]

The irrepressible Max Gritschneder, now general secretary of the Catholic *Filmliga*, characterized the league as a "*Volks* movement," intended to counter "the highly organized film industry with a correspondingly highly organized consumer group." While emphasizing that the league was designed to pressure the industry into acquiescing to the wishes of the Christian consumer, he also insisted that the "film industry should recognize thankfully that good films would be strongly attended and recommended."[91]

The trade association of the film industry strenuously protested the *Filmliga*, the solicitation of oaths, and the posting of Catholic film ratings on theater showcases as infringements on constitutionally protected democratic freedom. But the Catholic press responded that membership was voluntary and reminded the industry that film leagues were an invention of "America, the 'classic democracy,'" where they had functioned for twenty years.[92]

Furthermore, the strategy worked. Within two months, membership mushroomed to 1 million, in 1952 it reached 3 million, and by 1954 the Christian film leagues boasted 4 million members—nearly three times the combined membership of all German political parties, as one contemporary pointed out.[93] Indeed, the strength and economic impact of this "consumer group" pressured the German film industry to produce films that were morally and socially unobjectionable to the Catholic Film Commission throughout the 1950s.[94]

Transgressions could prove costly. A negative rating in the Catholic film journal typically resulted in slack business for the film outside of the major German cities. In smaller towns and rural villages, attendance at a film rejected by the Catholic film press could lead to public censure and suspicion of one's moral character. The clergy in the small Catholic towns of Altötting and Neuötting in Bavaria, for example, attempted to influence public behavior during the *Sünderin* campaign by insisting that those "who attended a film that glorified prostitutes betrayed a prostitute's spirit."[95] Film attendance was perceived as implied support of the values and messages the film allegedly conveyed. In this schema, consumption revealed character.[96]

Did the church leadership fear that consumption would replace contrition, religious or otherwise? Certainly they were reacting to both consumer culture and the political novelty of democracy. Their goal was somehow to stabilize their position and survive the onslaught of both. They did so by intervening between the media and the public. Public debates, demonstrations, and lobbying all served to determine the types of films screened in cinemas and to color the way German audiences interpreted what they saw and, indeed, the ways they decided what to see.

Church influence in film affairs was much greater after 1945 than it had been at any time previously. The churches adroitly capitalized on the circumstances of the early postwar period, bolstering their initially strong position as the sole remaining institutions in defeated Germany, forging close ties with the reigning Christian Democratic Party, encouraging lay involvement in party politics, and crafting their rhetoric to underscore the need to protect the national community during a time of exceptional material and moral crisis. Through these means, the churches assured for themselves a prominent voice in German cultural production and control. In effect, religious leaders were able to accomplish after 1945 what they had been striving for with little success and governmental support since the early 1920s: sustained influence over the types of films produced and marketed in West Germany, which would last through the heyday of postwar moviegoing.

Nevertheless, industry charges blaming the churches alone for German cultural provincialism remain problematic. In 1950 industry members once more looked to the state to bolster their industry and increase profitability—as they had during the crisis years of the Weimar Republic and the Third Reich. And once again industry reliance on postwar *Bürgschaften* encouraged both bureaucratic meddling and continuities in film style, genre, and personnel. As one film historian has noted: "Naturally a *Staatsfilm* emerged, however not in the sense [indicated] by many . . . critics, rather as the expression of the mentality of the no-experiments-society."[97]

Moreover, the second program of federal *Filmbürgschaften*, which extended from 1953 through the end of 1955, had a serious structural impact on the film industry. This time around, instead of financing individual films, the federal government funded only groups of films. This move was intended to minimize losses and encourage the economic health and long-range planning of larger, more stable firms. In practice, however, it weakened production companies, since most were small and lacked the resources to produce the required number of films annually. However, it worked to the advantage of distribution companies, which had made millions since the occupation distributing old German re-releases and foreign films. Film distributors thus enlisted various production companies to make the group of films for which they secured federal credit. In the process, film producers became dependent upon the demands of distribution companies (who sought to maximize market potential) and the mandates of state credit commissions. Moreover, since the profits of one production were used to neutralize the losses of another in any given group, production companies that scored big at the box office were denied financial rewards if they belonged to a group that included box-office bombs belonging to another producer.[98]

The industry thus exhibited little tendency to produce socially or formally innovative work through the 1950s and rarely attempted to confront political and social issues outside of the melodramatic form. Willi Forst—in spite of his call for a new type of German film—never delivered on his word and shortly afterward resorted to making his own brand of sentimental kitsch in the form of *Im weißen Rößl* (*The White Horse Inn*). Released the year after *Die Sünderin*, *Im weißen Rößl* was a musical film that showcased Austrian imperial traditions, the natural beauty of the Salzkammergut, and the cultural distinction between country and city life. In effect, it shared striking similarities with that critically disdained postwar genre, the *Heimatfilm*.

The peculiarly German genre of the *Heimatfilm*, the picture "postcard panorama" set in the rural hills of the Black Forest or the heathered fields of the Lüneburger Heide, became the staple domestic fare of West German cinema during the 1950s. Fully one-fifth of all German productions were devoted to this genre, which celebrated the beauty of the German landscape, featured close-knit communities and townsfolk in traditional dress, and contained the requisite festival celebrating local traditions from an unproblematic—and unmarred—past. As Eric Rentschler has pointed out, the genre provided postwar West Germans with a "reverse image of the period" in which "untouched nature replaces ruined cities, church bells resound instead of ubiquitous jackhammers, quaint panel houses offer a homeyness the city's ugly and quickly erected concrete edifices could not."[99]

In large measure, the *Heimatfilm* itself reinvented a reassuring, though unauthentic, German tradition for consumption by the postwar German viewer.[100] These films offered the public—and the newly arrived ethnic Germans from the eastern reaches of the former Reich—the opportunity to visually participate for a couple of hours in a never-never land of lost local tradition and ritual, or at least a generic cinematic version of it. Moreover, the genre suited the conservative agenda for the depiction of social, and particularly gender, relations since *Heimatfilme*, through mid-decade, consistently featured the spiritual repatriation of a young, attractive woman who abandons the marketplace for the home and affirms community and matrimony over autonomy. Metaphorically speaking, then, *Heimatfilme* portray the social redemption of Marina, the protagonist of *Die Sünderin*.

By the early 1950s, the *Heimatfilm* emerged as both the reigning film genre in West Germany and the national product of Bonn. This triumph of cinematic provinciality represents a striking about-face from Goebbels's grand plan to beat Hollywood at its own game by surpassing the "quality, cultural boldness, and feel for the modern" of American products in order to both dominate international markets and shape consumer identities. After the war, German elites abandoned the quest to cultivate German cinematic superiority abroad. West German officials had no ambitions to build an industry that could compete with Hollywood, in part because of the material devastation but more importantly because many feared the domestic social and cultural consequences of the kind of cinematic cosmopolitanism they assumed it would take to market their celluloid internationally.

Unlike the Nazi period, after 1945 there was no determined drive by state officials to invest energies or resources in the construction of an all-encompassing "imaginary reality" (to borrow from Ian Kershaw) that would serve as both a vehicle for consumer desire and a psychic balm for the material shortcomings of the present. The *Heimatfilm* became the national product of Bonn not because this genre was specifically pushed by state and church officials (in fact, some dismissed it as cinematic kitsch) but because it did not offend, promised a happy ending, and quickly developed a proven track record with audiences. Ultimately, state officials opted for a modest economic renewal of the industry and used funding policy to encourage the development of a domestic product that was morally and socially uncontroversial.[101] Nonetheless, although West German film production through the 1950s may have struck some as bland and others as saccharine, in retrospect it did—at least temporarily—appeal to the postwar public's need for both entertainment and psychic solace.

POPULAR CINEMA, SPECTATORSHIP, AND IDENTITY IN THE EARLY 1950s

Spectatorship is not only the act of watching a film, but also the ways one takes pleasure in the experience, or not; the means by which watching becomes a passion, or a leisure-time activity like any other. Spectatorship refers to how film-going and the consumption of movies and their myths are symbolic activities, culturally significant events. . . . Spectatorship is not just the relationship that occurs between the viewer and the screen, but also and especially how that relationship lives on once the spectator leaves the theater.—Judith Mayne, *Cinema and Spectatorship*

Within a year of the founding of the new West German state, its national cinema was already well on the way to developing an unenviable reputation. As early as 1950, even before the *Sünderin* controversy, a number of critics had surveyed the postwar film scene, denounced the prevalence of tearjerkers, musical revues, and *Heimatfilme*, and declared a state of cinematic crisis. Detractors ridiculed the "swollen Teutonic heroism, Gretchen romanticism, and little Moritz sentimentalism" of postwar production and regretted filmmakers' partiality to studio shots, ignorance of symbolism, and predilection for heavy-handed musical scores. Over the next few years, complaints about the quality of domestic films escalated, and the *Heimatfilm* became emblematic of all that was wrong with West German cinema.[1]

Criticism was fueled by disappointment at how rapidly West German film betrayed its initial promise. Some of the best postwar German films had been the earliest; and these seemed to draw inspiration from critically respected European filmmaking traditions rather than the commercial formulas of UFA or Hollywood. The very first postwar attempt, Wolfgang Staudte's *Die Mörder sind unter uns* (*The Murderers Are among Us*, 1946), held out the hope of a reinvigorated German style. Set against the backdrop of the Berlin ruins and filmed in black-and-white with heavy shadowing, Staudte's film had none of the polish of the earlier UFA productions. Rather, it appeared to be a nearly involuntary—and artistically fortuitous—merging of Italian neorealism and Weimar expressionism,[2] for the surreal, symbolic setting was no studio construction but the dramatic remnants of the recent war. Moreover, it attempted social commentary by grappling with themes like despair, physical and psychic survival, and moral bankruptcy.[3] Indeed, *Mörder* was the first of a number of early productions that came to be known as *Trümmerfilme*, or rubble films. Although it was made under a Soviet license, *Mörder* received positive critical reviews and did well at the box office in all zones. But the gritty realism of *Trümmerfilme* soon wore thin, and German audiences began to demand films that corresponded more to their fantasies than mundane social realities. By early 1948, the genre was bust.

The problem, then, was not merely the lack of creativity among German filmmakers but the film-viewing preferences of the West German public. As film professionals liked to point out, their hands were tied by the demands of a national audience that was becoming progressively younger and more feminized. One well-known German critic observed that while "youth prefer crime films, Westerns, revue films and the like; . . . the generally less-demanding female audience is led by emotion in its need to be moved and 'elevated,' and prefers to consume principally sentimental and . . . kitschy subjects (for the most part in color); whereas viewers *masculini generis* are more critically disposed (. . . less bent on color . . .), and incline more to serious material—these symptoms shouldn't be taken to hold for Germany alone."[4] National cinematic culture was understood to be suffering from the effects of the shoddy taste of a consumer group that was not sufficiently cultured—not sufficiently "masculine," that is—in its critical faculties. The problem, moreover, was not specific to Hitler's former pupils but stemmed from the fact that German audiences were beginning to display the same behavior as other modern Western publics. This, critics anticipated, would result in an ongoing decline in the quality of the domestic product and an increasing interest in the international—and especially the internationalizing American—product.

Film histories published through the present consistently tell the story of West German cinema as an extension of World War II, describing military defeat as merely the prelude to a much more serious cultural emasculation by Hollywood. Hollywood's thrust into the West German market, it has been claimed, stunted the development of a native national cinema by monopolizing domestic screentime, shutting West German films out of the international (and especially European) market, and colonizing the consciousness of West German citizens by transforming them into American-style consumers. Thus, film consumption habits were understood to have implications for the cultural recovery and cultural integrity of the new democratic German nation.

Without attempting to construct a new narrative, I would like to draw upon some recent theorizing about film spectatorship in order to question this interpretation. In the process, we will need to consider both actual postwar film-viewing behavior in West Germany through the mid-1950s and the meanings it may have had for postwar German identity. Rather than facilely assuming an appalling lack of taste among postwar German audiences, I will begin by taking another look at that most popular—if most critically ridiculed—genre of the *Heimatfilm* in order to investigate possible reasons for its immense audience loyalty and to assess its cultural significance. In doing so, I follow the lead of Janet Staiger, who suggested that "what we are interested in . . . is not a so-called correct reading of a particular film but the range of possible readings and reading processes at particular moments and their relation . . . to groups of historical spectators."[5]

The following discussion, then, is intended to be suggestive rather than exhaustive. The point of this somewhat inexact exercise is to puzzle out the meanings that German audiences attached to their consumption of films and to speculate on the relation of film viewing to both the process of identity construction and the historical context that framed audiences' lives.

Since its modern incarnation in the late nineteenth century, "Heimat" has served as an "integrative symbol" that "endowed the nation with continuity and causality": a shared past, that is, and shared meaning. *Heimat* celebrates the local, the mundane, the domestic; it refers to geographical place of birth but also the peculiar landscape, dialect, customs, and traditions attached to that locality. As such, it has a strong emotional component, since it is invested with all of the sentimental content of one's childhood. Encompassing both communal and personal identity, it denotes homeland, home, and hearth—with all of their myriad meanings and emotional associations.[6]

Contrasted with the masculine and martial connotations of "fatherland" and "nation," then, *Heimat* represents a feminized communal ideal. As Alon Confino has suggested, Fatherland or Nation "could go to war, while *Heimat* could never do that. *Heimat* was something one fought for, never something that participated in battle." Since the turn of the century, *Heimat* was imagined as the sentimental separate sphere that offered "respite from everyday social and political conflicts" by Germans from both ends of the political spectrum.[7]

By its very definition, then, *Heimat* was something that could—and would—survive political fluctuations and military defeat. Indeed, the decade after World War II witnessed the penning of a plethora of paeans to *Heimat*. As one contemporary commented, "One cannot speak enough of Heimat: it is something like heaven, a nonrational, deep soulfulness." Not a place, "neither mountain nor valley, . . . tree nor hill," but a "rootedness in the earth," "it is . . . the original comfort from which all else flows. . . . So let the world do as it will—the Heimat loves and confirms you without question, as its child."[8]

Symbolizing the unchanging, "essential," even spiritual, German nation, *Heimat* became a central cultural construct in the early postwar period. At once consoling, forgiving, and rehabilitative, as Celia Applegate has emphasized in her book on the subject, it was used to facilitate the messy process of political and moral reconstruction. "Pulled out of the rubble of the Nazi Reich as a victim, not a perpetrator," it was designated the bedrock upon which the new democratic German nation would be based, as evidenced in a remarkable speech that was given in the early 1946 Landrat of Rhineland-Pfalz:

> Out of destruction and want and disgrace and guilt we have saved one thing: our glowing heart for *Heimat*! . . . It lies here before us: wineland and tilled land, mountain and valley and stream, cities and villages, all bleeding from many wounds, torn apart by thousands of scars. . . . Hatred, injustice, revenge, force, terror, sycophancy, and knavery have all passed over us, but of one thing we can be sure, we did not betray our *Heimat*—in our hearts we resisted. And our *Heimat* will expiate our sins. . . . Heart, soul, *Heimat*, your best sons stand before you, caught up in your distress, laboring and creating with you, suffering and sacrificing with you, rising with you out of destruction to the rights of humanity. People of my *Heimat*, I call to you, hand to hand, heart to heart, victim to victim, hope to hope, love to love, with belief in the highest good: democracy and freedom for our Pfalzer *Heimat*.

Thus, *Heimat*, according to Applegate, "came to embody the political and social community that could be salvaged from the Nazi ruins."[9]

After 1945, *Heimat* represented a new political and cultural orientation, and *Heimatfilme*, too, seemed to serve as social and psychic balm. As one study on the film genre argued, "This rural cinematic *Heimat*-idyll became to some extent a substitute for . . . fatherland and nation, after both concepts were misused by national socialism." Public presentation of the beauty of the German countryside, color shots panning the distinctive natural treasures of the provinces, reassured West Germans that their "new state was not all that bad"; "the sight of this idyll made the audience proud of their *Heimat*, which was enormously consoling even for those who lived in the cities. The *Heimatfilm* made it easier for *Bundesdeutschen* to make a real home [*Heimat*] out of the provisional Federal Republic."[10] *Heimat* solved two postwar dilemmas with great economy: it provided an affirmative representation of the German nation and at the same time jettisoned the unsavory aspects of the German past. Given the postwar political climate, the immense popularity of the *Heimatfilm* through the mid-1950s should surprise no one.

The *Heimatfilm* offered the German public escape on a number of levels.

First, and perhaps foremost, it provided temporary relief through entertainment and visual spectacle. *Heimatfilme* were produced, after all, for the commercial market; and the overwhelming success of the first issues meant that films like Hans Deppe's *Schwarzwaldmädel* (*Black Forest Girl*, 1950) and *Grün ist die Heide* (*Green Is the Heath*, 1951) established the standards and contours of the cinematic genre. What is perhaps most striking to the contemporary viewer is the odd presence of visual "excess" that does nothing to advance the plot. In the 1951 film, *Grün ist die Heide*, for example, the audience is treated to an extended sequence filmed inside the circus big top, complete with clowns, comedy routines, acrobats, magicians, and animal acts. In this case, performance really does become little more than pleasurable distraction—from both the problems internal to the film's plot and those more pressing concerns located outside the walls of the cinema.

Heimatfilme also showcased musical performance; indeed, no film was complete without a handful of traditional *Volkslieder* and sentimental hits, which were simultaneously marketed on radio and records. The ever-present folk songs served to cement the bonds of the cinematic community or celebrate the budding romance of the leading stars and thus played a more integral role in the narrative. Folk songs appear as a part of oral tradition, passed from generation to generation according to a cyclical calendar of local celebration. Thus, they underscored the idea that *Heimat* grew out of a historic cultural heritage grounded in affective ties of matrimony, family, and community. At the same time, however, many *Heimatfilme*, like the 1950 production *Schwarzwaldmädel*, employed popular Nazi-era film stars and cinematic conventions (the musical and operetta) and spawned marketable melodies to seal their commercial success. Through their sentimental content and modern form, then, *Heimatfilme* allowed audiences to indulge in nostalgia—or fantasy—about a happier communal or individual past by simultaneously affirming cultural traditions forged across a hazy *longue durée* and recalling the personal pleasures of film spectatorship during the Third Reich.

Although they drew on popular commercial film forms, stars, and notions of community marketed during the Third Reich, these films did not mark a simple reversion to Nazi filmmaking tradition. Rather, they prepared for the future by celebrating a depoliticized local past; by taming, displacing, or destroying a criminal or ailing past, personalized in the form of an aging masculinity and psychologized as unmastered memory; and by reinventing models of youthful femininity and masculinity charged with reinvigorating Germany and reorienting it toward a democratic and prosperous future.

While stressing the interplay between past and present, *Heimatfilme* are nonetheless riddled with gaps, ellipses, and silences. They emphasize history and tradition but only in its vaguest form; they contain few specific references to the more recent national past, yet such references are not completely absent. *Heimatfilme* never mention politics and are stone silent on national socialism, yet allusions to the war do appear (albeit in the most oblique form) in a couple of the most popular films.

In *Grün ist die Heide*, for example, the action revolves around a dutiful daughter, Helga Lüdersen (played by Sonja Ziemann), and her father, Lüder Lüdersen (Hans Stüwe), a former Pomeranian landowner, who have been driven west by the war. They have taken up residence in their relative's country manor on the unscarred Lüneburger Heide and are trying to adjust to their new *Heimat* when the film opens. The father vastly complicates the process of assimilation by his uncontrollable compulsion to hunt deer, the one aspect of his past life that he is unable to surrender. In their new homeland, hunting is prohibited, and Lüdersen is tracked through the woods to the manor by the new forester, Walter Rainer (Rudolf Prack), who promptly falls in love with Lüdersen's daughter.

The war, then, is part of an unportrayed past. Like a natural catastrophe, it has no author but unsettling repercussions: the unexplained loss of Helga's mother, the blow to the Pomeranian patriarch's privilege and identity, the need to accept a new authority, new laws, and a new life. The war's aftershocks need to be weathered and the nonnative male self needs to be disciplined to insure the reemergence of social and emotional equilibrium. Indeed, toward the end of the film, after Walter gains evidence of Lüdersen's poaching but refrains from reporting the older man for his daughter's sake, Lüdersen's farewell speech at a local festival indicates that he is nearing the end of his struggle, that he is well on his way to mastering his unruly self:

> My dear friends, allow me to say a few words before I take leave of you. . . . I speak not for me alone, but for the many others who have found a second home [*Heimat*] here among you. I will never forget the days I was allowed to be with you in the *Heide*, in the *Heide* that has also become my second home.
>
> Do not be too hard on the people who have fled to you. Whoever has not been compelled to leave his home cannot know what it means to be without one [*Heimatlos*]. I know that we also have not always been as we should. But we have been most severely punished.
>
> When I was in the forest here, often I felt as if I were at home again. The natural beauty comforted me and made me forget what I have lost.
>
> I was close to losing myself. But through the goodwill and understanding you have shown me, I have found myself again.
>
> I thank you. I thank you from the bottom of my heart for all of the good things you have permitted me to know.

Helga Lüdersen (Sonja Ziemann) and Walter Rainer (Rudolf Prack) on the Lüneburger Heide in Hans Deppe's *Grün ist die Heide*. (Courtesy of the Stiftung Deutsche Kinemathek, Berlin)

Lüdersen's postwar experience necessitated a rediscovery of self, which was facilitated by the compassion and acceptance extended him by the locals. Indeed, Lüdersen's speech repackages German refugees—like himself—as the war's true victims, in need of forbearance and understanding.

Yet Lüdersen's status does not suffer too much in his new *Heimat;* he inhabits a new landed estate with nearly absentee owners, and the film shows him greeted with respect and friendship by the local dignitaries at their weekly *Stammtisch.* Thus, in this film, as in other *Heimatfilme*, the real problems involved in the assimilation of the refugee millions in West Germany—material destitution, social and political conflicts, mutual resentments—go unthematized.[11] Lüdersen's words serve as a not-so-subtle sermon of social reconciliation to both groups. And although "Lüdersen the Nonnative" must submit to the cultural and legal norms of his new *Heimat*, "Lüdersen the Man" is redeemed by his noble spirit and heroic action (as he is shot in the last minutes of the film pursuing a criminal on the heath). Ultimately, then, the success of postwar reconstruction depends on a test of male character. Fortunately, in this case, after much vacillation, it appears to hold up.

In fact, a specific sort of male character emerges in these (and other popular) films as the ideal type for the German romantic lead—the man, that is, who will take Germany into the future. Like the forester, Walter Rainer, the ideal German has a code of honor. He is law-abiding to a point but not to a fault. In *Grün ist die Heide*, Walter resists having Lüdersen arrested for poaching out of concern for the shame it will bring Helga. Instead, he is satisfied when Helga promises to leave the province and move to the city with her as yet undisciplined father. Thus, the dilemma is solved, and Walter avoids becoming yet another unfeeling civil servant "just following orders." A bit of legal latitude goes a long way after national socialism, and Walter is intended to be perceived as a principled humanitarian, a man with a heart—something that signals his difference from the Nazi film hero. Moreover, the film suggests that principled behavior has its price: in allowing the pair to leave, Walter will be sacrificing his chance for a life with his beloved Helga.

Other films were even bolder in resurrecting a moral masculinity, explicitly referring to the recent German past. Hans Wolff's *Am Brunnen vor dem Tore* (*At the Fountain near the City Gate*), a popular *Heimatfilm* from the 1951–52 season also starring Sonja Ziemann, introduces us first to the character of Kurt Kramer (Paul Klinger), who generously shares his lunchtime bowl of soup with a few wandering minstrel-tramps (Hans Richter, Kurt Reimann, and Ludwig Schmitz) when they stop by his gas station on the outskirts of scenic Dinkelsbühl. A few scenes later, Kurt assists a mysterious young man who appears at his shop, pens a letter, and begs Kurt to deliver it to an Inge Bachner (Sonja Ziemann). Kurt complies out of compassion for the man's evident state of desperation, meets Inge, and pledges, at her inexplicable request, to tell no one of his encounter with the young man. Kurt fulfills his pledge admirably; when the police show up at his station sometime later to inquire about the young man, he pleads ignorance and returns to tell Inge. Only then does she reveal that the mystery man is her brother (Fritz Kösling), wrongly accused of art theft, who is trying to avoid arrest. Kurt comforts the distraught damsel-in-distress and promises assistance. This he provides above and beyond the call of duty over the course of the film—even after Inge resumes her engagement to a British pilot (Fritz Wagner) whom she met during the occupation but subsequently lost contact with when he returned home.

The love triangle, then, has national-political complications and is played out in a most interesting way. To begin with, the young men never overtly compete for Inge's affections. In fact, until the very end, Robert, the British pilot, has no idea that Kurt is in love with his fiancée because Kurt's sense of honor will not allow him to make his emotions clear to either Robert or Inge. The reason for his silence is the bond of friendship Kurt feels for Robert. When we first see Robert, he too has stumbled upon Kurt's station and stops for gas. The shop, however, is empty; Kurt is nowhere to be seen, and Robert's eyes are drawn to the wall, where a broken propeller blade is mounted. Kurt enters, and an intent

Robert questions him about the blade. Is it from a fighter? Yes, answers Kurt, an English Spitfire. Where did it come from? How did he get possession of it? Kurt shrugs off the questions, saying, "Oh, it's a long story," but Robert insists. Kurt matter-of-factly relates that on his twenty-fifth mission he fired on a British fighter that went down. He landed his plane next to it and could see that the pilot was unconscious, so he pulled him from the burning craft. Did he know what happened to the pilot? Well, he heard he was brought to a hospital and recovered fully. At this point, Robert urges Kurt to look closely at him. "I," announces Robert, "am that pilot. And I've been searching for you all over." He heartily thanks Kurt for saving his life (who responds demurely that "it was nothing") and invites him for a celebration that evening.

In this remarkable and understated scene, the German pilot is redeemed as the unsung hero, a humble guardian of human life who returns to a modest living after the war. The experience of the war becomes the glue that seals their friendship, since no one sees fit to point out that Kurt could save Robert only because he shot him down in the first place. Kurt is congratulated on displaying compassion within the context of an impersonal war. The exchange between Robert and Kurt suggests that the hostilities were not, after all, personal, since they are not mentioned beyond the fact of the attack. The rescue, however, he performed as a man, and Kurt appears all the more likable because he is clearly an unboastful, reluctant hero.

Moreover, Kurt has a tragic edge, which imparts moral weight to his character. The evening of their chance meeting, the two go to Inge's inn to celebrate its opening and meet Robert's fiancée. Kurt is crestfallen to realize that Inge is his friend's intended, and he suffers silently through the festivities. Robert, however, senses neither his friend's nor Inge's sorrow at the renewed engagement and smiles naively throughout. Kurt's personal suffering only deepens his compassion, which he later exercises in response to Inge's considerably older third suitor, Herr Straaten (Hans Stüwe).

In offering audiences a new model of moral masculinity, *Heimatfilme* tended to set the romantic hero against an older rival for the desired woman's affections. Thus, the past reasserts itself in the form of this older male character, whose romantic interest in the younger woman is invariably portrayed as fundamentally misguided or naive. In *Brunnen*, Straaten, a local notable, returns to his opulent house from vacation in Italy to be informed by his housekeeper that Inge—who had been staying with them while her inn was used by British occupation officials—has taken repossession of her property. Straaten visits Inge at the inn, shows her a picture of a villa he has rented in Italy, and invites her to accompany him there for a vacation. She declines, explaining that she belongs in the inn, which she needs to ready for reopening. Straaten watches warily as Inge's friendship with Kurt develops and later mourns the news that Robert has returned to renew his engagement with her. In a scene at Straaten's house, we learn that the jealous older suitor had intercepted Robert's letters to Inge from England, which had led Inge to conclude that their engagement was off. Moreover, some sleuthing by Kurt uncovers the fact that the seemingly noble Straaten perpetrated the art theft unjustly attributed to Inge's brother. When confronted, Straaten confesses to Kurt, who is incensed that the older man would intentionally cause Inge such pain. But Kurt becomes compassionate as Straaten urges his accuser to look closely at the stolen portrait, which bears an uncanny resemblance to Inge. Straaten explains he was driven to possess the painting because it reminded him of Inge, who in turn resembles his beloved dead wife! His compulsive and dishonest behavior, then, was the result of an overwhelming emotional need to regain the irretrievable past.

Besides the fact of his age and nostalgic longing, Straaten is associated with the past in another way. After confessing to the crime, he begs Kurt to give him one more hour of freedom, after which he will return to his house to face arrest. Kurt accepts him at his word, and the older man hurries to the town festival, which dramatizes the city's rescue from destruction during the Thirty Years' War, when a local daughter led the town's children to the Swedish general to beg for mercy. Glimpsing a pleading child that reminded him of his dead son, the Swede embraced the boy and ordered the city spared. Thus, the festival was an annual ritual of thanksgiving for the survival of the community. Straaten, who was shown in an earlier scene both explaining and choreographing the drama, hurries to the town center and unexpectedly assumes the role of the Swedish general. Entering on horseback through the city gates, Straaten is confronted by Inge, shepherding a mass of children. After listening to her heartfelt plea, Straaten abruptly alters the script and lifts the startled Inge to meet his lips in a tender kiss. Releasing her, he gallops off and returns home, where Kurt awaits him. Excusing himself one last time, Straaten exits the room and we hear a gunshot. In a last redeeming move, he dispatches himself and his criminal past.

Thus, Straaten makes amends first symbolically, then sacrificially. Indeed, his performance at the festival anticipates his ultimate action. He saves the community a second time in its history by both embodying and destroying its problematic past. His kiss with Inge is at once an expression of his unrequited yearning, a farewell, and a plea for forgiveness. His suicide becomes the noble action that expiates the sins of the father, as the sound of his gunshot is drowned out by a drumroll that draws the visual focus away from his personal tragedy and back to the festival, where the parade is under way. And at that moment, Straaten tellingly evaporates along with his act; the film chronicles neither the announcement of nor the reaction to his death. There are no messy remnants, no repercussions, no need to examine the meaning of the act; the past simply and mercifully disappears.

Straaten represents an imperfect and aging masculinity that needs to be surmounted. The past is thus depoliticized and "softened" into a personal failing, a generational miscalculation. Straaten's tragic flaw is that he had no feel for what was appropriate to the present. He had outlived his time; he could not adapt, forget, move on. He had to pass into the past to liberate the present.

Yet the *Heimatfilm* offered audiences more than just the romantic triumph of the "son" and a new generation of moral masculinity; it also recognized the pathos involved in release from the past, which may account for its popularity with older viewers.[12] Even when the older man does not die—as in the smash hit comedy, *Schwarzwaldmädel*, in which an elderly Black Forest *Kapellmeister* (choir director/composer) is rejuvenated when Bärbel, a young woman from Baden-Baden, becomes his temporary housekeeper—the moment of realization that his affections have been inappropriate and misplaced is one of poignancy, not humor. Moreover, this moment again coincides with a local festival. This time, however, the old man (Paul Hörbiger) is encouraged by another of his generation to "come, sit with us old folks; we'll watch the young people dance." After a shot of the enchanting Bärbel (again played by Sonja Ziemann) dancing with the young artist, Hans (Rudolf Prack), the camera moves in for a medium close-up of the seated old man. With a downturned head and a sorrowful expression, he slowly begins to sing: "You can ponder it for a long time, but then your heart will break." Thus, the generational eclipse is portrayed as personally painful but necessary; the past must be cleared away—or at least set aside—before the present can thrive unencumbered.

Studies of *Heimatfilme* have commented on the recurrent theme of male generational conflict, but as yet no attention has been paid to the related phenomena of father-daughter relationships or the problem of the missing mother. *Heimatfilme* of the early 1950s focused on the romantic or familial dilemma of an attractive yet compassionate young virgin who enlivens and inspires her elderly admirers. In *Grün ist die Heide*, Helga fills in for her missing mother and remains steadfast in her commitment to her wayward father, even when his behavior threatens social expulsion and dashed romantic hopes. The daughter must bridge the gap between past and future; she must convince her father to surrender his past privileges to become an equal member of the new democratic community. In *Schwarzwaldmädel*, Bärbel's entry into the *Kapellmeister's* household—to fill in as housekeeper while her spinster aunt takes a rare vacation—is set against a prior, comic scene in which the domineering aunt interrupts the composer's work and his beloved cigar smoking with her incessant, overzealous cleaning. Bärbel, in contrast, transfixes the *Kapellmeister* with her fresh beauty, hums through her light tidying, and inspires him to interrupt work on a hymn to play a waltz on his piano, which provokes her to dance. Characters like Bärbel are loyal, nonjudgmental caretakers, and their youth releases them of responsibility for the past, although not initially for their older charges. As midwives to the future, Bärbel and Helga promise a fresh start. They embody youthful energy and joyfulness and are soft and vulnerable nurturers. Uniting the desirable with the maternal, they spark an optimism for the future in a way that tired old mothers could not.

This characterization carried over to popular films outside the genre as well. Josef von Baky's *Das doppelte Löttchen* (*Little Lotty Times Two*, 1950), which was written by Erich Kästner and awarded the first Federal Film Prize (Bundesfilmpreis) in 1951, opens *Heimat*-style with shots of an unnamed Bavarian lake and mountains but soon settles on an institution for girls nestled among the natural grandeur. A home for war orphans? No; rather, a resort, to which the overresponsible little Lotty (Jutta Günther) has been sent by her mother (Antje Weisgerber) to learn to be a child again. There Lotty stumbles upon her unknown identical twin (Isa Günther), who lives with their well-meaning but self-absorbed composer-father (Peter Mosbacher), and the girls hatch a plan to switch identities so they can each meet the unknown half of their former parental pair. Inevitably, of course, the diligent daughter makes an emotional home for her father and weans him from his destructive devotion to self-indulgent self-expression (both artistic and sexual). In the end, he reunites with his wife, not because of any apparent rekindled attraction to the struggling working mother but because of his unintended devotion to his little Lotty, whose efforts on behalf of her father reduce her to a state of physical and emotional collapse. Disruption was not political but familial and was due not to a war of aggression but to the personal and professional hubris of the father. Thus, the film leads us on a fantastic journey from an untouched, scenic *Heimat* to the reconstructed security of *Heim*, where the devoted daughter could first save the sinful father and then regain her childlike innocence.

The nature of this much-thematized girlish femininity merits a closer look. In the tellingly titled *Schwarzwaldmädel*, when we first spy Bärbel, she is wearing a charming dirndl. She is not, however, in the Black Forest village but at a masquerade party in the resort town, Baden-Baden, where, we later learn, she works in a jeweler's shop. At the masquerade, she bumps into the artist, Hans, who upsets a basket of apples she carries. Bending to help her collect the fruit, Hans asks, "Are these real [*echt*]?" The answer is that they are, and so, of course, is she—*ein echtes Mädel aus dem Schwarzwald*, whom the cosmopolitan and ennui-ridden Hans immediately falls for. But before this match can be made, he has to extricate himself from an ongoing, uninspired relationship with Malwina (Gretl Schörg), a well-known singer and entertainer who draws male admirers like flies to honey. One admirer is a jeweler, Bärbel's boss, who tries to impress Malwina by loaning her an expensive piece of jewelry to wear in her act. In this case, the accessory—like its wearer—is not *echt*, which helps precipitate a good-natured romp to the Black Forest and the jealous Malwina's futile struggle to win back her beau.

Bärbel is contrasted with both the elderly aunt and the flirtatious, sophisticated singer and shines in comparison. She is earnest and sweet—a breath of fresh air, whether in the well-scrubbed village home or in the resort nightclub. She makes the *Kapellmeister* feel young again, brings joy to his household, and sparks long-abandoned hopes for romance. As he shows her the contents of the small *Heimatmuseum* he has assembled, he takes a traditional woman's headdress from the case. This, he says, will be worn by the "bride" in the upcoming festival, and in a gesture that betrays his swelling emotions, he begins to place the bonnet on her head. Bärbel represents the promise of regeneration. But as the *Kapellmeister's* action is interrupted by the unexpected arrival of the town's mayor, the film foreshadows the fact that this will not be the tale of this particular man's personal renewal. His time, we learn later at the festival, has passed.

Bärbel's promise of regeneration is, instead, communal. After a series of comic episodes and miscommunications that cause her to leave the village, she does, indeed, return to the Schwarzwald. Moreover, her portrait by Hans becomes the basis for a poster that advertises the village festival, where she, ultimately, is crowned festival bride. Pure and genuine, she symbolizes the very essence of *Heimat* and (like Inge in *Am Brunnen vor dem Tore*) becomes the center of a communal celebration of tradition, renewal, and optimism. Moreover, her image, fixed not only on paper but also on Hans's mind, draws him back to the Schwarzwald as well. His return to *Heimat*, then, becomes a quest to retrieve Bärbel and the values she embodies.

This film is, however, no wholehearted paean to provincialism. In fact, the innkeeper who changes hats to become mayor at one moment and police chief the next, draws chuckles due to his jealous monopoly on authority in the tiny community and his energetic efforts to marry off his daughter to the wealthy jeweler from the city. The trappings of *Heimat* are not fully immune from merrymaking, for although the *Heimatmuseum* is the site of Bärbel's and Hans's first kiss, it is also associated with the *Kapellmeister's* misplaced affections and the jeweler's comic transvestite transformation into an elderly female villager. Finally, although we first meet Bärbel in the more cosmopolitan Baden-Baden, she nonetheless beats out the dutiful (but comically diminutive, shrill-voiced, and barrel-bodied) daughter of the local innkeeper as festival bride.

Thus, it seems, the *Heimatfilm* was neither an exhortation to return to the past nor to simple village life. In fact, Bärbel is rewarded for her *echt* nature before she even leaves the masquerade in Baden-Baden, when the raffle ticket that Hans has bought her wins her the party's grand prize: a shiny red Ford! It is in this very Ford that she sets out for the provinces of the Black Forest. And in

Bärbel (Sonja Ziemann) wins a red Ford convertible in Hans Deppe's *Schwarzwaldmädel*. (Courtesy of the Stiftung Deutsche Kinemathek, Berlin)

case we are unsure about what to make of this pricey acquisition, we are offered a shot of her gray-haired Hausfrau-landlady bubbling over with excitement at Bärbel's good fortune, as she wishes her tenant a good trip. Moreover, it is behind the wheel of the Ford, with the convertible top down and the *Kapell-meister* in tow, that Bärbel first charms his heart—to the tune of a waltz on the radio. This, then, was the desired postwar German woman: a portrait of female vitality that could straddle the past and the future, that could speak to—and reconcile—both.

Heimatfilme suggested to female audiences that their role in German regeneration did not necessitate a return to their mothers' lives. In fact, they were feted for being somehow different, and better. They could run an inn, work in a jewelry store, enjoy desired goods, and travel and still not capitulate to materialism or allow it to distract them from what was truly important. Bärbel's car quietly disappears from view after it has worked its magic by transforming her into a modern woman sporting traditional values. Moreover, when Bärbel and Hans finally embrace in dance at the end of the festival (and the film), we never question that it will result in matrimony and never doubt that they will return to Baden-Baden. Thus, these films assure us that *Heimat* is something you carry with you—provided you remain within national boundaries. In *Am Brun-*

Popular Cinema, Spectatorship, and Identity 161

nen vor dem Tore, for example, Inge is greeted by a returned Robert, bearing gifts in the form of an expensive necklace and the promise of a life in England "fit for a queen." Although she accepts the former, in the end she opts for the love of the handsome but humble homegrown hero, who can offer her only a modest nosegay of violets, his hard work, and his heart.

Bärbel and Inge seem to be driven by an inner force that draws them to—and keeps them within—the embrace of *Heimat.* In *Grün ist die Heide,* the dramatic tension derives from the imminent danger that this bond will be broken. Helga fears forcible rejection from the community that has become her new home because of her father's compulsive, illegal behavior. But Helga's yearning for home and *Heimat* is set against the response of her girlhood friend, Nora von Buckwitz (Maria Holst), who arrives one day with the traveling circus and meets Helga by chance in the pharmacy where she works. Nora is a charming and attractive woman whose classy equestrian act is clearly out of place among the circus clowns and acrobats. But her stint there is temporary; she will leave Germany for the United States at the earliest possible date. Soon it becomes clear that her cultivated happy-go-lucky attitude and determination to flee Germany are the brave facade of an emotionally numbed woman who has lost everything in the war and is afraid to invest any sentiment in place or community again. Throughout the film, she is genially pursued by the local judge (Willy Fritsch), who, with charm and candor, tries to persuade her to establish emotional roots in the verdant soil of the Lüneburger Heide. She smiles through his pleas but insists on going, an independent streak and spunky show of will that enhance both the strength of her character and our admiration. In the end, of course, she remains. A fall from her horse in the last dramatic moments of the film results in a leg injury that delays her trip and, we suspect, allows the engaging judge just enough time to persuade her to stay for good. Thus, fate, turning bad fortune to good, permits her to follow her heart without injury to her pride. Both Fritsch's character and the film take for granted that Nora is part of the *Heimat* and that she carries it inside her, whether she is willing to extend that fact conscious recognition or not. Emigration, then, appears not as a political choice but as a psychological state of denial that would have dreadful emotional consequences for the emigrant as well as those left behind.

Through the early 1950s, *Heimatfilme* included gestures of sensitivity to postwar emotions of nostalgia, loss, and personal pain. Like their youthful heroines, these films were good-natured in their treatment of flawed characters, all of whom were likable because they were fundamentally good at heart. None was intentionally hurtful; evil was psychologized and forgiven; deceit and deception were diagnosed as due to unhealed psychic wounds.

Thus, viewers would find no condemnation here. *Heimatfilme* recognized that the present contains traces of the past, but these traces were never overtly political. *Heimatfilme* focused on the postwar healing process but confined it to an emotional or spiritual exercise and doled out sympathy in generous portions. *Heimatfilme* constructed no Manichaean moral universe; rather, they offered consolation, compassion, and the prospect of reconciliation and inclusion.

"It still astounds," wrote one commentator on the *Heimatfilm*, "how quickly these films found their audience of millions despite the competition from Hollywood."[13] But I have tried to suggest that their commercial success was the outgrowth of a particular time and form of address. After all, the *Heimatfilm* could—and did—address German audiences as potential consumers, but Hollywood never addressed German audiences as Germans, with reference to their national past, present, or future.

Through the early 1950s, in fact, German films—both new productions and rereleases from the Weimar and Nazi periods—surpassed Hollywood and European imports in popularity on the West German market. Nearly 70 percent of those polled in 1951 preferred German entertainment films of any vintage, compared to 17 percent who opted for American, 8 percent for British, 5 percent for French, and 2 percent for Italian films. As late as mid-decade, one study that focused on film attendance in a "middling city of 30,000" noted that the average adult audience exhibited limited interest in foreign films, preferring to attend an unknown German film over any import. And in polls conducted through 1956, the *Heimatfilm* led the list of favorite film genres.[14]

Heimatfilme, like their Hollywood counterparts, held out a fantasy of the future. They showed what a German *Wohlstandsgesellschaft*, or prosperous society, would look like "long before it became reality for the broad German public." In these films, unlike in real life, housing, clothing, and food were never the object of concern. *Schwarzwaldmädel, Grün ist die Heide*, and *Am Brunnen vor dem Tore* all featured worlds unencumbered by material want, in which the begging of musical vagabonds is politely and generously answered with free food, beer, and social acceptance. In this case, mendicancy is romanticized as a life-style choice,[15] and the freedom of the road becomes a metaphor for self-realization in the developing democracy of plenty.

Through the mid-1950s, *Heimatfilme* enticed millions of German viewers with a vision of the future in which Germans could regain both their prosperity and their pride. *Heimatfilme* guaranteed personal and national redemption, forgiveness and forgetfulness. They therefore offered the postwar German viewer something that Hollywood films could not.

Although the *Heimatfilm* was considered family entertainment, anecdotal and industry sources suggest that German women were especially keen fans of the genre.[16] A generic breakdown of audience demographics is unavailable;

nevertheless, women may have been attracted to the genre for several reasons. Women, after all, were posited as the libidinal center of the *Heimatfilm*'s universe; they were the vortex around which all action, concern, and fantasy swirled. Yet they were no mere objects of desire; they received both recognition and credit for their efforts at caretaking, were lauded for their loyalty and strength, and drew sympathy for their contributions on the home and work fronts. The three *Heimatfilme* under discussion all shared a common feature: a working woman who struggled to construct a life as well as a home, who was as strong-willed and determined as she was sweet—and whose men noticed and admired this state of affairs. Moreover, the films rehabilitated the German man as an attentive, sensitive, and compassionate mate and suggested that he could provide a stable home life in the midst of an anxiety-ridden (and divorce-prone) reality. *Heimatfilme* may well have appealed to women's romantic and consumerist fantasies, but they also must have appealed to their need for recognition and security. And women doubtlessly found no cause for complaint in the fact that their celluloid counterparts were celebrated as the genuine basis for the postwar moral and social order.

The *Heimatfilm*, in its peculiar postwar form, emerged and peaked at a specific historical moment—during a period of political and economic uncertainty and emotional and social upheaval. In 1950, the year of *Schwarzwaldmädel's* release, the unemployment rate stood at 11 percent and refugees constituted almost 17 percent of the population of the country. When interest in the genre (and movie attendance in general) began its gradual decline in 1956, the unemployment rate was under 4 percent, wages had increased 66 to 75 percent over their 1950 levels (freeing most households from destitution for the first time in German history), the five-day work week had been instituted, and consumer goods like refrigerators, vacuum cleaners, washing machines, phonographs, and cameras were making their way into German homes. The *Wohlstandsgesellschaft* was becoming a reality. Indeed, *Heimatfilme* themselves seemed to change with the times; those produced after mid-decade struck some as little more than advertisements for domestic tourist destinations.[17]

The heyday of *Heimatfilme* indicates that the American film product dominated neither the West German market nor the consciousness of most German consumers through the mid-1950s. Yet the national picture tells us little about the diversity of film viewing and its manifold meanings. We can gain some insight into this by taking a closer look at the German market, which, like most modern commercial markets, was segregated according to class and education, generation and gender.

After currency reform and the return of commercial distribution in 1948, the German film industry claimed to detect a noticeable shift in consumer behavior. Since money was now valuable—hence scarcer—Germans "stopped going to the flicks and started attending films," as one industry insider put it. Germans, that is, began making informed choices about the films they saw and demanded a certain level of quality. This led to fears that Hollywood would dominate the German market, since after 1948, with profits convertible to hard currency, annual American imports more than doubled and Hollywood began to send quality features like *The Best Years of Our Lives* and *Gone with the Wind*. Concern about audience attrition intensified when surveys showed that consumer choice appeared to be linked to educational and social status. One 1951 poll registered that while 60 percent of viewers from the lowest educational level preferred German films, only 50 percent of those with "mid-level" education and 33 percent of "highly educated" Germans expressed the same preference.[18]

Producers' nervousness was fueled by what they identified as a marked shift in the class composition of the cinema audience. Industry insiders noted an increase in attendance by the newly "pauperized" educated classes as well as those of higher socioeconomic standing. Doctors, lawyers, civil servants, white-collar workers, and university students who had, until recently, preferred the theater were now lured to the cinema as much by the engaging programs as by the cheaper admission price. These groups also constituted a large proportion of the audience for quality American films. They should not be classified too readily as willing subjects for cultural Americanization, however, for although they were avid consumers of quality films, they exhibited no firm preference for any particular national product.[19] After Hitler, in fact, cinematic cosmopolitanism became the mark of an enlightened new German who was seeking to shed the chauvinism of a shameful past.

With the first signs of economic recovery, film consumption became more deeply conditioned by generation and gender. Although the most frequent filmgoers were under the age of forty, the most faithful spectators for Hollywood films were young and male. In mid-sized cities and smaller towns, young men between the ages of eighteen and thirty—who by the mid-1950s had increasing amounts of leisure time and disposable income—dominated the audiences of the late show on Saturday, which typically featured Hollywood Westerns, crime films, and "sensational" films. The same shows would often be screened at Sunday matinees for another, more youthful male audience of *Volksschüler*, apprentices, and workers between the ages of ten and sixteen. The most beloved stars among this set included Errol Flynn, John Wayne, Alan Ladd, Rita Hayworth, and, later, Marilyn Monroe, Marlon Brando, and James Dean.[20]

By the mid-1950s, young Germans began to identify German film with their parents and the National Socialist past: it seemed outmoded, authoritarian, and thoroughly unacceptable in comparison to the more "modern" impulses from the United States. Gerhard Bliersbach's reminiscences of his youthful film attendance during the 1950s suggest that it served as an expression of autonomy and a challenge to postwar styles of socialization. He described the noise and excitement of an audience unencumbered by parents. As the Hollywood film was about to roll, the cinema owner issued a "German call to order," but to no effect: "Here, adults were powerless. We screamed, we groaned, we clapped, we moaned, we rejoiced. . . . What I loved about American film was to be able to mature to a fast-paced tempo and a happy ending; it had the speed of my daydreams. Like no other cinema, Hollywood captured the strains of adolescence—the anxieties and conflicts, the fantasies and desires."[21]

Moreover, Bliersbach indicates that, as in previous generations, young Germans looked to Hollywood for a new model of male identity: "The virile stars taught a masculine lesson: Cary Grant, Robert Mitchum, Tony Curtis, Victor Mature. American actors possessed a physical presence that their German counterparts lacked."[22] Bliersbach claims to have rejected German films—and particularly *Heimatfilme*—as a boy because he detected in them an unsure or inadequately developed masculinity. He complains of an unnaturally prolonged bonding to mother figures and an insufficiently oedipal response to fathers: "I was disturbed by the physical ineptness of West German actors. These weren't real men. But rather mommy's little boys, who give way at the first sign of roughhousing."[23] In fact, in the most popular *Heimatfilme* of the early 1950s, the male lead did vacillate at the first sign of resistance and was quick to capitulate to competition from an older man for the love of the desired woman. Forester Walter Rainer in *Grün ist die Heide*, for example, wins Helga by default when her father is shot while confronting a murderer on the heath. And in *Am Brunnen vor dem Tore*, Kurt is finally paired with Inge by her British beau but only after Straaten commits suicide and Inge's brother plants doubt in Robert's mind about whether he is the actual object of her affections. Thus, the happy ending that ultimately unites the young couple results from a twist of fate or fortuitous intervention, not the volition of a German hero.

Since World War I, American culture was periodically looked to as the source for a modern model of male subjectivity. The process of crossing the Atlantic for cultural clues to aid gender development was not an innovation of the 1950s. In the early 1920s, as previously discussed, young male intellectuals celebrated American culture for its "naturalness" and unreflected self-confidence, which made earlier Wilhelminian culture appear effete, particularly in view of the recent military humiliation. Bertolt Brecht admired the American boxer because he was "hard, tough, and trained to the core" and held out the promise of cultural and self-renewal. Under Hitler, American culture was again employed as a basis for a new male identity—this time to counter the discipline and drilled conformism of the Hitler Youth. The urban working-class youths who collected into renegade groups like the Edelweiss Pirates, Navajos, and Roving Dudes shed their received identities and transformed themselves into rugged individuals modeled on their favorite cowboy or gangster hero.

American culture had remained a consistent tool of generational protest against the specific form and content of male socialization since the Weimar period. In the aftermath of Germany's second defeat in just over a generation, German boys who came of age under Adenauer turned to American stars for yet another "radically modern" model of masculinity. This time the sources of inspiration were Montgomery Clift, Marlon Brando, James Dean, Bill Haley, and Elvis Presley—young men with a working-class aura who became the physical expression of an uninhibited, even "informal," masculinity. In the summer of 1957, for example, the beloved German fan magazine, *Bravo*, featured Marlon Brando on its cover when the star was in the Federal Republic filming *The Young Lions*. A medium close-up of Brando in a sporty shirt and a civilian hat dominated the page, flanked by two minute shots—pushed to the upper and lower corner margins—of Brando in character, uniformed as a Nazi officer. The caption declared approvingly: "Brando is such a casual civilian, he feels fundamentally ill-at-ease in any uniform."[24]

Through casual clothes and youthful self-assurance, Brando and other American male stars represented a romantic, rebellious macho—a brand of antiheroic individuality and self-expression attractive for its generational- and class-specific packaging. Set against the cultural stereotype of the socially formal, physically stiff, "soldierly" German male of the Nazi period and the softer, more humble postwar version projected in *Heimatfilme*, it spoke to them of adventure and sexual expression, freedom from restriction and want.

Limited evidence also suggests that by the late 1950s teenage girls were affected by this generational struggle. One woman recalls: "An often-heard sentence from my life in the 'fifties: 'Turn the radio down, daddy's working.' Elvis Presley versus my father. Superficially, my father won. But the upbeat, provocative, stimulating music quietly wormed its way into my dreams. Elvis supplied my fantasies for a future as woman and wife . . . with a crucial erotic explosiveness. An alarming but hidden explosiveness that . . . recurred as I put on my first pair of nylons and high-heeled shoes."[25] Like their young male counterparts, some teenage girls turned to American-style culture and consumer goods to construct new social and sexual identities. In this case, Hollywood stars like Rita Hayworth, Ava Gardner, and Marilyn Monroe may have offered teenage girls a mature and sexualized feminine ideal that attracted precisely because of its difference from the maternal—and infinitely more respectable—brand of German womanhood showcased in *Heimatfilme*. What Jackie Stacey has argued for female filmgoers in postwar Britain may well apply to young women in 1950s West Germany: that "Hollywood stars were . . .

contested terrains of competing cultural discourses for femininity. . . . The reproduction of self-image through consumption was perceived as a way of producing new forms of 'American' feminine identity which were exciting, sexual, pleasurable and in some ways, transgressive."[26]

By the mid-1950s, then, German teenagers began to seek a transformation of identity through a "transformation of the body." Although attention to how the body is "clothed and presented" has been a central signifier of a girl's maturation to "adult femininity" in consumer societies, by the late Adenauer period in West Germany, young Germans of both sexes began to alter their appearances as a way to experiment with alternative identities. Self-transformation, moreover, rapidly translated into social practice as a highly visible minority of young Germans offered themselves for public display (and widespread public censure) by consciously manipulating the cultural meanings and national associations of dress and demeanor. Thus, consumption, personal style, and leisure activity took on symbolic significance as German youth employed American culture to mark their difference from received notions of German identity.[27] With the advent of the *Wirtschaftswunder* and increased disposable income, then, American-style consumption became the weapon of choice in the postwar generation's protest against parental prescriptions for proper socialization.[28]

As Bliersbach has observed, "American cinema had no sense of shame." To the youth of the late 1950s, Hollywood films seem to have represented both an escape from a reprehensible German past and a disavowal of German fathers, who, Bliersbach argues, "have never been especially presentable" and became even less so in the aftermath of national socialism.[29]

6

FROM FECKLESS MASSES TO ENGAGED CRITICS
GERMAN FILM CLUBS AND THE QUEST FOR CULTURAL RENEWAL

The film clubs are the connection between film criticism and the masses. Film club members insure that the masses do not remain anonymous. Through [them], . . . the public achieves a demanding and cultivated countenance.
—Kurt Joachim Fischer, organizer, Mannheim film festival, [1953]

By the late 1940s, cinematic fascination convinced a small but significant group of self-cultivated filmgoers that the medium could make a decisive contribution to the cultural renewal of the new democratic Germany. An artistically reinvigorated German cinema, some claimed, could efface the results of the dozen years the industry had spent pandering to the National Socialist state and assist in forging an acceptable cultural identity for postwar West Germans. Moreover, these film products—issuing from a new democratic identity and cleansed of the traces of the fascist past—could be proudly marketed abroad. By these means, West Germany could again gain admittance to the community of nations, not as a political or military power but as a cultural contender—a position well suited to the fatherland of Schiller and Goethe.

But this was only possible if the German public could be trained to demand a better domestic product. The barrier on the road to international cultural respectability was not primarily the much-heralded flawed collective German character. The problem, according to these film enthusiasts, was consumer taste, which many an intellectual found to be sadly lacking in postwar West Germany. Germany's cultural dilemma was understood to be rooted in the broader trends of the industrial West, whose publics lacked the means to discern quality products from trash. Germans departed from other Western societies only insofar as they were limited to consuming ideologically tainted native products during the war and thus were out of touch with the latest international developments. What they initially needed, then, was sustained contact with the best examples of international film.

During the occupation, film clubs were organized to fill this cultural lacuna. Begun under French guidance, German clubs deliberately turned a blind eye to the political implications of film, preferring to focus solely on film's artistic merits. In the ensuing years, however, the clubs developed internal differences over the role of film—and cultural criticism—in the young democracy. The increasing involvement of university students in the club movement altered the parameters and content of its agenda and led to schisms that set the younger generation apart from the older leadership. The former deserted the national film club association in the second half of the 1950s because of their insistence on a more critical engagement with film aesthetics and politics. This younger generation, raised on the exotic fare of the film clubs, matured to become the influential film critics, filmmakers, and founders of film institutes in the 1960s and the vanguard who fought for the rejuvenation of German film through a rejection of "Papa's" cinema. Club membership proved to be a fertile formative experience for these outspoken "angry young men,"[1] who based their criticism on aesthetic and political responses they developed while viewing French, Italian, Soviet, and Weimar film products in the film clubs of the 1950s.[2]

The club movement's attempt to rejuvenate film as a cultural force ran up against both the cultural legacy of the Nazi past and the prevailing institutional and economic organization of the film industry. The international reputation of German film—once renowned for its artistic and formalistic creativity during the Weimar period—had been badly compromised by the censorship policies and ideological tamperings of Goebbels. Nazi cultural policy effectively squelched a diverse domestic film culture by prohibiting a wide range of activity, including film criticism in the press, film production by companies with leftist agendas, seminars on international trends and the avant-garde, and art or "repertoire" cinemas, which exhibited films ignored by commercial distributors. Postwar cinematic and cultural renewal demanded not only the artistic and ideological diversification of an industry "coordinated" to conform to Nazi precepts but the resurrection of a public film culture as well.

Cinephiles had their work cut out for them. Film critics, intellectuals, and educators joined the clergy and state officials in censuring postwar German filmmaking, directing their contempt at its aesthetic and creative rather than moral paucity. Wolfdietrich Schnurre, a film critic from the *Deutschen Rundschau*, blasted the abysmal quality of postwar German films in his 1950 pamphlet, *Rettung des deutschen Films: Eine Streitschrift* (*Recovery of German Film: A Polemic*), complaining that he had waited in vain for the rehabilitation of artistic film production in Germany and was rewarded with banal old forms that insulted the spectator. Although he traced the decline of the film industry to Hitler, he regretted the complacency of postwar filmmakers who had failed to seize the opportunity to create a new expressive medium in the modern style. He called for salvation based upon European styles of filmmaking, holding up Italian and French productions and native Weimar cinema for emulation. According to Schnurre, there were no current German directors who exhibited the talent of Roberto Rossellini or René Clair or of earlier native directors such as F. W. Murnau, G. W. Pabst, Frank Wysbar, or Wilhelm Dieterle. Contemporary German filmmakers, he maintained, served up the same old gruel from the Goebbels era, suffused with a "wishful-thinking view of reality" and packaged in a slick style.[3]

By the end of the occupation, then, cinephiles joined religious and state leaders in calling for public support of "the good film," a rather undefined concept that was nonetheless advocated as an alternative to film's present low quality. Unlike social conservatives, who judged films on the basis of moral and social messages "read" from narrative content, film enthusiasts focused on the aesthetic and formal qualities of film. Like the social conservatives, however, film enthusiasts were judged by the commercial industry to be meddling antagonists, especially when substantial numbers joined organizations designed to educate the public in matters of taste.

Although organized on a nationwide scale by 1949, film clubs never became a mass movement. According to the most optimistic estimates, they reached a peak membership of 150,000 in the mid-1950s, which was dispersed among some 180 adult clubs, 144 youth clubs, and 12 university clubs located in over 200 German cities. Nevertheless, the national club movement achieved an influence far exceeding its small numbers.[4] This was due in part to the composition of its leadership, which tended to be dominated by secondary school teachers, municipal cultural officers, and university professors—educators, that is, who had the opportunity to recruit young adults into the clubs.[5] In addition, film club leaders became expert at achieving a high public profile for their activities and identified themselves as the voice of the discriminating film public. In the process, they successfully solicited the support of federal and state governments for their agenda.[6]

Undoubtedly, the clubs' public visibility and cultivation of government favor worried industry representatives. Yet the German film industry found the film clubs particularly troubling because they originated during the occupation under foreign sponsorship and regularly screened international products to their memberships. In the early postwar years, these concerns appear justified. German club members enthusiastically consumed images that had been forbidden during the late years of the Third Reich. To be considered cultured in postwar West Germany, one had to be conversant with international products. Industry members resented the equation of foreign origin with quality and suspected that their commercial interests would be compromised by the activities of the film clubs. Sensitive to its weakened position on the world market, the German film industry feared the loss of its home market as well.

The first film clubs were founded by French cultural officers during the occupation, who modeled the German variety after their homegrown *ciné-clubs*. French *ciné-clubs* were organized in Paris shortly after the end of World War I by Louis Delluc, a filmmaker and critic. Begun as loose associations of avant-garde filmmakers, artists, intellectuals, and film critics, these *ciné-clubs* were closed to all but invited members and were not intended to cultivate a broader public taste for film. Members sought to establish the medium as the "seventh art" and assembled to view films and discuss the specific formal and aesthetic problems of cinema. Unlike similar gatherings in the Soviet Union in the early 1920s, the French *ciné-clubs* developed theory based on issues of film viewing rather than filmmaking. Over the next several years, clubs expanded their study to include films denied general release in France, becoming in effect an exhibition forum for films excluded from the commercial cinemas.[7]

In 1925 Charles Léger, avant-garde painter and filmmaker, founded the first debate-style film club, which would become the model for the post-1945 German clubs. Léger's "Le Tribune libre du cinema" sponsored biweekly film screenings and accompanying lectures for the public, followed by open audience discussion. This format, which encouraged public participation, would be carried over to the German clubs in the late 1940s.

In interwar France, *ciné-clubs* faltered with the introduction of sound; by 1930 many intellectuals abandoned the clubs in disgust, considering the new technology an artistic abomination. But some clubs survived with the help of Jean Mitry, film theoretician and director of short films, and director Georges Franju and by 1935 began to supplement their screenings with film "classics" in an effort to build a must-see repertoire of serious, artistic cinema. Film club activity in France ended with the Nazi occupation. After the war, *ciné-clubs* were resurrected in Paris with the support of Jean Pailévès, the general director of the French film industry, who created a national organization of film clubs.[8] This supportive relationship between the commercial industry and the film clubs would not, however, find a parallel in West Germany.

The early German film clubs operated in the French tradition: they were intended to foster appreciation for film as art and met to investigate film aesthetics, form, and technology. Members were trained to understand and evaluate film as a medium wholly different from the more traditional arts. Thus, the German film clubs were initially much less concerned than the churches with exploring the social consequences of *Filmwirkung*. Their primary goal was to create a critical distance from which viewers could distinguish cinematic pabulum from haute cuisine.

The activities of Albert Tanguy, an officer of the Bureau de la Culture Populaire in Baden-Baden and a key figure in the film club movement in the French zone, serves as an example of the French perspective. Tanguy and his cohorts were not primarily interested in the use of film for political democratization. Rather, in keeping with the general aims of the French educational program in Germany, they were committed to expanding the cultural horizons of the German public: "They saw the isolation of the German mind as the greatest danger . . . and set as their main aim bringing the Germans back into the mainstream of European culture." The French quite comfortably assumed the role of cultural masters and concentrated on showcasing the fruits of their own national legacy that illustrated—according to one contemporary—those newly resurrected, enlightened eighteenth-century values upon which modern European life should be based: "the dignity of man" and "that universalism which is the vocation of the French spirit."[9]

Thus, film screenings were promoted as cultural events. French cultural officers, unlike their American counterparts in "information control," soft-pedaled their reeducation program and relied on the more subtle—and healing —effects of cultural contact.[10] Despite the hostility expressed by German adults regarding the putatively punitive approach to the management of material conditions in the French occupation zone, many young Germans became willing pupils when they perceived themselves to be treated as something other than willfully immoral, psychologically flawed subjects by this longtime enemy nation. As one participant in the early days of the film clubs recalled:

All of the occupation powers had film bureaus after the war. . . . But what separated the French from the others was that they did not only operate according to this American aim of "reeducation," they had an artistic ambition as well. That was what was special about people like Albert Tanguy— they were not simply occupiers, but human beings with a cultural awareness, with cultural objectives. If one looks at the lists [of films screened by] these three occupation powers, it soon becomes apparent that in respect to the French films distributed, the artistic and cultural were stressed, while the political and topical remained very much in the background.[11]

In 1949 Tanguy initiated the *Filmtreffen*, an annual international film club meeting hosted for the first three years of its existence by the French, after which it shifted to German sponsorship. In these early years, French and German film club members, film critics, and film directors and producers dominated the scene. The first meeting at the scenic Titisee in the Black Forest was an immense success. It was wistfully recalled in the mid-1950s as the "golden past" of the German film club movement, a characterization confirmed by one participant's enthusiastic description:

> It began in Titisee [1949], Schluchsee [1950], and Bacharach [1951]. At that time it was intended, above all, to surmount a . . . long intellectual isolation [*geistige Internierung*]. For twelve years we were cut off from the world; and the younger [among us] lacked entirely a perspective of nearly all of the history of film art, the most striking representations of which had been stigmatized as degenerate during the Third Reich. It was necessary to address this; and therefore the first film meetings were predominantly devoted to a fascinating taking of stock. In those days, we enjoyed an oversupply of filmic delicacies. We sat on hard benches in front of a improvised screen and watched the works of the French avant-garde, the great films of Carné, Renoir, and Feyder, representatives of the English documentary school, American realism, and Italian neorealism. . . . Direct contact with the works of art and the artists occupied the limelight, and subsequently discussions were passionate and spontaneous.[12]

Reports on the Titisee meeting stressed the growth of French-German fellowship, and the exchange of cinematic knowledge between French filmmakers and their German pupils left the latter dazzled. Enamored by the cultural contact, German club representatives praised French filmmaking in their unofficial organ, *Filmforum*. Indeed, French sponsorship of the early *Filmtreffen* encouraged German members to use French film classics and aesthetics as the standard for quality filmmaking. Moreover, they took as their intellectual model the French journal, *Cahiers du Cinema*, which appeared in 1951 and regularly featured articles by André Bazin, Eric Rohmer, Jean-Luc Godard, Jean Domarchi, François Truffaut, Jacques Rivette, and Claude Chabrol.[13] In 1950s Germany, film theory followed French trends, and the choice of films screened in the local German film clubs closely conformed to those analyzed in the influential French film journal.[14]

The British also founded film clubs in their sector, although German club members have been less rapturous in their praise of British involvement in cultural matters. This was largely due to the fact that Britain's cinematic contribution was limited to the documentary film; they had no tradition of art film production that could rival that of the French.

British-sponsored film clubs in Germany were based upon the film societies that had sprung up in England in the 1930s. The purpose of the British clubs was different from that of the French. They were dominated by individuals who were unhappy with Hollywood's predominance in the British market and intent on viewing films that did not reach the commercial theaters.[15] British film societies represented a reaction against foreign domination of domestic screens and therefore reflected a certain quiet defiance of the increasingly popular and exportable American cultural product. Although the French clubs were not formed explicitly to counter the influence of Hollywood, they did share the British clubs' dissatisfaction with the film program exhibited in the commercial cinemas and implicitly represented a challenge to the commercial fare.

In the U.S. zone of Germany, occupation officials never threw their energies into organizing film clubs, in part because such organizations did not have a tradition in the United States. Furthermore, American film officers had been plagued by problems in convincing Hollywood film companies to send their best quality products to Germany due to difficulties involving currency conversion and industry unhappiness with official American encouragement of renewed German film production. As a result, the cultural stock of the United States was rapidly sinking, as German film critics increasingly bemoaned the low quality of Hollywood products flooding their market. As late as 1948, one German critic summed up the postwar situation in the U.S. zone with the ironic retort: "National trash is, happily, dead. Long live international trash."[16] Such perceptions might have been overcome if American film officers had possessed the inclination. But the Americans were operating according to a different system than the French. U.S. officials were much more concerned with regulating the German film product and containing the influence of the state on the media. As we have seen, they were quite insistent on determining the institutional base of film censorship. Their attention was fixed on refashioning industry structure and control—on regulating the cultural producers. Unlike the French, they had little interest in satisfying German viewers' hunger for cultural delicacies. This they entrusted to profit-conscious industry members and the vagaries of the market, which they perceived as an outgrowth of public taste.

Thus, the early days of the film clubs, between 1946 and 1948, were marked by zonal organization and foreign leadership. By 1948, Germans increasingly seized the initiative and began establishing their own clubs. German-run film clubs continued the tradition begun by French and British cultural officers. Membership was open to anyone over sixteen years old who paid the annual dues of anywhere from 12 to 36 marks. Local clubs typically met once a month on Sunday mornings for a film screening, which was free of charge to members. An informed club member—usually also the leader of the club or, much less frequently, a visiting film scholar or filmmaker—would introduce that month's feature and provide background on the film's production, director, and place in cinema history. After the screening, the speaker would lead a discussion, the level of sophistication of which varied from club to club. Film aesthetics, style, or technique might be discussed, or discussions could become mired in a concentration on story line.[17] The expressed goal of the clubs was, however, invariable: to view as many quality films as possible. This was an ambitious and oftentimes difficult undertaking during the occupation, when attempts to procure some of the film classics—of both older and more recent vintage—were hindered by the limited stock of the Allied cultural centers and German film distributors.

Despite the openness with which members admitted to embracing the club movement to overcome their self-professed "intellectual imprisonment" under Hitler, their national president, Johannes Eckardt, emphasized the unideological nature of this pursuit. According to Eckardt, the clubs observed political neutrality in their efforts to acquaint Germans with "the essential films of all nations and states, even if some of these films perchance express the political perspectives of totalitarian regimes. In such cases, [the clubs] . . . guard against identifying with the ideologies of such production centers, even though . . . the artistic features of the theme must be recognized. The international perspective is at all times essential for the German film clubs."[18] Turning their backs on discussions concerning the social role of the mass media, national film club leaders represented their organization as benignly internationalistic in an increasingly politically charged atmosphere. Theirs, they argued, was an association of apolitical film enthusiasts who assembled to further the cause of art. Although club members in Munich explicitly stressed the democratic nature of their pursuit, referring to themselves as the postwar "intellectual vanguard" committed to facilitating creative freedom, all clubs treated film as a cultural form and aesthetic object, not as an ideological vehicle. Consequently, they demanded the right to view any important product of international cinema.

Through the 1950s, local clubs screened Soviet classics by Sergei Eisenstein and Dziga Vertov, as well as more recent documentaries, animated films, and features from "East Bloc" countries like Poland, Czechoslovakia, Hungary, and Yugoslavia. Moreover, there was a keen interest in domestic commercial classics, like *Das Kabinett des Dr. Caligari*, *Der blaue Engel*, and *Mädchen im Uniform* (*Girls in Uniform*), as well as the social realism of "proletarian cinema" from the Weimar period, such as *Mutter Krausen's Fahrt ins Glück* and *Kuhle Wampe*—all of which made frequent appearances on club programs. These were supplemented with a few well-regarded postwar efforts, such as Harald Braun's *Nachtwache*, Helmut Käutner's *In jenen Tag*, and anything by Wolfgang Staudte, who worked in both Germanies—East and West. Finally, the clubs seized the opportunity to screen highly controversial films like Käutner's *Der Apfel ist ab*, Roberto Rossellini's *Rome Open City*, which had been denounced for potentially damaging Germany's relations with other states, and Staudte's *Der Untertan* (*The Subject*), which, made in 1951 East Germany, was barred from release in the West on the prompting of the federal minister of the interior, who censured its highly critical view of German history and elite culture. As Eckardt emphasized, the clubs could appreciate the artistic value of a film in spite of its politics.[19]

Of course, it was not that simple; the recent German past belied this naive separation of art and politics. Indeed, such a marked disavowal of the ideological function of the mass media seems disingenuous after Hitler, particularly in the strained atmosphere of Cold War Germany. Perhaps, then, the studied apolitical approach was an intentional strategy. After all, it echoed the political push for European cooperation and unity and, moreover, reflected a certain pragmatism, since it was doubtless easier and less controversial simply to avoid the messy and unpopular issue of the relationship between politics and culture, especially if engagement with it could compromise the financial support of the clubs by state governments.

Perhaps the most telling illustration of the national club leadership's insensitivity to the politics of film was the scheduling of a Russian folk dance film to follow immediately the screening of *Night and Fog*, French director Alain Resnais's understated and chilling account of the Nazi death camps. The decision not only reflected the club leadership's reluctance to explore, in an open forum, the pernicious politics of the recent past—in this case, the officially sponsored murder of millions during the Third Reich—but also suggested an unwillingness to broach the cultural politics of the present, in terms of both the film's production and its reception. The screening offered an unutilized opportunity to stimulate public discussion on the sensitive political, ethical, and aesthetic issues connected to the cinematic representation of mass murder and to explore the manner in which the new West German government officially received the finished product. The latter would have provided for the uninitiated an especially telling introduction to the links between culture and politics. The West German Foreign Office considered the wrenching documentary a potential threat to German international rehabilitation (through a frictionless integration into the newly minted Western Alliance system) and demanded that France withdraw *Night and Fog* from official competition at the 1955 Cannes International Film Festival on the grounds that it would poison West Germany's relations with other states. The French complied, for reasons connected to their desire to cover traces of their own collaborationist past. Resnais's reaction perfectly captured the unsettling impression of historical continuity that West German officials had been so eager to avoid but nonetheless provoked through their strong-arm censorship action: "Naturally, I hadn't realized," he quipped, "that the National Socialist regime would be represented in Cannes. But now, of course, I do."[20]

Although film club leaders were fundamentally concerned with resurrecting a respectable cultural environment in West Germany, they neglected to frame this problem in its political context or deal explicitly with the difficult legacy of the recent past. Moreover, they ignored the politics of film production and control to focus on the problem of public reception. The clubs were based on the assumption that the German people needed to sharpen their critical and analytical skills, which had been dulled by the state control of cultural production during the Third Reich. This condition was taken to apply even to professional critics, for by 1936, legitimate film criticism had been stilled in the press; reviewers were permitted merely to "describe" German films to the public—which degenerated into a form of advertisement—and were prohibited from engaging in even the most superficial aesthetic, formal, or ideological analysis.[21] The postwar film clubs seemed to accept without question the image of a German public of passive subjects led astray by Nazi masters. They sought to counteract the cultural spoon-feeding of Goebbels by training Germans to develop their own critical assessments of film so they could become, in effect, discerning citizens in a new democratic world of consumer choice. This required that German filmgoers be able to "distance" themselves emotionally from the narrative in order to analyze and evaluate the artistic and technical merits of films. The German public, that is, had to learn to respond with their heads and not their hearts. In the process, film club leaders hoped to redeem both the medium and the masses and prove that the term "mass medium" need not be a pejorative one.[22]

The first German-led film clubs were private affairs, founded to explore issues of artistic or commercial production and facilitate professional contacts during the occupation period. One of the earliest clubs appeared in Frankfurt in the summer of 1945, without the support or knowledge of the U.S. Military Government. Led by Ella Bergmann-Michel, a Bauhaus painter and director of "social" documentaries until 1933, and Paul Sauerlaender, a film historian and educational filmmaker, this group of ten or twenty artists, journalists, writers, and film-loving intellectuals met once a week, salon-style, in Sauerlaender's apartment to view films he had "saved from the bombs and from Allied seizure."[23] Other such clubs were established in the British sector of Berlin in 1946 and in Munich in 1947, but they remained anomalies. Unlike the later German clubs that would coalesce into a national organization, these clubs included large numbers of filmmakers due to these cities' vying status as Germany's film production capital. In keeping with the interests of their constituency, the clubs' stated purpose was to screen films, inform members about trends in domestic and international production, and facilitate contact between artistic and technical personnel concerned with new German film production in order to "encourage and ease the work of all filmmakers."[24] This latter goal found little resonance in other areas of West Germany due to the absence of commercial studios outside of Berlin, Munich, and Hamburg. Indeed, the creation of the Berlin club appears to have been an early attempt by filmmakers to establish an informal professional organization where filmmakers could renew and maintain contacts after the war—and exchange rumors on Allied policy. By 1948 and the Berlin blockade, the Berlin club's membership declined drastically when Berlin filmmakers immigrated to Munich or Hamburg, where work could continue uninterrupted by Cold War politics. Thus, the contest was ended, and Munich became the new film capital of West Germany.[25]

A more typical German film club was founded in June 1948 by Walter Hagemann, a noted film sociologist at the University of Münster and director of the Institut für Publizistik there. The Münster club reportedly enjoyed a socially diverse, though mostly middle-class, membership, including "workers, salaried employees, civil servants, artists and . . . professors," which was said to reflect "the character" of the university city.[26] The forty-eight-year-old Hagemann was voted president of the Münster club and later became president of the Film Club Association for the British zone. Shortly thereafter, he started a chapter of the film club at the university. Over the course of the next few years, student film clubs caught on in a number of university towns, including Bonn, Heidelberg, Munich, and Frankfurt. These clubs were characterized by a socially middling but educationally elite membership and a dynamic cultural exchange, and by the early 1950s, they became the source of challenges to the dominant club philosophy.[27]

Another influential club was founded in Bavarian Augsburg by Johannes Eckardt. This club also claimed to reflect the city's social composition, with its broad industrial base. In fact, Eckardt boasted that his club was no haven for intellectuals; along with the usual teachers, professionals, civil servants, and students, it included a large number of factory workers and skilled tradespeople as well. Eckardt thought this an important point to stress, particularly to the commercial film industry, whose members periodically sought to undermine the influence of the club movement in cultural matters by dismissing it as a narrow group of eggheads and aesthetes who represented neither the views nor the taste of the broader moviegoing public. In a letter to the industry trade association, Eckardt excoriated this response by suggesting that industry members were borrowing a strategy, perfected by Goebbels's Propaganda Ministry, of "denouncing to the nation as 'destructive intellectuals' " any groups or individuals who developed "an independent judgment and expressed it freely." After taking the ideological high ground in favor of democratic freedoms, Eckardt nonetheless felt it necessary to refute the charge of intellectualism by emphasizing that the movement was diverse, hence socially representative. Betraying a long-standing (and widely held) *bürgerliche* bias regarding gender and class, he assured the industry that the movement indeed corresponded to popular taste since it contained "numerous women—whose judgment certainly relies more on the heart than cool reason—, . . . and many manual laborers from the lower social orders."[28]

Eckardt's involvement with public education and the pedagogical uses of film extended back to the early 1920s, when he began to build a career combining these with an interest in film art. At the end of World War I, Eckardt left his native Austria for Munich and within a few years was commissioned by the Bavarian Cultural Ministry to establish and manage the Bavarian Landesfilm-bühne, a state-sponsored organization that procured and exhibited "educationally worthwhile" films for local Bavarian communities. He moved to Berlin in 1930, where he led the Deutsche Gesellschaft für Ton und Bild (DEGETO) and became involved in the production and distribution of Kulturfilme, those technically polished documentaries unencumbered by attention to messy social realities that became a German specialty on the world market.[29] Eckardt successfully pursued this career throughout the Nazi period and taught film seminars on international and avant-garde film at the Lessing Hochschule in Berlin until Goebbels blocked the importation of foreign films. Despite his cosmopolitan cultural proclivities, Eckardt—like many other non-Jewish German film professionals—fell quietly into line during the period of Gleichschaltung. He accepted an appointment as adviser (Referent) to the Reich Union of German Film Offices, Kulturfilm, and Commercial Film Producers (Reichsvereinigung deutscher Lichtbildstellen, Kultur- und Werbefilmhersteller), which he eventually parlayed into a position overseeing the production and distribution of Kulturfilme. After the war, Eckardt spent the early occupation years in the U.S. zone cultivating official support for educational film programs for youth and the broader public and helped to found both the Institute for Educational Film (Institut für den Unterrichtsfilm) in Munich and the trizonal Institut für Film und Bild in Wissenschaft und Unterricht, a research and educational institute for film and photography.[30]

By 1949, the sixty-two-year-old Eckardt brought the film club movement to the U.S. zone and rapidly succeeded in outmaneuvering Hagemann to become the president and public spokesperson for the Association of German Film Clubs (Verband der deutschen Filmclubs).[31] Eckardt would remain president for thirteen years, until 1962, when he finally surrendered the post at the age of seventy-five. The longevity of his presidency insured organizational stability, an unchanging philosophy, and, some detractors would argue, an inflexible approach and petrification of purpose. Walter Hagemann, in fact, and the association's business manager resigned their offices within six months due to conflicts with the "authoritarian and public-profile-conscious Eckardt."[32]

The exuberance of the early annual meetings dwindled once sponsorship of the clubs was transferred from the French to the Germans. Club members and journalists complained that Eckardt firmly controlled association meetings and peopled the program with invited experts, who lectured members on topics designated by the Executive Committee. In contrast to the French, Eckardt failed to facilitate audience participation, even when the audience was composed of professionals whose experience could provide the basis for a "stimulating exchange."[33] This change was sardonically described by a Swiss journalist who attended the first German-run meeting at Bad Ems in 1953 and encountered a scene characterized more by bourgeois restraint than by the earlier élan:

> Horn-rimmed glasses and briefcases dominated among the festival participants. There was no extravagance to be seen, no existentialists with wild haircuts and fanatical eyes, no *Wandervögel* in short pants and open collars, no ironical types, holding tired cigarettes in the corners of their mouths, and no women, sitting elegantly with legs crossed while carefully applying their red lipstick during the leisure time devoted to lectures and endless discussions. . . . A mild, unrevolutionary middle class was gathered, . . . filled with the mission to educate with "Films from Yesterday, the Public of Tomorrow." . . . In short, it was all very fine and beneficial, and the little teacher [*Handarbeitslehrerin*] who sat next to me could fill her little notebook with many useful notes.[34]

The description of the "little teacher" busily taking notes provided an apt, although reverse-gendered, metaphor for a predominantly earnest, educated, and youthful middle-class male membership, which responded, at least initially, with respect and passivity to its elderly, trained elite.

In terms of age and outlook, the national film club leaders had more in common with church film commissioners and state leaders than with their studious charges. Since these groups shared a commitment to improving the cultural climate of postwar West Germany, Eckardt cultivated a close working relationship with church and state interests. From the beginning, film clubs received modest financial subsidies from municipal and state governments, and Allied, state, and federal officials underscored their support for the clubs by attending the association's organizational and annual meetings.[35] At the 1950 meeting in Hannover, Arno Hennig, a member of the Parliamentary Committee for Press, Radio, and Film and later the cultural minister of Hesse, heralded the clubs as the "the public conscience" of postwar cinematic culture and indicated their importance to political and economic renewal: "Only under the beneficent pressure of critical public opinion . . . will German film be . . . resurrected from the sensation of the *Kasenstück* and propaganda film. . . . [German filmmakers] can be helped only if they once again sense that the public conscience stands behind them. The film clubs must be this conscience; they must awaken and strengthen . . . an interest in and feeling for genuinely good film in all sectors of the population."[36] By the following year, the federal Interior Ministry institutionalized the voice of the film club movement as the "public's conscience" by granting Johannes Eckardt a seat on the selection committee for the ministry's newly founded annual Federal Film Prize, which was awarded to the year's best German film production. Moreover, Eckardt was invited by the federal minister of the interior to represent the film clubs on the FBS, which awarded distinctions and tax breaks to "worthwhile films," and was named a state representative to the film censorship board by the Bavarian Cultural Ministry.[37]

Eckardt and the Christian film commissioners developed a close working relationship as well. Eckardt attended the Protestant-sponsored 1950 film conference in Schwalbach, and Protestant and Catholic film commissioners Werner Hess and Anton Kochs regularly appeared at the clubs' organizational and annual meetings. Hess, in particular, became a permanent fixture on the program of the clubs' annual international film meetings, delivering lectures on such topics as "Church and Film" (Augsburg, 1949), "Youth and Film" (Bad Ems, 1953), and "The Problem of Religious Films" (Bad Ems, 1957).

Despite the shared commitment to improving the German film product and challenging the market orientation of the industry, Anton Kochs defended the institutional separation of Eckardt's film clubs from the Christian film leagues. Each was, after all, a different sort of consumer pressure group. The film clubs were interested in cinema as an art form—as an object of study in itself—and so screened films regardless of their moral content, provided they had aesthetic or formal appeal or a place in the rapidly developing film canon. For the *Filmliga*, however, the governing criteria were religious and ethical concerns. Thus, although Kochs agreed that "ideally" people should judge the merits of a film on their own, he concluded that this was in practice impossible, since "there is no 'own judgment' without first financing the film through the purchase of a ticket."[38]

Kochs insisted that "proper" film criticism was dependent on specialized training and commended the film clubs on their efforts to disseminate knowledge and cultivate good judgment among their members. Using critical pedagogical methods, he added, could strip even unacceptable films of their "psychical and spiritual danger," since the danger lay in naive viewing and insufficient critical training. "One could even screen *Die Sünderin* within the framework of an evening parish meeting," he ventured, "if afterward the pros and cons were explored in an earnest discussion."[39] The Catholic church, however, never opted to employ such an experiment in audience autodidacticism. Although the clubs were congratulated for cultivating more critical consumers, the fact that their members represented only a small percentage of the film-viewing public argued for the sustained need for the *Filmliga*, whose members ascribed to the decisions of the Catholic Film Commission—Germany's moral conscience.

The relationship of the film clubs and their leadership to the film industry was somewhat more complex. The transfer of the clubs to German control and the establishment of a superzonal association brought an addition to the clubs' agenda: to assist their national cinema in its economic and artistic recovery. Club leaders expected their campaign on behalf of "the good film" to both reinvigorate their national film culture on the international market and prompt it to serve its domestic public in a responsible way.

Club leaders believed that the most effective way to lobby for a better German film product was to bring public pressure to bear on their native industry. As Eckardt argued from the beginning, their only hope lay in the ambitious project of transforming the taste of the broad and diverse moviegoing public. The idea was to alter consumption habits—and hence the commercial product—by forging an organized group of informed and demanding consumers. Consumer expectation would then compel the industry to both respect its customers and produce a "more responsible" product.

Beginning in 1949, then, the film clubs occupied a somewhat ambivalent relationship to the industry. On the one hand, film club leaders recognized the material difficulties plaguing the industry and pledged their support in its quest for state credit, tax breaks, and an enhanced position in the national economy. Moreover, as cinephiles, they lobbied on behalf of less burdensome entertainment taxes for cinema and, in effect, a more equitable status in the cultural economy. Arguing that "communities have a cultural responsibility to film," Eckardt hinted that film should benefit from state and local subsidies similar to those awarded theater, music, and other arts. In sum, he portrayed the clubs as industry boosters and advocates for a rejuvenated national film culture.[40]

On the other hand, the clubs set high standards for the quality of new German film production—holding up the best examples of international (and particularly European) filmmaking as the desired model—and were not reticent to blast industry members for betraying their expectations. The clubs' roles as both nurturer and critic created a palpable tension between them and the commercial industry, and industry members tended to perceive the clubs' talent as lying primarily in the latter area.[41]

Predictably, the film industry blamed unschooled public taste for perpetuating the German cinematic "crisis." As one successful German distributor remarked, "the public taste is even worse" than the quality of German films would suggest. Moreover, many industry members confessed skepticism that the public taste could be improved. As more than one cineast noted, this was a problem that transcended the German situation: "The German commercial film . . . isn't enjoyed in America. American commercial films of the same quality are rejected in Germany. Every country insists on its own kitsch. Yet they are united in the rejection of the artistic film. Against that, an international front has been constructed."[42] Fritz Kortner penned these caustic lines for the 1949 German film club meeting in Augsburg. Cinematic mediocrity was attributed to the medium's status as mass culture. The problem of unrefined public taste was not peculiar to Germany or the direct result of National Socialist rule, according to industry spokespeople. Rather, they argued, all national audiences favored their own particular brand of pap.[43]

Club members countered that German audiences were "better than their reputation." The lead article in a 1952 issue of *Filmforum*, based upon a study by Walter Hagemann's Institut für Publizistik, highlighted viewers' desires to have *Kulturfilme* and newsreels screened before main features. The author interpreted this as a sign of the audience's good judgment and maturity, since these film genres had been heralded since the 1920s as quality film products of which German producers were clear masters. They represented German filmmaking finesse and had won international prestige.[44] It is not surprising that club supporters insisted that the German film-viewing public was "turning away from the factory of dreams," despite the continued popularity of knockoff *Heimatfilme* and revues. They needed, after all, to prove that their efforts to influence public taste were making a perceptible difference in order to legitimize their own position as both spokespeople for a broader German public and advocates for German film art.

The public profile of the film club association was enhanced when industry leader Curt Oertel extended his substantial support. Best known for the *Kulturfilme* he made on the lives of Michelangelo (*Michelangelo*, 1940) and Martin Luther (*Der gehorsame Rebell*, 1952), Oertel had been appointed the first postwar president of the German Film Producers' Association by the U.S. Military Government, became a leading officer in the SPIO, and assisted in the creation of the industry self-censorship board. He occupied, then, a highly visible position in the German film industry during the occupation. By 1950, however, he became increasingly critical of the industry's politics and commercial preoccupations and in effect "jumped ship" by resigning his SPIO office at the annual film club meeting that year to become second officer of the film club association under Eckardt.[45] As a *Kulturfilm*maker, Oertel differentiated his interests from those of commercial feature film producers and represented his professional move as a vote for quality over commerce. Culturally and professionally, he was more disposed to Eckardt, who, not incidentally, had produced his internationally renowned *Michelangelo* and with whom he had a long-standing professional relationship. They were united in their commitment to educational films and international contact as well as in their sense of separateness from the commercial industry.[46]

In order to rejuvenate German culture, Oertel and Eckardt required public clout and industry cooperation. Eckardt doggedly maneuvered to make the film club leaders "players" in negotiations concerning film matters and financing and by 1955 moved the film club business office to Wiesbaden, the seat of the industry trade association (SPIO), the film censorship board (FSK), and the industry-sponsored German Institute for Film Studies (Deutsches Institut für Filmkunde). These efforts did little, however, to alter the clubs' strained relationship with the industry. The industry continued to frustrate club members by remaining distant from the annual club meetings and generally treating decisions regarding film production as a matter of business rather than cultural renewal. Press coverage of the annual international meetings invariably bemoaned the absence of German filmmakers and the minimal amount of practical support they provided: "Above all, one reflects upon the marked aloofness of the German film industry, which sent along a scornfully smiling representative, but hardly a film. They still have not grasped the kind of economically valuable preview service the film club . . . can provide for them. The foreigners conducted themselves in an altogether more intelligent and understanding manner. They brought along a whole collection of rare and noteworthy films."[47]

The commercial industry suspected the international character of club screenings. Indeed, most feared that their products would suffer by comparison, that screenings at the annual meeting would result in bad press, public humiliation, and lower box-office receipts.[48] The president of the industry trade association charged that the clubs' real purpose was to cultivate a German audience for foreign films and pointed to the club's bylaws to substantiate industry members' position: "We fail to find any hint that the film club organization has thought to dedicate special attention to German film and its development. . . . In practice, the film clubs actually dedicate special attention to exceptional foreign films, and interest . . . is especially great in foreign films that are not accessible to the German public. Special advertisements . . . are even placed in public."[49]

Industry wariness extended beyond the threat of foreign competition and elevated consumer taste. Industry members considered the exhibition activities of the clubs a direct challenge to industry practices and institutions. Theater owners charged that the clubs were little more than "Besucherorganisationen," or subscription viewing clubs, designed to undercut the commercial interests of the exhibitors.

By 1950, Eckardt made a bid to placate industry concerns and establish a closer working relationship with the commercial sector. He claimed that this strategy was dictated by practical concerns: he needed industry assistance in securing films for the clubs' monthly showings. To win industry favor, Eckardt agreed to limit the annual number of new films exhibited at meetings to twelve and to mandate that an introduction and a concluding discussion accompany each screening.[50] These measures were meant to convince the skeptical industry that the clubs were no mere *Besucherorganisationen*.

Such assurances did not, however, suffice. Shortly after the agreement was concluded in early 1950, SPIO members voted to revoke it, unconvinced that the clubs would not become a competing forum for exhibiting national and international films. Anxious to forge closer ties to the industry, Eckardt invited the SPIO president to the 1950 annual film club meeting in Hannover to work out their differences. An agreement was reached in a closed session, which Eckardt then presented to the film club membership for approval.

The agreement, in essence, subjected the program of the local film clubs to industry approval and required that all films screened in the clubs' closed sessions gain clearance by the FSK. This stipulation guaranteed that the clubs would not enjoy an advantage over the commercial theaters, whose offerings were subject to censorship approval. By submitting to these terms, the club leaders integrated their movement into the commercial-institutional framework.[51]

Journalists attending the conference detected in the agreement an unwelcome new course for the German film club movement. They warned that the clubs' true vocation should be to serve as monitors and counterweights to the increasing cooperation between the industry and the state, which was gaining undue influence over cultural matters due to its role as financier of the film credit program. "The phantoms," wrote one observer, "dance on a thin, golden wire, and it's a pity that the film clubs have allowed themselves to be linked to this mechanism. Or will they, here and there, have the courage to crawl out from under the . . . comfortable cover of the [Film Club] Association, should they come to the realization . . . that freedom should not be surrendered so carelessly?"[52] Critics faulted the club leadership for renouncing their role as critical industry outsiders and in the process surrendering the opportunity to develop a more democratic alternative for film selection and consumption—one that would bypass the commercial controls of the distribution and exhibition branches as well as the moral controls of the censorship apparatus and potentially offer the public a more politically and aesthetically diverse fare than that playing at the local movie house.

Eckardt's attempt to cultivate the favor of the industry did, in fact, draw the ire of some club members. One of the more vocal opponents was Edmund Schopen, president of the Munich Film Club. Acting on behalf of his club membership, Schopen pilloried the agreement as sacrificial subordination to industry interests, which, he argued, must "be ended as soon as possible by means of the self-regulation of German film clubs. . . . This movement should represent public opinion and the conscience of the *Volk* vis-à-vis the film industry. . . . We can only be justified in this task . . . if we have a clear conscience . . . and if we confront the film industry as a film culture movement with internal—as well as external—independence."[53] In the view of both disgruntled club members and sympathetic journalists, the purpose of the film clubs was to protect the interests of art and national culture against a profit-hungry Goliath that, with the support of state subsidies, spurned the creation of cultural treasures in favor of tried-and-true formulas and melodramatic mediocrities. The rallying cry of these dissidents became art versus economics. Schopen appealed for a more democratic-style film club that could demand the right of access to films denied commercial distribution despite—or because of—their artistic merit, avant-garde character, or controversial nature. In place of product homogenization, he lobbied for diversity; in place of regulation, he called for unrestrained choice. Praising the clubs as "representatives of cultural liberalism . . . and enemies of censorship," Schopen castigated Eckardt for subordinating club programs to the review of the censorship board, which, he claimed, had been "conceived solely as a internal organ to secure the industry against official censorship" but was now "gradually enhancing itself into a type of film authority in its efforts to achieve omnipotence over all areas concerned with film."[54] For Schopen and like-minded critics, then, cultural renewal was dependent upon unregulated consumer freedom.[55]

To reinforce this point, Schopen's club seceded from the national association, formed the Independent Munich Film Club, and encouraged others in the association to follow its example. Eckardt eventually succeeded in staving off wholesale mutiny by convincing club leaders that the agreement to subject closed club programs to review by the FSK was an affirmation of "democratic" censorship over state control. Admittedly, the censorship board was coming under increasing attack at this time by state and church interests—particularly within the context of the *Sünderin* affair. Yet Eckardt's flurry of correspondence to the Bavarian Cultural Ministry over Schopen's revolt, and his failure to allay state officials' unsubstantiated suspicions that Schopen's real aim was to secure the uncensored exhibition in West Germany of "propaganda films from the East zone," suggests that he was as concerned to protect his reputation as a reliable ally of state interests as he was to limit state meddling in cultural matters.[56]

Over the course of the early 1950s, another form of industry "cooperation" nearly resulted in fatal competition for the clubs. This time, the proliferation of film art theaters—offering programs dominated by quality films of international origin—caused journalists, film critics, and some club members to question whether the clubs had become superfluous. Walter Talmon-Gros founded the first French-style postwar art cinema in the Schwabing section of Munich in

1951 and within two years established a League of German Art Cinemas (Gilde deutscher Filmkunsttheater), which by 1955 encompassed fifty-two art cinemas located in cities and large towns across West Germany. Although local club leaders feared the art cinemas as competitors, Eckardt praised their efforts and urged cooperation. This response was no doubt conditioned by his own earlier involvement in founding Parisian-style art or "repertoire" cinemas in Munich (the Urania) and Berlin (Kamera unter den Linden and Die Kurbel) in the late 1920s and early 1930s.[57]

In 1953 Eckardt secured the participation of the League of German Art Cinemas at the annual club meeting at Bad Ems. The league's attendance drew sharp criticism from the German commercial theater owners association, but an unruffled Talmon-Gros dismissed their "battle cry" as shortsighted. The commercial theater owners, he maintained, "apparently have not noticed that the . . . art cinemas have accomplished something much more effective . . . namely to—so to speak—neutralize the film clubs, that is, to refer them back to their original limits and furthermore curb [their activities] through collaboration."[58] Art cinema owners, in contrast to their mainstream commercial counterparts, worked with the clubs to build a dependable clientele and often benefited directly from the clubs' efforts to bring culture to the public. An art cinema on the outskirts of Regensburg, for example, sold few tickets to the Japanese film *Jiguko-Mon* (*Gate of Hell*, 1953) until the local film club decided to attend a screening and advertised the film in the local press. Afterward, it played to a full house.[59]

Art cinemas represented a curious combination of ally and competitor of the German film clubs. Despite signs of mutual assistance, the proliferation of urban art cinemas in the mid-1950s—and the institution of weekly art film screenings at some commercial cinemas—pressured the film clubs to differentiate their programs and rethink their purpose. They needed to prove they were more than screening facilities for foreign or classic film offerings, that they had not become redundant.[60]

The most serious blow to Eckardt's authority, however, emerged in the form of youthful protest against his studied neglect of ideological analysis at club meetings. Indeed, the "politics of generation" was more hazardous to Eckardt's association than Schopen's secession or any amount of art cinema competition or industry inattention. By mid-decade, a sizable contingent of university students started circulating complaints about Eckardt's management of annual meetings. These detractors did not dispute the worthiness of Eckardt's project to improve the public's taste. Rather, they attacked his authoritarian style, uninspired programming, and naive and pernicious separation of politics and culture.[61]

As early as 1953, a Swiss journalist compared the German film clubs' annual meeting at Bad Ems unfavorably with the scene at the internationally famous Cannes film festival, depicting a staid atmosphere lacking passion and a feel for the artistic:

> In Cannes, the discussions and conferences were wild improvisations. People gathered there in the small overcrowded press room, sat on stools, tables, or on the floor, stood or leaned against the wall, came and went when they liked, smoked and flicked the ashes inattentively on the floor. Here at Ems one sat in an academically proper position around a lectern, which was decorated with palms. One persevered, one was patient. One brought along an ashtray when one wanted to smoke. One nearly put aside the artistic and discussed with solemnity "What is a genius?" or the contributions of cities to the work of the film clubs. One spoke about the use of the entertainment tax, and about a law for the protection of youth. . . . "Film as an educational force" was discussed, but it was overlooked that the artistic has to be a first concern . . . , and that the "educational"—what a truly German concern, by the way!—can only arise . . . as a by-product.[62]

One suspects that this critique was conditioned as much by national stereotypes as the experience of the festival. Yet it captured the disgruntled spirit of student film club members who chafed at the stilted atmosphere of annual meetings after the clubs passed to German sponsorship. The students, increasingly influenced by Bazin's *Cahiers du Cinema*, detected a difference in vibrancy between the national film cultures of the two countries and began to articulate their displeasure at the unwillingness of their native leadership to broaden their discussions to entertain more controversial subjects.

By 1956, a group of "angry young men" seceded from the club movement, convinced that a critical approach to film culture could be constructed only outside of the clubs. Their revolt was at once gendered, generational, and ideological. The dissatisfied students who broke with Eckardt's organization were all male; apparently there were no female rebels in the club movement, or at least none that were able to make their voices heard. Indeed, both the club movement and the renegades, like the universities they sprang from, were dominated by men.

Women were active in some film clubs but rarely received recognition for their efforts. This was due in part to the attitude of many male colleagues who believed that women engaged in such extradomestic work merely as a distraction. It also stemmed, however, from the women's own priorities, at least as articulated by two of the most prominent women in the film club movement. Eva Schmid taught film seminars and led film clubs in the Ruhr area in the 1950s and was cofounder of the Oberhausen film festival (see chapter 7). She was consumed by a passion for film and devoted many hours to it but was torn by another calling, which she did not wish to neglect: "It was a lot of work, always something to do. It fascinated me, I invested a lot in it, I sacrificed a lot of sleep on account of it. But I never wanted my family life to suffer because of it. I was married—being mother and housewife was my first profession—and I believe, despite all my activities outside the home, that I always remained that. For that reason I never wanted a full-time job. And for that reason I never fought for my own interests. I always found it strange that the men often thought that I 'worked' because I had an 'unhappy' marriage."[63] Another notable woman is Fee Vaillant, who began as a film club "pioneer" in Bünde-Ennigloh in the 1950s and by the 1970s became director of the Mannheim film festival. Her involvement with film grew out of her experiences at the cinema with her daughter. Vaillant became convinced that children needed to be educated to become critical viewers of commercial film fare and organized a film club that offered weekly screenings and subsequent discussions of "appropriate" films for the local schoolchildren. Thus, her engagement with film derived from maternal concern and was directed toward the cultivation of discerning film-viewing minors.

These women had different demands on their time than did the university men, who would parlay their dissatisfactions into enterprises that would launch their careers as journalists, film critics, and cultural commentators. When Schmid was asked to describe her reaction to this group of renegades, she replied: "I found the work of these film critics incredibly important. What I didn't agree with was that they had no sense of humor whatsoever and didn't like comedies." Both women, in fact, seemed reluctant to combine their cultural work with political objectives. Schmid, for example, explained that she surrendered the leadership of a film club when she was scolded by a member for showing a "communist" film, Vittorio De Sica's *Miracle in Milan*: "Such a thing happened more than once, and when it occurred more frequently, I had the feeling that it served no purpose, that it negatively affected the work [of the club], that someone should do it differently." For Schmid, the point was not to provoke political passions or stimulate political debate. Politics, to her, poisoned the process. Having been trained in art and literature, she preferred to confine herself to an analysis of film aesthetics and style.[64]

Schmid's male counterparts were much less reticent about unleashing controversy, perhaps as a function of their youthful independence and judgmental idealism. The yawning age gap between the association leadership and the student rebels was a significant factor in their growing disenchantment with club activities.[65] Also, complaints about Eckardt's stodginess were targeted at more than his advanced years, for the marked difference in age coincided with a more fundamental disagreement regarding the social role of film criticism.

The inaugural issue of the leftist film journal, *Filmkritik*, which became the mouthpiece of the angry young student secessionists, opened with a challenge to the practices of the old guard:

> We agree with Walter Benjamin: The public is constantly judged incorrectly and yet feels itself to be represented correctly by the critics. Typical film criticism, insofar as it is not an appendix to the advertising section or practiced by volunteers, turns this sentence on its head: it says to the public what it already knows but can't formulate so elegantly. Oscar Wilde's observation applies to their best representatives: They have nothing to say, but they say it delightfully.
>
> Nothing is as outmoded as belletristic art criticism, which notes impressions and fancies instead of identifying structures, which describes instead of interpreting, which "celebrates" and "pans" instead of leading the reader to the proper understanding, which prefers to see the film "only as a film" instead of within its social context, which inquires into the "intentions of the artist" instead of making demands. [The critics] place their trust in the preexisting taste and reserve intellect for the discovery of stylish bons mots.[66]

One of the founders of this journal was Enno Patalas, a twenty-six-year-old doctoral candidate working under Walter Hagemann at the University of Münster. Patalas had been recruited into the film club by Hagemann, who convinced the younger man and a number of other students to accompany him to the annual meeting at Schluchsee in 1950. Stimulated by the atmosphere of international intellectual exchange there, Patalas threw himself into the film club movement, presiding over the University of Münster film club, attending annual meetings, and becoming a regular contributor to the association's official publication, *Filmforum*.

By the mid-1950s, however, Patalas became increasingly disillusioned with the complacency of the club movement in addressing broader issues of German reconstruction. In particular, he criticized the leadership for its lack of interest in changing the cultural situation in the Federal Republic. This state of affairs was reflected in editorial constraints imposed by the association's journal, *Filmforum*, which Eckardt heralded as an open "forum" for intellectual exchange and debate. Given such advertisement, Patalas bristled at the treatment his articles received from editors who stripped his submissions of their political slant. In order to articulate issues that went unaddressed in *Filmforum*, Patalas and fellow students Theodor Kotulla and Benno Klapp in 1956 founded a film journal, *film 56*, which they funded out of their personal savings. Although the journal was distributed with the help of the Arbeitsgemeinschaft der Studentfilmclubs, an association of student film clubs, the students received no encouragement from the film club movement leadership. In fact, Walter Hagemann, by now Patalas's doctoral adviser at the university, had so little sympathy for the project that he refused to supervise Patalas's thesis.[67] Patalas ended his university studies and continued work on the journal, but only three issues appeared before the money ran out. Within a year, however, the students were able to negotiate a deal with a Frankfurt company to publish a new journal, *Filmkritik*. Funding was tight, but Patalas demonstrated that if the 300 subscribers to the defunct *film 56* were carried over, subscriptions would pay for the cost of the printing. Patalas, however, worked for free.[68]

Filmkritik, then, was heir to *film 56*, which was conceived as a politically oriented, left-leaning journal. Patalas and friends drew upon the cultural criticism of Frankfurt School theorists Theodor Adorno and Max Horkheimer and sympathizers Walter Benjamin and Siegfried Kracauer. Like their Marxist-inspired predecessors, these students eschewed organized party-political activity in favor of intellectual endeavor. They sought to pierce the "apparent" order of things to uncover structures and mechanisms normally hidden from sight. More precisely, they wanted to subject to analysis the material, structural, and ideological underpinnings of postwar German film production and to draw attention to the cultural politics of the new democratic state. Drawing on the writings-in-exile of Adorno, Horkheimer, and Kracauer, they speculated also on the psychosocial effects of the cinematic "Kulturindustrie," which held out the promise of consumer freedom and individuality but delivered only illusory relief from oppressive reality and bolstered capitalist relations in the process. Although they published excerpts from Horkheimer and Adorno's *Dialectic of the Enlightenment* (1947), they eschewed class analysis to focus on national questions of ideological continuity in Germany's cultural production.[69]

The second issue of *film 56*, for example, featured a talk Patalas had given at the 1955 annual film club meeting in Bad Ems entitled "From Caligari to Canaris: Authority and Revolt in German Film." Originally sponsored by the Filmarbeitsgemeinschaft an den deutschen Hochschulen, an association comprised of college seminar groups interested in investigating practical and theoretical problems connected with film, the talk had its theoretical basis in Siegfried Kracauer's now well-known study of the authoritarian tendencies of Weimar film. According to Patalas, it was poorly received by the leadership of the association. Expanding on Kracauer, Patalas argued that the myth of authoritarianism had been propagated in German film from Weimar through Hitler and was now experiencing a "restoration" in the postwar period.[70] Patalas's contention that "the notion of an unpolitical film not driven by ideology is itself a piece of ideology" rubbed against the grain of the professedly apolitical club.

The talk discomforted the film club leadership because it sought to elucidate cultural continuities in German film from the Weimar Republic, through Hitler, to the present. Patalas reintroduced politics into culture, an unwelcome intrusion for a club leadership bent on examining "art for art's sake." His insistence on the sustained presence of authoritarianism in postwar German film culture suggested that Hitler's totalitarian regime was hardly a historical aberration that had been forever dispatched but was a disturbing phenomenon more firmly anchored in the peculiarities of German culture. To accept the Patalas-Kracauer thesis, one would need to commit to a program of national soul-searching; it was easier for the older leadership—as cinephiles with professional résumés that reached back to the interwar period—to deny or ignore the intimate connection between culture and politics.

Patalas and friends, however, continued to provoke. By the early 1960s, they highlighted articles criticizing state intervention in film culture, a phenomenon they had experienced firsthand during their early engagement with film. As a leader of the student film club in Münster, Patalas had encountered vexing difficulties importing films from East Bloc countries. According to federal regulations, all films entering West Germany from socialist countries—whether intended for public exhibition or private screenings—were required to be submitted for review within twenty-four hours to the Interministerial Committee of the federal Ministry of Economics.[71] The Münster student club considered this an infringement of democratic freedoms and circumvented the regulation by exhibiting such films the same day they were received, shipping them back before the twenty-four deadline. Only through such tactics were they able to subvert the unwelcome, and some would later argue unconstitutional, interference of the state in film exhibition.[72]

While chafing at official regulation of film exhibition, the editors of *Filmkritik* also criticized the film censorship board for releasing films prohibited under the occupation, such as Willi Birgel's . . . *reitet für Deutschland* ([He] *Rides for Germany*, 1941), which, they argued, advocated Nazi ideology. That this development was connected to the return of centralized government in the Western zones fueled the fear that the new democratic government was shockingly lax in snuffing out the cultural remnants of Nazism. In 1957 an article in *Filmkritik* warned that "under pressure from the general political development of the Federal Republic, the criteria for judging films has so fundamentally changed over the past four years, that today one can already speak of a perceptible tendency toward softening the political tenets" on which the censorship organization was based.[73] Pointing to Kracauer's thesis regarding the importance of film in preparing the way for national socialism's triumph, Patalas hinted at the dangers such policies could have for the new democracy. The problem was not just the resurrection of Nazi films, which did not in any case last long at the box office, but the contamination of the new film production. Documentaries such as *Beiderseits der Rollbahn* (*Both Ends of the Runway*) and *So war der deutsche Landser* (*Such Was the German Soldier*), which represented war outside of its political context from the viewpoint of a "simple soldier," were blasted by Patalas, along with a group of commercial products that showed similar characteristics of thematic bias.[74] Patalas cataloged films that resurrected the imperial period as a golden age dominated by good society (such as Josef von Baky's *Hotel Adlon*, 1955), films that falsified the political and military history of Germany (such as Wolfgang Liebeneiner's *Königin Luise* [*Queen Luise*], 1956, and Alfred Weidenmann's *Stern von Africa* [*The Star of Africa*], 1956), and treatments of the more recent past in which Western Allies' efforts to build a democratic Germany became the subject of ironic criticism (such as Eduard von Borsody's *Der Major und die Stiere* [*The Major and the Bulls*], 1955).

Patalas called upon the FSK to control this "flood" of films that enticed by their easy sentimentality and emotional appeal. Far from prodding the audience to examine recent German history in a critical fashion, he argued, these films sought to reassure German audiences with a romanticized or distorted view of an otherwise deeply troubling German past. This sentimentalized view not only thwarted criticism and reassessment but also provided a comfortable alternative German identity with insidious ideological continuities from the Nazi period. Patalas's response to this dilemma was to advocate stricter enforcement of censorship—a peculiar position for a left-leaning intellectual who favored democratic forms of government: "The FSK must find the strength not to surrender to conformity, and to abandon the attempt to rescue every film by means of editing when suppression as a precedent has been long justified. More decisiveness is necessary in order to act against impertinent provocations . . . and withdraw from the position of being ever ready to talk about decisions—which only encourages applicants to ever new attacks."[75] For Patalas, then, democratic debate had its limits; pushed too far, it could result in a spineless submission to bullying industry interests, which would have more serious repercussions for national democratic renewal. Clearly, then, the concept of *Filmwirkung* was as convincing to the cultural left as to the cultural right. In this case, arguments for heightened cultural watchfulness grew out of the assumption that the masses were incapable of identifying the ideological thrust of German films. They were still passive consumers, highly susceptible to manipulation, who needed to be trained both to perceive the political uses to which films could be put and to evaluate each film within its sociopolitical context. As a result, Patalas argued that the FSK should be more vigilant in policing for politically regressive tendencies in German film—tendencies that would reinforce unwelcomed cultural and ideological continuities between the Nazi and postwar orders.

Reviews in *Filmkritik* often strove to make such continuities explicit. One of the more biting attacks on the FSK and state cultural policies appeared in the form of a film review of Veit Harlan's *Anders als du und ich (Das dritte Geschlecht)* (*Different from You and Me [The Third Sex]*, 1957). Harlan was a successful film director during the Third Reich and is perhaps best remembered for scripting and directing the notorious *Jud Süss* (1940), a falsified historical account of Joseph Süss-Oppenheimer, the Jewish financial adviser to the duke of Württemberg in the 1730s. In the film, Süss robs the population of their prosperity, their cultural patrimony, and their racial purity by overtaxing the people, turning Württemberg into the "Promised Land," and brutally raping the beautiful daughter of the duchy's chief minister.[76] When Harlan first reappeared on the film scene in 1949 to direct his premiere postwar picture, *Unsterbliche Geliebte* (*Immortal Beloved*, 1950), he was brought to court twice, first in the Hamburg Denazification Chamber and then before a regular court, accused of membership in Nazi organizations and "crimes against humanity" for his work on *Jud Süss*. In both cases, he was acquitted since the prosecution could not prove with any degree of certainty that the anti-Semitic film succeeded in provoking either audience response or sympathy.[77] Both Harlan's lurid filmmaking past and the content and treatment of his latest effort, *Anders als du und ich*, provided the editors at *Filmkritik* with a perfect example of the lurking persistence of "prefascistic hostility toward intellect [*Geistfeindschaft*]."[78]

Harlan's film tells the story of Klaus (Christian Wolff), a young Gymnasium student and aspiring artist whose parents fear that he is developing homosexual proclivities when he becomes involved with a group of young men centered around Boris Winkler (Friedrich Joloff). The film opens with a long shot of a courtroom, in which Klaus's mother (Paula Wessely) is being tried for *Kuppelei*, or sexual procurement, for her son. The story is told in flashbacks, spurred by the judge's request for a chronological rendering of events leading up to the crime. Klaus meets Winkler through his school friend, Manfred (Günter Thiel), who occupies himself by penning poetry and pursuing Klaus. Klaus's visits with Manfred, spent reading poems and listening to electronic music in the latter's room, are parallel edited with scenes depicting Klaus's parents, Herr and Frau Teichmann, delaying dinner to await their son's belated arrival. Dinner finally is served without Klaus at his furious father's request.

That evening, after hearing his wife describe Klaus as talented, Herr Teichmann (Paul Dahlke) confides to Klaus's Uncle Max (Hans Nielsen) that he wishes his son were "less talented and more normal," adding later that his son is "not interested in girls." This exchange spurs Klaus's mother to consult first books, then doctors, in a quest for expert advice on an antidote for homosexuality—which she refers to, in dated Hirschfeldian fashion, as "the third sex [*das dritte Geschlecht*]," that intermediary biological state between manhood and womanhood.[79] In Harlan's film, however, Klaus's homosexual tendencies appear to be other than inborn, since unlike Manfred, who seems incapable of defending himself, Klaus jumps into the fray to defend his friend against bullies at school. Like the Nazi state, the film insisted upon maintaining a distinction between the "seducer" and the "seduced"—"between those with 'strong' and 'weak' homosexual tendencies."[80] Klaus, we are led to believe, belongs firmly with the latter; his sexual inclinations are attributable to social influences and therefore subject to modification.

After a heated confrontation between Klaus and his father, Frau Teichmann insists they should do something to "cure" their son rather than simply disciplining him. When her husband locks Klaus in his room to keep him from his "unhealthy" friends, Frau Teichmann declares her son too sensitive for such treatment and begins to seek her own remedy. A child psychologist points to the generational conflict between father and son and tells Frau Teichmann that she, as a mother, can "do more." The family doctor provides another tip: that the only solution is "die echte Liebe einer Frau," the true love of a woman. Armed with this advice and spurred by an offhand observation by Uncle Max about their "little housekeeper," Frau Teichmann hints to the beautiful young Gerda (Ingrid Stenn), a German refugee who is fond of Klaus, that she may be able to exercise some womanly "power" over the ailing young man. Having set the scene, Frau Teichmann and her husband take a trip, leaving Gerda at home alone with their son.

Klaus, the movie has convinced us by this time, is in dire need of rescue. Manfred is unhealthily dependent on him and obsessively jealous of any time Klaus spends out of his company. The more serious threat, however, is Manfred's onetime mentor, Boris Winkler, a man of about fifty who invites Klaus to his home, compliments him profusely on his artwork, and physically subdues him with a lingering look of longing—a close-up shot that convinces us of his potent hold over the boy.

Accessible only through admittance by a discreet butler, Winkler's home is a darkly lit, dramatically decorated den of Uranism. After an overture of musique concrète, Winkler explains that the Greeks stressed both mind and body—Geist und Körper—and the evening's entertainment begins. The camera tilts as two well-built men enter the room, remove their robes, and, clad only in bikinis, begin to wrestle. We watch the action briefly before the camera moves to Winkler, who perches on the arm of the chair occupied by his latest initiate. Winkler, the shot suggests, threatens to become a surrogate father to Klaus; but instead of paternal love, he is motivated by libidinal attraction.

Unlike Herr Teichmann, Winkler values and praises Klaus's artistic talents—drawing comparisons to Picasso and Kandinsky—and encourages him to develop his own vision and identity. If Klaus trusts his imagination, Winkler

A poster for Veit Harlan's *Anders als du und ich* romanticizes the heterosexual relationship under the guard of a watchful mother. (Courtesy of the Stiftung Deutsche Kinemathek, Berlin)

The dramatically lit Klaus (Christian Wolff) and Dr. Boris Winkler (Friedrich Joloff) in *Anders als du und ich*. (Courtesy of the Stiftung Deutsche Kinemathek, Berlin)

predicts, "there *really will be* a Klaus Teichmann." Winkler has obviously hit his mark, and Klaus, beaming with pride and pleasure, replies: "You are the first to tell me that. . . . That is the best thing you could say to me." Klaus is convinced that the cosmopolitan Winkler, in contrast to his *bürgerlichen* banker father, understands and appreciates him.

In the end, however, heterosexuality triumphs. When Klaus's parents leave for vacation, Gerda promptly ejects the visiting Manfred from the house. Bored, Klaus attempts to sketch Gerda but finds no inspiration until she loosens her bathrobe. Suddenly, he responds not as an artist but as an uninhibited, sexually charged, heterosexual man. Gerda becomes scared and flees, but he pursues her until she relents. The next day, Klaus's masculinity is restored. He is active and buoyant, shows no patience with Manfred or his jealousy, and appears intent only on repeating his episode with Gerda.

Rejected, Manfred does some spying and informs Winkler of Klaus's transformation. Winkler takes revenge by accusing Frau Teichmann of procurement, which leads to her arrest. The police question the underage Gerda, who bashfully confirms that she "did everything a woman in loves does" with Klaus—a scene that redeems her in spite of her act. At the trial, the judge (Otto Graf)

The morning after: a night of heterosexual sex has "cured" the son's unsure masculinity in *Anders als du und ich*. (Courtesy of the Deutsches Institut für Filmkunde, Frankfurt)

recognizes that Frau Teichmann was acting out of maternal concern but chastises her for ignoring Gerda's "human worth." In the original version of the film, prohibited from release in West Germany by the film censorship board, she is sentenced to six months in prison and Klaus begs her forgiveness, which is immediately and lovingly granted. In the version revised for domestic release, the prison sentence is mitigated to probation, allowing the family and its future to be saved without further sacrifice from the mother.[81]

The *Filmkritik* reviewer charged that Harlan's film used the subject of homosexuality to create a "characteristic simplification" of the normal and the abnormal, which was linked to the character's sexual preference and then expanded to his whole milieu. The effect was to stigmatize homosexuality along with "modern painting, electronic music, and any pursuit of things intellectual." This, he added, was a favorite strategy of Nazi propagandists, who contrasted "degenerate" culture—which they associated with urban life, intellectuals, and Jews—with the pure, natural, spiritual simplicity of the German *Volk*.

The reviewer detected an identical tendency in Harlan's work. The normal, for Harlan, was represented by "primitive emotion, which has been neither reflected upon nor sublimated" and which found its expression in "above all, the [hetero]sexual act." Harlan's film gradually returns the "homosexually endangered" Klaus to the "straight path sexually"—a transformation that is complete when he renounces his proclivity for painting in an abstract style. Thus, the plot explicitly equates "degenerate" culture and "degenerate" sexuality. With a somewhat more subtle technical effect, Harlan associates modern music with the character's sexual deviance and dispels both as the electronic sounds accompanying the homoerotic scenes dissolve into a romantic Chopin piece.

The reviewer also speculated whether Klaus's cosmopolitan friend, Boris Winkler, "presumably the seducer . . . is perhaps not also a Jew—thereby completing the Nazi enemy of the *Volk*." That charge, it seems, was a little more tenuous but not completely unwarranted. The film did, after all, link Winkler to internationalism—both in his artistic references and his futile attempt to flee Germany for Rome. Moreover, it insinuated that homosexuals delighted in playing the vengeful conspirators against enemies or turncoats, a characterization applied to both Jews and Marxists during the Third Reich by the Nazi Party, which, as early as 1928, fervently asserted the "indissoluble joining of marxism, pederasty, and systematic Jewish contamination."[82] Citing the charges brought against Harlan in 1949 and 1950, the *Filmkritik* review proclaimed it "an injustice that the members of the tribunal called him a 'conscious Nazi.' He was and is, rather, an unconscious Nazi . . . who shared the intellect and idiocy [*Geist und Ungeist*] of the rulers."[83]

By focusing narrowly on the ways in which the film could be considered an extension of Nazi filmmaking conventions, the reviewer missed much, including the tried-and-true themes of maternal sacrifice and feminine seduction and even a surprising scene involving the father, Uncle Max, and a transvestite act at a nightclub that humorously suggests the possibility that ambisexual attraction is not incompatible with "normal" heterosexuality. Ironically, given the criticisms of Harlan that surfaced in *Filmkritik* as well as in the mainstream and homosexual press, the film had been subjected to two rounds of revisions to subdue its putatively *pro*-homosexual bias before it was approved for release by the FSK. Catholic and Protestant clergy, in fact, denounced it as overt agitation against §175 of the West German penal code and charged that it set the issue of homosexuality before the public in order to prepare the way for its legalization. Their suspicions were no doubt fed by the fact that Harlan had enlisted the advice of Hans Giese for the project. Director of the Institute for Sexual Research in Frankfurt, Giese since the early 1950s had urged the reform of §175. Although the exact content and extent of Giese's input on the film cannot be determined, his professional presence no doubt alarmed the postwar guardians of West Germany's social and moral order. In the end, the FSK demanded that sympathetic portrayals of moral and monogamous homosexuals in the film be excised. As a result, homosexuals were represented exclusively as wily cowards and pedophiliac criminals "who bring calamity to mothers and corruption to youth."[84] Although this rendition of events does not absolve Harlan from the sins of ideological continuity alleged by the youthful *Filmkritikers*, it does suggest that the reigning sexual ideology of the Adenauer era, as expressed through the FSK, shared some of the same assumptions underlying the Nazi-era legislation it was so eager to endorse. As Robert Moeller has noted regarding the postwar decision to uphold §175, "The Federal Republic's break with the past was anything but clean." Given the reasons behind the FSK ban on the first two versions of the film, one can only wonder why the *Filmkritik* reviewer directed none of his indignant venom at that institution.[85]

Homophobia aside, of the numerous areas of critical neglect, perhaps the most striking is the theme of parental—and particularly paternal—guilt, especially in view of the generational nature of the *Filmkritik* attack. At the end of the film, just after Frau Teichmann is sentenced, she turns to her husband and says, "You too were guilty, and you don't even realize it." Herr Teichmann, his wife implies, forced her—the vigilant mother—to take drastic action due to his reliance on authoritarian, but completely ineffectual, bombast. From the first domestic scenes in the film, she contrasts her constructive desire to "cure" her son to her husband's resort to yelling. Even toward the end, Herr Teichmann attempts to solve the problem of his son's unsure sexuality by threatening Winkler and initiating legal action against him; but this, too, is exposed as fatuous bluster when the complaint is thrown out due to insufficient evidence. What Teichmann does succeed in doing is provoking Winkler to lodge a complaint of his own against Teichmann's wife, which Winkler will not withdraw—even at Klaus's pleading—once he knows that Klaus has engaged in heterosexual intercourse. The crime (albeit a different one in Winkler's eyes and those of the court) has been committed. As the grim defense lawyer vows to try his best, but regrets he cannot make her innocent, Frau Teichmann answers: "No one can take away *our* guilt."

As much as homosexuality, then, this film thematizes the gaping postwar generational divide, resulting from an absence of trust, respect, and communication between father and son (more than mother and child). This was a theme that resonated with Harlan's professional and personal life. The *Filmkritikers* derisively dismissed Harlan and his work as ideological holdovers from the past. Despite his repeated and strenuous attempts to convince the world that he was (and always had been) an apolitical artist, Harlan convinced few of the younger generation. This deep-seated suspicion of fathers was shared by his own, now estranged, son from his first marriage, Thomas Harlan, who traveled to Israel in 1953 to make a documentary on that new state as "atonement for the earlier National Socialistic attitudes of his father."[86] Communication between generations appeared at an impasse. If Harlan's film indicated that the father also needed to change, he appears not to have taken the message to heart.

The *Filmkritik* condemnation stood in sharp contrast to another article about Harlan, published in 1955 by association president Johannes Eckardt in *Filmforum*, which attempted to rehabilitate the director. Eckardt defended Harlan after Patalas used his film, *Der Große König* (*The Great King*, 1942), as an illustration for a film club talk on ideological continuities in German film. Eckardt's article included lengthy quotations from letters he received from Harlan, explaining the extraordinary pressure the director felt to cooperate with the Third Reich and his lack of artistic control due to Goebbels's meddling. According to Eckardt, this situation so frustrated Harlan that when he was contracted to film *Jud Süss*, he attempted to escape the project by volunteering for the military. Harlan claimed that Goebbels was determined to use his filmmaking talents and threatened that if Harlan enlisted, he would serve his time on the front: "Goebbels screamed at me, as you can read in my judgment [from the 1950 trial for crimes against humanity], upon hearing my refusal: 'I can crush you like a bug on the wall.' "[87]

After citing numerous examples of Harlan's victimization by Goebbels, Eckardt indicated his trust in the veracity of Harlan's representation, explaining that he published the letter "because it provides a further insight into the relentless control of German film work during the Third Reich and explains much of that which, in itself, appears to be incomprehensible."[88] Eckardt, in effect, delivered a clear and unveiled apology for Harlan's behavior and work under Hitler. Not content to leave it there, he quoted Harlan's complaint that, despite judicial exoneration, he was barred from making "artistically worth-while films." Harlan wrote: "I am very unhappy that still today I live without freedom and am not permitted to make films in the way that I must make them, in the way that I want to make them."[89] Unwilling to let Harlan speak for himself, Eckardt appended this with an expression of support and sympathy for the outcast director: "It appears to be justifiable for humane reasons to give a filmmaker the opportunity to declare publicly what he is striving for. One should remember these words of Veit Harlan's when the films that he still hopes to make come up for judgment." Through a facile treatment of the issue of individual responsibility under an authoritarian regime, Eckardt trans-formed a filmmaker who propagated Nazi ideology and received a handsome profit for his troubles into a victim deserving the sympathy of German au-diences.[90] Eckardt's strategy of reducing the issue to the personal and human level sought to deflect attention from the symbiosis between culture and poli-tics. Rather than respond to Patalas's position on its own terms, Eckardt shifted the focus from the political meanings and uses of cultural products to the plight and personality of the cultural producer.

Eckardt's sleight of hand could not mask the continuities between the cul-tural life of Nazi and postwar Germany, however. At the opening of a German Film Week in Hamburg, that city's press chief and *Senatsdirector*, Erich Lueth, called for a boycott of Harlan's new film, *Unsterbliche Geliebte*: "Anyone who has been as outstanding a director of Nazi movies as the co-creator of *Jud Süss* . . . should be blackballed in disgust by all decent Germans mindful of the tears that still flow at millions of Jewish graves. . . . Harlan's re-emergence will open wounds which have hardly closed. . . . It is the duty even more than the right of all decent Germans to be ready, not only to protest against—but to boycott—Veit Harlan."[91] Harlan took Lueth to court for his statement, and the latter was ordered to "abstain from calling for a boycott on the pain of fines and jail sentence." Lueth immediately filed an appeal, and a sizable number of German individuals and organizations supported his call for a boycott. Further-more, demonstrations against the film were held on the streets of Berlin and Munich.[92]

Eckardt's willingness to facilitate Harlan's rehabilitation may in fact have derived from his own experience in the Third Reich. Although that period is glossed over in biographical material on Eckardt, it is certain that he prospered during the Third Reich through his affiliation with DEGETO and the Tobis film company. A bit more light was shed on Eckardt's past at the annual film club meeting in 1962. Club members surreptitiously circulated a piece of paper that bore an excerpt from a 1936 speech in which Eckardt praised "the filmic natural-ness of 'our Führer' and set it up as a general postulate for German film."[93] The skeletons in Eckardt's closet may have caused him to be less outraged when confronted with Harlan's. In any case, that situation only served to underscore Patalas's concern about the political implications of the continuities in style, form, and personnel from the Nazi period that he detected in postwar German film culture.

If Patalas used Harlan as the personification of the persistence of "prefascist" and Nazi tendencies in German culture, he used the example of Wolfgang Staudte, another German film director whose career was a study in Cold War politics, as an example of "how and where German film was manipulated . . . , and still is." Staudte made the first postwar German film, *Die Mörder sind unter uns (The Murderers Are among Us)*, with a Soviet license in 1946. As a result, he became an inadvertent founding father of DEFA, the state-run film monopoly of the future German Democratic Republic. While acknowledging Staudte's negative experiences with Soviet and East German authorities, Patalas counseled West Germans that they had no reason for complacency or self-congratulation. Staudte's story, he claimed, was an "all-German tale *[ein gesamtdeutsches Märchen]*," which illustrated "how little one can speak of freedom of artistic expression in film even in this country."[94]

Patalas invited the reader to draw parallels between the cultural management and control practices of Western democracies and communist regimes by explicitly comparing Staudte's treatment by the governments of West and East Germany. Asserting that the "case of Staudte was a chain reaction of missed opportunities, political stupidities, and authoritarian arrogance on both sides of the 'Iron Curtain,'" Patalas suggested that democratic notions of freedom were as insufficiently instilled in the West German leadership as in the East.

Patalas's article cataloged the tribulations Wolfgang Staudte faced in his quest to reactivate his career after 1945. He considered the story particularly poignant because he judged Staudte one of the few postwar German directors capable of quality work. According to Patalas, Staudte's troubles began in 1945, when he attempted to interest Western Allied film officers in his screenplay for *Die Mörder sind unter uns*, which chronicled the spiritual suffering of a physician returning to Berlin from the war, who, imprisoned by memories of the past, is unable to confront the present. Despite a clean political profile and the strong anti-Nazi tone of his screenplay, Staudte was reportedly unable to win the support of any of the Western Allies for his project and turned to the Soviets, who permitted its realization. The film, to quote at length from Eric Rentschler's well-crafted summary, "from its very first shot"

> thematizes the relationship between the past and present: the camera fixes on a grave, rising to gaze out a long lane where Mertens, the dazed physician . . . staggers toward the mound and a group of playing children. Framed by the specter of war's devastation, but surrounded by youth and hopes for the

future, Mertens will take flight into a bar from which honky-tonk music issues. His persistent outings into night clubs are an escape from the past and a postponement of the future, a step into a realm of excitement and gaiety where time is of little importance. Pursued by the recollection of a massacre he sought to prevent while in Poland, the physician cannot recycle the past with the ease of his ex-superior Brückner, the man responsible for the killings who has in the meanwhile settled into a smug and comfortable existence as head of a factory where steel helmets are made into pots and pans.[95]

Die Mörder sind unter uns was completed in 1946, the first German production of the postwar period. "And so Staudte became a DEFA director," commented Patalas. But things were not quite that simple in the early days of the Cold War. Incensed by the tampering of a Soviet film officer who cut a crucial political scene from his next film, *Rotation*, Staudte returned to the West to make his next film. He later moved east again in order to realize his controversial film, *Der Untertan*, which had been blocked by West German film producers. *Der Untertan* was based upon a novel by Heinrich Mann and explored the authoritarian, nationalistic, and sycophantic character of a bourgeois citizen in imperial Germany. According to Harlan, the film was meant as a "warning": "This theme has never been more current than at the present time, since the military-minded are again strategizing in beer halls and want to believe that the honor of a nation can be secured on the battlefield with blood and iron; with blood, spilled for the profit of a handful of men [*Herren*]."[96]

Although the film was completed and released in East Germany in 1951, its official West German release was blocked until 1957 by the Ministry of the Interior. It was shown, however, in closed screenings by a number of student film clubs prior to 1957. Government officials were outraged by the film's implicit suggestion that authoritarianism had deep historical roots in Germany and that Hitler was perhaps less an aberration than a culmination. As Rentschler so aptly describes it, the film

stops at crucial junctures in the life of Diederich Hessling, showing how his blind worship of authority stems from a cultural heritage full of military marches, heroic portraiture, and impassioned patriotism. The authoritarian factory owner, Hessling, worships his kaiser every bit as ardently as he expects absolute allegiance from his workers. In the film's most striking sequence, the sycophant follows his ruler to Rome. Staudte stages the confrontation between sovereign and dutiful subject in a stunning montage sequence that climaxes in Hessling's chase after the royal coach, bowing with hat in hand, screaming hurrahs, framed as a pitiful lackey between the revolving spokes of the coach wheels. A final passage updates Mann's novel of 1913 to the postwar present: the monument of Kaiser Wilhelm II that

"The Subject," complete with bandaged face, after a youthful duel as a university student in Wolfgang Staudte's controversial film parody of the German past, *Der Untertan*. (Courtesy of the Deutsches Institut für Filmkunde, Frankfurt)

Hessling helped erect in his hometown square stands in the midst of rubble as the voice-over narrator insists that the spirit that bore Hessling lives on.[97]

Staudte had a great deal of difficulty working in the West following the East German release of *Der Untertan*. Although he contracted to direct a detective story about surreptitious animal killings, *Gift im Zoo* (*Poison in the Zoo*), a telegram from the federal Ministry of the Interior to the production company threatened the withdrawal of federal credits for the film if Staudte did not sever all ties with DEFA. Staudte resigned from the project and returned to the East. His "defiant" acceptance of the "National Prize of the Soviet Union" from the hands of Walter Ulbricht transformed "the best German director in the West" into "a persona non grata for all time." Staudte was unable to work again in West Germany until the federal program of film credits ended in 1956. The end of federal credits brought with it the end of the official ability to prohibit, through the power of the purse, the production of films bearing messages of dissent.[98]

Patalas's tale of Staudte was at once a condemnation of political suppression of artistic freedom in West Germany, a chronicle of state interference in cultural matters, and a testament to the shaky foothold democratic principles had in West German society. Patalas challenged the hypocrisy of Cold War politics, alleging that the elevation of communists to the status of enemies of the state allowed "unconscious" former Nazis to slip through the back door and set the cultural agenda. His contribution was to reveal the political implications of postwar cultural production and control. The *Filmkritiker*s illustrated that political renewal was intimately linked to cultural renewal and that without the latter, the former was incomplete.

In retrospect, however, it appears that Patalas and his group had to ignore something of the past to participate in Staudte's postwar cultural coronation. Staudte had entered the profession as a stage actor, had participated in productions of Erwin Piscator and Max Reinhardt, and was affiliated with the Berlin *Volksbühne*, which led the new Nazi government to group him with the cultural left and ban him, temporarily, from the stage in 1933. But he quickly made peace with his new masters, found work as a radio announcer, and wrote and made short filmed advertisements that won him a contract as a director-in-training with Tobis. With the outbreak of the war, he maneuvered to remain in the profession and avoided both military service and the dreaded experience of the front. Although he described himself as a lifelong pacifist, he later admitted that "during this time, I had very little interest in politics."[99]

Like Harlan, Staudte was tainted by cultural collaboration with the Nazi regime. Staudte, in fact, acted in Harlan's *Jud Süss* and in *Reitet für Deutschland*—two of the most notorious hate films of the period. He too described himself as an unwilling participant who sought only to save his skin. "To reject a movie role at that time," he recalled in 1966, "meant a call to military service—and I did not want that under any circumstances." His main aim, he candidly confessed, was to "keep my head above water as inconspicuously as possible."[100]

Also like Harlan, he considered himself an apolitical artist, intent only on working. Even after 1945, filmmaking—not politics—took precedence for Staudte. In 1945, with the screenplay for *Die Mörder sind unter uns* completed, the thirty-nine-year-old director went off to seek a license: "I wanted to make the film, it didn't matter in whose zone." He had, in fact, been awarded a British license but had no money to realize his project. That problem led him to the Soviets, who supplied him with both.[101]

Staudte was certainly no communist, but he was no unproblematic antifascist either. He was easier to rehabilitate because—unlike Harlan—he did not become a household name in the Nazi period and appeared to be unjustly maligned after 1945. Indeed, the Cold War paranoia that led West German officials to target Staudte as a communist sympathizer only added to his allure, and younger intellectuals admired him for his presumed commitment and integrity. Moreover, his work became increasingly politicized in the postwar period. Staudte tackled sensitive topics tied to the recent past and suggested that

German reconstruction was blighted by both historical continuities and widespread social amnesia. The critiques embodied in films like *Der Untertan* and *Rosen für den Staatsanwalt* (*Roses for the Prosecutor*, 1959)—a political satire on the reemergence of Nazis to positions of importance in the postwar West German judicial system—led many outraged West Germans in the press and state to charge Staudte with "fouling his own nest." This effect was heightened —along with the point of his films—when he refused to accept the 1960 Federal Film Prize for *Rosen für den Staatsanwalt* from "the hands of that one-time SA man," Minister of the Interior Gerhard Schöder. By now, Staudte's provocative pictures had succeeded in stimulating both recognition abroad and public debate at home. The young *Filmkritiker*s praised him for providing a much-needed public service that would force Germans to confront the repercussions of the recent past on the present.

In 1960 Staudte teamed up with Helmut Käutner and Harald Braun to make *Kirmes* (*Fairgrounds*), a highly disturbing study in stark black and white that revisited the "unmastered past."[102] The film opens with a shot of a village wall plastered with advertisements, and the camera comes to rest on a prominent poster for the CDU featuring Konrad Adenauer and his successful election slogan, "No Experiments [*Keine Experimente*]." To this postwar pastiche is added an announcement for the fair, which, in tight close-up, becomes the film's title. The little village has clearly survived the war to experience happier, more prosperous times, and the townsfolk are setting up for a carnival. As they dig to anchor the carousel, however, they uncover the bones of a young German soldier. They are the remains of Robert, who deserted in the last days of the war and returned home, only to be driven to despair and, ultimately, his death by a fearful father, an uncertain clergy, and an unyielding local Nazi functionary. The disinterred past shatters the comfortable complacency of the present, forcing survivors to confront both the memory and consequences of their earlier actions. Bad conscience, moreover, appears less political than deeply personal, for the greatest failing in the tragic story occurs within that most intimate social circle, the family. Robert's parents can neither protect their son nor hide him; his father feels endangered and fears discovery. When Robert finally shoots himself in desperation one evening at home in his parents' presence, they give no thought to providing a proper burial but hurriedly drag his body through darkness and artillery fire and roll it to rest in a flooded bomb crater. Only his body's unearthing—physical proof of the past and their past deeds—breaks the wall of repressed silence and shakes them out of their self-imposed stupor by reminding them that their hands are stained with the blood of an abandoned and betrayed son whom they lacked the courage and moral conviction to save.

Like the film, the young intellectuals at *Filmkritik* denounced the social amnesia of a postwar consumer society that was built on an unacknowledged

Robert Mertens (Götz George), a youthful deserter from the German Wehrmacht, finds no shelter in his hometown in Wolfgang Staudte's *Kirmes*. (Courtesy of the Stiftung Deutsche Kinemathek, Berlin)

past and the betrayal of its future. What the *Filmkritik*ers protested was the cultural cowardice of filmmaking fathers who renounced an honest taking-of-stock in favor of the tried-and-true formulas of the past. They admired Staudte's bold approach, his drive to expose the underside of complacent post-war life; they forgave his political passivity during the Third Reich because of his provocative productivity afterward. They, too, after all, chose cultural commentary over political activity, and they lobbied for a common goal: cinematic renewal and the realization of film's artistic potential.

As early as 1947, Staudte argued that Germans, unlike other filmmaking nations, have only one "trump in the hand": "The chance to begin again! . . . We stand at the crossroads. Will [German] film choose the laborious hike on the narrow paths of art's domain, bearing the burden of an inner accountability? or will it again carry a light parcel of wretched irresponsibility on its merry march down the comfortable street of cheap effects in the empire [*Reich*] of a mediocre entertainment industry?"[103] Staudte represented the path of culture and cultivation, a commitment to the artistic and the intellectual. Harlan offended because he represented the vulgar. His film derided both artistic and intellectual endeavor as a form of deviance, which made the *Filmkritikers* suspect him of two offenses: first, of ongoing ideological sympathy with national socialism, and second, of a lowly commitment to cinema as mere commercial entertainment.

For Patalas and his group, cultural renewal could not be based on old commercial genres and filmmaking styles that had been developed under the guidance of the huge film companies of the 1920s and perfected under Hitler. What was needed was a critical distance from the past, and this required an influx of new filmmaking talent uncompromised by association with Goebbels's Film Chamber. Yet the ongoing attempts in West Germany to discredit Staudte, the realities of film financing, and the self-satisfied complacency of active filmmakers made it difficult for Patalas's group to envision a scenario for such a rejuvenation—until, that is, a young group of filmmaking "rebels" threw down the gauntlet at Oberhausen in 1962 and held out the hope that a German film culture untainted by both commercial considerations and the unhappy politics of the past might finally reach fruition.[104]

LOCAL CHALLENGES TO
THE DOMINANT CULTURE
MANNHEIM, OBERHAUSEN, AND THE
STIRRINGS OF YOUNG GERMAN CINEMA

The hall [at Oberhausen] was full of people. There weren't any seats, and everyone was standing all around. One knew beforehand that there would be people who would make all kinds of malicious remarks. . . . We stood together as a group. We felt like the accused, although we were causing the stir. . . . I believe . . . that the text [of the manifesto] was already known. It had been reproduced and distributed. I can no longer remember the arguments [raised], but I remember the shrill voices, the agitated, spiteful . . . remarks of men and women who were older than us and appeared to be so competent. There was nothing for us to do, but to move closer together. We stood there that way, side by side. . . . I remember that the group became a group there for the first time, because we were standing shoulder to shoulder and each was holding firmly onto the other. . . . It was due only to this stance that one could summon the courage to counter-attack. . . . [Alexander] Kluge was the one who . . . did most of the talking, and we merely stood behind him with pale faces, looking defiant.—Edgar Reitz, filmmaker

For the past thirty years, the name "Oberhausen" has been heralded —by film historians and filmmakers alike—as the birthplace of Young German Cinema and the artistic renewal of national film culture. In that city in 1962 a rather amorphous group of young filmmakers, who were united by optimism, idealism, and the rejection of reigning commercial cinematic forms, promulgated their Oberhausen Manifesto and announced the dawn of a new era of filmmaking in West Germany.[1]

Young German Cinema was more of an improvisation than a movement. The Oberhausen rebels shared no particular political or ideological outlook. In fact, the reminiscences of Edgar Reitz suggest that the young filmmakers first developed a group identity in response to the angry, vocal reception they re-

The rebels of Oberhausen, 1962. (Courtesy of the Deutsches Institut für Filmkunde, Frankfurt)

ceived at the press conference they held to publicize their views. Their youth and sense of separateness from the film establishment were crucial in forging their identity as a group but most significant were their cultural aspirations. They united in opposition to the old, dominant forms of "Papa's" cinema, which appeared at last to be in its death throes, suffering from a dramatic decline in attendance, a reduced share of the domestic market, and embarrassing international publicity of its substandard quality.[2] Impatient with the gradual demise their aged competition, the Oberhauseners attempted a coup. Their manifesto was at once a declaration of war and of artistic, financial, and ideological independence:

> The future of German film lies in the hands of those who have proven that they speak a new film language. Just as in other countries, the short film has become in Germany a school and experimental basis for the feature film.
> We declare our intention to create the new German feature film.
> This new film needs new freedoms. Freedom from the conventions of the established industry. Freedom from outside influence of commercial partners. Freedom from the control of special interest groups.
> We have concrete intellectual, formal, and economic conceptions about

the production of the new German film. We are as a collective prepared to take economic risks.

The old film is dead. We believe in the new one.[3]

Although signed and publicized at Oberhausen on 28 February 1962, the manifesto was in fact composed in a Chinese restaurant in Munich, which had displaced Berlin as the German film capital in the West. As Alexander Kluge put it: "Whoever wanted to make films at that time gravitated to Munich." The signatories were, however, underfinanced industry outsiders, unable to break into the "hermetic, stylish society held over from the UFA era." Lacking the financial backing to make feature films, they began to experiment with short films.[4] In the process, they resurrected and reinvigorated the *Kulturfilm*, an important current in German filmmaking in the interwar period, recasting the genre to highlight its potential for sociopolitical commentary. Advancing a vision of cultural renewal based upon the international examples of Italian neorealism, the French and Polish New Wave, the British Free Cinema, and the work of Weimar filmmakers, these young renegades strove to create a native art cinema to counter the leveling influences of international commercial culture. Their efforts represented a push for cultural diversity and were launched at the local level.

Contrary to popular representations, this well-publicized challenge to the commercial film industry was not based upon a generational split that surfaced suddenly in the early 1960s. Rather, it grew out of dissident voices, such as those of Enno Patalas and Wilfried Berghahn, that emerged from the student branch of the film club movement of the 1950s. It also grew out of the *Kulturfilm* festivals in Mannheim and Oberhausen, which were founded to foster public appreciation for a film genre neglected by commercial cinemas. These festivals advocated *Kultur* over commerce, and by identifying film with *Kultur*, they implicitly constructed an alternative vision regarding the purpose of film in postwar German society. City sponsorship of the *Kulturfilm* became, to borrow the words of Thomas Elsaesser from a different context, "part of the politics of culture, where independent cinema is a protected enclave, indicative of the will to create and preserve a national film . . . *ecology* amidst an ever-expanding international film . . . *economy*."[5]

The Mannheim and Oberhausen festivals were shaped according to the political affiliations of each city's mayor. The conservative values of Christian Democracy reigned in Mannheim, while the Social Democratic politics of Oberhausen's mayor informed the cultural politics of that city's festival. Consequently, Oberhausen was more open to alternatives to dominant forms and invited cultural exchange with the East. Yet both festivals opened a space outside the commercial circuit where aspiring young filmmakers could acquaint themselves with artistic developments in other European countries and critique the native product against international trends. A fortunate few would be provided the opportunity to exhibit their own films, which otherwise were smothered by the disinterest of profit-conscious commercial distributors.[6]

At the 1953 annual film club meeting in Bad Ems, Werner Uhde, cultural adviser of Augsburg and a member of the Cultural Committee of the Council of German Cities (Deutscher Städtetag), proposed that cities actively support the goals of the German film clubs by exhibiting worthwhile films in their communities. Cinema owners quickly protested that city involvement would suggest to the public that "municipal cinemas exhibit artistic films" while commercial theaters "show flicks."[7] In fact, theater owners were right to fear for their image. Municipal involvement in film matters was motivated by cultural ambitions and the desire to provide an alternative to the popular film fare offered in commercial cinemas.

In the early 1950s, numerous cities sponsored film screenings and seminars through local educational and cultural institutions.[8] This was consistent with the active role town governments historically had played in subsidizing culture in Germany. However, they departed from their traditional role by expanding their previously narrow focus on elite culture to include mass culture.[9]

In the early postwar period, municipal support for film grew out of expectations regarding its value for popular education. The impetus for such involvement was frequently based on the personal interests of an incumbent mayor or an energetic secondary school instructor, as was the case with the two communal film festivals founded in Mannheim and Oberhausen in the early 1950s. The events at Mannheim and Oberhausen expanded far beyond the limited commitment to film culture in other cities to become annual affairs and achieved a measure of national and international recognition unprecedented for community-sponsored film events.

The first of these festivals, the Mannheim Kulturfilm Week (Mannheimer Kulturfilmwoche), was held in 1952 at the suggestion of the mayor, Hermann Heimerich, who drew his inspiration from a film art conference sponsored by the Heidelberg student film club in 1950. Heimerich was struck by the pedagogical possibilities of film exhibition and decided to initiate a city-sponsored film festival in Mannheim. He mandated that the Mannheim festival should be limited to the screening of Kulturfilme, a genre that he and others identified as "volksbildend," or educational at a popular level, and one that, he regretfully noted, had disappeared from the postwar programs of commercial cinemas.[10]

This characterization of the Kulturfilm was based upon both the conventional content of the genre as well as its exhibition history in interwar Germany. The *Kulturfilm* developed as a German specialty on the world market in the mid-1920s, at a time when economic instability temporarily led German firms to reduce their production of full-length feature films. To compensate, the large film company, UFA, stepped up its production of short-subject films. Conceived primarily to "enrich . . . knowledge, promote . . . understanding of other peoples and countries, [and] enliven . . . scientific research,"[11] these *Kulturfilme* were frequently supported by government funding. They depicted anything from industrial processes to sculpted athletes engaged in sport, from deer in rut to "fire worshipers and Tibetan monasteries." By the mid-1920s, with the cultivation of their trademark feuilletonistic style, they reached a broad audience. *Kulturfilm* shorts became a regular part of the prefeature show in commercial cinemas, and special theaters devoted to exhibiting feature-length examples of the genre appeared in larger cities such as Berlin, Hamburg, Düsseldorf, Leipzig, Dresden, Stuttgart, and Munich. UFA, moreover, developed its own *Kulturfilm* section and began to exploit its material to its fullest commercial potential by issuing some films in three versions: "academic [for screening in universities], pedagogical [for schools], and popular [for screening in cinemas]." Thus, the more notable *Kulturfilme* received wide distribution and became popular vehicles for education and entertainment.[12]

The identification of the *Kulturfilm* as an important educational tool for use both inside and outside the classroom continued into the second postwar period and derived from the typical subject matter of this genre. The *Kulturfilm* acted as a filmic encyclopedia, visually guiding the spectator through a fascinating universe of biological, technical, geographic, and cultural diversity. As one film critic pointed out, the genre delivered an "unbelievable abundance." Mannheim schoolchildren in the 1950s "could, for two hours, get a glimpse of the world— . . . far away lands, antarctic regions, sun-shimmering deserts, uncanny jungles, bodies of water, mountains, cities, castles, cathedrals, works of art, technical things—from the first railway to the atom bomb, people from all regions, all races, animals, nearly the entire fauna, all of this and even more came to them in the dark room by means of the great medium film."[13]

In its early years, the festival was explicitly aimed at the youth of Mannheim. The festival's motto, "Um das Publikum von morgen" ("For the public of tomorrow"), coined in the second year, emphasized the pedagogical orientation of Mannheim's sponsors. Yet organizers were well aware that the *Kulturfilm*, the star of their festival, had become—at least in Germany—a "sick child" that needed special tending.[14] One well-known film critic depicted Mannheim's agenda in martial terms, as a cultural crusade that could be won only by securing the loyalties of postwar German youth: "The *Kulturfilm* is being fought for in the present, it must be fought for. There is a significant outpost in this battle and it is Mannheim. And there are assault troops, fighting troops, whose strength should not be undervalued, and who will win this war in the end—that is the youth. . . . [Their support] must be secured for film—for good film."[15] In order for the genre to recover, it would be necessary to stimulate the interest of the filmgoing public of the future.

Educators and *Kulturfilm*makers tended to articulate their demands for official support of this genre on national and moral grounds. Eberhard Tautz, head of the Mannheim-Ludwigshafen Film Club, which cosponsored the festival, commented that the organizers "wanted, above all, to lead the youth to an [appreciation for] good film and away from the insipid productions of the 'dream factory' and Wild West films."[16] The cultivation of good taste in German audiences, then, demanded instilling a preference for "quality" *Kulturfilme* over Hollywood-style commercial film products.

The identification of the *Kulturfilm* with quality and public education, and of Hollywood products with amoral commercialism, was widespread in the early 1950s. German filmmaker Alf Zengerling, for example, appealed for state support for the *Kulturfilm* on moral grounds by trotting out the old argument concerning the need to shelter German youth from bad influences. This, he claimed, was particularly necessary in a period of free competition and open markets: "The distributors of feature films are not interested in films made solely for youth, because they cannot earn that much with them. On the other hand, there are more than enough adventure, Wild West, . . . and crime films available for youth to see. What do the children get from such films? . . . When one looks at American films such as 'Sinbad the Sailor' . . . with [its] half-naked harem girls, which is screened as a film designated for youth, one must ask oneself what all of this will lead to."[17] The *Kulturfilm* became an important symbol of German cultural identity in a period dominated by the internationalizing culture produced in the United States—especially as "Hollywood" became shorthand for sex, violence, and immorality. In the early 1950s, communities like Mannheim attempted to resuscitate the familiar German genre as a moral national bulwark against those pernicious foreign influences.

Short documentaries had been a mandatory part of the cinema program under Hitler, screened before the feature film at every commercial theater. With German defeat, however, state support of the genre ceased, and the production and exhibition of the *Kulturfilm* declined with the emergence of a liberal market economy. *Kulturfilm*makers were unable to secure financial backing from commercial firms, which foresaw no market for these wares after the state ceased to require their exhibition.[18]

This fact was not lost on representatives of the federal government. In an opening address at the fourth annual Mannheim festival in 1955, Richard Muckermann, a Christian Democratic representative in the Bundestag and member of the Parliamentary Committee for Press, Radio, and Film, underscored the importance of *Kulturfilme* for the recovery of German film culture: "Already in the 1920s the German *Kulturfilm* was spoken about around the world, and its didactic character was recognized by the state. Film culture in Germany thrived with the support of the *Kulturfilm*, and this *Kulturfilm* has proved that it can again culturally fertilize the new era of German filmmaking. . . . A new era calls for new directions and new methods but does not mean that origins should be renounced or accumulated experience should be tossed overboard. . . . [The *Kulturfilm* must again become] the pearl on the film industry's cravat."[19]

In advocating the *Kulturfilm* in Mannheim, Mayor Heimerich was responding to his earlier viewing experience, the international reputation this genre had enjoyed abroad two decades earlier, and the official Nazi equation of German *Kulturfilme* with quality. The *Kulturfilm*, for Heimerich and those of his generation, was synonymous with German cultural prestige and economic might. It was recognized on the world market since the 1920s as a predominantly German film form, or at least one that the German film industry had perfected through its "scientific thoroughness and competent photography."[20] Support for the *Kulturfilm* implied a commitment to the resurrection of German culture and economy.

The presumed educational and moral value of *Kulturfilme* caused some admirers to release the genre from the aesthetic and formal demands typically made of film products. One critic suggested that the *Kulturfilm*'s social and cultural importance dictated that "absolute, film-artistic criteria have no validity here. It concerns the factual, the subject matter: it revolves around [the capacity] to offer the young something that they otherwise would rarely see, to make the *Kulturfilm* accessible in its astounding freshness of life."[21] Despite the opinions of such enthusiasts, festival organizers and film critics in the 1950s did not push uncritically for resumed production of old-style UFA *Kulturfilme*. German film culture needed to be refashioned to appeal to the postwar audience.

Supporters in the Federal Republic blamed the declining quality of German *Kulturfilme* in part on the limited amount of financial help received from the state and federal governments. To bolster their arguments, they focused on the generous support the French and Italian governments extended their documentary artists and, more ominously, indicated German inability to compete with the unlimited resources available to their colleagues in the East.[22] Others pointed to the advances in avant-garde documentary production made in small countries such as Belgium without the benefit of such resources. To these critics, the problem was a crisis of creativity and reflected the inability of West German artists to develop new cultural forms that would speak to the present generation.

By 1956, the fifth year of the Mannheim film festival, organizer Kurt Joachim Fischer declared a state of emergency for the German *Kulturfilm*. This was not because the genre itself was threatened but because a decline in German dominance of the genre, both in terms of quality and international standing, had been indisputably revealed. Fischer maintained that financing alone could not be blamed for the poor quality of German *Kulturfilme*; their producers had increasingly received support in the form of film prizes, awards, and credits from the federal and state governments.[23] Much more important was filmmakers' lack of imagination regarding subject matter and stubborn adherence to old forms. Arguing that "the herring have finally become tired of being filmed for the two-hundredth time!," Fischer calculated that in the past ten years since 1946, "blast furnaces [appeared] 247 times, ocean fishing 189 times, road-safety campaigns 176 times." In addition, German filmmakers fashioned "156 films on mountains, 134 on rivers, and 129 films on cities."[24] As further comment on this sad state, Fischer quoted *Kulturfilm* director Curt Oertel, who insisted that for "two years we haven't had a *Kulturfilm* we could market abroad. We have fallen asleep behind our cameras. When we awaken, we busy ourselves as if headmasters in the deepest provinces. We have hardly anything left to show that displays quality."[25]

Clearly, the Mannheim organizers faced an uphill struggle in their quest to support this genre. Studies on the reception of the *Kulturfilm* showed that Germans above the age of thirty would greet its return to the commercial theaters with enthusiasm, and school-age children showed interest when exposed to *Kulturfilme*. But young Germans between the ages of seventeen and twenty-five, who were the most avid moviegoers, rejected its old-style didacticism.[26]

The municipal festivals themselves generated increasing public ire at the German *Kulturfilm*. The festivals provided one of the few public forums for *Kulturfilme*, where they were screened alongside their international counterparts. This, however, facilitated comparisons of national style and quality, which had serious implications for the reception of the German product. As Fischer pointed out, "The Mannheim public, which has become extraordinarily demanding, no longer wants to see German films. . . . A group of German films was again booed this year."[27]

The cure for this malady was for filmmakers to learn from their more creative colleagues abroad. Throughout the decade, critics and supporters alike insisted that the resurrection of a quality film culture—indeed, a German culture—depended upon the assimilation of foreign discoveries, technologies, and impulses. Fischer, for example, praised the work of Polish, Russian, Czechoslovakian, Italian, British, Belgian, Dutch, and French documentary makers and pointed in particular to Albert Lamorisse's *Le Ballon rouge*, which provoked an incredibly enthusiastic response from the Mannheim festival audience. Such a response, Fischer maintained, was at once encouraging and depressing because it illustrated the audience's sophisticated understanding of the film medium but also demonstrated just how "hopeless" the state of the German film industry was: "We Germans at one time invented the UFA-scheme and are now, after thirty years, smothered by it. The innovative is alien to us, because we cling to survival. Risk-taking is out, because economic security matters above all. The courageous decision either to give up filming altogether or to begin again in a completely new manner . . . is nowhere to be found. . . . The *Wirtschaftswunder* has allowed us to become poor in film-intellect [*film-geistig arm*]. . . . Filmmaking is not dependent solely on money. . . . The creative spirit is much more important."[28]

The low esteem accorded German *Kulturfilme* and declining attendance ultimately forced Mannheim organizers to reevaluate their program. In 1960, after a great deal of negotiation, they opted to rename the festival International Film Week Mannheim (Internationale Filmwoche Mannheim) and broaden their program to include the first feature film of *Kulturfilm*makers or documentary filmmakers. Pressure to repackage the festival was not merely the outgrowth of the German *Kulturfilm* crisis, however. Rather, it derived from the increasingly critical reviews leveled at its annual program as well as differences that surfaced among the festival's organizers.

The Mannheim festival had shown signs of stagnation by 1957. Internal differences of philosophy and conflicting ambitions among the festival organizers had provoked a period of self-conscious reassessment and readjustment. Much criticism was leveled at Fischer and his ambitious designs for the festival. From the festival's beginnings, Fischer energetically strove to broaden its appeal and attract an ever-increasing number of international guests and journalists. This strategy served his career and brought a large measure of recognition to the industrial city of Mannheim but was antithetical to the original vision of Mayor Heimerich. Heimerich had presented a clear mandate to the festival in 1951: it was to serve the local population, above all the youth. It was not to become an attraction for "throngs of international visitors," the site of "congresses, and the awarding of prizes," or a promotional tool for the city. By 1958, Fischer's ambitious plans for the festival were clearly winning out. Mannheim had received recognition as an international festival by the Paris-based International Film Producers' Federation (Fédération Internationale des Associations de Producteurs de Films [FIAPF]), and the festival became a juried competition, awarding prizes of gold ducats, embossed with the festival's title, to the best entries.[29]

Responding to a perceptible drop in local attendance, continued public complaints about the quality of films exhibited at the festival, and the ever-increasing number of foreign guests, journalists, and officials, the city government decided to take action.[30] Arguing that they could no longer spend their limited funds to finance a festival that increasingly catered to the interests of film-makers, journalists, and, incidentally, Fischer's career, festival organizer Christoph Andritzky and Mayor Hans Retschke pressured Fischer to resign. They then attempted to change the orientation of the festival by recruiting Johannes Eckardt and the Association of German Film Clubs as cosponsors.[31] They had opted, for the moment, to revert to the festival's original function as a forum for raising public awareness of quality domestic and international film. In the process, they identified the festival more closely with the aging Eckardt and the national film club movement, which was also suffering from a depleted public image and declining membership by the turn of the decade. The mayor's right-leaning politics and Eckardt's official presence gave the Mannheim festival a conservative pall that was off-putting to some of the younger, more spirited film enthusiasts.

Mannheim's woes were compounded by the competition offered by the Oberhausen West German Kulturfilm Meeting (Westdeutsche Kulturfilmtage), founded in 1954, two years after the start of the Mannheim festival. The organizers of the two festivals initially greeted each other as friends and allies, but by the late 1950s, Oberhausen's influence had clearly surpassed Mannheim's.[32] Oberhausen became known as the "Mecca" of the modern short film, acquiring in the process a reputation as host to a more lively festival, which drew young, politically engaged filmmakers, critics, and enthusiasts who shunned the more stodgy Mannheim event.[33]

The Oberhausen festival began, similarly to Mannheim, with city sponsorship and was based upon the cooperative efforts of Hilmar Hoffmann and Eva Schmid, two adult education instructors. Hoffmann and Schmid initially organized the event as a seminar for film instructors from the Volkshochschulen of North Rhine Westphalia,[34] a fact reflected in the festival's early mottoes, "Way to Education [Weg zur Bildung]" (1954), "The Educational Powers of Kulturfilm [Bildungsmacht Kulturfilm]" (1956), and "Film Experience—Educational Experience [Filmerlebnis—Bildungserlebnis]" (1957). At first, Oberhausen was a "purely national" affair, exhibiting mostly German Kulturfilme in the old style, including "the first animal films by Sielmann, . . . films by Cürlis about graphic arts."[35] Despite its humble beginnings—only 112 instructors attended the first meeting along with a handful of journalists and two foreign guests—Oberhausen rapidly surpassed Mannheim in drawing foreign and domestic participants. Hoffmann and Schmid studied the programs of competing documentary film festivals in Cork, Annecy, and Mannheim, intending to broaden their scope. In 1958 they coined the motto "Path to Neighbors [Weg zum Nachbarn]," highlighting Oberhausen's international program and Hoffmann's ambitions to achieve international recognition for it as a serious film festival. The next year, the festival was renamed the West German Short Film Festival (Westdeutsche Kurzfilmtage), which reflected the organizers' desire to distance their event from the nationalist and outdated connotations associated with the term, "Kulturfilm."[36] By 1960, Oberhausen received recognition from the FIAPF in Paris, a sure sign that it had arrived on the international scene.[37]

Oberhausen's reputation as the more dynamic of the German festivals stemmed partly from the leadership of Hilmar Hoffmann. Just twenty-nine years old in 1954, Hoffmann gave the impression of youth, vitality, and expertise. His aggressive strategy of attending the better-known international European film festivals at Edinburgh, Brussels, Cannes, Venice, and Locarno suggested that he had his finger on the pulse of new filmmaking trends. In addition, Hoffmann provided international prestige and publicity for the festival by recruiting well-known talent. Jean Mitry attended the first year and brought along his films *Pacific 231* and *Image pour Debussy* for screening and discussion. The works of the British documentary filmmaker John Grierson were shown, and he later became a reliable participant, presiding over Oberhausen's international jury in 1960. Bert Haanstra, a Dutch filmmaker who won an American Academy Award in 1958 for his short film *Glass*, was also secured for the festival as an exhibitor and jury president. This expanding stable of filmmaking notables assured the festival national and international press coverage and would work to Oberhausen's advantage in its periodic conflicts with the government in Bonn.[38]

The political openness of the Oberhausen festival also attracted young German filmmakers, critics, and enthusiasts. Indeed, throughout the 1950s, Oberhausen provided more fertile ground than Mannheim for the cultivation of cultural pluralism in German cinema. Hilmar Hoffmann and the mayor of Oberhausen were Social Democrats at a time when culture was dominated by Christian Democrats, as was the case in Mannheim. Because the festival organizers decided to forego federal funding in order to maintain their independence from the dictates of Bonn, ideologically and aesthetically diverse films could be shown with little interference in Oberhausen. This often extended to the controversial.[39] In 1957, for example, two years after the West German Foreign Ministry lodged a formal protest against the showing of Alain Resnais's *Night and Fog* at the Cannes film festival for fear that it would "disturb the international harmony of the festival by its emphatic reminder of the painful past,"[40] the film was awarded a prize at Oberhausen. Oberhausen provided a more politically congenial forum for film screenings and discussions and exhibited an independence of action that many found refreshing.[41]

Despite the perception of Oberhausen as "progressive," Hoffmann's stated aims for the festival did not differ fundamentally from those of Johannes Eckardt, the German Film Club Association president, who insisted that artistic film should be viewed in spite of its politics. Hoffmann, however, expanded on this argument (and his festival's motto) and, by stressing film's importance as cultural ambassador, provided an implicit critique of the cultural politics of the Bonn government:

> One should not understand "neighbor" only in its geographical sense. . . . [It] also refers to . . . those who live differently, who act differently, who think differently, in Christian terms, one's fellow man [den Nächsten]. . . . The countries that meet together in Oberhausen are all neighbors. . . . Each is the other's neighbor, and even if one rejects the political ideology of a person or another state, one should still be acquainted with their characters. . . . Political education, when based on taboos and fictions, cannot hold its own. The films of . . . other lands have the power to reveal what kind of answers we have. Perhaps they can also show why and to what extent our answers have been insufficient until now. Because people have been offered few opportunities to come together, and are left in the modern world to the mercy of fate, they should at least try to get to know each other in as direct a way as possible.[42]

Such an approach made possible a cultural opening to the East. In the first years of the festival, French, British, and Canadian films were heavily represented. During the second year, a controversial decision was made to include films from Eastern Europe in the program. The Czechoslovakian filmmaker Jiří Trnka sent his puppet films, and a number of Prague cartoons "of a revolutionary character" were exhibited as well.[43] Over the course of the next few years, the festival expanded Eastern representation, securing submissions from Poland, Hungary, Romania, Yugoslavia, the Soviet Union, and the German Democratic Republic.[44]

The festival became known as "Red Oberhausen" among anticommunist detractors and conservative politicians in Bonn, who feared the influx of socialist culture into the Federal Republic. They complained that the East Bloc countries reserved their very best products for successful display in the West or, worse yet, produced films specifically for the festival. On several occasions, West German authorities attempted to counter the increasing Eastern influence at the festival by withholding visas from visiting East European filmmakers, as was the case in a 1956 action against Trnka, who was becoming an Oberhausen regular. In such circumstances, pressure from international and national filmmakers and the press usually settled the matter in the festival's favor.[45]

In fact, the participation of East European filmmakers increased over the course of the late 1950s and early 1960s, drawing, in addition to Trnka, such luminaries as Walerian Borowczyk, Jan Lenica, and Jerzy Bossak of Poland,

István Szabó of Hungary, Dušan Vukotić of Yugoslavia, and Roman Karmen of the Soviet Union. Nervousness over the large contingent of Eastern Europeans at the festival did not, however, diminish, and in 1958 some German newspapers decried the fact that Poland, Czechoslovakia, the Soviet Union, and the German Democratic Republic had voting representatives on the Oberhausen jury. They were especially shocked that the East German's affiliation was listed as "the German Democratic Republic," which implied a diplomatic recognition of East German sovereignty that continued to be officially withheld by Bonn.[46]

Despite the festival's reputation as "red," the audience at Oberhausen contained individuals of all political stripes, including a good number of "Cold Warriors." Eva Schmid remembered one incident in which film historian Jerzy Toeplitz's observation that "Poland also belongs to Europe!" was met with a shout from the crowd: "But I prefer the Poland of Chopin to the Poland of Gomulka!"[47] Given the tensions that divided Germany, the Western orientation of the federal government, the large number of Polish-Germans in the industrial Ruhr area, and the increasing Eastern orientation of the program, the festival's proceedings were highly politicized.

Oberhausen became the gateway to the East in both cultural and economic terms. The festival attracted serious filmmakers and distributors from across Europe, the United States, and Canada who wanted a glimpse at artistic developments behind the "Iron Curtain": "Western buyers from New York and London came to view the Eastern product. West German television bought East European shorts and ran them at regular intervals, primarily on Eva Hoffmann's Second Channel program, 'The International Short Film.' Polish Film Weeks in West Germany grew out of the gatherings; friendlier relations developed between artists from East and West; and young West German filmmakers turned, perceptively, from French models to Czech and Polish directors for inspiration."[48]

The young West German filmmakers who were influenced by the French and Eastern European films shown at Oberhausen were, for the most part, makers of cultural short films who rejected the "escapist neutrality" of old-style *Kulturfilme* "that showed only sunsets, beekeepers, and industrial process." "In our films," recalled Peter Schamoni, "we wanted to depict our present—films as documents to aid comprehension of the times."[49] Oberhausen drew the likes of Bernhard Dörries, Rob Houwer, Alexander Kluge, Dieter Lemmel, Edgar Reitz, Peter Schamoni, Haro Senft, Herbert Vesely, and Wolf Wirth, who engaged in discussions on filmmaking, exhibited their works, and, in 1962, clustered together to present their manifesto to a hostile audience of self-satisfied feuilletonists.

These filmmakers transformed the *Kulturfilm* by infusing it with a measure of social consciousness or sharpening it with political or social critique. Lemmel's *Sie waren leider nicht gemeint* (*You Were Unfortunately Not Intended,* 1961), for example, explored the social effects of old age by focusing on the loneliness of an old woman; and Kluge and Schamoni's *Brutalität in Stein/Die Ewigkeit von Gestern* (*Brutality in Stone/Yesterday Goes on Forever,* 1960) "subverted the *Kulturfilm*" genre by "deconstructing the Nazi past" through a visual analysis of its monumental architecture.[50] Other films attempted to comment on the numbing effects of consumer culture, advertising, and technology on individual identity, the human spirit, or interpersonal relations. Dörries's *Das Mannequin* (*The Fashion Model,* 1961), for example, chronicled the interaction between a professional photographer and a fashion model on a location shoot in the countryside. By focusing on the photographer's fastidious preparations and his cold, mechanical approach to both his work and his subject, Dörries sought to convey "how technical achievements affect the spiritual existence of humans. Over the course of the film, the soul of the model is murdered by the camera, and the visible vitality of the girl is extinguished by the photographic material."[51] By the 1961 festival, the contributions of these young filmmakers provoked the international jury to issue a statement of recognition, praising this "group of previously unknown creators" who have "brought new impulses to short filmmaking [*Kurzfilme*] in the Federal Republic."[52]

These "creators" were "previously unknown" because they were young (between twenty-eight and thirty-two years old), worked outside of the established industry, and had a correspondingly precarious economic base. The Oberhausen rebels were centered in Munich but had no access to West Germany's most modern film studios at Munich-Geiselgasteig. They developed their identities as filmmakers and their ideas about the creative process of filmmaking in opposition to the culture industry headquartered across the Isar River at Geiselgasteig.[53]

The Oberhauseners shared other characteristics as well. All, to begin with, were men. This is consistent with the "virtual absence" of women filmmakers in German cinematic history through the early 1960s. There were, of course, some notable exceptions, but of these, Leni Riefenstahl and Hanna Henning, an early silent film director, were the only female film directors to make more than one or two feature films prior to the 1960s. Even after 1962, as Julia Knight has noted, women were "acutely underrepresented within the New German Cinema." The "decisive breakthrough" did not come until 1977, when five female directors released well-received feature films, and the top Federal Film Prize went, for the first time in its history, to a woman, Helma Sanders-Brahms.[54] Tellingly, Sanders-Brahms and Helke Sanders—who would become the noted female directors of the late 1970s and 1980s—were on the average five to ten years younger than the Oberhauseners and had entered the profession through acting schools in the late 1950s and early 1960s, the one proven avenue for women interested in film.[55]

The "angry young men" of Oberhausen also sprang from similar social backgrounds. Most came from middling to upper middle-class backgrounds, completed their *Arbitur*, and went on to university study, a privilege reserved for a small (mostly male) minority in the 1950s. Some in the group, in fact, renewed acquaintances in Munich they had originally made during their university years: "The group's formation was an organic process [and], . . . above all, a Schwabinger process. It was, strictly speaking, a collection of friends and acquaintances. No one was a stranger in this group."[56] All inhabited a shared intellectual milieu centered around Munich's Schwabing cafés, the Chronos-Filmstudio, Fritz Falter's art cinema on Occamstraße, and Enno Patalas's Munich-based periodical, *Filmkritik*. Like the *Filmkritik*ers, these were highly educated young men who received their early training in the audiences of film club and art cinema screenings. They constituted the tiny minority of the West German filmgoing public that sought out quality foreign films like Vittorio De Sica's *Bicycle Thieves* and considered themselves—due to their powers of discernment and analysis—the new generation of film intellectuals.

The group had already been formed by the time Alexander Kluge joined. Kluge was a lawyer and the published author of a book of fiction entitled *Lebensläufe (Life Stories)* by this time; he had also been a member of Gruppe 47, the group of postwar writers who had sought the regeneration of German literature. One suspects that he commanded considerable cultural authority, given these credentials, and he reportedly attempted to give the group of aspiring filmmakers a "political dimension" by introducing them to the ideas of Theodor Adorno and other theorists affiliated with the Frankfurt School. Nonetheless, participant Edgar Reitz noted that "it was neither a politically cohesive group nor a group with specific aesthetic principles. What united us was simply the rejection of what was showing at the cinemas at the time and the fact that we were outside looking in. We saw that the 'New Wave' was possible in France, that there was a Young Czech and a Young Polish Cinema. We were depressed because of our own situation but optimistic enough to believe that something similar could also be possible in Germany."[57]

The Oberhausen group framed its protest as aesthetic, ideological, and, above all, generational. The dilemma, as Enno Patalas later remarked, was one peculiar to post-Nazi Germany: "The sons must first beget their fathers." To accomplish this, these young German independents adopted foreign fathers, modeling their work on the short experimental films of Jean Mitry, Alain Resnais, François Truffaut, and Bert Haanstra, as well as a number of Eastern European filmmakers they encountered at the Oberhausen festival. Or they dug deeper into their national past and resurrected their grandfathers, those critically respected filmmakers from the Weimar period.[58]

Edgar Reitz recalled being surrounded by the "rubble of the war in the 1950s. . . . We were inspired by the operatic beauty of the ruins. One day Jean Cocteau came to Munich and said, 'Someone must make a film about these ruins.' . . . Such a voice seemed like a wake-up call." They scared up some film negative from a camera assistant who was working on a Billy Wilder production and went to work. Reitz and his friends made *Kurzfilme* out of financial necessity; production costs were a major consideration, as were the limited avenues of distribution. But the creative spark came from abroad. The filmmakers soon learned through the process of experimentation the genre's potential for artistic expression and sociopolitical commentary.

The Oberhausen festival proved itself invaluable to the professional development of independent filmmakers. It was a place to make contacts, exchange opinions, and sample the products from Western and Eastern Europe. Furthermore, it guaranteed talented German filmmakers an opportunity to screen their works to an international audience. Such screenings could win recognition, access to international festivals, and professional "legitimacy" for young filmmakers that could be crucial in obtaining financing for future projects. The Oberhausen signatories were aware of the need for self-promotion, both for personal ambitions and in order to stimulate cultural renewal.[59] They appended their 1962 manifesto with a list of their film awards and participation at festivals in order to verify their professional qualifications and support their demands for state-assisted financing.[60]

Herbert Vesely, who achieved a measure of stardom on the international festival circuit, is an informative case in point. Vesely, who originally hailed from Vienna, began to make 16mm films during his high school years. In 1951, at the age of twenty, he completed a half-hour experimental film based upon Georg Trakl's poem "Die junge Magd" ("The Young Maiden") entitled *An diesen Abend* (*This Evening*). Vesely submitted it to the Vienna Film Academy as part of his application to attend that school but was rejected, reportedly due to the film's "expressionist black-and-white photography and montage of sounds [musique concrète]." The next year, he took the film to West Germany and exhibited it at a festival sponsored by the Heidelberg Film Club. This screening opened doors for Vesely; he was invited to a festival in New York City, where he won first prize for the film. The resulting recognition secured him financial backers in West Germany for his first feature film, *nicht mehr fliehen* (*Stop Running*, 1955). The cost of the production was covered by equal investments by the Cultural Ministry Fund of North Rhine Westphalia and the Göttingen commercial company, Filmaufbau, headed by Hans Abich. Abich's willingness to underwrite a young independent director's project was highly unusual, since such decisions were usually vetoed because of profit considerations. Based upon Vesely's earlier work, Abich could not have deceived himself about the improbability of finding a distributor for the film. *nicht mehr fliehen* was hardly commercial fare but rather an avant-garde attempt to combine "fragmented narrative, existential philosophy, and (for the first time) radical politics."[61]

Set in a barren surreal world that some have compared to a Chirico painting, the film, according to one reviewer, was an existentialist study in "despair, which is indirectly compared to the position of people confronting the explosion of an atomic bomb":

> Two people are forced—physically and psychically—to contemplate point zero. The man reacts with numbed activity, and appears to be a prototype of the machine age; the woman understands nothing and thinks only about her cosmetics. The conflict appears in the form of a girl, a being of instinctual nature, who provokes her own rape and can be understood as the onslaught of the animalistic. The "redeeming act," the revolt in response to absurdity, is executed by the man who shoots the girl. The police, who come by at the that moment [*Sekunde Null*], let the man be, since a murder committed from a sense of absurdity is [morally] neutral according to Camus's conception. The retreating jeep that leaves the man behind works as a symbol of the triumph of a deified technology.

Premiered at the 1955 annual film club meeting in Bad Ems and screened at film festivals in Mannheim and Berlin, *nicht mehr fliehen* became the first postwar German film to be shown in the West German art cinemas. Although Patalas praised it as an example of filmic art true to its medium —one that "makes visible a whole new world"—the critical reception of the film was mixed.[62]

Vesely went on to make a feature-length film of Heinrich Böll's *Das Brot der frühen Jahre* (*The Bread of the Early Years*), which was released in 1962, the same year as the Oberhausen Manifesto, and was received as the premiere issue of Young German Cinema. In total, four Oberhauseners were involved in the production (Vesely as director, Hans-Jürgen Pohland as producer, Wolf Wirth on camera, and Christian Doermer in the leading role), and Heinrich Böll lent his support by writing the screenplay. The black-and-white film introduces Walter Fendrich (Christian Doermer), age twenty-four, an electrical mechanic who specializes in repairing washing machines, and focuses on a particular day in his life—"Monday, March 16th"—when the "past and present intermingle" in a way that provokes Walter to make some drastic changes.[63]

The film seeks to acquaint us with Walter by juxtaposing scenes shot variously from a third-person narrative perspective, a documentary perspective, and his interior, subjective perspective. The drama neither unfolds nor unravels

Spiritual desolation in Herbert Vesely's early effort, *nicht mehr fliehen*. (Courtesy of the Deutsches Institut für Filmkunde, Frankfurt)

but is chopped into initially incomprehensible scenes, which are flung at the audience without reference to chronological order and repeated two or three times over the course of the film. The result is a disturbing sense of confusion and dislocation; time and place are out of joint. We do not know where we are, when we are, who we are. We are forced to defer our desire for the immediate gratification of a coherent narrative and must patiently piece together the story of Walter's dilemma using snatches of conversations and bits of action, unsure at the moment whether we are observing something that corresponds to "social reality," Walter's subjective experience, or his reflections, reminiscences, even fantasies.

The film opens with a shot of train tracks, as the camera moves through an industrial district of Berlin on a wet, gray, dreary day. A woman's voice-over remarks, "Then he said he was going to the train station, at least that's what he said." Inside the train station, we see the close-up of a hand lighting a cigar, the camera tilts to reveal a loudspeaker overhead, then comes a close-up of a telephone dial and the partial face of a woman inside a phone booth. We hear another snatch of conversation before the camera shakily leads us down the steps of the deserted station. We again see empty tracks, the cigar being lit, and the upturned shot to the loudspeaker. Life is governed by ubiquitous technology, depressing monotony, a strange emptiness; the only element of surprise is a distressing disappearance—of Walter, we later learn. The woman in the phone booth will be identified as Ulla (Vera Tschechow), Walter's fiancée and the daughter of his boss, who cannot comprehend Walter's disappearance and bitterly dubs him an "ungrateful brute," for whom she's done everything. Ulla, it soon becomes clear, thinks in practical, material terms. She is certain that Walter's happiness will be sealed by money, entertainment, and a new car and manages their intimate relationship with the dispassion of an accountant—realizing only after it is too late that her unquestioned adoption of her businessman father's values has extinguished all ardor and spontaneity in their relationship.

Walter, however, suffers from a "hunger" that cannot be satisfied with the rewards of a *Wohlstandsgesellschaft*. Moreover, the hunger seems to represent both an emotional emptiness, symbolized by his relationship with Ulla, and an overwhelming insatiable desire sparked on the day of his disappearance by an unplanned reunion with Hedwig (Karen Blanguernon), a twenty-year-old woman from his hometown in East Germany whom he barely remembers from his youth as a skinny young girl. Hedwig, then, is immediately linked to Walter's nearly effaced personal past. But she evokes a suppressed national memory as well. For when Walter first approaches her at the train station, she asks him for directions to "Judenstraße"—the street of the Jews. This scene of their meeting is revisited a few moments later, but this time Walter responds to her question with a blank stare; "Judenstraße, Judenstraße," he repeats. Then finally comes the flicker of recognition: "Ah, Judenstraße. Yes, come with me."

Hedwig's appearance acts as a reminder of a long-forgotten individual and communal past, causing Walter to abandon his thoroughly planned present and a life that lay before him "like an open book . . . all arranged, all provided for." "If I hadn't met Hedwig," Walter muses, "I would have climbed into another life. Like taking another train . . . like living the life of a twin." Upon seeing Hedwig, Walter's amnesia is transferred to his current life and the plans made with Ulla: "I remember nothing of the future that will never be the present." Walter pursues Hedwig as a way to recapture his historical self. He wants to seduce her because she seems somehow "familiar" and because, we learn, she knew his father—a "cheerful and proud" teacher, reduced by circumstances to beg for bread; the man Walter both admired and abandoned to come West. The film is a meditation on identity, belonging, and longing, developed through the interplay of the personal and political, the past and the present, remembering and forgetting.

But identity fashioned from a recaptured past proves elusive, and Walter finds himself pursuing a reluctant Hedwig. From their first meeting in the train station, she is placed at a distance, tucked into a corner with her back to Walter and her eyes cast downward. When he visits her later with flowers in hand, she is again in the corner across the room from the doorway he enters. The camera zooms in on Hedwig, closing the distance and displaying Walter's attraction. We watch the nude caresses of the couple making love. But the scene is betrayed as Walter's fantasy through a discrepancy between the image and the soundtrack. Hedwig's voice repeatedly insists that Walter "go now," while Walter suggests that the flowers be put in water. The dialogue continues when the lovemaking scene disappears, and Hedwig is still in the corner, completely clothed. Reversing the zoom shot, the camera draws us back from Hedwig to the place where Walter stands, reestablishing the emotional distance she insists on maintaining.

Walter seeks in Hedwig something he could not find in Ulla. He believes that they understand one another, that they share a common experience. Unlike Ulla, in her world of cafés and cigarettes, cars and cosmetics, Hedwig, he claims, knows the meaning of bread and hunger. But Hedwig, too, has a hunger, and it differs from Walter's. Toward the end of the film, after a brief disappearance of her own, Hedwig repeatedly and obsessively describes her fleeting encounter with a man on a Berlin street: "I lived a whole life in this minute," she insisted. She could see herself married to him; they had children, they celebrated his raise, he bought her a new hat. As snapshots of this fantasy life flash before our eyes, we catch a glimpse of Hitler's portrait and hear her voice-over repeat, "He should have held out; just one minute more." The film concludes with the replay of a scene in which a relieved Walter finds and embraces the missing Hedwig on the neon-lit streets of Berlin, as a soundtrack of marching feet fades into the lonely echo of footsteps.

Vesely's film indicated that there would be no genuine meeting of the souls. The quest for shared understanding and intimacy was quixotic; happy endings were illusory. Identities remain unstable; human relations, fragile and problematic. The film may contrast the affective ties of family in the East with the techno-consumer sterility of the West, but Hedwig wanted nothing to do with the noble suffering that Walter recalls in his memories of his father. Hitler's portrait and the sounds of the goose step suggest that national socialism damaged and divided German identity, leaving a gaping emotional void. Moreover, the mention of Judenstraße—and a Star of David in the brickwork of the walkway Walter paces while pursuing Hedwig—evokes an even greater physical and cultural destruction. Ultimately, then, Walter cannot rediscover or remake himself through Hedwig, the daughter of the East, who nurses disappointed dreams of her own. The blinking neon light outside Walter's window, which alternatingly illuminates then extinguishes first Hedwig's, then Walter's, mirrored reflection, indicates that they must remain isolated, incomplete individuals. Thus, although Walter, Hedwig, and even Ulla attain some self-knowledge, they are powerless to either bridge their existential alienation or surrender their desires. As Walter announces, "We are in the desert and the wilds," and at the end of the film, he clings desperately to the distraught Hedwig.

The pessimistic tone of the film and its experimental formal qualities— which depart from conventional film-editing and storytelling strategies—made the film difficult to follow and therefore a commercial, and for the most part critical, flop. Yet *Das Brot der frühen Jahre* was recognized as an ambitious artistic effort, was nominated as the German entry for the Cannes film festival, and was awarded five Federal Film Prizes.[64]

This type of recognition emboldened the Oberhausen rebels to request a onetime loan of 5 million marks from the Federal Republic to be used as "start-up capital" for new-style productions. In return, they promised to complete ten films with the money, which would be sufficient to cover the costs of only three films produced by a commercial firm. The Oberhauseners were offering the state a bargain: ten films for the price of three and a promise of cultural diversity. As Enno Patalas pointed out, "The request for the 5 million [marks] was not as illusory as it sounded." The federal and state governments had already decided to provide financial support to the ailing commercial film industry. But at least initially, they did not entertain the offer of the young independent filmmakers.[65]

Artur Brauner, head of CCC-Film, however, did. He announced the creation of a *Kulturfilm* section in his company and offered to finance three films at the cost of 350,000 marks each, provided the films dealt with "provocative material [*riskante Stoff*]." Brauner demanded thematic control of the projects but claimed that the filmmakers would enjoy "artistic freedom." In response, the Oberhauseners published "Ten Questions for Artur Brauner" in the Hamburg *Film-Telegramm*, sarcastically inquiring whether Brauner believed that artistic freedom overrode profit considerations and whether directors should enjoy full artistic control unencumbered by the meddling of producers and company executives, ending with the question: "Do you want a renewal of German film or [merely] to surmount current economic difficulties?"[66]

The young filmmakers sought more than immediate financing, as their manifesto made clear. They demanded the creation of both a permanent institutional base and a film school, a foundation that would "enable each new generation of German filmmakers to complete their first feature films, [provided they] . . . proved [themselves] in the short-film realm." They also demanded a separate subsidy program for the independent short film—"the natural experimental field of film" and "the private school . . . of independent impulses and reformist endeavor." Short film was considered an emancipating genre that encouraged cinematic experimentation, creativity, and diversity. The young filmmakers did not want it squelched.[67]

By 1962, their battle had just begun. Kluge drew upon his legal training to lead supporters on an energetic crusade to secure state funds for independent filmmakers. Within two years, their efforts paid off. The federal Ministry of the Interior established the Kuratorium junger deutscher Film in 1964, designed to support the first and second projects of "debutant" filmmakers. Support came in the form of interest-free loans, which averaged about 300,000 marks for each of the twenty films financed in its first three years of operation.[68] The effect of the loans was almost immediate: Alexander Kluge's first feature film, *Abschied von Gestern* (*Yesterday's Girl*, 1966)—about the troubled toils of Anita G., a young woman of Jewish descent who arrives in the West from East Germany—became the first postwar German film to receive an award (the Silver Lion) at the Venice Biennial. Similar to Vesely's 1962 film, Kluge's was a literary adaptation (of a story in his *Lebensläufe*), a formal experiment, and a meditation on the "inescapable" relationship between the past and the present—a theme evident in the more literal translation of the film's ironic title, "Taking Leave of Yesterday," and one that applies as much to West German society as to the central character. Here, too, narrative scenes are "intermittent and often highly oblique," "an elliptical sequence of episodes that switch from fiction to documentary, from the surreal to the naturalistic."[69] The film again drew critical attention but had little popular appeal. The same year as Kluge's effort, three other "New German" films were enthusiastically received at Cannes: Ulrich Schamoni's *Es* (*It*, 1965), Volker Schlöndorff's *Der junge Törless* (*Young Törless*, 1966), and Jean-Marie Straub's *Nicht versöhnt* (*Not Reconciled*, 1965).[70]

By the mid-1960s, the federal government finally acknowledged artistically ambitious independent filmmaking as a national cultural resource worthy of its support, in part because of the Cold War competition from the "other" Germany. State support for young independents was encouraged by officials who feared that the diminished quality of the domestic commercial product would result in an embarrassing decline in West Germany's cultural stock vis-à-vis its Eastern adversary. Interest-free loans served as notice of the state's intent to foster a "national film *ecology* amidst an ever-expanding international film *economy*,"[71] a goal set by festival organizers in Mannheim and Oberhausen over a decade earlier.

Aspiring as well as practicing independent filmmakers were energized by the international cultural contact offered at the municipal film festivals of the 1950s. The festivals were created to provide a cultural counterweight to the standardized film products appearing in commercial cinemas. Implicit in this campaign was a critique of Hollywood, the midwife of American mass culture.

Heimerich, a CDU member and mayor of Mannheim, promoted the old German *Kulturfilm* as an educational tool. The influence of the Hollywood-style product was thus met with a "native" genre associated with the glory days of UFA and therefore with German economic and cultural strength. The festival rapidly developed into an international event under the able direction of Kurt Fischer, and the inadequacy of the old-style *Kulturfilm* to stimulate interest, much less challenge the popular commercial film fare, was dismally revealed.

The leftist politics of the Oberhausen festival leadership, on the other hand, allowed for a film program of greater political and artistic diversity. This led to tumultuous discussions and periodic uproars but also provided a nurturing environment for different forms of cultural expression and cinematic style. Here, the Munich filmmakers learned from contact with European avant-gardists to update and politicize the *Kulturfilm* to create the artistic short film. Outside the sanctuary of the festival and film clubs, however, they ran up against the brick wall of commercial distribution and audience expectation.[72] A handful of "New German" directors were able to craft international reputations for themselves at festivals in Cannes, Venice, and New York City, which provoked talk of a German cinematic revival. But the attempt to displace the standardized products of the culture industry failed, and even today, all but the most accessible examples of New German Cinema remain ghettoized from mainstream culture. Unlike the representatives of "Papa's" cinema and Hollywood, the young German independents had elevated intellectual and artistic aspirations for their medium and displayed these through unfamiliar formal strategies. These were highly educated connoisseurs of haute film art, who preferred to provoke rather than entertain. Their films demanded an investment of faith and forbearance that most viewers were unwilling to make. As a result, New German Cinema has never won the broad home market. But due in part to state and federal sponsorship, a dynamic alternative film culture, which stubbornly took root at festivals, film clubs, and art cinemas in the late 1950s, has persisted.

8

MASS CULTURE AND
COLD WAR POLITICS
THE BERLIN FILM FESTIVAL
OF THE 1950s

It began in Berlin! And what is perhaps more crucial—one began in Berlin! From Garbo to Marlene Dietrich to Ingrid Bergman. From Ernst Lubitsch to Dieterle, actors, directors, composers, and technicians of film, a long list of brilliant names, every one a piece of international film history, and every one also a piece of Berlin!—*Der Tag*, 6 June 1951

State sponsorship of film as mass culture was renewed in earnest in the first years of the Bonn Republic. Beginning in the early 1950s, officials earmarked federal funds to subsidize an annual film festival in the western sectors of Berlin. Like the festivals in Mannheim and Oberhausen, the Berlin event exhibited an international array of products. But the similarity stopped there. This was no art festival, aimed at cultivating public appreciation for neglected film genres or experimental films. The majority of films shown in Berlin were commercial feature films readily accessible at one's local theater. Bonn officials were not at Berlin to encourage cultural diversity. Nor were they primarily interested in the festival as a means to bolster Berlin's ailing film industry, segregated both from the West German "mainland" and the international market. Their ambitions were overwhelmingly political.

Following the lead of American cultural officers, Bonn officials sculpted the Berlin festival as a cultural accompaniment to their pro-Western, anticommunist politics. Berlin became an important symbol of West Germany's democratic renewal. The festival was conceived as a way to revive the former capital's interwar reputation as an important European cultural center; and ultimately American and West German officials expected the image of a revitalized Berlin to serve as proof of Western economic superiority and cultural dynamism. Yet the Bonn government also fostered this image for national purposes, expecting a thriving "colony" in the East to lend a certain legitimacy to its claim to represent the best interests of all Germans—not just those residing in the West.

The opening of the fifth Berlin International Film Festival, 1955. (Courtesy of the Landes-bildstelle, Berlin)

Over the course of the 1950s, various West German federal ministries played out their version of Cold War politics to an international audience, eager to score a public relations coup by enticing East Berliners to film performances that excluded the products of socialist countries. Thus, federal officials carefully cultivated their stage in the East with an eye toward promoting the sovereignty of *their* Germany, in a way that flaunted their new Western political orientation.

In June 1951, the city of Berlin held its first annual film festival. It was a modest affair with a small budget.[1] Guests attending from twenty countries were plagued by poor weather and inconvenient accommodations, which forced them to commute long distances to the festival film houses. This was postwar Berlin, a city devastated by Allied bombings and fierce street fighting during the last months of the war. Defeat, occupation, and the victors' failure to agree on a peace settlement had reduced Berlin's political prominence to that of the former capital city of a nonexistent German Reich and had augured the end of Berlin's international reputation as *Kulturstadt*. Postwar Berlin became an embattled island of cultural provincialism that attracted a good number of curious artists and filmmakers—such as Roberto Rossellini and Billy Wilder—in search of authentic scenes of suffering, dislocation, and psychological trauma.[2] Few, however, were willing to subject themselves permanently to the strict rationing and volatile political atmosphere in order to spark a cultural renaissance.

Despite Berlin's obvious lack of appeal as a tourist destination in the early postwar period, the number of festival attendees grew from year to year. By the end of the decade, fifty-three countries were represented and Berlin had won recognition by the FIAPF as an "A" festival, an honor shared only by the older, renowned film festivals at Cannes and Venice.[3] Berlin's initial success in luring international notables and attracting the interest of the press was based on the peculiarities of the festival. The distinct political and ideological agenda of its early years separated it from its more overtly commercial equivalents in France and Italy. These festivals, in contrast, had developed into media spectacles dominated by film stars and their clusters of paparazzi or the less visible dealings of businesspeople hawking their latest products or movie concepts.

The Berlin festival (or "Berlinale," as it became known) was enthusiastically promoted as the "Western cultural showcase in the East." Berlin was not merely a symbol but also a site where political and ideological differences acquired a palpable presence in the form of physical and linguistic barriers, protected military compounds and airfields, even the distinct national uniforms of foreign occupiers. The economic union of the Western zones, the Soviet blockade, and the ensuing airlift further dramatized the East-West split. Media coverage in the West firmly established Berlin as a necessary democratic outpost in a no-man's-land of Soviet-sponsored totalitarianism. Berlin became the epicenter of the Cold War topography. Its festival was no mere commercial or cultural event but a celebration of Western values.

But the Berlin festival should not be reduced to a propaganda event underwritten by the American occupation authorities. Local interests also determined the character and development of the festival. Hoteliers and restaurateurs, for example, looked to the festival to increase tourism and stimulate an economic revival. Local filmmakers and technicians sought to resurrect interest in and contracts for their products and expertise. Although these local interest groups tended to support the American agenda, they added concerns of their own that would alter the event in substantial ways over the course of the decade. The festival became, in fact, the focus for the aspirations of Berlin government officials and artists who wished to rejuvenate the cultural traditions—and reputation—of the city.

These interests found a ready proponent in Alfred Bauer, who organized the Berlin film festival from its beginning in 1951. Perhaps best known as the author of the *Spielfilme-Almanach (Feature Film Almanac)*, Bauer worked for UFA in the last years of the war and as film adviser to the British Military Government in Germany between 1945 and 1950. In his capacity as the festival's director, Bauer sought to place Berlin back on the cultural map of Europe by reviving its reputation as "Filmmetropole"—an important center for film production and distribution.[4] His commitment to this agenda reached back to at least 1950, when he presented the Berlin Senate with a "seven-point petition" urging practical support to stimulate the city's film economy.[5]

Film industry members in Berlin considered it a matter of economic necessity and international prestige to revive the cultural heritage of Berlin as the "artistic home of German film."[6] With the division of Germany, Berlin filmmakers in the Western sectors were cut off from the Soviet-controlled Babelsberg and Johannisthal studios and deprived of access to the surrounding "hinterland." They feared the loss of their patrimony and livelihood, particularly during the Soviet blockade of Berlin, when many of their members headed west to build or expand new production centers in Munich, Hamburg, Wiesbaden, and Düsseldorf. Film distributors shifted their headquarters to Munich, Berlin's long-standing cultural rival, where Bavarian officials boasted that their capital city had become the film center of the new democratic Germany.[7] Lamenting the loss of their life's blood, the Berlin Film Workers' Union (Verband der Filmschaffenden) warned their mayor of the impending demise: "It is a fact that a film industry no longer exists in Berlin. . . . There are only a few production companies, steadily moving West in search of a distribution contract and federal credit for a film that they'd like to produce in Berlin. Or a production comes to Berlin to film, and takes its value away from Berlin with it. We no longer have a distribution company that supplies the whole country; Berlin is uninteresting since it represents only 8 percent of [a film's] possible financial yield. It is also unimportant as a premiere city."[8] Local filmmakers argued that a resuscitated Berlin film industry would benefit both industry members and the Berlin economy. The American and West German governments also had a good deal to gain from the image of a thriving Western metropolis in the midst of the communist East. In fact, Berlin filmmakers would later maintain that the public image, or the "gaze of the world" as one American film officer called it, mattered more to the festival's official sponsors than the reality of a depressed industry, careening toward cultural provincialism.[9]

The first Berlin film festival was heavily endorsed by American officials and may well have been the brainchild of Oscar Martay, a film officer of the Information Services Branch of the Office of the U.S. High Commissioner for Germany (HICOG), who is said to have received his inspiration while attending the Venice Biennial Film Festival. Martay worked closely with the Berlin senator of popular education, Professor Joachim Tiburtius, to secure the financial means to sponsor the festival.[10] Tiburtius would remain an influential voice in the Berlin affair, presiding over the Planning Committee throughout the 1950s. For the first several years, the Berlin Senate was listed as the sole official sponsor of the festival. Allied contributions were not publicly acknowledged, although American authorities contributed financially to the event and representatives of the three Western Allies sat on the organizing committee until 1954, when the West German federal government became an official cosponsor with the Senate.

From its beginnings, the festival was a carefully designed cultural event with broad political overtones. Western democracies were invited to exhibit their finest film products to insure that the festival would become a "magnificent series of great cinematic events."[11] The point was not to pummel viewers with pieces of overt political propaganda. Rather than explicitly reflect the interests of American foreign policy, film was to serve as a goodwill ambassador.[12] Audiences were appealed to as consumers, the single shared identity in capitalist mass society. The existence of a successful festival showing popularly acclaimed films was in itself a propaganda victory.

Martay and officials at the U.S. Information Services Branch insisted that the festival be organized as a discrete event exclusively devoted to film and vetoed the attempts of Berlin officials to graft the film festival onto a larger cultural Festival Week (Festspielwoche) being planned for September 1951 in conjunction with an industrial trade show. Film was to hold the spotlight. American authorities did not want the popular appeal of this medium to be buried in a larger program devoted to the elite arts and business deals. The showcase for democracy was to be based upon this most "democratic art":[13] "The initiators of the Berlin International Film Festival proceeded from the idea that the event should direct the attention of the world once again to the old film metropolis of Germany. Berlin, as the birthplace of German film, is better qualified than any other city to organize an International Film Week for Germany and mold it into a first-class cultural event. If film was to be built into the program as merely a part of a larger and multifaceted exhibition . . . the . . . main purpose . . . of placing Berlin and its film festival into the public view as the spiritual film center of Germany would be illusory [sic]."[14] Oscar Martay exploited the city's former reputation to sell the festival to the world, claiming the legacy of Lang and Murnau for West Berlin at a time when privately owned film companies there were competing for Berlin audiences with the state-owned, Soviet-sponsored film monopoly, DEFA.[15] The festival was to foster the image of a revitalized, democratic Berlin and serve as a tribute to Western cultural vitality.

Timing was also a consideration, since organizers believed it essential that the festival enjoy the undivided attention of the press and film world. In order to keep other events from stealing the thunder from the Berlin film festival, American officials firmly encouraged that the event be held in June rather than in September, as some Berlin officials favored. Martay explained that they wanted to preempt the festivals planned by various other German cities for later that summer. Moreover, Martay particularly wished to avoid scheduling the Berlin festival to follow the Venice Biennial, which was set for late summer. A September date, he argued, would allow Venice to take the "wind out of [Berlin's] sails."[16]

The most important consideration for Martay remained, however, political. American officials sought to use film in a "cultural offensive" designed to reach the populations to the East and counter the influence of officially sponsored popular events there.[17] The keystone of his argument to move the festival dates to June was based on

> the fact that shortly after the first press notice about our Berlin festival, the Eastern press announced an "International Youth Festival" for the summer of 1951 in East Berlin, which is heralded as a meeting of the International Association of Democratic Youth [Weltbundes der Demokratischen Jugend] and is to be run by the Free German Youth [Freie Deutsche Jugend]. I believe it . . . necessary, on the basis of this political consideration alone, to hold the Film Week without fail . . . in June. By doing so, the necessary counterweight would be created, as would—above all—an attraction for the East Berliners and the population of the East zone, and not least of all for the youth in the Eastern peoples' democracies.[18]

Martay's arguments were supported by the festival committee members. Alfred Bauer acknowledged their commitment to the political aims of the American officials of the Information Services Branch and emphasized that while the event would provide an international forum for film professionals, it was expected to work on a more popular and local level as well. It should be staged, he maintained, "for the wide circle of inhabitants in West and East Berlin . . . and should present a peaceful demonstration of the cultural offerings of the Western world."[19]

Throughout the 1950s, Bauer and the Berlin Senate sought to accentuate the uniqueness of their festival in comparison to the other major European film festivals at Cannes, Venice, and Locarno. Berlin was promoted as a popular affair, in contrast to the "opulence" and "glamour" that reigned at festivals to the South.[20] From the first year of the Berlin festival, a good deal of attention was devoted to attracting popular support and attendance. The organizing committee, with official American encouragement, arranged several "mass events" for the program, including a star parade, autograph sessions, and an evening film screening at the open-air Waldbühne. In addition, HICOG sponsored outdoor film screenings at Potsdamerplatz to lure an audience from the East for its cultural wares.[21]

By the second year of the festival, Senator Tiburtius and several members of the Berlin State Parliament (Abgeordnetenhaus) insisted that the organizing committee redouble its efforts to win the support of the people of Berlin—both East and West. Festival film screenings were organized in Neukölln and Wedding, sectors of the city that abutted East Berlin. Border areas were plastered with posters advertising festival events, and East Germans were offered festival tickets for the eye-opening exchange rate of one Ostmark for one Westmark.[22]

The organizing committee also discussed screening the German film, *Nachts auf den Straßen* (*Nights on the Road*, 1951), in the Waldbühne with a promise of a personal appearance by the film's star, Hans Albers. Berlin officials felt this would draw large numbers of spectators from the East and West since Albers—the beloved blond-haired, blue-eyed epitome of dynamic masculinity, the urbane John Wayne of German film in the 1930s—was a "concept" among both populations. Apparently they expected to cash in on nostalgia by appealing to a common cultural experience of the Nazi period to unite a divided population, even for just a few hours. The key element was not the film but the ever-marketable "schöner Hans," whose dual appeal as heartthrob and man of action helped transform him into an icon of an indivisible German cultural nation.[23]

The decision to broaden the popular appeal of the festival was not based purely on Cold War calculations, however. After the first year's festival, Berlin officials had come under fire from laborers and lower-income groups residing in the city's western sectors. If Berlin officials were going to sell their event as "the democratic festival," they needed to consider the class implications of this project. Parliamentary representatives from the SPD and the Liberal Party argued that the "working population attaches particular value [to the demand], and it is important, that they be included in the festival atmosphere. Already it has been very strongly protested in these circles . . . that the first festival was altogether too closed off" from them.[24] Special additional screenings organized for the *Randtheatern*, or border theaters, were designed to address this situation. Neukölln and Wedding were predominantly working-class districts and had been hard hit by the economic dislocations of the war. West Berlin, with an overall population of 2.1 million, contained as many as 300,000 unemployed, and tens of thousands were living off social welfare insurance or pensions. By extending the festival program to the margins of Berlin, officials hoped to conciliate a disgruntled working-class population and, by subsidizing tickets to such exhibitions, tempt East Berliners to cross the border.[25]

The project to broaden participation in the festival did not, however, receive the unanimous support of the organizing committee. Alfred Bauer, for example, noted that decentralized or multiple film screenings were highly unusual at international film festivals and pointed to the prohibitive costs involved. He also feared serious opposition from film producers, who would resent a second, uncompensated showing of their films in outlying areas of Berlin.

German heartthrob, Hans Albers, whose film stardom outlived the Weimar Republic and the Nazi regime. (Courtesy of the Stiftung Deutsche Kinemathek, Berlin)

Film industry members did indeed strenuously resist these steps to democratize the festival. The representative of the Film Distributors' Association objected to the exhibition of festival films to a public (in Wedding and Neukölln) that "was not so open to artistic films." His colleague from the German Film Theater Association concurred, adding that he rejected the screening of films anywhere but on the Kurfürstendamm, the main business boulevard in center city: "One must remain exclusive in international settings. . . . We are talking about a film festival, not a promotional show for wine at which samples are distributed; [this is,] rather, a distinguished cultural event. . . . In Berlin, the cinema provinces actually begin just behind the Kurfürstendamm. All artistically significant or great films (for example, . . . [De Sica's] *Bicycle Thieves* . . .) flop in the other theaters."[26] Industry representatives possessed a keen sense for the geographic parameters of the prestigious and had little appreciation for the possible political dividends to be gained from screenings in the Berlin "provinces." Their cultural and class biases, moreover, left them free to respond as businesspeople and fight the pernicious effects of democratic practices on their pocketbooks. Political considerations, however, won this round; industry representatives were unsuccessful in blocking the special screenings in the *Randtheatern*.[27]

Despite official efforts to democratize the festival, the border screenings, open-air events at the Waldbühne and Olympic Stadium, and autograph sessions at the Zoo or RIAS Park remained marginal to the real hub activity, which from the second year on centered around the once world-renowned Kurfürstendamm or "Ku'damm," the fashionable avenue that in Berlin's heyday was a consumer's paradise and the heart of the city's cultural life.[28] Even with an increasing crush of curious fans over the decade, the Ku'damm remained an elite enclave for international notables from the entertainment and business world.

Berlin's film public were corralled behind barricades as the ersatz royalty were ushered past in grand style to closed festival openings and industry-sponsored film balls. Berliners experienced the festivities vicariously, through press reports and newsreels. They were treated, for example, to stunning décolleté shots of the immaculately coiffed trio, Yvonne De Carlo, Sophia Loren, and Gina Lollobrigida, as well as reports about the comings and goings of Gary Cooper, William Holden, Trevor Howard, Yves Montand, Dieter Borsche, Curd Jürgens, Hardy Krüger, Bob Hope, Jeanne Moreau, Liselotte Pulver, Horst Buchholz, and Hildegarde Knef, among others. When film stars made personal appearances, the public encountered their fantasy objects only across the proscenium or a cordon of police. Hans Albers enlisted the aid of twenty police escorts to push back his fans when he went to retrieve his car. Maria Schell received homage at her hotel window, tossing flowers to her adoring but anonymous mass of admirers. And in a grand gesture of noblesse oblige, Jean Marais showered his public with neckties from his hotel fortress.[29]

The festival was clearly an elite construction, fashioned to satisfy political, economic, and cultural agendas centered on Berlin. The publicity that film personalities attracted only served to further these agendas. Despite the amount of attention lavished on visiting luminaries and the predictable distance maintained between these cultural elites and the Berlin masses, however, organizers successfully marketed it as a democratic festival, both domestically and abroad. Admittedly, the festival was democratic to the extent that it served as a showcase for the cultural products of Western democracies. But by 1952, Tiburtius and parliamentary representatives were determined to convince Berliners and the world alike that it was "democratic" in another sense. These officials proudly claimed that it functioned according to democratic principles, that it was a festival by and for the people, a genuine *Volksfest.*

This claim was based upon what was certainly the most unique aspect of the Berlin festival, the public vote. Audiences at the screenings of competing films were provided with ballots on which they were to rate each film's quality. A certificate was awarded to the film in each category that received the greatest percentage of positive evaluations. In 1951 Disney's *Cinderella* won top honors. That first year, however, public acclaim was merely advisory. The official competition was decided by an appointed jury of German educators, critics, artists, and theater owners, which awarded gold, silver, and bronze bears—the symbol of Berlin—to the top three films in each category (dramatic feature; comedy; detective or adventure film; musical; and documentary). The following year, the jury was dropped, and until 1956, when juried prizes were also conferred, the public vote alone determined the awards.[30]

The elimination of the official jury was not the result of an avid push for further democratization. It was, rather, a condition imposed by the FIAPF in return for its formal recognition of the festival. The FIAPF was an international organization of national film producer associations based in Paris and Rome. Members were committed to participating as associations in only those international film festivals that had received FIAPF approval.[31] FIAPF approval of the Berlin festival was expected to insure the steady participation of member associations in the event on an annual basis. As importantly, it was expected to improve the quality of films submitted to the festival by national industries. Bauer strongly felt that the continued success of the festival was dependent on the endorsement of the FIAPF.[32]

Securing the official recognition of the FIAPF for an international film festival was not an easy matter. This was particularly true in the early to mid-1950s, when the national film producer associations were confronted with a steadily increasing number of invitations to recently hatched festivals. One

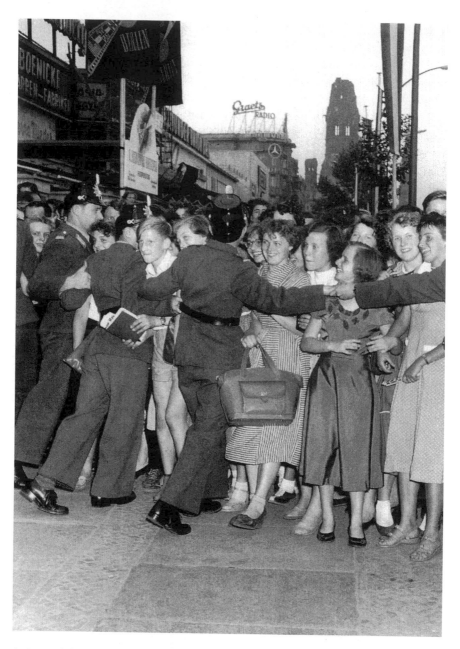

Autograph hunters on the Ku'damm during the 1955 Berlin International Film Festival.
(Courtesy of the Landesbildstelle, Berlin)

German representative in the FIAPF complained that "since the war . . . a considerable festival fatigue has occurred" in industry circles. "Almost every country, and in some countries even various cities, have attempted to gain permission to sponsor an international film festival." After assessing the expense of participating in these festivals, and the often-limited benefits they could reap in return, national film producer associations proposed an annual "Olympics of Film." This plan was designed to eliminate the multitude of national and regional film festivals in favor of a single, massive, competitive event. It was, however, heartily criticized and ultimately vetoed by officials in Venice and Cannes, who sought to retain the cultural and economic benefits of their own festivals. The Venice Biennial, with its twenty-year history, and the annual postwar festival at Cannes had become well-financed institutions with year-round staffs, supported by state and tourist industry funds.[33] Local businesspeople, city and state officials, and native film industry members guarded their prerogatives jealously and ultimately succeeded in protecting their interests. In the early 1950s, Cannes and Venice alone received the highly coveted FIAPF recognition as "A" festivals, which authorized them to appoint an international jury to judge the films in competition and award prizes.[34]

Berlin was able to win FIAPF designation as a "B" festival in 1952, which meant that it was an officially recognized festival without the right to constitute a jury or award prizes. FIAPF recognition of the Berlin festival was not won without a fight, however; FIAPF members needed to be persuaded to accept the "political grounds" for the festival.[35] Organizer Alfred Bauer realized that the appeal of the Berlin event and the reason it received the endorsement of the FIAPF were based precisely on the fact that it did not mimic the events at Cannes and Venice. Given the physical devastation of the war and its northern geographic location, the former German capital could not hope to compete with the enticements of luxury and sun that were so amply provided on the Riviera. In the early 1950s, Berlin had no obvious charms that would recommend it as a tourist location or playground for the wealthy.

Bauer and festival committee members resolved to stress the uniqueness of their festival in order to stimulate press interest and to set their event off from the "glitter" festivals that had come to dominate the international festival calendar. They promoted their event to the FIAPF, the film world, and the press as both a democratic and "serious"—or "working"—festival that integrated the public voice, as well as seminars and lectures by noted authorities, into a program of film screenings. This strategy was designed to provide a distinct identity for the festival, elicit international interest, and convince the FIAPF that recognition should be renewed annually. Bauer felt it essential to the success of the Berlin festival that it retain this "official" standing given the international festival glut of the 1950s.[36]

Festival officials were confronted with a greater challenge when they attempted to win the cooperation of the German film industry. In the first year of the festival, the Association of German Film Producers declined to participate in an official capacity, despite the entreaties of festival organizers and the Berlin Senate. The association's spokesman, H. B. Baum, blamed its reluctance to participate on the German film producers' weakened position on the world market and their inability to compete with the national products of the United States, France, and Italy.

The rationale for the association's decision involved more than a realistic assessment of the artistic quality of German films. It represented an unveiled protest against the film policies of the American occupiers. The German Film Producers' Association had noted American officials' keen interest and involvement in the Berlin film festival. German producers recognized that the festival served the political and propagandistic goals of U.S. foreign policy, as well as the interests of Hollywood producers, who were already well entrenched in the postwar European market. In a letter declining participation in the festival, Baum explained that "due to the film policies of the Allies, German film production has been placed at a tragic disadvantage in relation to foreign productions." The policies that created this unhappy situation derived from American insistence on the decartelization of the German film industry, which entailed the breakup of the huge UFI film monopoly and prohibited German film firms from involvement in more than one branch of the industry. This situation led to a proliferation of small production firms that had a great deal of difficulty securing financial backing for their projects and amortizing their films since they lacked other areas of diversification that would yield profits. Industry members lobbied for a more rational (vertical) organization of the industry, which would allow them to compete against the Hollywood giants.[37]

In addition to protesting the decartelization laws of the Western Allies and the subsequent effects on the position of German film in the international market, German film producers decried the massive influx of foreign films into their domestic market, which, they claimed, displaced their native products. Their most acerbic criticism was directed at Hollywood, which supplied twice as many films to German audiences in 1953 as did German producers.[38] In a letter explaining their decision to spurn the festival, Baum reiterated these concerns:

> You are also acquainted with the special measures prejudicial to the film industry as a whole [such as] the flooding of the German market with foreign films and the discounted release of reprises, which have impeded the development of German film in its entirety.
>
> These circumstances do not permit German film to compete successfully in an international show, such as that being planned in Berlin. On the con-

trary, such an exhibition . . . has a showcase effect and would work to the disadvantage of the German market.[39]

Fritz Podehl, a leading industry voice and head of the FSK, the industry-sponsored censorship board, elaborated on the inability of German films to compete with their more polished Hollywood competitors at the Berlin festival: "It would of course be important to know if other countries aside from the Americans are participating. In this case it would be probable that German films would have to be compared with German, and foreign films with foreign, if one did not want to come to a humiliating outcome for German production. Although the latter has improved in the last few years, the means are not at [our] disposal to be able to compete adequately on either the technical or artistic level with foreign productions."[40] In negotiations with festival authorities, industry representatives dropped broad hints that their members would be inclined to participate in the festival if the Berlin Senate and federal government were able to sweeten the deal by providing financial support for the ailing industry in the form of entertainment tax breaks and increased direct subsidies. In addition, they sought assistance in their dealings with American officials over the break-up of the UFI monopoly, which native producers feared would be sold to the highest foreign bidder.[41] Berlin officials denied that they had any influence over the UFI dismantling process; their hands were tied by decartelization laws imposed by the Allies. Federal officials were also apparently unable or unwilling to provide the types of incentives the film producers demanded.

Festival organizers, however, did try to placate the producers with a proposal to create a special program highlighting the best "30–40 German postwar feature films from 1946 to 1951" at the 1952 festival. The show would be targeted primarily at "foreign film buyers and journalists" attending the festival and would "belong to the official program . . . and serve the export of German film." Bauer was suggesting that the festival play a mediating role between the German commercial film industry and foreign buyers, functioning more overtly as a showcase and marketplace for the German film product. With this gesture, he hoped to prove to German film producers that the festival was not merely a vehicle for foreign products but could serve their financial interests as well.[42]

Bauer appealed to the federal Ministry of Economics to subsidize the exhibition, but the request was refused. As a result, the special exhibition of German films was scrapped. The industry did, however, sponsor a small-scale film fair that featured its most marketable products.[43] The lack of official support frustrated industry members, however, and did little to alter their impression of the festival as a foreign-dominated event. Consequently, German industry participation remained low, both in terms of members' attendance at the festival and their willingness to submit film entries for the competition. This situation did not change until the mid-1950s, when the industry recovered its confidence and a sizable part of the domestic market for family-style entertainment. By 1955, it became a minority sponsor of the event, along with the Berlin Senate and the West German federal government, thus allowing industry representatives a greater voice in planning.[44]

The federal Ministry of the Interior did take steps to support and publicize the native film product within West Germany and Berlin. Beginning in 1951, the Ministry of the Interior annually designated a jury composed of "personalities from public, cultural, and intellectual life" to award a German "Oscar," the Bundesfilmpreis, to the best feature and documentary films of the production year. Industry representatives, federal officials, film critics, and educators sat on the jury that presented the award, initially during a separately scheduled "special program" at the Berlin film festival. Only after 1953 did it become an official part of the program.[45] The Bundesfilmpreis provided an official seal of approval to a handful of films at a time when the German film industry was struggling for a place on the international—and domestic—market. By including the ceremony in the festival's official program, federal and industry officials apparently sought to increase the visibility of their native product in the hopes of boosting export revenues. Annual awards did favor box-office hits with proven appeal among (at least) German audiences.[46]

Industry revival was not, however, the primary aim of the film awards. The award ceremony at Berlin provided an irresistible opportunity to engage in ideological showmanship. Predictably, given Berlin's location at the geographical heart of the Cold War, the conservative politics of the reigning Christian Democratic government in Bonn influenced the selection process. As one film historian has pointed out, "The political bias of the awards was unmistakable; the Minister [of the Interior] regularly honoured films with a distinct anti-communist and pro-NATO slant, usually stories dealing with Germany's divided state from a Cold War perspective. When challenged on this, a Ministry spokesman tartly replied: 'these prizes are gifts. It is our right to choose to whom we want to present them.' "[47]

Federal officials were even more heavy-handed in the only other area of their involvement at the Berlin festival: the special screenings sponsored by the federal Ministry of Greater German Matters (Bundesministerium für Gesamtdeutsche Fragen). Far from being benign exhibitions, these politically tendentious shows revolved around themes such as those featured in *Film behind the Iron Curtain*, a documentary screened at the 1952 festival comprised of clips from feature and newsreel films produced in the Soviet Union and East Germany. In the following years, the ministry expanded the program by showing complete films from the "Soviet zone," which focused on such topics as daily life in East Germany and the effects of Soviet policies on East German art.[48] Although these exhibitions were not included on the official program, their obvious propagandistic thrust underscored the political nature of the festival. The ministry's exhibitions served to remind visitors that the real competition was not among films of the Western world. The stakes were much higher, as the German ministry pointed out in a series that chronicled the "loss" of compatriots in the East to Stalinism. This loss involved the spread of communist influence as well as national truncation and cultural emasculation.

The federal government's decision to commit more resources to the festival was made after the June 1953 uprising in East Berlin, which began just one day before that year's festival. Senator Tiburtius opened the 1953 festival with a "memorial to the victims of the demonstration for freedom." The next year, Bonn's contribution to the festival was substantially increased and the ministers of the interior and economics, as well as the vice chancellor, personally attended the festival in an unprecedented show of federal support.[49]

Ironically, the festival was forced to abandon the most overtly political aspects of its program in 1955, the same year that the federal government was officially listed as cosponsor. In order to retain recognition from the FIAPF, Berlin was required to adhere to FIAPF rules that sought to guarantee the political neutrality of all FIAPF-approved film festivals. Festival authorities were therefore requested to renounce the screening of all politically tendentious films.[50] Beginning in 1955, the propaganda shows sponsored by the federal Ministry of Greater German Matters were suspended, as was the David O. Selznick Silberlorbeerpreis, which had been awarded annually by a jury of international journalists to the German-language film that "best served international understanding."[51]

The reduction of overt displays of Cold War propaganda at the festival belied the intense political jockeying that went on behind the scenes during preparations for the event. With federal sponsorship, the festival acquired status as "the official German film festival," and representatives of the Foreign and Interior ministries kept a sharp eye on proceedings, concerned that festival organizers do nothing to compromise West German interests. Bonn officials won permanent seats on the organizing committee, and any decisions regarding invitations to East Bloc countries or screenings of "sensitive" films had to be cleared through the appropriate ministries.[52] As a result, committee meetings were often the sites of clashes between proponents of political considerations and those with predominantly cultural agendas.

Alfred Bauer had been committed from the beginning to organizing an impressive cultural event that would both attract the best international film products available and rejuvenate the city of Berlin as a cultural capital of Europe. The bestowal of the coveted "A" rating on the Berlinale by the FIAPF in 1956 indicated that Bauer was close to achieving his goals. Yet the "A" rating also brought with it a change in the nature of the festival. Organizers were compelled to decide whether to retain the popular vote as the mechanism to decide winning films or to assign this function to an international jury. By 1957, the public vote was dropped. The committee opted for cultural prestige over homey democratic practice. Berlin thus entered the exclusive inner circle formerly monopolized by Cannes and Venice.

By the late 1950s, however, even this inner circle had been riddled by sharp press criticism over the uneven quality of films screened for competition. Film critics complained that too few quality films were being produced worldwide to justify the overbooked international festival calendar. Berlin organizers, therefore, could not afford to become complacent. Bauer insisted that they had to address the critical comments of the press if they wished to retain their good reputation.

Perhaps the most persistent criticism involved the charge of partisanship in extending invitations to the Berlin festival. Immediately following Berlin's promotion to an "A" rating in 1956, journalists began to compare the guest list to that of Cannes, which was open to films of all interested countries, even those in the East Bloc. Countries with which France had diplomatic relations received their invitations to Cannes through the French Foreign Ministry. All others, such as the People's Republic of China and the Soviet Union, were invited to the festival by the French film producers' association.

By 1957, German journalists increasingly demanded that the Berlin festival be opened up to all nations, despite differences in ideology and political systems. Will Wehling, a journalist and press agent of the Oberhausen film festival, maintained in *Die Welt*:

> The era of the festival as a primarily cultural-political affair ("film showcase toward the East") of the early years is gone, now that it has achieved recognition as an A-festival. That does not however mean that it has an apolitical demeanor. But one doesn't need to stress that in relation to Berlin. Either an A-festival is organized with the possibility of participation by all countries, or, in the case of limited participation, Article 2 of the Berlin bylaws must be changed, which last year read: "The film festival intends to demonstrate to a broad public the development of film art, to bring together in Berlin the leading personalities of the film world for an exchange of views, and thus to contribute to the promotion of mutual understanding and friendship between peoples."[53]

Wehling's concerns, like Bauer's, were primarily cultural in orientation. This is not surprising given Wehling's affiliation with the Oberhausen festival, which had a reputation for displaying interesting examples of film art drawn from various nations, East and West, regardless of their ideological content or the reactions of Bonn.[54] His argument was based upon the desire to secure films of the best artistic quality for the festival. For Wehling and Bauer, the festival was primarily a cosmopolitan cultural event based upon the principles of international dialogue. It should be treated as a marketplace for the free exchange of ideas; geopolitics and ideology had no role there.[55]

Federal officials saw it differently, however. Bauer's plans to promote the festival as an elite forum for cultural exchange coincided with what was identified as a Soviet cultural offensive. Western officials had detected a change in Soviet tactics since 1955, when the Soviet Union switched from a hard-line adherence to Stalinism to a competitive posture abroad. A U.S. Information Agency pamphlet, for example, accused the Soviet Union of feigning a "posture of peace" to sell communism to the "free world." By 1957, "communist films" were no longer being distributed on a noncommercial basis through diplomatic channels and front organizations but were circulating "through conventional commercial channels in almost every market in the world." The Soviets were beginning to compete on capitalist terms, but they had one clear advantage: "communist interests" could use costly promotional devices such as film festivals to gain a foothold in foreign markets. Moreover, they utilized a number of profit guarantees "of the type that would be totally impractical for industries operating under the free enterprise system," offering films to exhibitors at reduced rates and occasionally extending nonrepayable "loans" to theater owners to cover the costs of advertisement.[56]

West German officials adamantly refused to offer the Soviets an entrée into their "free world" festival. Tension developed between this principle of political exclusion and the pressing need to secure good films. By 1956, the political and cultural standing of the Berlin festival appeared under attack by the East when the Karlovy Vary festival in Czechoslovakia received FIAPF recognition as an "A" festival, joining the exclusive ranks of Cannes, Venice, and Berlin. The federal Ministry of the Interior considered the Czechoslovakian festival a direct challenge and worried that Berlin would have to compete with the socialist festival for participants since rumors had been circulating in the press that Karlovy Vary would be scheduled in 1957 to coincide with the Berlin event.[57] Federal representatives on the organizing committee feared that developing countries currently participating in the Berlinale would be persuaded to shift their loyalties to the East, given the scathing reviews their national products were receiving from German critics. This was expected to result in a loss of prestige for the Berlinale but, more importantly, would serve to undermine Western claims regarding the superiority and benefits of political—and cultural—democracy.[58]

The controversy that arose in 1956 over the question of Soviet participation continued over the course of the decade. The Foreign Office stood firm against

Soviet involvement through 1957. For the 1958 festival, Alfred Bauer and a representative from the Berlin Senate's Office of Popular Education argued that Soviet films had been screened at the festival in Oberhausen and requested that the Ministry of the Interior allow the Berlin Senate to consider the issue of Soviet participation and make recommendations to the Foreign Office. Bauer maintained that it would be less harmful to screen Soviet films within the context of the Berlinale "than to allow . . . the Karlsbad [Karlovy Vary] festival advertise against Berlin and the Western world due to the fact that a large section of international film production remains closed off from the Berlin film festival because of Soviet nonparticipation."[59]

Federal officials continued to resist the demand to include the Soviets. They treated the Berlin festival as an "official" government event because of the sizable financial backing of Bonn but more importantly because it occurred in Berlin—the West German outpost in the East. For that reason, they demanded that festival invitations follow official etiquette and conform to federal government policy. Therefore, when federal officials "relented" and permitted Soviet Union participation in the festival, it had to be done on their terms; the invitation was tendered not by festival authorities but by the West German Foreign Office. The tactics of the ministry assured Soviet response in advance. The Soviets declined to participate since they did not recognize the West German federal government as possessing sovereignty over Berlin. The following year, a representative from the Ministry of the Interior assured the Berlin organizing committee that a number of Eastern European states would participate, but "only those with which we have diplomatic relations."[60]

Thus, German officials were responding to more than the dictates of Cold War cultural policy in their efforts to control East Bloc participation. A subtext to the debate was the issue of West German sovereignty—including Bonn's claim as legitimate heir of the old German Reich. Bonn officials were not merely battling the cultural forces of communism in Berlin; they needed to prove the justice of their political claims on this cultural "front."

Ultimately, the festival became highly successful in attracting hordes of East German visitors through the use of such strategies as reduced ticket prices and increased star presence at border screenings.[61] Yet, ironically, festival officials were less adept at keeping Western visitors from heading east. Members of the Berlin Senate and federal ministries chafed at reports of visiting notables crossing the border to tour state-run DEFA film studios in East Berlin. Their best suggestion for stemming the eastward tide was to "keep them busy" with a full festival program "so they wouldn't get bored"![62] Berlin officials zealously sought to root out the competing cultural influences of their compatriots in the East, prohibiting, for example, the screening of DEFA films in West Berlin cinemas for the duration of the festival.[63]

The Berlin festival became as much a display of West German economic vitality as a Western cultural showcase. By the end of the decade, the Berlinale more closely resembled the high-profile, "glitter" fests at Cannes and Venice and offered a schedule packed with trade shows, receptions, and industry association meetings. West German film companies optimistically set up export offices as well, still hoping for an entrée to the world market. And the Berlin film industry certainly profited from the publicity. After a flurry of contracts for sound synchronization and dubbing, Berlin film workers were producing a steady one-third of West German output by the end of the decade.[64]

Conceived as a cultural accompaniment to Cold War politics, the Berlinale became a tribute to Western capitalism, commercialism, and the popular allure of mass culture. Faced with a budget crunch in 1956, West German federal officials were shrewd enough to beef up the budget for international advertising and travel subsidies for movie stars attending the festival.[65] They understood that the manufactured images of these human commodities would insure popular interest for the event. The Berlin festival was an elite construction that peddled propaganda through spectacle. What was being sold was not merely an image of material abundance, leisure, individual fulfillment, and cultural superiority but a political system as well.

CONCLUSION

The Bonn government's celebration of American-style mass culture at the Berlin film festival was unique in the 1950s, differing considerably
from the typical response of West German elites, which was characterized by
marked antagonism to the commercial culture issuing from Hollywood. But
Berlin's political situation as a West German outpost in the ideologically inhos-
pitable East was also unique. Amid the rubble and reconstruction of early
postwar Berlin, American culture emblematized the wealth and wonders of the
Western world. Moreover, it supplied a visible promise of consumer vitality for
the West German future. Both symbolically and materially, it served to delimit
Berlin's Western sectors from the communist provinces of Eastern Europe.

West German officials exploited Berlin's position "behind enemy lines" to
open a new cultural front in the Cold War. By showcasing American films and
Hollywood stars, federal officials advertised the new Western orientation of
their postwar German state and its fundamental departure from the Nazi past.
But they also looked to the festival to further the causes of national unification
and sovereignty. Bonn officials had a keen interest in peddling the attractive
wares of Western culture to their poorer Eastern relations, who, they assumed,
would queue up eagerly to consume these images of prosperity and democracy.
Thus, dazzling film stars and Disney movies at the Waldbühne were expected to
sell the superiority of the Western system and West German society, when
compared to the gray social realism of East German cinematic culture.

In Berlin, the populations being plied with commercial culture were, in a
sense, peripheral; they were not a part of the West German mainland. On home
turf, state officials saw things considerably differently. There they joined forces
with religious leaders in order to define a German cultural nation in opposition
to American commercial culture. In West Germany proper, American culture

was not hailed as an alluring helpmate for national reconstruction and Western integration but excoriated as a force of social and sexual disintegration.

This response was shaped by the specific historical conditions that accompanied German defeat and occupation after World War II. As such, it expressed the deep-seated fears regarding the devastation of the war—be it physical, psychological, spiritual, or moral—and its effects on German men, women, and children, as well as similar concerns about the health of institutions like the family, the churches, and the state.

Official distrust also grew out of a longer history of public criticism regarding commercial cinema that reaches back to the beginning of the century and thus transcends the usual political periodization. This older debate too conditioned the responses and rhetoric of the post-1945 period. Even before the American film industry established a strong foothold in the German market after World War I, commercial culture—and cinema in particular—was condemned as the cultural excrescence of a rapidly urbanizing and industrializing modernity, which threatened to eradicate earlier bourgeois forms of class, gender, sexual, and familial relations. American commercial culture struck many interwar critics as a particularly virulent strain, in part, one suspects, because of the timing of its entry into the host market. German society, after all, was reeling from military defeat, suffering a period of protracted political, economic, and social crisis. "Fatherland" and "father" had been weakened by the war; political authority and patriarchy were under attack; economic, class, and sexual hierarchies were on the verge of collapse. Critics feared that American cinema would facilitate social disintegration by seducing the German public (and particularly German women) with its slick production style, consumer values, and Hollywood brand of hedonism. Persuaded that film influenced social behavior, they suspected Hollywood of encouraging individual fulfillment and pleasure seeking over social responsibility to family and nation. At issue, then, was the recovery of national health and social equilibrium.

In the aftermath of World War I, cultural integrity became a crucial aspect of Germany's interwar quest to regain national sovereignty and pride, and the regulation of cinematic representation became a prerequisite for restoring national vitality. In the film world, cultural integrity also implied economic recovery and the construction of a thriving national cinema with a healthy export profile. Begun during the Weimar Republic, this process reached its fullest potential only under Hitler, due to the support of the Nazi state and its murderous program of massive market expansion.

German defeat in 1945 and the international censure of Nazi crimes against humanity initiated an unprecedented period of national self-redefinition. The struggle for cultural integrity resumed with a vengeance with military occupation and the sudden reintroduction of American economic and cultural forms to territories closed off for half a decade by Hitler's autarkic policies. Packaged first as part of a foreign program of political reeducation, cinema again came to represent a broad cultural threat for many local leaders, precisely because Germany's nature and future were unstable and in flux. At such a historical juncture, insubstantial streams of light appeared capable of wreaking grave social and psychological damage, particularly since these appealed to the postwar public directly, bypassing the mediation of state and church authorities. It was precisely this characteristic that frustrated traditional elites, who strenuously attempted to construct a national identity based upon the family, Christian values, and old notions of a German moral community as a bulwark to hold back the flow.

In the process, they enlisted the aid of the German film industry, which again looked to the state to provide the economic assurances and protection it had enjoyed under Hitler. In exchange for limited state guarantees—and in order to build a domestic market for a national cinematic culture distinct from the American internationalizing variety—the industry resurrected old film forms developed during the 1920s and 1930s. For a short period of time, this strategy worked. The *Heimatfilm*, a peculiarly German genre with interwar antecedents, became a sure money-maker as family entertainment. If the industry experienced a brief golden age between 1950 and 1956 on the domestic market, the national nature of its products prevented its large-scale export abroad. Domestic commercial success was due in large measure to the way these films recycled German film genres and stars and thus referred back to the pleasures of film spectatorship during the Weimar Republic and the Third Reich. Yet it was also due to the altered appeal of the these postwar films, which reformulated earlier filmmaking conventions to suit the emotional and entertainment requirements of post-Nazi Germans, engaged in a process of national and cultural reconstruction.

Tellingly, the heyday of the *Heimatfilm* ended with the decade. By the late 1950s, young Germans began to identify it with their parents and the National Socialist past; it appeared cramped, outmoded, and thoroughly unacceptable compared to the modern cultural impulses from the United States.[1] Thus, German cinema of the 1950s could ultimately issue no challenge to an American commercial culture with its international, cross-generational, and transgender appeal.

American culture therefore played a central role in a second wave of postwar redefinition. In the wake of the *Wirtschaftswunder*, consumer choice (and preference for foreign imports) was used to spawn youth cultures that expressed solidarity on the basis of generation rather than nationality and thus implicitly criticized received forms of German identity. Nonetheless, if American culture assisted members of the postwar generation in forging social identities distinct from those of their elders, its consumption also highlighted the cleavages in economic and social status in the Federal Republic. Cultural consumption, after all, was influenced by factors like class, social status, educational level, and sex. As a result, it became important for both indicating and expressing one's social position, self-image, aspirations, and fantasies.

The new Hollywood heroes of the late 1950s—like Elvis Presley, James Dean, and Marlon Brando—became important models for rebellious young men from working and lower middle-class milieus and the romantic fantasy figures for young women seeking a release from the social and cultural restrictions of the parental home. Highly educated middle-class to upper-class youth may have enjoyed Hollywood movies and American rock and roll as individuals, but their group identity was based upon cultural consumption and physical styles that advertised the fact that they—unlike their "social inferiors" decked out in leather jackets and jeans—enjoyed elevated European-style tastes. Their cultural preference was consciously "nicht-Amerikanisch." In opposition to the machismo of the "Halbstarken" or young punks who ran wild in the streets after seeing Bill Haley's *Rock around the Clock*, these reluctant Germans tended to exhibit their cosmopolitan openness by listening to cool jazz in dark coffeehouses, studying and discussing cinematic "art," and taking on the personal style of the French existentialists. As self-conscious intellectuals, they spurned the stereotypical "philistine addiction to order" and stiff conventionality of middle-class German respectability, but they did so in a way to differentiate themselves from the consumer masses.[2]

The young *Filmkritiker*s led by Enno Patalas and the independent filmmakers who denounced "Papa's" cinema appear to have shared this profile. They advocated a more intellectually demanding and aesthetically sophisticated alternative to American cinema, based on a "cerebral" or European style of filmmaking.[3] The clubs and festivals initially fostered artistic solidarity with French filmmakers, but individuals with leftist sympathies gradually expanded their definition of "European culture" to include the cinematic currents from Eastern Europe. Independent German filmmakers employed the lessons they learned primarily against their native "culture industry," which was suffering from declining audiences by the late 1950s.

The relationship of these young German filmmakers to American mass culture was, however, complex and deeply ambivalent.[4] Nurtured on American films, they nonetheless expressed an elitist distaste for the crudeness and standardization of American cultural conventions. Yet, following the trend set in André Bazin's *Cahiers du Cinema*, they were equally fascinated by uniquely

American myths and genres (especially Westerns) and the putatively highly "individual" visions of American auteurs like Howard Hawks and John Ford.

Ultimately, of course, the intellectually demanding products of Young German Cinema failed to capture the general West German audience, and American film has come to dominate the programs of German commercial cinemas. It is ironic, given the fact that the Oberhauseners grounded their revolt firmly within the "politics of generation," that their films never achieved a broad-based following among their peers, who, after all, continued as the most avid filmgoers in a period of decreasing attendance.[5] Their project of confronting and countering the cultural legacies of the national past found little resonance among a generation that increasingly turned away from questions of national identity to focus on the formulation of alternative social identities, firmly grounded in class and gender and articulated through individualized consumption.

By the 1960s, cultural critics began to shift their sights from film to television, scrutinizing the new medium for its effect on the impressionable viewer. Protestant film commissioner Werner Hess, for example, resigned his office in the early 1960s to become a television director at the Zweites Deutsches Fernsehen (ZDF). Although the cultural authority of the churches was beginning to abate in the early 1960s (due in part to highly publicized revelations regarding their role under national socialism), ecclesiastical influence did extend into the television era, and Hess vetoed Enno Patalas's application for a job as program director at the station on the grounds that Patalas was both a "leftist and a cineast"![6]

State and church intervention in cultural matters, overt campaigns to limit democratic freedoms, and characterization of the German public as passive, gullible "masses" beg the question of continuities with the Nazi past. Industry acquiescence to conservative cultural politics resulted in a persistence of older cultural forms, social ideologies, and personnel from the Nazi period. In the late 1950s, young film critics and filmmakers began exposing these holdovers and demanded that issues of cultural continuity be addressed in an open, honest manner. This initiated—or at least reflected—a gradually growing movement of antiauthoritarianism, variously expressed as a critical public inquiry into the relationship between the superficially democratic present and the Nazi past, in the case of these self-conscious young intellectuals, and as a less articulate but broader-based rejection of old-style German cultural forms, in the case of other, less theoretically engaged, young German consumers.

The consumption of commercial culture is not merely a form of self-indulgence but an avenue for self-definition. In postwar Germany, it was embraced as a way to chart a new identity. Because cinema is historically linked to national culture, political persuasion, and advertising technologies, consumer choice expressed a complex interaction between national, gender, and class identities. By the 1950s, the responses to cinematic consumption that emerged suggest the variety of ways postwar Germans positioned themselves in relation to their national past and cultural heritage.

APPENDIXES

APPENDIX A:
U.S. FILMS APPROVED FOR EXHIBITION
IN THE U.S. ZONE, 1945–1946

Abe Lincoln in Illinois (RKO, 1940)
Across the Pacific (Warner Bros., 1942)
Action in the North Atlantic (Warner Bros., 1943)
Air Force (Warner Bros., 1943)
All That Money Can Buy (RKO, 1941)
Appointment for Love (Universal, 1941)
Christmas in July (Paramount, 1940)
Corvette K-255 (Universal, 1943)
Dr. Ehrlich's Magic Bullet (1st National, 1940)
Going My Way (Paramount, 1944)
Gold Rush (UA, 1942 reissue with sound)
Hold Back the Dawn (Paramount, 1941)
The Human Comedy (MGM, 1943)
I Married a Witch (UA, 1942)
It Happened Tomorrow (UA, 1944)
It Started with Eve (Universal, 1941)
Madame Curie (MGM, 1944)
The Maltese Falcon (Warner Bros., 1941)
The More the Merrier (Columbia, 1943)
My Sister Eileen (Columbia, 1942)
The Navy Comes Through (RKO, 1942)
One Hundred Men and a Girl (Universal, 1937)
Pride and Prejudice (MGM, 1940)
Remember the Day (20th Century-Fox, 1942)
Seven Sweethearts (MGM, 1942)
Shadow of a Doubt (Universal, 1943)
The Sullivans (20th Century-Fox, 1944)
Tales of Manhattan (20th Century-Fox, 1942)
Thirty Seconds over Tokyo (MGM, 1945)
Tom, Dick, and Harry (RKO, 1941)
Young Tom Edison (MGM, 1940)
You Were Never Lovelier (Columbia, 1942)

Source: Robert Joseph, "Our Film Program in Germany: I. How Far Was It a Success?," *Hollywood Quarterly* 2, no. 2 (January 1947): 124–25.

APPENDIX B:
U.S. FILMS APPROVED FOR EXHIBITION
IN THE U.S. ZONE, JANUARY 1947–SEPTEMBER 1948

Adam Had Four Sons (Columbia, 1941)
The Adventures of Mark Twain (Warner Bros., 1944)
The Affairs of Susan (Paramount, 1945)
All This and Heaven Too (Warner Bros., 1940)
Always in My Heart (Warner Bros., 1942)
Anna and the King of Siam (20th Century-Fox, 1946)
Back Street (Universal, 1941)
The Bells of St. Mary's (RKO, 1945)
The Best Years of Our Lives (Samuel Goldwyn, 1946)
Boomtown (MGM, 1940)
Boys' Town (MGM, 1938)
The Bullfighters (20th Century-Fox, 1945)
Calcutta (Paramount, 1946)
Captain Kidd (Benedict Bogens, 1945)
The Constant Nymph (Warner Bros., 1943)
The Corn Is Green (Warner Bros., 1945)
The Corsican Brothers (Edward Small, 1942)
Destry Rides Again (Universal, 1939)
The Egg and I (UA, 1947)
The Enchanted Cottage (RKO, 1945)
Flesh and Fantasy (Universal, 1943)
Gaslight (MGM, 1944)
Gentleman Jim (Warner Bros., 1942)
The Great Victor Herbert (Paramount, 1939)
The Green Years (MGM, 1946)
Here Comes Mr. Jordan (Columbia, 1941)
His Butler's Sister (Universal, 1943)
Holiday Inn (Paramount, 1942)
The Hunchback of Notre Dame (RKO, 1939)
Jane Eyre (20th Century-Fox, 1943)
The Keys of the Kingdom (20th Century-Fox, 1944)
Kitty (Paramount, 1945)
Kitty Foyle (RKO, 1940)

Laura (20th Century-Fox, 1944)

The Lodger (20th Century-Fox, 1944)

Lost Angel (MGM, 1943)

Lost in a Harem (MGM, 1944)

The Lost Weekend (Paramount, 1945)

Love Letters (Paramount, 1945)

Lucky Partners (RKO, 1940)

The Mark of Zorro (20th Century-Fox, 1940)

The Men in Her Life (Columbia, 1941)

Moontide (20th Century-Fox, 1942)

Mr. Deeds Goes to Town (Columbia, 1936)

Mrs. Parkington (MGM, 1944)

Music for Millions (MGM, 1944)

Ninotchka (MGM, 1939)

No Time for Love (Paramount, 1943)

One Foot in Heaven (Warner Bros., 1941)

Our Town (Principal Artists, 1940)

Our Vines Have Tender Grapes (MGM, 1945)

Penny Serenade (Columbia, 1941)

The Rains Came (20th Century-Fox, 1939)

Random Harvest (MGM, 1942)

Rhapsody in Blue (Warner Bros., 1945)

Road to Morocco (Paramount, 1942)

The Sea Hawk (Warner Bros., 1940)

The Shop around the Corner (MGM, 1940)

Sister Kenny (RKO, 1946)

The Song of Bernadette (20th Century-Fox, 1943)

Song of Love (MGM, 1947)

A Song to Remember (Columbia, 1944)

Son of Fury (20th Century-Fox, 1942)

So Proudly We Hail (Paramount, 1943)

The Spiral Staircase (RKO, 1945)

State Fair (20th Century-Fox, 1945)

A Stolen Life (Paramount, 1939)

The Story of Louis Pasteur (Warner Bros., 1936)

Sunday Dinner for a Soldier (20th Century-Fox, 1944)

Sun Valley Serenade (20th Century-Fox, 1941)

Suspicion (RKO, 1941)

Tarzan and the Huntress (RKO, 1947)

Tarzan's New York Adventure (MGM, 1942)

To Each His Own (Paramount, 1946)

Together Again (Columbia, 1944)
Topper Returns (Hal Roach, 1941)
Two-Faced Woman (MGM, 1941)
Two Girls and a Sailor (MGM, 1944)
Two Years before the Mast (Paramount, 1946)
Union Pacific (Paramount, 1939)
The Valley of Decision (MGM, 1945)
Woman of the Year (MGM, 1942)
You Can't Take It with You (Columbia, 1938)
Ziegfeld Girl (MGM, 1941)

Source: Erich Pommer Collection, University of Southern California Cinema Library, Los Angeles, box B, #8, U.S. Information Services, "U.S. Feature Films Approved for Exhibition in U.S. Area of Control as of 30 September 1948."

NOTES

ABBREVIATIONS

In addition to the abbreviations used in the text, the following abbreviations are used in the notes.

BayHStA	Akten des Bayerischen Staatsministeriums für Unterricht und Kultus, Bayerisches Hauptstaatsarchiv, Munich
DIFF	Press clippings files and microfiche, Filmarchiv, Deutsches Institut für Filmkunde, Frankfurt
EP-USC	Erich Pommer Collection, University of Southern California Cinema Library, Los Angeles
FTM Branch	Film, Theater, and Music Control Branch
IFB File	Internationale Filmfestspiele Berlin File
LAB	Papers of the Senator für Wissenschaft und Kunst, Rep. #14, Landesarchiv Berlin
LBS	Presse-Archiv, Landesbildstelle Berlin
OMGUS Papers	Papers of the Office of the Military Government for Germany, United States, National Archives and Records Service, Suitland, Maryland
DO-ISD	Papers of the Director's Office, Information Services Division
MPB-ICD	Papers of the Motion Picture Branch, Information Control Division
MPB-ISD	Papers of the Motion Picture Branch, Information Services Division

INTRODUCTION

1. Ruhl, *Deutschland 1945*, 149–50, 153–94. See also Kleßmann, *Die doppelte Staatsgründung*, chap. 2, and Kramer, " 'Law-Abiding Germans'?" Please note that, unless otherwise indicated, all translations are my own.

2. See Petro, *Joyless Streets*, and Grossmann, "*Girlkultur*," "The New Woman," and " 'Satisfaction Is Domestic Happiness.' "

3. Adolf Hitler, *Mein Kampf*, quoted in Welch, *Propaganda and the German Cinema*, 40.

1. Italo Calvino, "Autobiografia di uno spettatore," quoted in Gundle, "From Neo-Realism to *Luci Rosse*," 199. Calvino's experience in the 1930s was not peculiar to film spectatorship in fascist Italy but was rather the result of the nature and technologies of filmmaking by that time. As German journalist and cultural critic Siegfried Kracauer observed in 1929, the task of the filmmaker lies in "shaping the cinematic material, as beautifully chaotic as life itself, into that unity for which life is indebted to art." Quoted in Hansen, "Decentric Perspectives," 59.

2. Stark, "Cinema, Society, and the State," 129.

3. Ibid., 129–34. See also Lenman, "Mass Culture and the State in Germany," and Kaes, "The Debate about Cinema," 14.

4. Stark, "Cinema, Society, and the State," 160; Welch, "A Medium for the Masses."

5. Kershaw, *The Hitler Myth*, 2.

6. Peukert, *Inside Nazi Germany*, 41–42.

7. Ibid., 244.

8. Kaes, *From Hitler to Heimat*, 4. In keeping with this argument, Kaes adds that "no other government has ever represented itself so obsessively on film."

9. Kaes, "The Debate about Cinema," 23–27; Lenman, "Mass Culture and the State in Germany," 51–52. On the emergence of mass culture, the commercialization of culture, and working-class consumption, see, for example, Abrams, *Workers' Culture in Imperial Germany*; Trommler, "Working-Class Culture"; and Jochen Schulte-Sasse, "Toward a 'Culture' for the Masses."

10. Murray, "Introduction to the Commercial Film Industry," 23. See also Hansen, "Early Silent Cinema," 159–63, and Stark, "Cinema, Society, and the State," 122–27.

11. A. M., "Siegeszug der Kinematographie," quoted in Kaes, "The Debate about Cinema," 20. See also Stark, "Cinema, Society, and the State," 125.

12. Murray, "Introduction to the Commercial Film Industry," 23; Stark, "Cinema, Society, and the State," 124–27. See also Abrams, *Workers' Culture in Imperial Germany*, 171–74.

13. Herman Kienzl, "Theater und Kinematograph" (1911–12), quoted in Kaes, "The Debate about Cinema," 12.

14. Kaes, "The Debate about Cinema," 10.

15. Ibid., 13–14; Stark, "Cinema, Society, and the State," 130.

16. Stark, "Cinema, Society, and the State," 128; Hansen, "Early Silent Cinema," 177.

17. Hansen, "Early Silent Cinema," 174; Kaes, *Kino-Debatte*, 38.

18. Hansen, "Early Silent Cinema," 173–74.

19. Victor Noack, "Die soziale Bedeutung des Kinematographen, 1909," in

Bredow and Zurek, *Film und Gesellschaft,* 54 (emphasis added). See also Albert Hellwig, "Die Schundfilms, ihr Wesen, ihre Gefahren, und ihre Bekämpfung, 1911," and Reg.-Rat Griebel, "Die Kinematographenzensur, 1913," both in ibid., 60–61, 67.

20. Hansen, "Early Silent Cinema," 174.

21. Memo, 8 March 1912, quoted in Stark, "Cinema, Society, and the State," 132.

22. Kaes, "The Debate about Cinema," 14–15 (emphasis added). See also Kaes, "Mass Culture and Modernity."

23. Stark, "Cinema, Society, and the State," 148–49.

24. Quoted in ibid., 153–54.

25. Kaes, "The Debate about Cinema," 7, 14. See also Kracauer, *From Caligari to Hitler,* 16, and Stark, "Cinema, Society, and the State," 148. For a discussion of working-class leisure and its commercialization in imperial Germany, see Abrams, *Workers' Culture in Imperial Germany.*

26. By the 1920s, in fact, one SPD functionary complained that workers "are proud of the fact that they can imitate everything bourgeois; for the most part they have bourgeois ideals: drinking, trashy literature, jazz, boxing, and so forth." Abrams, *Workers' Culture in Imperial Germany,* 142, 177, 181.

27. Abrams, *Workers' Culture in Imperial Germany,* 142–43.

28. Lenman, "Mass Culture and the State in Germany," 51–54. See also Abrams, *Workers' Culture in Imperial Germany,* esp. chap. 6.

29. Stark, "Cinema, Society, and the State," 127–54; Lenman, "Mass Culture and the State in Germany," 51–57.

30. Rentschler, "The Elemental, the Ornamental, the Instrumental," 172–73.

31. Hansen, "Early Silent Cinema," 151–58. See also Kracauer, *From Caligari to Hitler,* 17–18; Kaes, "Silent Cinema," 246–52; Murray, "Introduction to the Commercial Film Industry," 23; and Ruge, "Üb 'immer Treu' und Redlichkeit," 25–27.

32. Hansen, "Early Silent Cinema," 153.

33. Lyon, "Bertolt Brecht's Hollywood Years," 146–47.

34. An early, but sure, sign of the gradual elevation of film to serious consideration as an art form was the emergence of film criticism in the cultural sections of newspapers and periodicals in 1913, such as the review of the film adaptation of dramatist Paul Lindau's play, *Die Andere (The Other).* See Wollenberg, *Fifty Years of German Film,* 10. For a discussion of the emergence and development of German film criticism, see Hake, *The Cinema's Third Machine.*

35. Stark, "Cinema, Society, and the State," 161. See also Manfred Behn, "Krieg der Propagandisten," in Bock and Töteberg, *Das Ufa-Buch,* 28–29.

36. Stark, "Cinema, Society, and the State," 161; Wollenberg, *Fifty Years of German Film,* 12. See also Thompson, *Exporting Entertainment,* 87–97, and

Manfred Behn, "Filmfreunde: Die Gründung der Ufa 1917," in Bock and Töteberg, *Das Ufa-Buch*, 30–35.

37. Stark, "Cinema, Society, and the State," 161–62. See also Wollenberg, *Fifty Years of German Film*, 12, and Kracauer, *From Caligari to Hitler*, 35–36.

38. Stark, "Cinema, Society, and the State," 161–62.

39. Thompson, *Exporting Entertainment*, 76–81, 85–90.

40. Bild- und Filmamt, "Der Propagandafilm und seine Bedingungen, Ziele und Wege," in Bredow and Zurek, *Film und Gesellschaft*, 73–74. See also General Ludendorff, "Schreiben an das Königliche Kriegsministerium vom 4. Juli 1917," in ibid., 102–4.

41. Major van den Bergh, quoted in Welch, "A Medium for the Masses," 86–87. See also "Vom Kaiserreich zur Weimarer Republik," and Bild- und Filmamt, "Der Propagandafilm," both in Bredow and Zurek, *Film und Gesellschaft*, 17–22, 73–74; Wollenberg, *Fifty Years of German Film*, 7–9; and Hansen, "Early Silent Cinema," 159–60.

42. Quoted in Hansen, "Early Silent Cinema," 170–71.

43. Stark, "Cinema, Society, and the State," 154–60.

44. Bild- und Filmamt, "Der Propagandafilm," in Bredow and Zurek, *Film und Gesellschaft*, 76–81, 86–87.

45. Ibid., 75–80; Murray, "Introduction to the Commercial Film Industry," 25; Stark, "Cinema, Society, and the State," 161–62.

46. The minutes of the meeting from which this quote is drawn were translated and reprinted in Welch, "A Medium for the Masses," 85–87. For information on Deulig, BUFA, and UFA, see Ludendorff, "Schreiben an das Königliche Kriegsministerium," and Hans Traub, "Die Gründung der Ufa, 1943 (Ausschnitt)," both in Bredow and Zurek, *Film und Gesellschaft*, 102–4, 105–12. See also Behn, "Filmfreunde," "Großeinkauf: Die Grundlagen des Ufa-Konzern," and "Was will die Ufa," all in Bock and Töteberg, *Das Ufa-Buch*, 30–35, 36–40; Wollenberg, *Fifty Years of German Film*, 10–24; Kracauer, *From Caligari to Hitler*, 35–37; Stark, "Cinema, Society, and the State," 160–63; and Murray, "Introduction to the Commercial Film Industry," 23, 25. For a short synopsis of the creation of a viable German film industry by a participant, see the 1922 lecture by Ludwig Klitzsch, "Der deutsche Wiederaufbau und der Film," in Bredow and Zurek, *Film und Gesellschaft*, 113–15.

47. Wollenberg, *Fifty Years of German Film*, 12, 17. See also Hardt, "Erich Pommer," 1–9. Pommer had a long career in film, beginning in 1907, when he worked in the Berlin office of the French film company Leon Gaumont. He later transferred to Vienna to work for the French company Eclair, where he was responsible for sales and the production of newsreels in his capacity as general manager for Central Europe. With the onslaught of World War I, he was drafted into the German Army and served on the French front. On leave in 1915 he founded Decla-Film-Gesellschaft in Berlin. The next year, he was

transferred to the Balkans to edit newsreels and documentaries for the newly founded Film Propaganda Office of the General Army Supreme Command. After the war, he continued to expand Decla and in 1919 produced *Das Kabinett des Dr. Caligari*. In 1920 Decla merged with Bioscop and thereby gained access to the latter's movie theaters and studios in Berlin-Neubabelsberg. The following year, Decla was absorbed by UFA, where Pommer became head of feature film production. In that capacity, he continued to encourage the production of expressionist-style films, which he had helped develop at Decla. He was also a member of the UFA Executive Committee until 1926. In 1923, furthermore, he was elected president of the newly founded SPIO, the trade association of the German film industry. After a short hiatus in Hollywood in 1926–27, Pommer returned "to take charge of Ufa's most prestigious and expensive 'international' production unit, newly named the Erich-Pommer-Produktion." With the advent of sound, he "experimented with and perfected the *Filmoperette*" in such films as *Die Drei von der Tankstelle* (1930) and *Der Kongreß tanzt* (1931). He also produced *Der blaue Engel* (1930), which "reestablished Ufa's international reputation and catapulted film director [Josef von] Sternberg and female lead Marlene Dietrich to international stardom." Pommer's career took a downturn in 1933 when Goebbels's anti-Semitic politics forced him out of the Berlin film industry. He emigrated to France shortly thereafter. In 1934 he left France for the United States.

48. Saunders, "Comedy as Redemption," 254.

49. Wollenberg, *Fifty Years of German Film*, 11–17, 24, 37. See also Saunders, "Comedy as Redemption," 254, and his more recent *Hollywood in Berlin*, esp. chap. 8. For a detailed discussion of the Tobis venture, see Thompson, *Exporting Entertainment*, 148–58.

50. Thompson, *Exporting Entertainment*, 100–119, 148–54. See also Thomas Saunders, "Von Dafco zu Damra: Spekulation mit amerikanischen Film," in Bock and Töteberg, *Das Ufa-Buch*, 70–71. For a nuanced discussion of the relationship between Hollywood and German film interests, see the excellent study by Saunders, *Hollywood in Berlin*.

51. Thompson, *Exporting Entertainment*, 102–3. See also Jan-Christopher Horak, "Die Anti-Ufa," Ursula Hardt, "Kon-Fusion: Die Ufa übernimmt die Decla-Bioscop," and Thomas Elsaesser, "Kunst und Krise: Die Ufa in den 20er Jahren," all in Bock and Töteberg, *Das Ufa-Buch*, 78–79, 80–85, 96–105.

52. Kracauer, *From Caligari to Hitler*, 3, 61–76, 77–79, 149–50. See also Eisner, *The Haunted Screen*, and Coates, *The Gorgon's Gaze*.

53. Elsaesser, "Kunst und Krise," in Bock and Töteberg, *Das Ufa-Buch*, esp. 99–101. See also Ursula Hardt, "Kunst für Waschfrau Minna Schulze: Die Produktions-Konzepte des Erich Pommers," in ibid., 90–93.

54. For discussions of the cinematic landscape of Weimar Germany, see Wollenberg, *Fifty Years of German Film*; Kracauer, *From Caligari to Hitler*; and

Eisner, *The Haunted Screen*. More recent analyses are offered in Horak, "Die Anti-Ufa," and Elsaesser, "Kunst und Krise," both in Bock and Töteberg, *Das Ufa-Buch*, 78–79, 96–105. For statements by industry insiders, see Klitzsch, "Der deutsche Wiederaufbau und der Film," and Spitzenorganisation der Deutschen Filmindustrie, "Die kulturelle, politische, und wirtschaftliche Bedeutung der deutschen Filmindustrie," both in Bredow and Zurek, *Film und Gesellschaft*, 113–15, 116–17. Scholarship that calls into question the perception of a firmly national quality in German filmmaking includes Petro, *Joyless Streets*, which explores female spectatorship; de Grazia, "Mass Culture and Sovereignty," 53–87, which investigates the American cultural influences in Europe as well as self-proclaimed European (and especially fascist) alternatives to it; and most recently, Saunders, *Hollywood in Berlin*, which characterizes the relationship between Hollywood and Berlin film interests as a complex "dialectic" involving cooperation and competition.

55. Usborne, *Politics of the Body*, 78.

56. Kracauer, *From Caligari to Hitler*, 44–45; Murray, *Film and the German Left*, 27.

57. For a discussion of the film, its reception, and its social context, see Dyer, "Less and More Than Women and Men," 5–60. For a more general discussion of the history of the gay movement as well as conceptions of homosexuality in pre-1933 Germany, see Oosterhuis, *Homosexuality and Male Bonding in Pre-Nazi Germany*, esp. 1–27.

58. Abrams, *Workers' Culture in Imperial Germany*, 103–8, 169–71. On postwar concerns regarding moral decline, see Usborne, *Politics of the Body*, esp. 69–85.

59. The Independent Socialists did not support the legislation. Excerpt from Reichslichtspielgesetz quoted in Murray, "Introduction to the Commercial Film Industry," 26. See also Lenman, "Mass Culture and the State in Germany," 55–57; Mühl-Benninghaus, "Verbotene Leinwand"; Wollenberg, *Fifty Years of German Film*, 13–14; and Elsaesser, "Kunst und Krise," in Bock and Töteberg, *Das Ufa-Buch*, 96.

60. Quoted in Hake, "Chaplin Reception in Weimar Germany," 107. See also Kaes, "Mass Culture and Modernity," 323–26, and Saunders, "Comedy as Redemption," 253–55.

61. Kaes, "Mass Culture and Modernity," 323, 325.

62. Hermann Kasack wrote: "Americanism is the materialism of vitality . . . and in the figure of the sportsman is embodied the popular hero, the myth of the heroic." See Kasack, "Sport als Lebensgefühl" (1928), quoted in Bathrick, "Max Schmeling on the Canvas," 116.

63. Bathrick, "Max Schmeling on the Canvas," 117; Kurt Pinthus, "Männliche Literatur" (1929), quoted in ibid., 123.

64. Willi Haas 1926 review of Chaplin's *Gold Rush*, quoted in Saunders, "Comedy as Redemption," 269.

65. 1927 review of a Harold Lloyd film in *Deutsche Allegemeine Zeitung*, quoted in Saunders, "Comedy as Redemption," 273.

66. Quoted in Saunders, "Comedy as Redemption," 272.

67. Kaes, "Mass Culture and Modernity," 326.

68. Saunders, "Comedy as Redemption," 261; Hake, "Chaplin Reception in Weimar Germany," 95–101.

69. Saunders, "Comedy as Redemption," 261–67.

70. Ibid., 266 (emphasis added).

71. Kracauer, "Cult of Distraction," 94–95.

72. Saunders, "Comedy as Redemption," 266.

73. Quoted in Bredow and Zurek, *Film und Gesellschaft*, 23.

74. On filmmaking and the political left in Germany, see Murray, *Film and the German Left*, and Korte, *Film und Realität*.

75. *Reichsfilmblatt*, 20 September 1924, pp. 35–36, quoted in Saunders, *Hollywood in Berlin*, 130, and more generally, 126–30.

76. Quoted in Thompson, *Exporting Entertainment*, 100.

77. Saunders, "Von Dafco zu Damra," and Horak, "Die Anti-Ufa," both in Bock and Töteberg, *Das Ufa-Buch*, 70–71, 78–79. See also Saunders, *Hollywood in Berlin*, chaps. 2–4. Saunders points out that German film companies were jockeying for position among themselves as well. Thus, competition did not cut neatly along national lines.

78. Thompson points out that American films dominated the French and British markets through the late 1920s. American productions accounted for a staggering 90 percent of all films screened in Britain in the early 1920s, declining to 70 percent only in 1932. In France, American films commanded 85 percent of screentime in 1924, dropping off to just over 48 percent in 1929. See Thompson, *Exporting Entertainment*, 108–10, 125. See also Elsaesser, "Kunst und Krise," in Bock and Töteberg, *Das Ufa-Buch*, 102–4; Murray, "Introduction to the Commercial Film Industry," 29; and Prokop, *Soziologie des Films*, 90.

79. Quoted in Kaes, "Mass Culture and Modernity," 328. See also Saunders, *Hollywood in Berlin*, chaps. 4–5.

80. Saunders, *Hollywood in Berlin*, chaps. 2–4.

81. SPIO, "Die kulturelle, politische, und wirtschaftliche Bedeutung der deutschen Filmindustrie" (1925), quoted in Bredow and Zurek, *Film und Gesellschaft*, 117–18. See also de Grazia, "Mass Culture and Sovereignty," 60, on the Hollywood film's role in supplying consumer information as well as "attractive social identities" for women and men.

82. Thompson also points out that during World War I, the Creel Committee

assisted in shipping industrial films abroad that advertised the plants and products of companies like Beechnut, General Electric, Remington, and Ford. See Thompson, *Exporting Entertainment*, 95, 122–23.

83. Wollenberg, *Fifty Years of German Film*, 30–31.

84. Thompson, *Exporting Entertainment*, 104, 125, 131, 219.

85. Ibid., 104, 111–17, 125, 131, 219.

86. Quoted in ibid., 113. See also de Grazia, "Mass Culture and Sovereignty," 67–70, 76–81.

87. Murray, "Introduction to the Commercial Film Industry," 31; Wollenberg, *Fifty Years of German Film*, 30–34. Thomas Saunders investigated the German reception of American "hate films" of the mid- to late 1920s in "Hollywood's Great War and the Weimar Republic: *Hetze* or Enlightenment," paper presented at the German Studies Association Meeting, Milwaukee, 1989.

88. See Elsaesser, "Kunst und Krise," in Bock and Töteberg, *Das Ufa-Buch*, 96–105, esp. 104.

89. *Film-Kurier*, 28 August 1928, and *Reichsfilmblatt*, 20 February 1932, quoted in Hardt, "Kunst für Waschfrau Minna Schulze," in Bock and Töteberg, *Das Ufa-Buch*, 93.

90. Hardt, "Kunst für Waschfrau Minna Schulze," and Elsaesser, "Kunst und Krise," both in Bock and Töteberg, *Das Ufa-Buch*, 90–93, 96–105.

91. Hardt, "Kunst für Waschfrau Minna Schulze," Elsaesser, "Kunst und Krise," and Axel Schildt, "Auf Expansionskurs: Aus der Inflation in die Krise" and "Hugenberg ante portas: Rationalisierung mit nationalem Besen," all in Bock and Töteberg, *Das Ufa-Buch*, 90–93, 96–105, 170–73, 190–95. See also Hermann Kappelhoff, "Lebendiger Rhythmus der Welt: Die Erich-Pommer-Produktion der Ufa," in ibid., 208–13; Romani, *Tainted Goddesses*, 163; and Prokop, *Soziologie des Films*, 90.

92. See, for example, Welch, *Nazi Propaganda*; Lowry, *Pathos und Politik*; Labanyi, "Images of Fascism"; Golsan, *Fascism, Aesthetics, and Culture*; and Witte, "Visual Pleasure Inhibited."

93. See Kershaw, "How Effective Was Nazi Propaganda?"

94. Rentschler, "German Feature Films"; Lowry, *Pathos und Politik*, 30–34, 41.

95. Rentschler, "German Feature Films," 258, 260. See also Lowry, *Pathos und Politik*, 26–47, 115, 199, 202.

96. See, for example, Peukert, *Inside Nazi Germany*. Victoria de Grazia in "Mass Culture and Sovereignty" focuses on the cinema to explore the question of American "free-floating" culture and national sovereignty; and Eric Rentschler in "German Feature Films" appeals to scholars to consider the relationship between German cinema under Hitler and German cinema under Weimar on the one hand and the interplay between German cinema and Hollywood on the other.

97. For a discussion of film censorship and the organization of the German film industry under national socialism, see Welch, *Propaganda and the German Cinema*, esp. 6–38; Drewniak, *Der deutsche Film*; Albrecht, *National-sozialistische Filmpolitik*; Cadars and Courtade, *Geschichte des Films im Dritten Reich*; Bredow and Zurek, *Film und Gesellschaft*; Hull, *Film in the Third Reich*; Petley, *Capital and Culture*; Spiker, *Film und Kapital*; and Wollenberg, *Fifty Years of German Film*. For a selected bibliography on cinema during the Third Reich, see Rentschler, "German Feature Films," 263–66.

98. Lowry, *Pathos und Politik*, 4–14. See also Elsaesser, "Kunst und Krise," and Manfred Behn, "Gleichschritt in die 'neue Zeit': Filmpolitik zwischen SPIO und NS," both in Bock and Töteberg, *Das Ufa-Buch*, 105, 340–42.

99. Wollenberg, *Fifty Years of German Film*, 36–38. See also Lowry, *Pathos und Politik*, 12; de Grazia, "Mass Culture and Sovereignty," 77–78; and Welch, *Propaganda and the German Cinema*, 12–14.

100. Welch, *Propaganda and the German Cinema*, 17.

101. De Grazia, "Mass Culture and Sovereignty," 79. See also Wollenberg, *Fifty Years of German Film*, 37.

102. Leiser, *Nazi Cinema*, 12.

103. De Grazia, "Mass Culture and Sovereignty," 66, 78.

104. Rentschler, "The Triumph of Male Will," 15–23.

105. John Pommer, Erich's son, interview by author, Camarillo, California, 6–7 August 1992. For discussions of purged German film personnel, see Horak, *Fluchtpunkt Hollywood*, and Liebe, *Verehrt, verfolgt, vergessen*.

106. Lenman, "Mass Culture and the State in Germany," 57–58. See also Schäfer, *Das gespaltene Bewußtsein*.

107. Schäfer, *Das gespaltene Bewußtsein*, 114, 115–17.

108. Ibid., 119.

109. Ibid., 118, 119–30.

110. Thompson, *Exporting Entertainment*, 125, 220.

111. Quoted in Schäfer, *Das gespaltene Bewußtsein*, 129, 130, 132.

112. Ibid., 130–31.

113. Ibid., 123.

114. Quoted in Rentschler, "The Elemental, the Ornamental, the Instrumental," 173, 175.

115. Ibid., 174, 179.

116. Ibid., 173. See also Rentschler, "The Triumph of Male Will," and Linda Schulte-Sasse, "Retrieving the City as *Heimat*."

117. See, for example, Stacey, *Star Gazing*, and Weiss, *Vampires and Violets*.

118. Lowry has begun to investigate these questions in *Pathos und Politik*. See also Linda Schulte-Sasse, "Retrieving the City as *Heimat*," 184.

119. See Peukert, *Inside Nazi Germany*, 145–74, and "Youth in the Third Reich," and Schäfer, *Das gespaltene Bewußtsein*, 137.

120. See Kater, "Forbidden Fruit" and *Different Drummers.*

121. Peukert, *Inside Nazi Germany,* 247.

CHAPTER TWO

1. Wollenberg, *Fifty Years of German Film,* 46.

2. Chamberlin, *Kultur auf Trümmern,* 12–13.

3. Pleyer, *Deutscher Nachkriegsfilm,* 24–25.

4. Richard Griffith, quoted in Hoenisch, "Film as an Instrument of the U.S. Reeducation Program," 200.

5. Culbert, "American Film Policy," 181. On JCS 1067, see Gimbel, *American Occupation of Germany.*

6. Joseph Barnes, assistant director of OWI's Overseas Branch and deputy director for Atlantic operations, quoted in Pütz, "Business or Propaganda?," 398.

7. EP-USC, box B, #5, U.S. Film Branch, ICD, "Report on the Status of the Motion Picture Industry in Germany."

8. Ibid.; box B, #4, memo from film control officer to chief, FTM Branch, 9 October 1946.

9. Guback, *International Film Industry,* 128–29.

10. See Joseph, "Our Film Program in Germany," 124–26, and EP-USC, box B, #8–9, U.S. Information Services, "U.S. Feature Films Approved for Exhibition in U.S. Area of Control as of 30 September 1948" and "Annex L: Synchronization in U.S.-operated Studios as of 30 June 1949."

11. Cadars and Courtade, *Geschichte des Films im Dritten Reich,* 8.

12. Hollywood producer-director Walter Wanger, quoted in Pütz, "Business or Propaganda?," 401 (emphasis in original); Eric Johnston, quoted in Guback, "Shaping the Film Business in Postwar Germany," 252.

13. Joseph, "Our Film Program in Germany," 122–23. See also Pütz, "Business or Propaganda?," 400.

14. OMGUS Papers, DO-ISD #15, Davidson Taylor, chief, FTM Branch, "Report on Trip to Munich of 20 June through 26 June," 27 June 1945.

15. EP-USC, box B, #5, U.S. Film Branch, ICD, "Report on the Status of the Motion Picture Industry in Germany." See also Joseph, "Our Film Program in Germany," 123–24, 129. For a description of the content of *Welt im Film* and the French newsreel *Actualités,* see Regel, "Der Film als Instrument alliierter Besatzungspolitik," 44–49.

16. Culbert, "American Film Policy," 179; Hoenisch, "Film as an Instrument of the U.S. Reeducation Program."

17. OMGUS Papers, MPB-ISD #260, Research Department of the Foreign

Office, German and Austrian Section, "The Film Situation in All the Zones of Germany," 5 May 1946.

18. Quoted in Culbert, "American Film Policy," 179. During the occupation years, U.S. authorities persistently attempted to evaluate the success of re-education efforts by means of questionnaires, intelligence reports, and the like. Although this information alone did little to alter U.S. film policy in Germany, it was cited as support when other circumstances demanded that policy be reassessed.

19. Quoted in ibid. Regel cites an OMGUS survey that recorded a 12 percent Bavarian attendance rate for the film. See Regel, "Der Film als Instrument alliierter Besatzungspolitik," 43.

20. Hoenisch, "Film as an Instrument of the U.S. Reeducation Program," 200–201.

21. OMGUS Papers, MPB-ISD #277, memo from Robert Joseph, film officer, to ICD officer(s), 25 November 1945.

22. OMGUS Papers, DO-ISD #15, memo from William D. Patterson, chief of film production, to Heinz Roemheld, chief, FTM Branch, 24 November 1945.

23. The cases of Veit Harlan and Wolfgang Staudte will be discussed in chapter 6. For a discussion of other rehabilitated German filmmakers, see Hans-Peter Kochenrath, "Kontinuität im deutschen Film," in Bredow and Zurek, *Film und Gesellschaft*, 286–92, and Kreimeier, *Kino und Filmindustrie*, chap. 1.

24. Pleyer, *Deutscher Nachkriegsfilm*, 31–34.

25. For a brief description of this film and a discussion of Staudte's place in postwar German cinema, see chapter 6.

26. OMGUS Papers, MPB-ISD #275, secret report of Current Political Intelligence, 17 April 1946.

27. Ibid.

28. Ibid.

29. Ibid.

30. Pleyer, *Deutscher Nachkriegsfilm*, 34. The films were Wolfgang Staudte's *Die Mörder sind unter uns*, Gerhard Lamprecht's *Irgendwo in Berlin*, and Milos Harbich's "propaganda film" advocating land reform, *Freies Land*.

31. OMGUS Papers, MPB-ISD #259, minutes of General Information Control Meeting, 28 October 1946.

32. OMGUS Papers, MPB-ISD #260, Research Department of the Foreign Office, German and Austrian Section, "The Film Situation in All the Zones of Germany," 5 May 1946. See also Regel, "Der Film als Instrument alliierter Besatzungspolitik," 43; Hoenisch, "Film as an Instrument of the U.S. Reeducation Program," 205; and EP-USC, box I, #6, taped interview with Erich Pommer.

33. OMGUS Papers, MPB-ISD #260, confidential report from Robert Schmid, ODIC, Intelligence Branch, to FTM Branch, [1946].

34. Hoenisch, "Film as an Instrument of the U.S. Reeducation Program," 201.

35. Hardt, "Erich Pommer," 1–9. A 1926 article in the German film journal *Film-Kurier* congratulated Pommer on giving "the UFA trademark a name in the world. That means that he has presented exemplary works on the world market with a two-fold effect: The German film became worthy of debate in foreign countries, and the UFA films received world-wide recognition as highest achievements in international film art." Quoted in ibid., 7.

36. EP-USC, box A, #27, Horst Feldt, "So fing das damals an," 18.

37. EP-USC, box B, #3, letter from John Pommer to his father, Erich Pommer, 7 May 1947. John Pommer noted that a number of Hollywood companies had been exploring expansion possibilities in the South American market. He continued, "Obviously German pictures will never be able to obtain a large run in the U.S. proper or in Canada or other British territories, so the industry cannot be afraid of them appearing in these markets."

38. EP-USC, box B, #5, U.S. Film Branch, ICD, "Report on the Status of the Motion Picture Industry in Germany"; box B, #4, memo from the Decartelization Branch to the FTM Branch, "Reconstruction and New Organization of the German Film Industry," 3 December 1946; box A, #33, "Erich Pommer, Film and Future," translation of article in *Tagesspiegel*, 26 July 1946.

39. Riess, *Das gibt's nur einmal*; Hardt, "Erich Pommer," 210, 215.

40. Quoted in Hardt, "Erich Pommer," 17 (emphasis added).

41. Quoted in OMGUS Papers, MPB-ISD #287, draft of memo from Erich Pommer to R. A. McClure, 6 February 1947. See also OMGUS Papers, MPB-ISD #277, memo from R. A. McClure to War Department, War Department Special Staff, Civil Affairs Division, Reorientation Branch, Washington, D.C., 11 February 1947.

42. OMGUS Papers, MPB-ISD #287, draft of memo from Erich Pommer to R. A. McClure, 6 February 1947.

43. Ibid.

44. MPEA member companies were Columbia Pictures, Metro-Goldwyn-Mayer, Paramount, RKO, Twentieth Century-Fox, United Artists, Universal, and Warner Brothers. OMGUS Papers, DO-ISD #18, briefing memo to military governor regarding visit of Eric Johnston, president, MPAA, 7 July 1947. For a discussion of MPEA's postwar activities abroad, see Guback, *International Film Industry*.

45. OMGUS Papers, MPB-ISD #277, copy of "Pommer to Integrate German, Austrian Pix Trade," *Film Daily*, 6 September 1946, and letter from Edward L. Peeples for director of ICD to the War Department, Civil Affairs Division, and Reorientation Branch, 2 October 1946.

46. EP-USC, box B, #6, "Pommer's Kicking Around in H'wood Said to Influence His Germ Pic Plans," *Variety*, 7 May 1947; OMGUS Papers, MPB-ISD

#277, copy of "Pommer Hurls German Threat at Hollywood," *Variety*, 8 May 1947.

47. OMGUS Papers, MPB-ISD #261, copy of "Secret Anglo-U.S. Plan to Reestablish Reich Film Industry Bared," *Washington Evening Star*, 6 May 1947. See also EP-USC, box B, #6, copies of "German Film Revival Bared," *Los Angeles Examiner*, 6 May 1947, and "Pommer Reveals Plans for German Film," *Film Daily*, 12 May 1947.

48. EP-USC, box B, #6, MPEA typescript urging that German exports be banned, [1947]; OMGUS Papers, MPB-ISD #277, confidential report by Eric Clarke, chief, FTM Branch, 19 April 1947. Following a joint meeting of the ICD with the American and British film industries, Clarke reported being told by British film magnate Sir Arthur Rank's representative that "the British industry people . . . had agreed to support efforts by MPEA in Washington to have Mr. Pommer recalled to the United States." After meeting with the ICD the following day, the same British industry representative acknowledged that these informational meetings had given him a better appreciation of the existing situation in Germany and convinced him "that Mr. Pommer had been unwarrantably maligned"; he would recommend to Rank back home that they desist from having Pommer recalled.

49. OMGUS Papers, MPB-ISD #258, letter from Decartelization Branch, Economic Division, to Anti-Trust Division, Department of Justice, Washington, D.C., 5 June 1947, and "Unlikely for German Pix to Reach Here," *Film Daily*, 26 May 1947, p. 1.

50. OMGUS Papers, MPB-ISD #277, briefing memo regarding Eric Johnston's visit to the ICD, 8 July 1947.

51. OMGUS Papers, MPB-ISD #258, letter from Decartelization Branch, Economic Division, to Anti-Trust Division, Department of Justice, Washington, D.C., 5 June 1947.

52. OMGUS Papers, MPB-ISD #258, letter from Decartelization Branch, Economic Division, to Anti-Trust Division, Department of Justice, Washington, D.C., 5 June 1947. In fact, during 1948–49, 64 American films were released in Germany. In 1949–50, the number rose to 145, and in 1950–51, to 202. See Guback, *International Film Industry*, 133. The numbers differ slightly in Prokop, *Soziologie des Films*, 90.

53. OMGUS Papers, DO-ISD #30, Film Section report to chief, FTM Branch, 13 March 1947. See also OMGUS Papers, MPB-ISD #277, memo on meeting of MPEA at War Department, 1 July 1947. At this meeting, MPEA president Eric Johnston warned that if the Military Government allowed the export of German films, the MPEA would not be able to insure member support for the reeducation effort through the provision of "proper films" for exhibition in Germany. See Guback, *International Film Industry*, 126–33, and "Shaping the Film Business," 256, for a discussion of Hollywood's less than enthusiastic

support for the reeducation program in Germany when it felt its interests were not being considered.

54. OMGUS Papers, MPB-ISD #256, confidential memo to Civil Affairs Division, New York Office, 18 December 1947.

55. Guback, "Shaping the Film Business," 255–65, esp. 261, 264.

56. OMGUS Papers, DO-ISD #30, Film Section reports to chief, FTM Branch, 13 March, 22 May 1947. See also OMGUS Papers, MPB-ISD #282, confidential report to director, ICD, from Erich Pommer, 22 May 1947.

57. OMGUS Papers, MPB-ISD #278, minutes of the Economic Fusion of U.S. and British Zones Joint Film Policy Meeting, ICD, OMGUS, 31 March 1947.

58. Quoted in Hardt, "Erich Pommer," 199.

59. OMGUS Papers, MPB-ISD #292, translation of restricted memo from Willy Zeyn, 1 April 1947.

60. OMGUS Papers, MPB-ISD #287, memo from Dr. Werner Faasch to Erich Pommer, translated by Liaison and Protocol Section, OMGUS, 19 April 1947.

61. Ibid.

62. OMGUS Papers, ICD-MPB #287, memo from chief, Film Section, to chief, FTM Branch, 24 April 1947; EP-USC, box B, #5, U.S. Film Branch, ICD, "Report on the Status of the Motion Picture Industry in Germany."

63. OMGUS Papers, ICD-MPB #287, memo from chief, Film Section, to chief, FTM Branch, 24 April 1947.

64. Willis, *The French in Germany*, 47. In April 1947, French policy toward Germany was based upon a "six point thesis," namely that the Rhineland should be demilitarized and detached from Germany; the Ruhr should be separated from the rest of Germany and placed under international control; the Saar should be joined in an economic union with France; its neighbors should exploit Germany economically for their own benefit by exacting reparations, controlling the distribution of its coal and steel, and maintaining a low ceiling on its industrial production; by a thorough process of demilitarization and denazification, Germany should be made incapable of menacing its neighbors; and Germany should be reeducated and reorganized as a democratic, federal state (ibid., 45–46).

65. OMGUS Papers, MPB-ICD #287, memo from chief, Film Section, to chief, FTM Branch, 24 April 1947.

66. Ibid.

67. OMGUS Papers, MPB-ISD #10-14-2/3, memo from A. V. Chukayeff, secretariat, Information Committee, to Film Section, through Clarke, 29 May 1947.

68. Ibid.; OMGUS Papers, MPB-ISD #279, minutes of Meeting of Joint Anglo-American Film Production Control Board, 5 May, 17 July 1947. By late summer 1947, the Joint Anglo-American Film Production Control Board was created, and the British and Americans agreed to recommend the issuance of

joint film production licenses. In addition, the Americans were able to place the establishment of voluntary self-censorship by the German film industry on the agenda for their next meeting.

69. Kleßmann, *Die doppelte Staatsgründung,* 177–92.

70. OMGUS Papers, Berlin Information Services Branch, #109, private memo from Carl Winston, chief, U.S. Film Section, to Colonel Howley, 10 February 1948.

71. Ibid.; OMGUS Papers, MPB-ISD #287, memo from Dr. Werner Faasch to Erich Pommer, translated by Liaison and Protocol Section, OMGUS, 19 April 1947, and DO-ISD #15, confidential memo from Erich Pommer to chief, FTM Branch, "Reconstruction and New Organization of the German Film Industry," 15 October 1946.

72. OMGUS Papers, DO-ISD #15, memo to director, ICD, about status of decartelization negotiations, 3 June 1948.

73. A suggestion was made, undoubtedly by U.S. officials, that the Tripartite Film Committee be located in Wiesbaden in the U.S. zone. OMGUS Papers, ISD, Office of the Military Government, Bavaria, Division Headquarters, #2, memo of meeting of film and information officers of the American, French, and British zones, 31 August 1948.

74. OMGUS Papers, MPB-ISD #281, memo from Arthur Mayer, chief, MPB, to Henry Heymann, legal adviser, Bipartite Control Office, U.S. Decartelization Element, 21 March 1949.

75. OMGUS Papers, DO-ISD #15, confidential memo from Erich Pommer to chief, FTM Branch, "Reconstruction and New Organization of the German Film Industry," 15 October 1946, and #276, copy of "Minutes of Informal Meeting with U.S. Production Licensees on Saturday, 25 January 1947," 31 January 1947.

76. Although U.S. information officers devoted much attention to developing a self-censorship code, assistance was less forthcoming in response to the German film industry's material needs. A week after this meeting, Curt Oertel wrote to General McClure to request "that the Military Government not confine itself . . . to directives and recommendations but . . . help us by practical means to get production under way." German dissatisfaction with film financing continued throughout the occupation, with pleas for assistance again swelling in the summer of 1948 after the currency reform. OMGUS Papers, MPB-ISD #287, letter from Curt Oertel to General McClure, director, ICD, translated by Liaison and Protocol Section, OMGUS, 31 March 1947.

77. OMGUS Papers, MPB-ISD #287, "Translation of Summary of Events of the Meeting of Motion Picture Producers Licensed in the U.S. Zone of Germany, 20–25 March 1947," and #276, copy of "Minutes of Informal Meeting with U.S. Production Licensees on Saturday, 25 January 1947," 31 January 1947.

78. OMGUS Papers, MPB-ISD #287, "Translation of Summary of Events of

the Meeting of Motion Picture Producers Licensed in the U.S. Zone of Germany, 20–25 March 1947." ICD officials demanded that German producers provide input for the new censorship legislation within the week. Klagemann assured producers that he had already drawn up a draft and emphasized that licensed filmmakers should recognize that they enjoyed the "100% support of the Military Government."

79. OMGUS Papers, MPB-ISD #287, "Protokoll über die Tagung der U.S. lizensierten Produzenten am 20. März 1947," 21 March 1947. The juxtaposition of the implied imperative "must" and the adjective "voluntary" created a curious contradiction that set the tone for negotiations between the ICD and the German film producers and was not questioned in any legal sense until almost ten years later by jurist Johanne Noltenius. See Noltenius, *Die Freiwillige Selbstkontrolle.*

80. OMGUS Papers, MPB-ISD #287, "Protokoll über die Tagung der U.S. lizensierten Produzenten am 20. März 1947," 21 March 1947.

81. Walter Keim, "Die Freiwillige Selbstkontrolle der deutschen Filmwirtschaft," *Kulturarbeit* 9 (1949).

82. U.S. film officers had been reporting such activity since the autumn of 1946. See OMGUS Papers, DO-ISD #15, confidential memo from Erich Pommer to chief, FTM Branch, "Reconstruction and New Organization of the German Film Industry," 15 October 1946, and EP-USC, box B, #5, summary of U.S. administration of film matters in Germany, 30 April 1947.

83. OMGUS Papers, MPB-ISD #260, translation of report by H. W. Kubaschewsky to the ICD, 11 January 1946.

84. Welch, *Nazi Propaganda*, 73–78. See also "Film und Jugend," in Drewniak, *Der deutsche Film*, 579–603.

85. See Kershaw, *Popular Opinion and Political Dissent*, 182–84, 207. See also Blessing, " 'Deutschland in Not, wir im Glauben.' "

86. OMGUS Papers, MPB-ISD #260, memo from J. H. Hills, deputy director, ICD, 17 January 1946. See also memo from H. W. Kubaschwesky, manager of Allgemeiner Filmverleih, to the mayor of Plattling, Lower Bavaria, 25 January 1946, protesting the latter's posting of a sign at the local theater entrance prohibiting attendance by youth under the age of eighteen.

87. OMGUS Papers, DO-ISD #15, confidential report from Erich Pommer to chief, FTM Branch, "Reconstruction and New Organization of the German Film Industry," 15 October 1946. Pommer also noted a second challenge to U.S. policy by some Bavarian film unions, which requested "a decisive voice in respect to the artistic and cultural-political contents of German films." While Pommer professed U.S. intent to guarantee "absolute freedom and independence of filmmakers within the normal limits of Military Government's existing laws and future German legislation," he "turned down as impracticable" the unions' request that they be "allowed to have their own film production group

licensed whose pictures would represent their special ideas and aims." The union demands did not represent an attempt to exercise censorship control but merely indicated their desire to express a particular artistic and perhaps political point of view. Indeed, such initiatives by filmmaking interests did not pose as great a challenge to U.S. aims as did activities of local German government officials. Unlicensed filmmakers had no basis of authority and no influence over public opinion in occupied Bavaria, and U.S. disregard insured their inaccessibility to film rawstock, studio facilities, and distribution channels. Local German officials, however, were more difficult to control.

88. OMGUS Papers, DO-ISD #107, "German Information Control Legislation," 18 August 1947.

89. OMGUS Papers, MPB-ISD #256, memo from director, ICD, to chief, NYFO, 18 December 1947. Earlier that year, Pommer received a complaint concerning state involvement in film production from a U.S.-licensed filmmaker, Hubert Schonger, who specialized in children's films. See OMGUS Papers, MPB-ISD #261, translation of letter from Hubert Schonger to Erich Pommer, 29 April 1947.

90. OMGUS Papers, MPB-ISD #261, memo from Eric Clarke, chief, FTM Branch, to Information Control Branch, Berlin Sector, 2 July 1947. The advisory committee was to be consulted concerning the release of every film, domestic and foreign, proposed by OMGUS for exhibition in Germany. Despite the preliminary planning, the proposed advisory committee was not established. This was likely due to significant opposition by the MPEA, whose representative, Irving Maas, opposed the advisory committee on the grounds that it infringed upon an agreement reached between the MPEA and the Civil Affairs Division of the U.S. Military Government. He specifically objected to "any plan giving weight and influence to German groups such as press, German film industry, political parties, etc." See OMGUS Papers, MPB-ISD #256, response to Maas cable from director, [MPB?], to chief, NYFO, 18 December 1947.

91. OMGUS Papers, MPB-ISD #261, memo from Eric Clarke, chief, FTM Branch, to Information Control Branch, Berlin Sector, 2 July 1947.

92. Noltenius, *Die Freiwillige Selbstkontrolle*, 11.

93. OMGUS Papers, MPB-ISD #261, translation of "Film Censorship for Youths," *Jugendnachrichten*, 17 April 1947.

94. Included were the ministers of culture from Wiesbaden, Stuttgart, and Munich, the interior minister from Stuttgart, and the minister of employment (*Arbeitsministerium*) from Wiesbaden.

95. OMGUS Papers, MPB-ISD #287, Protokoll der Sitzung der Kommission zur Prüfung der Frage "Gefährdung der Jugend durch Filme," 23 January 1948. See also Noltenius, *Die Freiwillige Selbstkontrolle*, 11–12.

96. OMGUS Papers, MPB-ISD #281, translation of confidential report submitted to ICD, 3 April 1948.

97. OMGUS Papers, MPB-ISD #281, translation of radio announcement by Erwin Oehl, 3 April 1948; Noltenius, *Die Freiwillige Selbstkontrolle*, 21. In a radio announcement, Erwin Oehl, *Land* chairman of the Union of Intellectual and Cultural Workers, criticized Alois Hundhammer, the Bavarian minister of culture, education, and religious affairs, for treating cultural issues as "department matters concerning the Minister alone." Citing his union's aim "to protect the constitutional freedom of all intellectual and cultural activities" and its refusal to "have surprises sprung on the public as a steady practice," Oehl posed several crucial questions to Hundhammer regarding ministerial responsibility to insure democratic practice. Specifically, Oehl asked, "What guarantee is offered that the committee . . . will work in the interest of the entire nation and not in the interest of individual groups? On whose order and by what democratic mandate does this committee function? Does the appointment of this committee mean a sidestepping of the elected parliament?" Oehl's incisive questions did not provide a sufficient public challenge to alter the backroom nature of church and state strategic planning, nor was the union invited to participate. Nonetheless, later in 1948 Oehl's union appealed at a higher level for a seat on the FSK, as did other groups and federations, none of which gained inclusion.

98. OMGUS Papers, MPB-ISD #287, Protokoll der Sitzung der Kommission zur Prüfung der Frage "Gefährdung der Jugend durch Filme," 23 January 1948. See also Noltenius, *Die Freiwillige Selbstkontrolle*, 13–15. The principles for censorship would remain nearly identical to those presented at the meeting of the German Film Producers' Association in March 1947. The purpose of self-control was to insure that "negative influences on the moral, religious, and political areas would be avoided." Specifically, the FSK code prohibited films that offended religious or moral sentiments; that exhibited National Socialist, militarist, imperialist, or nationalistic tendencies or encouraged racial hatred; that endangered the relations of Germany with other states; that endangered the constitutional and civil rights of the German population; or that falsified historical fact by means of propagandistic or tendentious devices.

99. OMGUS Papers, MPB-ISD #287, minutes and summary for March 1947 meeting of the German motion picture producers licensed in the U.S. zone, and Verband deutscher Filmproduzenten, e.V., "Mitgliederrundschreiben #1/1948," 22 March 1948. Representatives of the German Film Producers' Association had already recognized the weakness and vulnerability of a branch censorship and had concluded that self-censorship "could be workable only if not only producers, but also distributors (and indeed also the foreign ones) and theater-owners willingly joined in the effort."

100. According to Noltenius's account of this proposal, the Jewish synagogues were not yet accorded representation along with the Catholic and Protestant churches. A representative of the Jewish faith was included on a rotating basis in the FSK upon its founding in July 1949.

101. OMGUS Papers, MPB-ISD #281, translation of letter from Dr. Reichstein, German Film Producers' Association, to Erich Pommer, MPB, 11 May 1948. The letter notes that representatives of the film producers', distributors', and exhibitors' associations from the British and U.S. zones took part in the May meeting.

102. EP-USC, box B, #5, U.S. Film Branch, ICD, "Report on the Status of the Motion Picture Industry in Germany."

103. OMGUS Papers, MPB-ISD #281, translation of letter from Dr. Reichstein, German Film Producers' Association, to Erich Pommer, 11 May 1948.

104. Keim, "Die Freiwillige Selbstkontrolle," 193.

105. See OMGUS Papers, MPB-ISD #281, letter from Helmut Käutner to ICD, Munich, 22 May 1948, Käutner to Max Gritschneder, 23 May 1948, Käutner to file, 24 May 1948, and teletype message from Colonel Textor, ICD, Berlin, to Clarke, ICD, Munich, 27 May 1948, and #282, telegram from Pleskow, ICD, Munich, to Clarke for van Wagoner, 29 May 1948.

106. "Angriff auf Gott?," in *Der Kurier, Berliner Abendzeitung*, 5 June 1948.

107. "Die kirchlichen Behörden zu Helmut Käutners 'Der Apfel ist ab,' " in *Der neue Film*, 30 November 1948; article in *Wiesbadener Kurier*, 5 June 1948; OMGUS Papers, MPB-ISD #281, translation of letter from Bishop Meiser to ICD, June 1948. Material on this controversy can also be found in BayHStA MK51750.

108. DIFF, microfiche of 1955 Camera Film/Herzog Film brochure on *Der Apfel ist ab*. See also DIFF, film review by Rolf Strehl in *7 Tage*, 24 December 1948.

109. The following discussion is based upon my viewing of the film (on video format at the Freie Universität Berlin, Theaterwissenschaft Abteilung) and DIFF, microfiche of 1955 Camera Film/Herzog Film brochure on *Der Apfel ist ab*.

110. DIFF, "Leserstellungnahme zu dem Film 'Der Apfel ist ab,' " and extensive quotes of Neuhäusler in "Angriff auf Gott?"

111. DIFF, press clippings on *Der Apfel ist ab*.

112. OMGUS Papers, MPB-ISD #282, typescript of Deutsche Nachrichtagentur, "Kultur: Katholische Kirche gegen Käutner-Film," 1 June 1948.

113. OMGUS Papers, MPB-ISD #281, translation of memo on meeting with the church representatives on film censorship, "Church Communique to the Press," 5 June 1948.

114. Boyens, "Die Kirchenpolitik der amerikanischen Besatzungsmacht," 35.

115. OMGUS Papers, MPB-ISD #281, translation of confidential report by Erika Beyfuss on meeting at the Ministry of Education, Culture, and Religious Affairs on 2 April 1948, 3 April 1948.

116. Noltenius, *Die Freiwillige Selbstkontrolle*, 14–17. Noltenius pointed out that this right of appeal was treated summarily in the bylaws of the organi-

zation and became significant only after the FSK began operation. Details of the appeal process were not worked out until the early 1950s.

117. OMGUS Papers, MPB-ICD #287, Berlin memo, 2 August 1949.

118. Over the course of 1948, yet another scheme had been proposed by an unknown author. This proposal envisioned a decentralized FSK and the creation of zonally based Vorkommissionen situated in Hamburg, Mainz, and Munich. The suggestion was not dismissed out of hand but was nevertheless ultimately rejected based upon the justification that the FSK should be near the seat of the Military Government and the recently created Spitzenorganisation der Filmwirtschaft in Wiesbaden, in the U.S. zone of occupation. See OMGUS Papers, MPB-ISD #287, letter from Curt Oertel, German Film Producers' Association, to Alois Hundhammer, Bavarian minister of education, culture, and religious affairs, 27 November 1948. See also Noltenius, *Die Freiwillige Selbstkontrolle*, 21–22, and EP-USC, box B, #5, U.S. Film Branch, ICD, "Report on the Status of the Motion Picture Industry in Germany."

119. OMGUS Papers, MPB-ISD #287, memo, 1 July 1949.

120. OMGUS Papers, MPB-ISD #287, memo, 10 June 1949.

121. Keim, "Die Freiwillige Selbstkontrolle," 193.

122. EP-USC, box B, #5, U.S. Film Branch, ICD, "Report on the Status of the Motion Picture Industry in Germany"; OMGUS Papers, DO-ISD #25, "Plans of the Bavarian Ministry of Economics to Control Film Production," 5 July 1949.

123. Noltenius, *Die Freiwillige Selbstkontrolle*, 17–18.

CHAPTER THREE

1. Quoted in Eisenführ, "Die Sünderin," 243.

2. "Hirtenwort des Kardinals Frings gegen den Spielfilm 'Die Sünderin,' 28. Februar 1951," quoted in Ruhl, *Frauen in der Nachkriegszeit*, 115–16. See also Eisenführ, "Die Sünderin," 249–95; *Filmblätter*, 26 January 1951, p. 78; and excerpt from *Der Spiegel* 26 (1951), quoted in Bessen, *Trümmer und Träume*, 184. Although it is not possible to determine the actual number of people involved in street demonstrations nationwide, press reports indicate that local action typically involved anywhere from several dozen to several hundred protesters. To a certain extent, the actual numbers do not matter. What was more important was that local and state government officials and the conservative and confessional press perceived and characterized the scattered demonstrations as widespread civil unrest.

3. From a film review by Werner Hess in *Evangelischer Film-Beobachter*, 1 February 1951, quoted in Eisenführ, "Die Sünderin," 247. See also Cardinal Frings's Palm Sunday address, quoted in ibid., 299.

4. See chapter 4 for an expanded discussion of these issues.

5. Petley, *Capital and Culture*, 20.

6. For a discussion of postwar German social policy affecting women and the family, see Moeller, *Protecting Motherhood*, "Reconstructing the Family," and "Protecting Mother's Work." See also Ruhl, *Frauen in der Nachkriegszeit*; Schubert, *Frauen in der deutschen Nachkriegszeit: Frauenarbeit, 1945–1949*; Kuhn, *Frauen in der deutschen Nachkriegszeit: Frauenpolitik, 1945–1949*; Vogel, "Familie"; and Frevert, *Women in German History*, 255–86.

7. Schubert, *Frauen in der deutschen Nachkriegszeit: Frauenarbeit, 1945–1949*, 34. See also Frevert, *Women in German History*, 257–58, 263–64.

8. Moeller, "Reconstructing the Family," 140. See also Meyer and Schulze, *Von Liebe sprach damals keiner*, and Diehl, *Thanks of the Fatherland*.

9. Erich Kuby, quoted in Schmidt-Harzbach, "Eine Woche im April," 55.

10. Helga Born, quoted in ibid., 56.

11. Tröger, "Between Rape and Prostitution," 102–4.

12. "Psychologische Streiflichter auf das Versorgungswesen," *Zentralblatt*, 16 August 1921, quoted in Whalen, *Bitter Wounds*, 187.

13. Michael von Faulhaber, *Das hohe Lied der Kriegsfürsorge* (1916), quoted in ibid., 187–88.

14. In August 1945, for example, Ursula von Kardorff exhorted women to "furnish the understanding, the emotional balance, the rebuilding of confidence, the encouragement needed now by so many totally beaten and desperate men." Quoted in Frevert, *Women in German History*, 262.

15. Quoted in Meyer and Schulze, " 'Als wir wieder zusammen waren,' " 314–15.

16. See Diehl, *Thanks of the Fatherland*, 54–86.

17. Meyer and Schulze, " 'Als wir wieder zusammen waren,' " 305–26. See also Willenbacher, "Zerrüttung und Bewährung der Nachkriegs-Familie."

18. "Der Publizist Walther von Hollander über Ehezerrüttung, Ehetrennung, Ehescheidung, 1946," quoted in Ruhl, *Frauen in der Nachkriegszeit*, 37.

19. See Tröger, "Between Rape and Prostitution," 105, 111–12; and Meyer and Schulze, *Wie wir das alles geschafft haben*, 51.

20. Tröger, "Between Rape and Prostitution," 109–10.

21. Frevert, *Women in German History*, 258.

22. Tröger, "Between Rape and Prostitution," 98–99. See also Meyer and Schulze, *Wie wir das alles geschafft haben*.

23. "Der Publizist Walther von Hollander über Ehezerrüttung, Ehetrennung, Ehescheidung, 1946," quoted in Ruhl, *Frauen in der Nachkriegszeit*, 37.

24. Quoted in Hoerning, "Frauen als Kriegsbeute," 340.

25. Ingrid Schmidt-Harzbach makes a similar point, dubbing the collective "rape syndrome" an "alibi of German men." See Schmidt-Harzbach, "Eine Woche im April," 55.

26. Rundschreiben des Stuttgarter Oberkirchenrats, 20 March 1946, quoted in Vollnhals, "Die Evangelische Kirche," 151–52.

27. "Der Publizist Walther von Hollander über Ehezerrüttung, Ehetrennung, Ehescheidung, 1946," quoted in Ruhl, *Frauen in der Nachkriegszeit*, 37. See Moeller, *Protecting Motherhood*, 12–14, for a discussion of women's tendency to portray themselves as victims of a masculine, militarist national socialism.

28. Ruhl, *Frauen in der Nachkriegszeit*, 107.

29. See "Klaus Mörsdorf über die hierarchische Struktur von Ehe und Familie, 1952," quoted in ibid., 116–17.

30. Vogel, "Familie," 99.

31. Erich Reisch, "Die Situation der Familie von heute," reprinted in Ruhl, *Frauen in der Nachkriegszeit*, 123–24.

32. Moeller, *Protecting Motherhood*, 62–108.

33. Moeller, "Reconstructing the Family," 146; Frevert, *Women in German History*, 265.

34. Moeller, "Reconstructing the Family," 162.

35. See ibid., and Moeller, "Protecting Mother's Work."

36. Frevert notes that this phrase gained currency in the early 1950s. See Frevert, *Women in German History*, 265. For a discussion of how the enlightenment, industrialization, socialism, and national socialism were linked in the minds and rhetoric of postwar German conservatives and rejected due to their secular, materialist basis, see Moeller, *Protecting Motherhood*, 64.

37. Reisch, "Die Situation der Familie," reprinted in Ruhl, *Frauen in der Nachkriegszeit*, 124–26.

38. Quoted in Eisenführ, "Die Sünderin," 281. This fear survived well into the 1950s. In 1956, for example, a speaker at a conference of Catholic women argued: "Not only is the dialectical materialism of the East a terrible danger, but so too is the materialism of the West that prepares the way for the former and that subordinates all values, even the religious, to questions of profit, and elevates the standard of living to an Idol." See "Die Frau in der Entscheidung zwischen Zeitgeist und christlicher Wertordnung, Januar 1956," quoted in Ruhl, *Frauen in der Nachkriegszeit*, 130.

39. Quoted in "Bischöfe fordern Jugendschutz-Gesetz," *Münchner Merkur*, 24 March 1950.

40. See Eisenführ, "Die Sünderin," 264.

41. Ibid., 167–68.

42. Ibid., 226–27.

43. Klaus Brüne, review of *Die Sünderin* in *Katholischer Film-Dienst*, 2 February 1951, reprinted in Hoffmann and Schobert, *Zwischen Gestern und Morgen*, 356.

44. The Working Committee of the FSK, which viewed the film for public

release, reproached Marina's return to prostitution "for reasons of convenience
. . . [as the] self-evident way out of her human and financial troubles." Specifically, it criticized "the episode in Naples, in which Marina submits to the gallery
owner to sell Alexander's painting . . . her walk through the Munich rubble,
during which she decides to earn money for Alexander's operation by means of
her old bar work [prostitution] . . . the particular part of the bar scene in which
Marina scolds herself . . . for being a failure . . . because she is no longer able to
interest men in her [sexually], . . . and the street scene . . . with Dr. Valentin . . .
and the following scene in the hotel room." Quoted in Eisenführ, "Die Sünderin," 226–27.

45. "Die Lage der Jugendlichen in Aachen, 1947: Sozialbericht der Stadt
Aachen über die Lage der Jugendlichen 1947, HSTA/Bestand NW 43/457,"
reprinted in Ruhl, *Frauen in der Nachkriegszeit*, 31–34.

46. BayHStA, MK51766, copy of letter from Dr. Kneuer, Regierungspräsident Oberbayern, to Bayerische Landesjugendamt, 24 April 1951. Kneuer
likely had no firsthand knowledge of the film, *Bitter Rice*, nor its notorious star,
Silvana Mangano, to judge from the consistency with which he misspelled her
name throughout his letter.

47. Meyer and Schulze, *Wie wir das alles geschafft haben*, 53.

48. Ibid., 127–28.

49. Quoted in Frevert, *Women in German History*, 263.

50. See, for example, the oral histories discussed in Meyer and Schulze, " 'Als
wir wieder zusammen waren,' " esp. 318–19. One woman described the burden
of interceding between a returned husband and resentful children. The oldest
child, a boy who had helped her provide for the family, begrudged his unproductive father's attempt to usurp household authority. The youngest boy, Rolf,
also harbored ill will. The mother described Rolf's reaction after the father said
something that infuriated him: "I can still see him. There [Rolf] stood, his fists
clenched and his head swelling with rage. He went around the table to his father
and said, 'You, you, you don't have any right to say anything here.' " The father
responded with military-style discipline, which did nothing to endear him to
his sons or wife. When Rolf had difficulty learning to read, for example, his
father made him perform twenty-five knee-bends.

51. See Schubert, *Frauen in der deutschen Nachkriegszeit: Frauenarbeit,
1945–1949*, 56.

52. After all, as Ute Frevert has argued, "the end of the Third Reich heralded
no new beginning, no *Stunde Null* . . . , but rather a continuation of [women's]
toil under straitened circumstances." See Frevert, *Women in German History*,
258. See also Schubert, *Frauen in der deutschen Nachkriegszeit: Frauenarbeit,
1945–1949*, 48–49, 66–67; Tröger, "Between Rape and Prostitution," 109–10;
and Meyer and Schulze, " 'Als wir wieder zusammen waren,' " 313.

53. See Freud, "The Psycho-Analytic View."

54. See Rentschler, "The Elemental, the Ornamental, the Instrumental," 179–80.

55. Quoted in Hoerning, "Frauen als Kriegsbeute," 335; SPD representative Dorothea Groener-Geyer, quoted in Moeller, *Protecting Motherhood*, 55.

56. Tröger, "Between Rape and Prostitution," 104; Hoerning, "Frauen als Kriegsbeute," 333–35.

57. I am indebted to Miriam Hansen for this observation. One of the earliest feature films during the Nazi period that portrayed a surreptitious female suicide was *Hitler Junge Quex* (1933). Although, admittedly, in this film the woman is a mother sacrificing herself for her son, the concealed and aestheticized nature of the act anticipates Marina's suicide in *Die Sünderin*.

58. BayHStA, MK51766, letter from Wilhelm Kummerle, Landpolizeibeamter, Lenggries, to Kulturausschuß, 24 May 1951 (emphasis in original).

59. BayHStA, MK51766, transcript of a public meeting called by the Evangelical Men's Club of Feuchtwangen, 11 April 1951.

60. Quoted in Eisenführ, "Die Sünderin," 281.

61. BayHStA, MK51766, letter from Regierungspräsident, Oberbayern, to Bayerisches Staatsministerium für Unterricht und Kultus, 4 March 1947.

62. Arbeitgemeinschaft der katholischen deutschen Frauen, "Die Frau zwischen Zeitgeist und christlicher Wertordnung," quoted in Ruhl, *Frauen in der Nachkriegszeit*, 107–8.

63. See Huyssen, "Mass Culture as Woman," for an analysis of discourse on "mass culture as woman" during the late nineteenth and early twentieth centuries. In West Germany, the prevailing sense that women could not adequately perform necessary tasks of social reproduction had enormous implications for the analysis of postwar policy decisions. Robert Moeller has pointed out that German sociology and family policy in the early 1950s were predicated on the assumption that women's proper place was in the home, not out in the labor force. Women's roles as nurturers of the family and socializers of children were particularly stressed: "At the same time that women's reproductive work was praised as essential to the smooth functioning of the 'market economy,' it was also women's responsibility to raise children to resist the consumer temptations that the economic miracle offered. . . . Inculcating children with the right values was clearly among a mother's tasks." Moeller, "Reconstructing the Family," 162.

64. See Carter, "Alice in Consumer Wonderland," 190, 193. Erica Carter points out that in postwar West Germany, "the explicit inscription of women as equal subjects in legal discourse was negotiated through their installation as consumers in a 'social market economy'; citizenship for women thus came to be defined through consumption on a capitalist mass market." Moreover, although "consumer freedom" was showcased as a "basic democratic right," its acceptable form was narrowly defined as a process in which "the consumer public exercises

its critical faculties in the 'rational' choice of those commodities which best correspond to its *needs*" (emphasis added). Thus, socially responsible forms of consumption were encouraged, while a more hedonistic style of consumption continued to be decried as socially dangerous.

65. BayHStA, MK51766, copy of letter from Bischöfliches Ordinariat Würzburg to Dr. Hans Erhard, Bayerischen Ministerpräsident, 6 March 1951.

66. Moeller, *Protecting Motherhood*, 217.

67. See Grossmann, "*Girlkultur* or Thoroughly Rationalized Female," and Petro, *Joyless Streets*.

68. Meyer and Schulze, *Wie wir das alles geschafft haben*, 133.

69. Quoted in "Bischöfe fordern Jugendschutz-Gesetz," *Münchner Merkur*, 24 March 1950.

70. See Lenman, "Mass Culture and the State in Germany," and Usborne, *Politics of the Body*, 76–81.

71. BayHStA, MK51766, letter from Schulrat, Schulamt Rosenheim, to Schulreferat, Stadtrat Rosenheim, 10 April 1951, quoting article in *Filmdienst* 4, no. 5, p. 6, and letter from Vereinigte Bürgerausschüsse der Stadt und des Landkreises Schwabach to the Bayerisches Staatsministerium für Unterricht und Kultus, 8 May 1951. In addition, administrators of the Catholic Girls' School in Rosenheim, frequent complainants and lobbyists to the Bavarian Ministry of Education and Culture, assembled a catalog of film-induced behaviors: "indifference to the educational influence of parents . . . and every authority, lack of respect, and craftiness . . . , rude behavior in public and against friends." They named *Die Sünderin* an offending film and proposed that the Bavarian Parliament permit children under the age of fourteen to attend only *Kulturfilme* and filmic fairytales and strictly control the types of films seen by children between the ages of fourteen and eighteen. See BayHStA, MK51766, letter from Schulpflegschaft der kathol. Mädchenschule Rosenheim to Bayerischem Landtag, 15 March 1951, and a similar letter sent by Evangel.-luth. Landeskirchenrat to Bay. Staatsministerium für Unterricht und Kultus.

72. BayHStA, MK51766, memos, 11, 20 June, 26 July 1951. Before federal legislation was enacted, the Bavarian Ministry of Education and Culture actively pursued legal remedies for limiting film attendance by children and adolescents. Bavarian state officials, in fact, expressed their impatience regarding the lack of progress by the federal government in this area during the early summer of 1951. The Bavarian Ministry of the Interior had determined some months earlier, in response to *Die Sünderin* demonstrations, that legal means did not exist for the prevention of attendance at films unauthorized for youth. Since proposed legislation in Bonn seemed to be at a standstill, the Bavarian Parliament resolved to begin drafting a Bavarian law for the protection of minors.

73. Ibid. During the second half of June, Bavarian Cultural Ministry papers reveal that Hundhammer's motion and a subsequent resolution by the Bavarian

Parliament to press for the expedient passage of a youth protection bill were again taken up. To pressure the Bonn government into action in this area, the Bavarian Parliament agreed to begin drafting a state law for the protection of minors.

74. Wuermeling's controversial speech on film was published under the title "Familie und Film" in *Filmforum* in March 1954 and was followed by a response from the German film industry's SPIO. See also "Die Jugendfreigabe von Filmen in der deutschen Bundesrepublik: Die neuen Vereinbarungen," *Internationale Film Revue* 2, no. 5 (1954/55): 222–24.

75. See, for example, "Die Jugendfilmarbeit in Bayern," *Jugend-Film-Fernsehen* 5, no. 4 (1961): 247–51, and Arbeitsgemeinschaft der deutschen Jugendfilmclubs und -gruppen im Verband der deutschen Film-Clubs, e.V., *Zur Entwicklung der Filmerziehung in den deutschen Jugendfilmclubs*.

76. Paula Linhart, "Zur Praxis des Filmjugendschutzes," *Jugend-Film-Fernsehen* 3, no. 4 (1959): 19–20.

77. Moeller, "Protecting Mother's Work," 420–32. See also Moeller, *Protecting Motherhood*.

78. Moeller, "Protecting Mother's Work," 413, 420, 431 (emphasis added).

79. See ibid., 413–25.

80. See Moeller, *Protecting Motherhood*.

CHAPTER FOUR

1. See Dost, Hopf, and Kluge, *Filmwirtschaft in der Bundesrepublik Deutschland*, 110, and Höfig, *Der deutsche Heimatfilm*, 449. This domestic cinematic renaissance was, however, followed by a precipitous drop at the end of the decade, when the novelty and convenience of television gradually—but irreversibly—began to entice viewers out of the movie theaters.

2. BayHStA, MK51750, press release of Kirchliche Hauptstelle für Bild- und Filmarbeit, 27 November 1948.

3. See Noltenius, *Die Freiwillige Selbstkontrolle*, 61–86, esp. 85.

4. Quoted in Vollnhals, "Die Evangelische Kirche," 113.

5. Spotts, *Churches and Politics in Germany*, 55. See also Blessing, "Deutschland in Not, wir im Glauben," 19–111; Braun, "Demographische Umschichtungen im deutschen Katholizismus nach 1945," 24–25; Connor, "Churches and the Refugee Problem," 399–421; and Vollnhals, "Die Evangelische Kirche," 113–67. This situation lasted until October 1946, when the Allied Control Authority allowed coverage of "domestic political problems" in the German press, "provided it did not undermine Allied unity," a stipulation that could be broadly interpreted. Over the next two years, with the gradual declaration of the Cold War, the press was allowed to publish criticisms of Soviet policy and commu-

nism, first in the U.S. zone in 1947, then in the British zone in 1948. See J. Farquharson's review of Kurt Koszyk, *Pressepolitik für Deutschland, 1945–1949*, in *American Historical Review* 93, no. 4 (October 1988): 1078.

6. Bavarian Cardinal Faulhaber reportedly had forms printed with a blank for the applicant's name to facilitate the denazification process. OMGUS Papers, DO-ISD, Intelligence #48, copy of "The Catholic Church in Bavaria," *Trend*, 10 September 1946, nos. 13/14 and supplement, pp. 17–31. See also Spotts, *Churches and Politics in Germany*, 96–103.

7. See Boyens, "Die Kirchenpolitik der amerikanischen Besatzungsmacht"; Greschat, "Kirche und Öffentlichkeit in der deutschen Nachkriegszeit," 107, 115–16; Blessing, " 'Deutschland in Not, wir im Glauben,' " 60–111; Vollnhals, "Die Evangelische Kirche"; Connor, "Churches and the Refugee Problem"; and Spotts, *Churches and Politics in Germany*, 149–58.

8. See Braun, "Demographische Umschichtungen im deutschen Katholizismus nach 1945," 12–15. Braun states that the millions of expellees who entered the German territory after the end of the war did not significantly change the confessional composition of the German population in the Western zones compared to 1939. Yet more Catholics were settled in formerly Protestant areas, giving North Germany at least the illusion of "Catholicization" at the local level. On the other hand, the new West German state had a much greater proportion of Catholics (45.2 percent in 1950) than the old German Reich (32.9 percent in 1933)—a situation that, according to Braun, helped facilitate the creation of an interconfessional political "partnership."

9. See Blessing, " 'Deutschland in Not, wir im Glauben,' " 60–71, and Spotts, *Churches and Politics in Germany*, 23–42, 97. Catholicism's spiritual head in Rome, Pius XII, a Germanophile dubbed "il papa tedesco" who had served as papal nuncio to Bavaria in 1917–25 and to Germany in 1920–29, set the tone for Catholic appraisal of the Nazi past in his 1945 address, "The Church and National Socialism." In it, he emphasized the church's moral integrity and resistance to national socialism and was careful to avoid any admission of guilt or responsibility.

10. Spotts, *Churches and Politics in Germany*, 10, 129; Vollnhals, "Die Evangelische Kirche." For detailed discussions of church-state relations and internal church conflict during the Third Reich, see Helmreich, *German Churches under Hitler*, and Baranowski, "Consent and Dissent." Men such as Dietrich Bonhoeffer condemned national socialism as a political and moral abomination, while others like Hans Meiser, bishop of Bavaria, opposed only Nazi intervention in internal church matters.

11. Forster, "Entwicklungslinien in den Beziehungen von Kirche und Staat," 41–68. See also Spotts, *Churches and Politics in Germany*, 13, 129, and Vollnhals, "Die Evangelische Kirche."

12. Spotts, *Churches and Politics in Germany*, 157. "Strength through

unity," not pluralism, "was the hierarchy's political formula." Although German Catholic bishops agreed after 1945 that it would be best for the clergy to avoid direct participation in politics, ecclesiastic guidance of the political laity, lay associations, and the Catholic press remained strong and insured that dissenters from the established Catholic line would not be allowed a voice in the Catholic lay and professional organizations and publications.

13. See Connor, "Churches and the Refugee Problem," 399–421.

14. See Schmitt, *Kirche und Film*; Ford, *Der Film und der Glaube*, 200–203; and Bamberger, *Christentum und Film*, 7–24, for discussions of early film activity by German ecclesiastics.

15. "Die Enzyklika 'Vigilanti cura' von Papst Pius XI (29.6.1936)," reprinted in Ford, *Der Film und der Glaube*, 39–48.

16. "On Motion Pictures," in *Sixteen Encyclicals of His Holiness Pope Pius XI*.

17. "Die Enzyklika 'Vigilanti cura' von Papst Pius XI (29.6.1936)," reprinted in Ford, *Der Film und der Glaube*, 11.

18. Ibid., 43.

19. Ibid., 48.

20. Ibid., 187. It is illustrative that despite attempts to create an internationally standardized Catholic classification system for films, one was never agreed upon. The best that could be produced at the 1954 International Catholic Congress in Cologne was a conversion chart for national rating systems. National and regional differences in social and cultural organization impeded the creation of a universal Catholic film-rating system. Papal pronouncements acted as a spur to Catholic film organization in Western Germany but could not efface the national variation in interpretation and implementation.

21. Schmitt, *Kirche und Film*, 64–87, 151–89, 205–30, 244–54.

22. Werner Hess, "Die Filmarbeit der Evangelischen Kirchen in Deutschland," *Internationale Film Revue* 2, no. 6 (1954/55): 42; Schmitt, *Kirche und Film*, 105–39.

23. Schmitt, *Kirche und Film*. Hess later stated that 1949 represented a turning point in the EKD's understanding of its responsibility for film content and control—perhaps due to censorship negotiations. For a general comparison of Catholic and Protestant assessments of film, see Karl-Heinz Wurm, "Die Urteile der kirchlichen Filmdienste—ein Vergleich," *Filmstudien* 3 (1957): 71–86.

24. See "Entschließung," in *Film und Kirche*, 39–40; "Film und Kirche," *Die Rhein-Neckar Zeitung*, 2 July 1950; Bühler, *Die Kirchen und die Massenmedien*, 95; and "Tagung 'Kirche und Film' in Bad Schwalbach," *Film-Korrespondenz*, 1 July 1950. In April 1948, the Evangelischer Presseverband Deutschland (Protestant Press Association) invited Catholic representatives and members of the film industry to Bad Salzdetfurth to discuss film matters. The next Protestant-sponsored conference was held in June 1950 in Bad Schwalbach.

25. Bühler, *Die Kirchen und die Massenmedien*, 94; Ford, *Der Film und der Glaube*, 240–41. The film was directed by Harald Braun, who also wrote the screenplay. Ford also pointed to Curt Oertel's film on the life of Martin Luther, entitled *Der gehorsame Rebell* (1952), which neutralized the portrayal of Luther's challenge to the Catholic church (and hence confessional conflict) by focusing on Luther's spiritual struggle while ignoring the historical context of the reformer's actions.

26. Anton Kochs, "Wunsch an den deutschen Film," *Film-Korrespondenz*, supplement, 1 August 1950, and "Kirche und Film in Westdeutschland," *Internationale Film Revue* 1, no. 4 (1951/52): 287–88. Church involvement in film production remained at a low level during the Adenauer era and, not surprisingly, never represented a challenge to the commercial film industry. The churches did entertain suggestions for scripts and film projects, even for the creation of Christian production and distribution companies. Members of the film industry made offers for cooperative ventures, which resulted in "lively but also . . . unfruitful" negotiations since the cooperation of commercial film companies was based upon the church underwriting the project with a rather large check. Pointing to the material and economic misery of the population, complicated by the task of absorbing millions of refugees, Kochs reasoned that ecclesiastical leaders could hardly "neglect the church and Christian charity to make films." In addition to the prohibitive cost of production, church initiatives were stymied by the lack of exhibition equipment available at the parish level. In comparison to Italy, which reportedly had 3,600 parish cinemas (*Pfarrkino*), and France, which had about 2,000, Kochs presented the picture of an underequipped and underfunded Christian film culture in Germany.

27. Ford, *Der Film und der Glaube*, 246.

28. "Entschließung," in *Film und Kirche*, 39–40. Specifically, the churches supported the industry's fight against an increased tax on films and called for the creation of a national system of film prizes accompanied by financial incentives.

29. "Tagung 'Kirche und Film' in Bad Schwalbach," *Film-Korrespondenz*, 1 July 1950. The meeting at Bad Schwalbach was attended by federal minister of the interior, Gustav Heinemann, and his assistant, Carl-Heinz Lüders; Parliamentary representative Rudolf Vogel; and Walter Keim, the general secretary representing the cultural ministries at the federal level. Film industry representatives included Curt Oertel, the honorary president of the SPIO; Dr. Aulich, director of the SPIO; two members of the FSK, the national film censorship board; a member of the Film Producers' Association; as well as various documentary and feature filmmakers, including Josef von Baky.

30. Schmitt, *Kirche und Film*, 182–88. See also Kochs, "Wunsch an den deutschen Film" and "Kirche und Film in Westdeutschland." Kochs's discussion closely follows Werner Hess's argument in his talk entitled "Gibt es den religiösen Film?," which was published in *Film und Kirche*, 18–38.

31. Werner Hess, "Der Wille der Kirche zur filmischen Gestaltung," *Kirche und Film*, 14 October 1949, p. 2.

32. Kochs, "Wunsch an den deutschen Film" and "Kirche und Film in Westdeutschland."

33. Noltenius, *Die Freiwillige Selbstkontrolle*, 83–84. See also OMGUS Papers, MPB-ISD #266, "Discussion of Suggestions Concerning the Establishment of Voluntary Self-Imposed Supervision of the German Film Industry," n.d.

34. Walter Keim, "Die Freiwillige Selbstkontrolle der deutschen Filmwirtschaft," *Kulturarbeit* 9 (1949).

35. Walter Keim, "Genießen wir Katholiken verfassungsmäßige Meinungsfreiheit auf dem Gebiet des Films?," *Münchner Katholische Kirchenzeitung*, 5, 12 March 1950, reprinted in *Film-Korrespondenz*, 1 May 1950, pp. 3–4.

36. In 1949, at a lay conference in Hamburg, a Pastor Wilken, an associate of Hess's, explained that the "church will be the one to bring back home the spiritual level of the *Volk* and thereby the filmmakers. Only where living communities internalize these values, will the advancing secularization of all spiritual forces be stopped." Quoted in Bühler, *Die Kirchen und die Massenmedien*, 95.

37. Bamberger, *Christentum und Film*, 26–27; Ford, *Der Film und der Glaube*, 204–6.

38. Shortly after the creation of the Catholic Film Commission, Rolf Meyer, a film producer from the Junge Film Union, lodged a legal complaint charging that the negative rating of one of his films by the Catholic Film Commission in its publication *Filmdienst* violated the constitutional guarantee of freedom of opinion and resulted in reduced business for the film. See the response to this complaint by Walter Keim in "Genießen wir Katholiken verfassungsmäßige Meinungsfreiheit auf dem Gebiet des Films?," 3–4.

39. BayHStA, MK51766.

40. Quoted in "Bischöfe fordern Jugendschutz-Gesetz," *Münchner Merkur*, 24 March 1950.

41. Quoted in Vollnhals, "Die Evangelische Kirche," 145.

42. Kochs, "Kirche und Film in Westdeutschland," 289.

43. Forst called *Die Sünderin* a "chronicle of real life [Reportage des wirklichen Lebens]" yet emphasized that his representation was mild compared to some Italian, French, and U.S. films. He had not, after all, depicted the "sin itself. . . . That he would never do!" See Eisenführ, "Die Sünderin," 228, 256. Forst apparently did not consider his film to be part of a longer tradition of cinematic social realism identified with leftist filmmaking in the late Weimar period. And, in fact, *Die Sünderin* remains mute on issues of class.

44. Ironically, aside from the inclusion of social problems such as prostitution, incest, adultery, and alcoholism, the film has no thematic or stylistic

similarities to Italian neorealism. Filmed in the studio, *Die Sünderin* is characterized by sanitized sets and treats social problems as melodrama.

45. Eisenführ, "Die Sünderin," 228.

46. During the summer of the previous year, criticisms of the FSK's ability to enforce its decisions regarding the rejection or contingent release of films surfaced in the Catholic film press. These articles demanded the enforcement of the FSK's decisions on a national level through recognition by the federal government. Apparently the modification made by the FSK in its bylaws in February 1950 providing for disciplinary measures to be taken by the appropriate branch associations of the film industry against infractors did not end infractions on the local level. See "Die Tätigkeit der Selbstkontrolle," *Film-Korrespondenz*, 1 June 1950; "Die befehdete Selbstkontrolle," *Film-Korrespondenz*, 15 June 1950; "Nachrichten aus der Filmwirtschaft," *Film-Korrespondenz*, 1 July 1950; as well as correspondence in BayHStA, MK51766.

47. According to Eisenführ, the committee suggested that Marina's promise to "work off" the money she borrowed from a former admirer be cut from the film. The committee refused to entertain other suggestions for cuts, since it could not test the validity of such recommendations, not being in possession of a copy of the script. This, in addition to the late submission of the film for consideration by the FSK, resulted in the "reprimand of the film's submitter"; however, in this case it worked in favor of the film's producers and distributors. Eisenführ, "Die Sünderin," 234.

48. "Zum Fall Sünderin," *Kirche und Film*, 1 February 1951; "Der Sünderin: Fall der Selbstkontrolle," *Filmblätter*, 26 January 1951, p. 77; "Filmkontrolle ohne Evangelische Kirche?," *Evangelischer Film-Beobachter*, 1 February 1951, pp. 17–18; Eisenführ, "Die Sünderin," 246. Kochs apparently had not anticipated taking such action until he heard of Hess's resignation; indeed, he even attended the Frankfurt premiere of *Die Sünderin* and told the film production company representative that the film would receive a higher rating by the Catholic Film Commission than it ultimately did in the thick of the controversy. Thus, the change in the Catholic rating of the film (from the penultimate to the worst rating) and in Kochs's attitude occurred in response to the news of Hess's resignation and represented a display of Christian solidarity against the film industry.

49. Eisenführ, "Die Sünderin," 249–50.

50. A historical precedent existed for the lobbing of stink bombs and release of mice in German movie theaters; precisely the same tactics were employed by the Nazi SA against the U.S. film *All Quiet on the Western Front* upon its release in Berlin in late 1930. See Eksteins, "War, Memory, and Politics."

51. See "Klinkhammer-Prozeß in Düsseldorf," *Kölnische Rundschau*, 16 October 1952. Father Klinkhammer was arrested and accused of disturbing the public peace, disseminating stink bombs, and impeding police activity. Klink-

hammer countered that the police physically and verbally abused him due to their antireligious bias and explained that he was stimulated to act against the film locally after he heard a pastoral letter of the cardinal and archbishop of Cologne in February 1951 and a sermon of the cardinal's, both calling for the defense of the church. The article noted that the cardinal had not objected to his behavior in this instance.

52. This concern that a film could threaten national reconstruction in fact expressed "deep fears about the political behavior of the so-called 'masses,'" which were exacerbated by the unprecedented influx of refugees into West German territory at the end of the war. Catholic leaders, in particular, feared that mass immigration would result in social and political destabilization and the "complete dechristianization of many village communities." Their response of *Menschenführung* was directed against both the presumed disruptions to German reconstruction caused by refugee populations as well as those issuing from commercial cinema that addressed the viewer directly, without the mediation of traditional cultural elites. See Connor, "Churches and the Refugee Problem."

53. *Filmblätter*, 26 January 1951, p. 78.

54. Eisenführ, "Die Sünderin," provides a lengthy treatment of the Regensburg protests based upon contemporary newspaper reports. My discussion relies on her detailed description of events.

55. Quoted in ibid., 273.

56. Eisenführ identifies this as an allusion to the East German Socialist youth organization, the Freie Deutsche Jugend. See ibid.

57. Quoted in ibid., 258.

58. See Wilmont Haacke, "Filmkontrolle und Meinungsfreiheit: Kommentar zur 'Film-Umfrage 1952' des Instituts für Publizistik an der Universität Münster," *Kulturarbeit* 7 (1952): 124–25.

59. Eisenführ, "Die Sünderin," 283–84.

60. "Schutz zugelassener Filmvorführungen," *Film-Echo*, 30 January 1951, p. 97.

61. *Münchner Merkur*, quoted in "Presse-Echo zur . . . ," *Film-Echo*, 30 January 1951, p. 98.

62. Pfarrer Robert Geisendörfer, "Filmselbstkontrolle ohne Evangelische Kirche?," *Evangelischer Film-Beobachter*, 1 February 1951, p. 18.

63. For discussions of the postwar reconstruction of the German film industry, see Dost, Hopf, and Kluge, *Filmwirtschaft in der Bundesrepublik Deutschland*; Pleyer, *Deutscher Nachkriegsfilm*; Höfig, *Der deutsche Heimatfilm*; Kreimeier, *Kino und Filmindustrie in der BRD*; Bredow and Zurek, *Film und Gesellschaft*, 237–371; Heerman, "Die Entwicklung der deutschen Filmwirtschaft"; Guback, *International Film Industry*; Hoffmann and Schobert, *Zwischen Gestern und Morgen*; and Bessen, *Trümmer und Träume*.

64. See "Der Strudel," *Filmblätter*, 26 January 1951, p. 79, and "Lassen Sie mich nicht in Stich," *Film-Echo*, 27 January 1951, 74.

65. Quoted in *Film-Echo*, 27 January 1951, p. 74.

66. Eisenführ, "Die Sünderin," 229–30. See also Hess, "Gibt es den religiösen Film?"; Kochs, "Kirche und Film in Westdeutschland"; "Der Strudel," *Filmblätter*, 26 January 1951, p. 79; and Bühler, *Die Kirchen und die Massenmedien*, 40–41.

67. "Notes on *Die Sünderin*," from confidential papers of the FSK, quoted in Eisenführ, "Die Sünderin," 240.

68. The *Sünderin* affair opened up the federal and state film subsidy programs to public scrutiny, and over the next year, the press picked up stories alleging poor investment strategies and unethical business conduct on the part of board and bank members responsible for subsidy decisions. Ironically, the public funds in this case had been well invested, and the government did not lose a *Groschen*. Eisenführ, "Die Sünderin," 251. See also "Ein Film jagt den anderen," *Der Spiegel*, 12 October 1951, and Walter Panofsky, "Enttäuschte Träume um die Traum: Der bayerische Staat hat fünfzehn Millionen Mark an Filmbürgschaften verloren," *Süddeutsche Zeitung*, 28 December 1952.

69. Eisenführ, "Die Sünderin," 253–54. The representative for the state of North Rhine Westphalia, Professor Walter Hagemann (at the time a member of the CDU), had not been present at the decisive meeting but resigned from the FSK the following week. Complaining that the FSK permitted the release of films "whose moral tendencies are not unobjectionable," he called for a change in the structure of the body, advocating an increased voice for public and social institutions (such as the churches, political parties, unions, and youth organizations) in order to challenge the dominant voice of the film industry in censorship decisions.

70. See *Film-Echo*, 30 January 1951, p. 97.

71. Eisenführ, "Die Sünderin," 313–21. The SPIO rejected the Catholic demand that both confessions have permanent seats in the Main Committee, arguing that church interests would be represented by the confessionally oriented state and youth organization representatives. The SPIO, however, did concur with demands by both churches to regulate the timely submission of completed films to the FSK for consideration, to strengthen the executive function of the FSK, and to review film advertising material. It further assented to a change in the appeal procedure.

72. The number of votes needed for an appeal was also changed to make it easier for dissenting public representatives to invoke the appeal process. However, the number and distribution of seats on the Main Committee, as well as the ratio of votes required for appeal, remained the same. The new bylaws took effect on 25 August 1951, and the same day church representatives reclaimed their seats in the FSK.

73. Eisenführ, "Die Sünderin," 313–20. See also *Film-Echo*, 30 January 1951, pp. 97–99.

74. See Presse Archiv Sammlung der Bayerischen Staatsregierung, Munich, #17, 1950, "Gemeinwohl geht vor Individualismus," and BayHStA, MK51766. The Bavarian Cultural Ministry officials indicated in notes and missives that the possibility for action on these points was greatly limited by constitutional law but confirmed their strong support for the promulgation of legislation to protect the youth.

75. Eisenführ, "Die Sünderin," 251, 253, 259, 284; "Professor Hagemann und die Selbstkontrolle," *Filmpresse* (February 1951): 6–7.

76. BayHStA, MK51766, letter from the Vereinigte Bürgerausschüsse der Stadt und des Landkreises Schwabach to the Bayerisches Staatsministerium für Unterricht und Kultus, 8 May 1951.

77. "Plakate: Untere Busenhälfte sichtbar," *Der Spiegel*, 19 December 1951, p. 27.

78. Ibid.

79. Ibid., 22–27.

80. See "Berichte: Der Film im deutschen Bundestag," *Internationale Film Revue* 2, no. 1 (1954/55): 38–40; and Dost, Hopf, and Kluge, *Filmwirtschaft in der Bundesrepublik Deutschland*, 102. In a January 1954 speech in Düsseldorf, Wuermeling blamed film for destroying the German family and the principle of marriage and, appealing to article 6 of the Basic Law, which places these institutions under state protection, called for a "Volkszensur." Members of the SPD understood this to entail the reintroduction of state censorship and strongly denounced his action.

81. "Untere Busenhälfte sichtbar," *Der Spiegel*, 19 December 1951, p. 27.

82. For a sketchy assessment of the success of the campaign to clean up film posters and advertisements, see Kurt Joachim Fischer, "Die Problematik der deutschen Filmplakate," *Kulturarbeit* 8 (1953): 143–44.

83. See Robert Liebig, "Filmbürgschaften aus Frankfurt," and Reinold E. Thiel, "Filmförderung oder Schnulzenkartell?," both in Stettner, *Kino in der Stadt*, 40–43, 44–46. See also Berger, "Bürgen heißt zahlen." For Bavaria, see Presse Archiv Sammlung der Bayerischen Staatsregierung, #17, 1950, "Gemeinwohl geht vor Individualismus," and BayHStA, MK51766. For more general discussions, see Höfig, *Der deutsche Heimatfilm*, 88–90, and Bredow and Zurek, *Film und Gesellschaft*, 239–47. Bredow and Zurek indicate that in 1950–51, a third of West German feature films received federal subsidies covering 35 percent of production costs.

84. Eisenführ, "Die Sünderin," 8.

85. "Die Freiheit des Regisseurs," *Filmforum* 10, no. 2 (July 1953).

86. Thiel, "Filmförderung oder Schnulzenkartell?," 46.

87. Quoted in Eisenführ, "Die Sünderin," 7.

88. The FBW began operation on 20 August 1951, but the need for such an organization had been under discussion by the German states since 1950. The actual proposal for a unified film-evaluating body with national jurisdiction occurred only in April 1951, no doubt spurred along by the *Sünderin* affair. See Roeber and Jacoby, *Handbuch der filmwirtschaftlichen Medienbereiche*, 483–87.

89. See Krings, *Was heißt wertvoll*, 14–17; Pflaum and Prinzler, *Film in der Bundesrepublik Deutschland*, 105–6; Roeber and Jacoby, *Handbuch der film-wirtschaftlichen Medienbereiche*, 483–87; and Kochs, "Kirche und Film in Westdeutschland," 289. The evaluation board of the FBW was comprised of government officials (40 percent), professionals in private practices (*freien Berufen*) (30 percent), film journalists (19 percent), and representatives of the film industry (11 percent). The churches were also represented, apparently in an advisory capacity.

90. The oath read as follows: "I promise to attend no film that contradicts Christian beliefs or morals. I recognize that it is my duty to inform myself in a timely manner about the church's position on films I would like to see. I will not frequent movie theaters that consciously and regularly show films that are rejected by the Catholic Film Commission for Germany. I will assiduously support, by means of attendance and recommendation, good and worthwhile films." Quoted in Bühler, *Die Kirchen und die Massenmedien*, 42.

91. Max Gritschneder, "Bilanz der katholischen Filmarbeit," *Petrusblatt*, 15 July 1952.

92. Keim, "Genießen wir Katholiken verfassungsmäßige Meinungsfreiheit auf dem Gebiet des Films?"

93. These figures are quoted in Bühler, *Die Kirchen und die Massenmedien*, 42, and in "Die Filmdebatte des Bundestages," *Filmforum* 3, no. 8 (May 1954): 5. In comparison, total membership for all political parties is estimated at 1,180,818 in 1946 and 944,551 in 1955. See Padgett and Burkett, *Political Parties and Elections in West Germany*, 293. For further discussion of the *Filmliga*, see "Die Ziele der Katholischen Filmliga," *Nürnberger Nachrichten*, 4 July 1951; Max Gritschneder, "Bilanz der katholischen Filmarbeit"; "Wo liegen die Grenzen?," *Filmwoche*, 10 May 1952; BayHStA, MK51763, "Hirtenwort der deutschen Bischöfe zur Filmfrage"; and Eisenführ, "Die Sünderin," 303–4. The Evangelical church founded a similar organization, the *Filmgilde*, with less public fanfare and fewer members. For an explanation of the organization and activities of the *Filmgilde*, see Werner Hess, "Evangelische Filmgilde," *Kirche und Film*, 1 November 1951, p. 4.

94. An article in *Kirche und Film* in 1954 noted that "between 30 and 35 percent of all theater owners can no longer decide to screen films that have been rejected by one of the two churches [Catholic or Evangelical]; in small cities and rural areas, this percentage has already reached 45 percent." Furthermore, dis-

tributors estimated that films rejected by the churches showed profits of up to a third less than what otherwise would have been expected. See "Kirchliche 'Streitmacht für den guten Film,'" *Kirche und Film* 4 (April 1954): 7. For a discussion of the tendency of Catholics to favor film control—especially on moral grounds—at a ratio of 2:1 over Protestants, see Haacke, "Filmkontrolle und Meinungsfreiheit." He also discusses differences according to age and geography.

95. Quoted in Eisenführ, "Die Sünderin," 294.

96. Helga Haftendorn indicates that rejection or praise by Catholic or Protestant clergy (often expressed from the pulpit) *did* make a difference in the success of a movie's run in the unidentified city of 30,000 for her study. See Haftendorn, "Zusammensetzung und Verhalten des Filmtheaterpublikums," 22.

97. Berger, "Bürgen heißt zahlen," 80.

98. See the interview with Hamburg producer, F. A. Mainz, in Thiel, "Filmförderung oder Schnulzenkartell?," 45–46.

99. Rentschler, "Germany," 215. See also Höfig, *Der deutsche Heimatfilm*; Hoffmann and Schobert, *Zwischen Gestern und Morgen*; Bessen, *Trümmer und Träume*; Seidl, *Der deutsche Film der fünfziger Jahre*, 52–102; and Bliersbach, *So grün war die Heide*.

100. See Hobsbawm, "Introduction: Inventing Traditions," and Thelan, "Memory and American History."

101. In the first *Bürgschaftsaktion* (1950–53), the genres most frequently financed were revues and operettas, musical comedies, comedies, and *Problemfilme*, or films that focused on contemporary social problems. For a list of films that were approved or rejected for federal credit, see Berger, "Bürgen heißt zahlen," 92–95, and Höfig, *Der deutsche Heimatfilm*, 446.

CHAPTER FIVE

1. Schnurre, *Rettung des deutschen Films*. See also Höfig, *Der deutsche Heimatfilm*, 132–34.

2. Eric Rentschler also makes this observation in "Germany," 119.

3. For a further description of this film and director Wolfgang Staudte's work, see chapter 6.

4. Ludwig Thome, "Der Film und sein Publikum: Der deutsche Filmbesucher," *Internationale Film Revue* 1, no. 4 (1951/52): 280.

5. Janet Staiger, "'The Handmaiden of Villainy,'" quoted in Mayne, *Cinema and Spectatorship*, 67.

6. Confino, "The Nation as a Local Metaphor," 73–74. See also "Heimat," in Projektgruppe deutscher Heimatfilm, *Der deutsche Heimatfilm*, 15–32, and Applegate, *A Nation of Provincials*.

7. Confino, "The Nation as a Local Metaphor," 73–74.

8. Wilhelm Michel, "Lob der Heimat," *Pfalz und Pfälzer* 1 (August 1950): 13–14, quoted in Applegate, *A Nation of Provincials*, 235–36.

9. Applegate, *A Nation of Provincials*, 229, 243–44.

10. Projektgruppe deutscher Heimatfilm, *Der deutsche Heimatfilm*, 82; Seidl, *Der deutsche Film der fünfziger Jahre*, 66.

11. Projektgruppe deutscher Heimatfilm, *Der deutsche Heimatfilm*, 82.

12. Anecdotal evidence from the 1950s suggests that older moviegoers were drawn to *Heimatfilme*. Industry statistics published in 1961 indicate that nearly 50 percent of Germans polled between the ages of 55 and 65 identified the *Heimatfilm* as their favorite film genre. Percentages for other age groups are as follows: 46 percent for ages 45–54, 36 percent for ages 35–44, 33 percent for ages 25–34, and 26 percent for ages 16–24. See table 12 in Höfig, *Der deutsche Heimatfilm*, 452.

13. Wolfgang Kaschuba, "Bildwelten als Weltbilder," in Projektgruppe deutscher Heimatfilm, *Der deutsche Heimatfilm*, 11.

14. Thome, "Der Film und sein Publikum," 280; Haftendorn, "Zusammensetzung und Verhalten des Filmtheaterpublikums," 20–21; Höfig, *Der deutsche Heimatfilm*, 135, 451.

15. See Projektgruppe deutscher Heimatfilm, *Der deutsche Heimatfilm,* 82–84; Seidl, *Der deutsche Film der fünfziger Jahre*; and Bliersbach, *So grün war die Heide*.

16. Höfig, *Der deutsche Heimatfilm*, 135.

17. Abelshauser, *Die langen fünfziger Jahre*, 80–81; Maase, *Bravo Amerika*, 65–69; Projektgruppe deutscher Heimatfilm, *Der deutsche Heimatfilm*, 87.

18. Thome, "Der Film und sein Publikum," 280.

19. Hans Abich, "Die Filmproduktion in Deutschland: Ihre Struktur, Ihre Hauptprobleme, Ihre Thematik," *Internationale Film Revue* 1, no. 4 (1951/52): 253–58. See also Thome, "Der Film und sein Publikum," 279–81, and EP-USC, box B, #8, OMGUS, ICD, Opinion Surveys, "The Moving Picture Audience in AMZON," 28 April 1948.

20. Haftendorn, "Zusammensetzung und Verhalten des Filmtheaterpublikums," 15–22; Bliersbach, *So grün war die Heide*, 40–41.

21. Bliersbach, *So grün war die Heide*, 38–40.

22. Ibid., 41.

23. Ibid., 53.

24. Maase, *Bravo Amerika*, 83–137, esp. 113–15.

25. Ibid., 81, 96, 118, 137.

26. Stacey, *Star Gazing*, 205. See also Christine Bartram and Heinz-Hermann Krüger, "Vom Backfisch zum Teenager: Mädchensozialisation in den 50er Jahren," in Krüger, "*Die Elvis-Tolle*," 84–101, and Zinnecker, *Jugendkultur*. Uta Poiger is currently studying the female response to U.S. popular culture in both

East and West Germany in her doctoral dissertation, "Taming the Wild West: East and West German Encounters with American Popular Culture, 1949–1962" (Brown University).

27. I am indebted to Jackie Stacey's discussion of these issues in her excellent work on the meanings of female spectatorship in postwar Britain. See Stacey, *Star Gazing*, 198, 206–7.

28. Maase, *Bravo Amerika*, 96–101. This change was abrupt. In a 1955 poll on dance and music, 77 percent of respondents favored the waltz, tango, and fox-trot, and only 8 percent listed the boogie-woogie and jitterbug; the most popular categories of music were operas, operettas, and choral, spiritual, and folk music. Within three years—after Elvis Presley's "Jailhouse Rock" and Bill Haley's "Rock around the Clock" took West German youth (particularly those from the lower social milieu) by storm, provoking riots in a number of cities—Maase argues that such a response would have been "unimaginable."

29. Bliersbach, *So grün war die Heide*, 53; Maase, *Bravo Amerika*, chaps. 5–8.

CHAPTER SIX

1. H. C. Opfermann employed this appellation in his pamphlet *Deutsche Filmkrise*.

2. Anna Paech has reached a similar conclusion concerning the significance of the film clubs as "schools" for students who would go on to become the influential film critics, filmmakers, film historians, and directors of film institutes of the 1960s and 1970s. See Paech, "Schule der Zuschauer."

3. Schnurre, *Rettung des deutschen Films*, 1–41.

4. These figures come from Paech, "Schule der Zuschauer," 227. Paech does not cite her source for the numbers, which appear to be exceedingly high compared to those reported in newspaper accounts of film club activities. In 1957, which seems to have been a peak year for club membership, a film publication covering the annual meeting numbered the clubs at 300 and the total membership at approximately 80,000. See "In Bad Ems: Jeder gezeigte Film ein Treffer," *Filmblätter*, 18 October 1957; Johannes Eckardt, "Die Film-Club-Bewegung im Bundesgebiet," *Schwäbische Landeszeitung* (Augsburg), 24 April 1954; and numerous articles in the film club files located in the press clipping sections of the LBS and the DIFF.

5. Fee Vaillant, former film club organizer in Bünde-Ennigloh and current codirector of the Mannheim Filmwoche, interview by author, Mannheim, 1 June 1987; Enno Patalas, former officer of the student film club at the University of Münster, film historian, film critic, cofounder of *Filmkritik*, and director

of the Filmmuseum of the Munich Stadtmuseum, interview by author, Munich, 4 August 1987.

6. Johannes Eckardt secured annual sums of money from the Bavarian Cultural Ministry for his club in Augsburg and for the Association of German Film Clubs. The Independent Munich Film Club was also granted funds from this source. BayHStA, MK51780, "Filmclubs und München, 1948–52."

7. In November 1921, Delluc organized a screening of *Das Kabinett des Dr. Caligari* (1919), the German expressionist film produced by Erich Pommer's Decla Company, at the Colisée Cinema in Paris. This was the first public screening of a German film in France since World War I. See Abel, *French Cinema*, 251–52.

8. After the establishment of the first club in November 1944, film clubs in France numbered 185 by June 1948, with an estimated 100,000 members. For a short synopsis of the film club movement in France, see H. H. Wollenberg, "Die Film-Club Bewegung," *Schwäbischen Landeszeitung* (Augsburg), 16 September 1949. See also "Erbe einer großen Vergangenheit," *Filmforum* 11, no. 5 (August 1956): 8; Abel, *French Cinema*, 251–57; and Paech, "Schule der Zuschauer," 227–28.

9. Willis, *The French in Germany*, 247.

10. This assessment is based upon remarks made by Enno Patalas, interview by author, Munich, 4 August 1987.

11. Herbert Stettner, quoted in Paech, "Schule der Zuschauer," 228.

12. Dieter Krusche, "Rückblicke und Ausblicke zum 10. Internationalen Filmtreffen," *Filmforum* 10 (July 1956), quoted in Paech, "Schule der Zuschauer," 237–38.

13. Hiller, *Cahiers du Cinema*, 2–4.

14. Preferred directors included Clair, Clément, Clouzot, Cocteau, Eisenstein, Flaherty, Ford, Hawks, Hitchcock, Lang, Lubitsch, Pabst, Rossellini, and Visconti and somewhat later Buñuel, Chabrol, Franju, Resnais, and Truffaut.

15. See Wollenberg, "Die Film-Club Bewegung." Enno Patalas also mentioned that the British influence in encouraging German film clubs was important, especially in creating interest in documentary films. The British cultural centers in Germany, the *Brücke*, screened mainly documentary films for their German audiences. Enno Patalas, interview by author, Munich, 4 August 1987.

16. Quoted from the *Münchner Merkur*, in OMGUS Papers, MPB-ICD #256, copy of Editorial Survey by Walter N. Brockmann in English translation, 19 April 1948. See also OMGUS Papers, MPB-ICD #256, letter from James A. Clark to Col. Gordon Textor, 17 April 1948.

17. See Eva Schmid's reminiscences about her involvement in the film club movement in Schlüpmann, " 'Das Leben ist viel zu kurz.' "

18. Johannes Eckardt, "Die deutschen Film-Clubs," *Internationale Film Re-*

vue 1, no. 4 (1951/52): 284. See also BayHStA, MK51780, Bylaws for the Film-Club Augsburg, e.V.

19. BayHStA, MK51780, film clubs file. Also see the film club files for various cities in the press clipping archives of the DIFF for descriptions of film club programs.

20. Due to the reaction of the audience to *Night and Fog*, the dance film was mercifully canceled. See Schlüpmann, " 'Das Leben ist viel zu kurz,' " 71. For a discussion of the official reaction of the West German government to the film and its attempts to have it banned from the Cannes film festival in 1955, see Ungureit, "Filmpolitik in der Bundesrepublik," 9.

21. See Welch, *Propaganda and the German Cinema*, 22–23. "On 13 May 1936 Goebbels issued a proclamation that banned the writing of critical reviews on the same evening of the performance (*Nachtkritik*). . . . Such measures were clearly intended as a warning to critics not to question by means of hostile reviews . . . officially approved artistic works." By November of that year, Goebbels banned all film criticism, except for "descriptive reviews," and required critics to obtain a special license from the Reichskulturkammer before they could practice their profession. See also Cadars and Courtade, *Geschichte des Films im Dritten Reich*, 18–20, and Petley, *Capital and Culture*, 96–98.

22. See, for example, Robert Bernauer and Willi Vöbel, "Das Filmstudio an der Johann-Wolfgang-Goethe-Universität (II). Und wie es dann weitergang," in Stettner, *Kino in der Stadt*, esp. 64–65.

23. Frank Sauerlaender, "Filmclub Frankfurt am Main, e.V.," in Stettner, *Kino in der Stadt*, 67.

24. Quoted in Paech, "Schule der Zuschauer," 229.

25. König and Hintz, *10 Jahre Berliner Filmclub*. See also BayHStA, MK51780, letter from Johannes Eckardt to Bayerisches Staatsministerium für Unterricht und Kultus, 19 July 1949. A film club was also founded in Munich in May 1949, and by July clubs were formed in Coburg, Hof, Nuremberg, and Starnberg and were in preparation in Bayreuth, Kaufbeuren, Würzburg, Rosenheim, and Passau in the U.S. zone.

26. *Der Film-Club* (1949), quoted in Paech, "Schule der Zuschauer," 230.

27. Students at the university in Frankfurt, for example, began by exhibiting films but later developed their own film seminars since none were offered in the university curriculum. See Günther Vogt, "Von der Leinwand die Kunst erleben," *Frankfurter Allgemeine Zeitung*, 31 March 1962. See also Stettner, *Kino in der Stadt*, especially Ivar Rabeneck, "Das Film-Studio an der Johann-Wolfgang-Goethe-Universität," 58–64; Bernauer and Vöbel, "Das Filmstudio an der Johann-Wolfgang-Goethe-Universität," 64–66; Sauerlaender, "Filmclub Frankfurt am Main, e.V.," 67–69; and Herbert Stettner, "Engagiert für den zeitkritischen Film: Der Filmkreis im Frankfurter Bund für Volksbildung," 69–73.

28. BayHStA, MK51780, letter from Johannes Eckardt to the SPIO, 26 Sep-

tember 1950. See also "Verblüffender Aufstieg: Fünf Jahre Film-Club Augsburg," *Filmforum* 3, no. 9 (June 1954): 7.

29. Siegfried Kracauer asserts that the *Kulturfilme* of the 1920s and early 1930s "excelled in evasiveness. They mirrored the beautiful world; but their concern with the beauty of 'nimble-footed Chinese before palanquins' made them overlook the misery these beautiful coolies endured. They mirrored 'the confusion of the time'; but instead of penetrating the confusion, they gloated over it, thus leaving the audience more confused than ever. They spread information on wild buffalo herds and fire-worshippers; but their insistence upon exotic matters of no use to the spectator enabled them to withhold from him any essential information regarding everyday life." Kracauer, *From Caligari to Hitler*, 143. See also my discussion in chapter 7.

30. "Sein Lebenslauf ist ein Stück Filmgeschichte," *Filmforum* 7, no. 6 (April 1957): 1–2.

31. BayHStA, MK51780, letter from Edmund Schopen to Curt Oertel, 30 June 1950. Eckardt's rise in the postwar film club movement was rapid. A month after founding a local club in Augsburg in the U.S. zone in April 1949, Eckardt attended a film club meeting in Hamburg at which all three Western zones were represented. Aboard the hotel-ship *St. Louis*, the delegates of fifteen German film clubs announced the creation of the Association of German Film Clubs (Verband der deutschen Filmclubs). Walter Hagemann, who represented the British zone, was elected president of the association, and Eckardt was appointed to the Executive Committee. Four months later, Eckardt arranged another meeting of the film clubs in his home city of Augsburg, at which he was elected president of the association, replacing Hagemann.

32. BayHStA, MK51780, letter from Johannes Eckardt to Bayerisches Staatsministerium für Unterricht und Kultus, 19 July 1949. See also "50 deutsche Film Clubs," *Schwäbische Landeszeitung* (Augsburg), 16 September 1949, and Paech, "Schule der Zuschauer," 232, 234.

33. "Die Schatten tanzen am goldenen Faden . . . Zweite Tagung des Verbandes der deutschen Film-Clubs," *Aachener Nachrichten*, 24 May 1950. Eckardt's rather unyielding style is evident in the minutes of the Hannover film club meeting, 20 May 1950, in the Hannover Film Club file at DIFF.

34. "Festival der Elite," *National Zeitung Basel*, film supplement, 17 October 1953.

35. BayHStA, MK51780, letter from Johannes Eckardt to Bayerisches Staatsministerium für Unterricht und Kultus, 19 July 1949. See also BayHStA, MK51781, Band 2, Filmclubs 1.1.53–24.6.63, AZ:14a41. The Bavarian Cultural Ministry, for example, annually contributed small amounts (500–2,500 marks) to the Association of German Film Clubs and the local Munich Film Club.

36. DIFF, Hannover Film Club file, minutes of the Hannover film club meeting, 20 May 1950.

37. "Filmclubs keine Besucherorganisationen," *Die Illustrierte Filmwoche*, 3 June 1950; "Sein Lebenslauf ist ein Stück Filmgeschichte," p. 2; BayHStA, MK51780, letter from Johannes Eckardt to the SPIO, 26 September 1950.

38. Anton Kochs, "Filmliga und Filmclub," *Filmforum* 3, no. 1 (December 1951).

39. Ibid.

40. Eckardt, "Die Film-Club-Bewegung im Bundesgebiet."

41. "Die Schatten tanzen am goldenen Faden."

42. Fritz Kortner, "Bulletin der Leinwand," *Schwäbische Landeszeitung* (Augsburg), 16 September 1949.

43. "Wo wirklich geheuchelt wird," *Filmforum* 7, no. 1 (January 1958): 1. The low opinion of the German viewing public was expressed by a spokesperson from Gloria Film Verleih, a major postwar German film distributor.

44. Michael Bruck, "Filmbesuch—besser als ihr Ruf," *Filmforum* 1, no. 7 (April 1952): 1. See also Ludwig Thome, "Der Film und sein Publikum: Der deutsche Filmbesucher," *Internationale Film Revue* 1, no. 4 (1951/52): 279–81. Thome attacked the notion that the public had an identifiable taste and argued that the popularity of film genres changes over time, based upon fashion. In favor of the "maturity" argument, he cited the statistic that 7 out of 10 Germans surveyed actively selected the films they attended rather than simply seeing any film showing at their local theater, a practice that he assumed marked a departure from interwar and wartime behavior. Finally, he contextualized the problem of audience responsibility for commercial film quality by suggesting that similar developments could be observed in the United States.

45. He was named honorary president of the German film clubs for his efforts on their behalf.

46. Oertel described his sense of alienation from the commercial film industry as early as 1948 in his article, "Schicksal des Großkulturfilmes," *Der neue Film*, 7 May 1948, typescript copy in BayHStA, MK51818. See also "Wesentliches demokratisches Element," *Westfälische Rundschau*, 13 October 1950, and OMGUS Papers, MPB-ISD #259, "Basic Information, Film Control," 10 May 1947.

47. Hannes Schmidt, "Diskutieren oder Dinieren?," *Filmforum* 9, no. 1 (June 1952). Some of the noteworthy films included Orson Welles's *Citizen Kane*, Sergei Eisenstein's *Alexander Nevsky*, Max Ophüls's *Le Plaisir*, Luis Buñuel's *Un Chien andalou*, and Jean Mitry's *Pacific 231* as well as films by Sidney Meyers, René Clair, André Michel, Pietro Germi, Curzio Malaparte, Ingmar Bergman, and Dziga Vertov. French and Italian filmmakers generally continued to participate regularly in the Association of German Film Clubs' international meetings.

48. This did not, however, hold true across the board; the early annual meetings were not spurned by all members of the German film industry. Actor

Dieter Borsche and a handful of well-known film directors—including Harald Braun, Josef von Baky, and Helmut Käutner—attended in 1950, along with Wolfgang Staudte, who by that time had left the West in frustration to establish a career in the German Democratic Republic. These artists supported the international focus of the clubs, and Käutner, in keeping with the spirit of the meeting, presented a proposal calling on UNESCO to underwrite the production, distribution, and exhibition of artistic films. Käutner's proposal addressed both the financial woes of postwar European film production and the cultural corruption of the "Hollywood dream factory" as well as other national sources of kitsch, which, he claimed, undermined significant film art. His suggestions were enthusiastically reported by the French, Swiss, and South German radio stations, but French representatives at the meeting effectively scrapped the proposal by indicating that UNESCO was unable to implement such an ambitious project. See "Kunst contra Geschäft," *Westdeutsches Tagesblatt*, 19 March 1950.

49. LAB, "Filmbewertungsstelle den Länder der Bundesrepublik, April 1950–März 1954," transcript of letter from Aulich, president, SPIO, to Johannes Eckardt, 8 August 1950.

50. "Filmclubs tagten in Augsburg," *Illustrierte Filmwoche*, 1 October 1949.

51. See Helmut Lüssow, "Filmclubs suchen neue Wege," *Der neue Film*, 30 May 1950; "Filmclubs keine Besucherorganisationen"; and "Die Schatten tanzen am goldenen Faden." See also DIFF, Hannover Film Club file, minutes of the Hannover film club meeting, 20 May 1950, and memo from Aulich to SPIO member organizations, 22 May 1950; and Johannes Eckardt, "Graf Perponcher zum Gedenken," *Filmforum* 7, no. 2 (February 1958).

52. "Die Schatten tanzen am goldenen Faden."

53. DIFF, Hannover Film Club file, minutes of the Hannover film club meeting, 20 May 1950.

54. BayHStA, MK51780, letter from Edmund Schopen to Curt Oertel, 30 June 1950.

55. Schopen's arguments were not, however, completely disinterested. Schopen was an SPIO member, a Munich cinema owner, and the chairman of the Bavarian Theater Owners' Association. He argued for democratic renewal through cultural liberalization—provided it did not undermine cinema owners' interests. In Schopen's view, clubs should disavow the status of subscription organization to become centers of cultural discussion that would highlight exceptional films that received no commercial exposure. He argued that the clubs should remain autonomous since their influence resided in their "uncompromised idealism." They could only promote public interest in worthwhile films—and thus provide the latter with a market—if they "distanced themselves from the industry and appeared to be completely independent." The "capture and domestication of this free-roaming dog" would, on the other hand, accord-

ing to Schopen, spell the end of public and press support for the clubs. Nonetheless, industry members did not find Schopen sufficiently profit oriented and blasted his demand for club independence in their trade papers. See BayHStA, MK51780, "Sinn und Ziele des Münchners Filmclubs," and letter from Edmund Schopen to Curt Oertel, 30 June 1950; and DIFF, Hannover Film Club file, minutes of the Hannover film club meeting, 20 May 1950. See also "Ein merkwürdiger Entschluß: Filmclub München setzt sich ab," *Der neue Film*, 5 June 1950.

56. BayHStA, MK51780, correspondence from Johannes Eckardt to the Bavarian Cultural Ministry and the leader of the Heidelberg Film Club, June–September 1950.

57. In the 1950s, he also helped to establish an art cinema in Augsburg that was run in conjunction with the city, the film clubs, the Hochschule, and the Catholic *Filmliga* and Protestant *Filmgilde*. "Sein Lebenslauf ist ein Stück Filmgeschichte," 1–2.

58. Bestand: Filmwoche #10, Stadtarchiv, Mannheim, memo from Walter Talmon-Gros to the Information Office of the League of German Art Cinemas, 23 October 1953.

59. Johannes Eckardt, "Film-Clubs und Filmkunst-Theater," *Filmforum* 4, no. 8 (May 1955): 5.

60. In 1956 Eckardt tried to buttress his position, and that of the film club movement, by creating a centralized Deutscher Rat für Filmkunde, a sort of interest group for public institutions concerned with film matters. Members of the commercial film industry attempted to block the creation of the council, objecting that it sought to oppose their interests. Eckardt, of course, denied these charges. But his intention to strengthen and unify the "public voice" in its dealings with the industry is suggested by the composition of the council, which included representatives from German schools, film clubs, and research institutions as well as from the film offices of the churches and municipal art cinemas. Under Eckardt's leadership, the council won official recognition to act as the institutional center for public advocates of "the good film." Despite his efforts, the council never amounted to much—perhaps because by the time it got started, film attendance was falling off among large sectors of the public. See BayHStA, MK51692, "Niederschrift über die Sitzung am 7. März 1957 im Bayerischen Staatsministerium für Unterricht und Kultus wegen Fragen der Freiwilligen Selbstkontrolle der Filmwirtschaft," 5. See also Johannes Eckardt, "Echter Partner in fruchtbarem Gespräch," *Filmforum* 5, no. 10 (July 1956). The Executive Committee officers were President Johannes Eckardt (Association of German Film Clubs), Vice President Bernhard Künzig (Gilde deutscher Filmkunsttheater), Second Vice President Hilmar Hoffmann (Volkshochschulverband), and General Secretary Walter Talmon-Gros (Freunde der Gilde);

the members of the Executive Committee were Eberhard Hauff (Deutsches Institut für Film und Fernsehen, Munich), pastor Werner Hess, and director Anton Kochs.

61. Enno Patalas, interview by author, Munich, 4 August 1987. In a 1961 article in *Filmkritik*, Patalas quoted Eckardt's comments concerning the lack of discussion following film screenings at the annual meetings, which Patalas claimed was proof of the ennui overtaking the club movement. Eckardt complained, "We Germans are apparently no longer able to hold a discussion." Enno Patalas, "Kommentare: Eine Chance für die Filmclubs," *Filmkritik*, no. 4 (April 1961): 177. See also Patalas, "Filmclubs in Plüschfauteuil," *Filmkritik*, no. 11 (November 1957): 161–62, and Heinz Ungureit, "Kommentar: Filmclubs ohne Programm," *Filmkritik*, no. 5 (May 1962): 193.

62. "Festival der Elite," *National Zeitung Basel*, film supplement, 17 October 1953.

63. Quoted in Schlüpmann, " 'Das Leben ist viel zu kurz."

64. Interview with Schmid, in ibid., 71–75. See also Fee Vaillant, interview by author, Mannheim, 7 June 1987.

65. Throughout the 1950s, the national film club leadership was, without exception, male and on the whole considerably older than its membership. As noted, Johannes Eckardt was sixty-two years old when he became president of the Film Club Association, and he continued to serve in that elected office until he turned seventy-five. The managing director of the association and founder of the Bonn Film Club, Friedrich Carl Graf von Perponcher, was fifty-three when he began his tenure in 1949.

66. "Anstelle eines Programms," *Filmkritik*, no. 1 (January 1957): 1.

67. Enno Patalas, interview by author, Munich, 4 August, 5 October 1987. Hagemann refused to continue serving as Patalas's adviser despite the fact that Patalas's thesis topic had already been approved. Hagemann had a history of involvement in conservative politics and has been described as a convinced Catholic and German nationalist who, after 1945, favored German reunification. A member of the Catholic Center Party before 1933, he was involved in founding the CDU after the war and remained politically active in it until the mid-1950s. Curiously, he began propagandizing for the German Democratic Republic sometime after 1956 and fled there in the late 1950s, remaining until his death.

68. Enno Patalas, interview by author, Munich, 4 August 1987.

69. Enno Patalas denounced postwar film's superficiality and "weepy sentimentality," which promised viewers that "the sun will come out tomorrow." This, he claimed, indicated a flight from reality that extended to many other areas of daily life and accounted for the popularity of magazines and the soccer lottery. See Patalas, "Vom deutschen Nachkriegsfilm," 27–28.

70. See a synopsis of Patalas's talk in the 1955 Bad Ems film club meeting file

deposited at DIFF. See also Enno Patalas, "Von Caligari bis Canaris: Autorität und Revolte im deutschen Film," *film 56*, no. 2 (February 1956): 56–66. For Eckardt's reaction, see Johannes Eckardt, "Joseph Goebbels und Veit Harlan," *Filmforum* 5, no. 3 (December 1955): 4.

71. Ungureit, "Filmpolitik in der Bundesrepublik."

72. Enno Patalas, interview by author, Munich, 4 August 1987.

73. "Hat die Filmselbstkontrolle versagt?," *Filmkritik*, no. 9 (September 1957).

74. Such films were supplemented by printed pulp, like the adventure stories popular among veterans that described the actions of commanders and soldiers during World War II in heroic terms. See Mosse, "Two World Wars," 491–513.

75. "Hat die Filmselbstkontrolle versagt?"

76. *Jud Süss* was the sixth most popular feature film in the Nazi period, drawing a total of 20.3 million viewers. See Gerd Albrecht, "Auch Unterhaltung ist staatspolitisch wichtig," *Das Parlament*, 18, 25 April 1987, p. 4.

77. See Schwab-Felisch, "Die Affäre Harlan"; Muhlen, "The Return of Goebbels's Filmmakers"; and Welch, *Propaganda and the German Cinema*, 307.

78. Although initially denied release in West Germany by the censorship board, the film was eventually approved after cuts were made. It premiered in the more "tolerant" Austria, as the reviewer in *Filmkritik* sarcastically observed. See review of *Anders als du und ich* in *Filmkritik*, no. 12 (December 1957).

79. For a discussion of theories of homosexuality at the turn of the century, and particularly sexologist Magnus Hirschfeld's understanding of "uranism," see Oosterhuis, *Homosexuality and Male Bonding*, 1–2. In Hirschfeld's "widely publicized theory, homosexuality was an inborn mental and physical condition of a specific minority, the so-called 'third sex,' which he described as an intermediate human species between full-blown men and women, comparable to androgynes, hermaphrodites, and transvestites."

80. See Moeller, "The Homosexual Man Is a 'Man,' " 403.

81. For a discussion of the cuts mandated by the FSK, see Theis, " 'Anders als du und ich,' " 56–75. See also a psychologist's expert report on the film deposited in the "Anders als du und ich" file, Schriftgutarchiv, Stiftung Deutsche Kinematek, Berlin.

82. *Völkischer Beobachter*, 31 October 1928, quoted in Moeller, "The Homosexual Man Is a 'Man,' " 400.

83. See review of *Anders als du und ich* in *Filmkritik*, no. 12 (December 1957).

84. See Theis, " 'Anders als du und ich,' " 56–75, for recent comment on critical reactions at the time. For a discussion of the legal debates about homosexuality and §175, as well as contemporary assumptions regarding the link

between sexual behavior and social order in postwar West Germany, see Moeller, "The Homosexual Man Is a 'Man,'" 395–429.

85. Moeller, "The Homosexual Man Is a 'Man,'" 427.

86. Thomas said at the time that he maintained no contact with his father. "Harlans Sohn will Israel-Film drehen," *Filmforum* 2, no. 10 (July 1953).

87. Quoted in Eckardt, "Joseph Goebbels und Veit Harlan," 4. See also Theis, "'Anders als du und ich,'" 61. Theis notes that after 1945, "Goebbels was stylised into the bearer of all guilt, the demon who pulled all the strings and from whom there was no escape."

88. Eckardt, "Joseph Goebbels und Veit Harlan," 4.

89. Quoted in ibid. Harlan complained that the projects he was involved with in the 1950s were denied federal and state credit for political reasons. Despite his protestations, the record shows that he was still able to direct some ten films over the course of the 1950s. See Helt and Helt, *West German Cinema since 1945*, 40, 69, 70, 169, 194, 230, 292, 446, 488, 499.

90. Arguments such as Eckardt's were not confined to the German press. An article on the reemergence of Veit Harlan and Werner Krauss on the German cultural scene in *Commentary* stated:

Totalitarianism always involves, and corrupts, a majority of people. That an advocate of mass murder like Streicher was to be silenced forever, every decent German agreed . . . but opinion is split with regard to the tens of thousands of Krausses, exactly because people who have themselves lived under Nazism—including many who fought against it—recognize how difficult it was for the individual not to be corrupted to some degree. To turn all these people into perennial outcasts, to exclude from the new society even those who may be willing honestly to mend their ways and break with the past would be to encourage hostility against the young German republic and limit significant possibilities for the regeneration of individual Germans and German society. Totalitarianism brands whole groups of people as eternal enemies. Can democracy, which believes in—and is based upon—the improvability and potential decency of the individual and society, rightfully insist that all sinners against civilized morality, even if they have committed no legally punishable acts of criminality, be condemned to lifelong punishment, denied a second chance? This is the dilemma posed by the cases of Harlan and Krauss.

See Muhlen, "The Return of Goebbels's Filmmakers," 250.

91. Ibid., 247.

92. Ibid., 247; Schwab-Felisch, "Die Affäre Harlan." On the street demonstrations in Munich, see the *Filmdemonstrationen* file in the Akten des Bürgermeisters und Rats, #2722 (1951–52), Stadtarchiv, Munich. See also newspaper clippings on the film and its impact on microfiche at the DIFF.

93. Ungureit, "Kommentar: Filmclubs ohne Programm," p. 193.

94. Enno Patalas, "Die Staudte-Story, ein gesamtdeutsches Märchen," *Filmkritik*, no. 3 (March 1957).

95. Rentschler, "Germany," 119. See Orbanz and Prinzler, *Staudte*, for the director's description of the film and the changes that were required in the screenplay for its realization.

96. Quoted in Knietzsch, *Wolfgang Staudte*, 23.

97. Rentschler, "Germany," 127. See also Silberman, "Semper fidelis."

98. See Patalas, "Die Staudte-Story." Staudte, however, did achieve international recognition in the form of the Silver Lion at the 1955 Venice film festival for his work on a Dutch coproduction.

99. Egon Netenjakob, "Ein Leben gegen die Zeit," in Orbanz and Prinzler, *Staudte*, 19. See also "Interview," in ibid., 132.

100. Netenjakob, "Ein Leben gegen die Zeit," 18–19.

101. Ibid., 22–24; "Interview," in Orbanz and Prinzler, *Staudte*, 132–33.

102. This is Staudte's own representation of the film. See his "Ein Kommentar: Zur Thematik von *Kirmes*," in Orbanz and Prinzler, *Staudte*, 161–63.

103. "Eine Antwort: Auf die Frage, Deutscher Film—wohin?," in Orbanz and Prinzler, *Staudte*, 158.

104. See Enno Patalas, "Die Chance," *Filmkritik*, no. 4 (April 1962): 146–50.

CHAPTER SEVEN

1. For a discussion of Young German Cinema and New German Cinema, see, among others, Corrigan, *New German Film*; Elsaesser, *New German Cinema*; Franklin, *New German Cinema*; Frieden et al., *Gender and German Cinema*, vols. 1 and 2; Knight, *Women and the New German Cinema*; Rentschler, *West German Film in the Course of Time* and *West German Filmmakers on Film*; and Sandford, *New German Cinema*. For reminiscences by Edgar Reitz, see Jung, "Das Kino der frühen Jahre," and Dawson, "A Labyrinth of Subsidies."

2. Between 1960 and 1962, the German film industry's share of the shrinking domestic market slipped from 43.3 percent to 28.5 percent, and German film producer Artur Brauner was quoted by Enno Patalas as saying: "A sense of panic dominates German film. One is merely attempting to keep the offices [going]." Moreover, the selection committee of the Venice Biennial Film Festival rejected all five of the films nominated for screening by the West German government in 1961. For an indication of the severely weakened position of German film production and distribution companies by the beginning of the 1960s, see "Weniger Filme—mehr Qualität?," *Filmkritik*, no. 7 (July 1961): 322–23, and Enno Patalas, "Die Chance," *Filmkritik*, no. 4 (April 1962): 146–47.

The above figures are cited in Koch, *Die Bedeutung des "Oberhauseners Manifestes*," 32–33.

3. Quoted in Rentschler, *West German Filmmakers on Film*, 2. The Oberhausen Manifesto was signed by Bodo Blüthner, Boris von Borresholm, Christian Doermer, Bernhard Dörries, Heinz Furchner, Rob Houwer, Ferdinand Khittl, Alexander Kluge, Pitt Koch, Walter Krüttner, Dieter Lemmel, Hans Loeper, Ronald Martini, Hans-Jürgen Pohland, Raimond Ruehl, Edgar Reitz, Peter Schamoni, Detten Schleiermacher, Fritz Schwennicke, Haro Senft, Franz-Josef Spieker, Hans Rolf Strobel, Heinz Tichawsky, Wolfgang Urchs, Herbert Vesely, and Wolf Wirth.

4. Koch, *Die Bedeutung des "Oberhauseners Manifestes*," 68–70.

5. Elsaesser was referring to the effect of state film subsidies in West Germany in the 1970s, but his analysis is applicable to the rationale behind city sponsorship of *Kulturfilm* festivals in the 1950s as well. Elsaesser, *New German Cinema*, 3 (emphasis in original).

6. Independent filmmaker Herbert Vesely's *Autobahn* (1957), for example, was picked up by Bavaria Film for distribution in the Federal Republic only after it had won prizes at several international festivals and the Ministry of the Interior's Bundesfilmprämie in 1958. See Jung, "Das Kino der frühen Jahre," 325.

7. "Die kulturellen Aufgabe gerecht werden," *Film-Echo*, 17 October 1953, p. 1.

8. For a description of some of this activity, see Schlüpmann, " 'Das Leben ist viel zu kurz.' " For Association of German Film Clubs president Johannes Eckardt's efforts in Augsburg, see "Sein Lebenslauf ist ein Stück Filmgeschichte," *Filmforum* 7, no. 6 (April 1957): 1–2.

9. For a discussion of municipal cultural policies in the postwar period, see Horn, *Kulturpolitik in Düsseldorf*. Horn discusses the philosophy behind the founding of the Deutscher Städtetag, which was based upon a commitment to the "cultural tradition of the cities." In the preamble to its 1952 "Leitsätze zur kommunalen Kulturarbeit," the Städtetag identified the cultivation of culture as an "important and pressing task" and broadened its sphere of interest to include film and radio in addition to its traditional focus on adult and youth education, bookstores, theater, music, art, museums, and public monuments.

10. The educational aim of the festival was underscored by the constellation of individuals and groups involved in its organization. The festival was initially placed under the leadership of Christoph Andritzky, the city's cultural adviser (*Kulturreferent*). Andritzky was assisted by Kurt Fischer, who was active in leading film seminars at the Mannheim Adult School (Volkshochschule), and Bernhard Künzig, the owner of a local art cinema and member of the Executive Committee of the League of German Art Cinemas. The Mannheim-Ludwigs-

hafen Film Club cosponsored the festival. Kurt Fischer, who later directed the festival, also enlisted the support and ongoing participation of Johannes Eckardt. For a short history of the Mannheim Kultur- und Dokumentarfilmwoche (later known as the Internationale Filmwoche Mannheim), see Christoph Andritzky, "1951–1961: Die Mannheimer Filmwoche von der Geburt bis zu ihrem 10. Lebensjahr," in *Dokumentation: XXV Internationale Filmwoche Mannheim*, 9. See also Wilhelm Varnholt, "Dreißig Jahre Internationale Filmwoche Mannheim," Fee Vaillant and Hans Maier, "Gedanken und Fragen zur Bilanz dreißig Jahre Filmwoche Mannheim," and Ulrich Gregor, "Stationen eines Festivals," all in *Dokumentation: 30 Jahre Internationale Filmwoche Mannheim, 1951–1981*, 5–6, 7–13, 26–45. See also Tautz, "Die zweite Mannheimer Kultur- und Dokumentarfilmwoche," 35–36, and Kurt Joachim Fischer, "Mannheim wird wohl nur ein Beispiel bleiben," *Internationale Film Revue* 3, no. 2 (1956): 93–94, and "Gilt die Festivalneuordnung auch für Mannheim?," *Rhein-Neckar Revue* 10 (1970): 11–12.

11. Curt Oertel, "Schicksal des Großkulturfilmes," *Der neue Film*, 7 May 1948.

12. The first *Kulturfilm* to win attention abroad was UFA's *Wege zu Kraft und Schönheit* (*Ways to Health and Beauty*, 1925), a feature-length film promoting the "regeneration of the human race" through sport, dance, calisthenics, and aestheticized nudity. See Kracauer, *From Caligari to Hitler*, 142–43, 151–52. See also Oertel, "Schicksal des Großkulturfilmes"; Michael Töteberg, "Wie werde ich stark: Die Kulturfilm-Abteilung," "Schöne nackte Körper: *Wege zu Kraft und Schönheit*," and "Im Auftrag der Partei: Deutsche Kulturfilm-Zentrale und Ufa-Sonderproduktion," all in Bock and Töteberg, *Das Ufa-Buch*, 64–67, 152–55, 438–43; and "Sein Lebenslauf ist ein Stück Filmgeschichte," pp. 1–2.

13. Ludwig Thome, "Für fünfzig Pfennig die ganze Welt," *Filmforum* 3, no. 10 (July 1954). See also Töteberg, "Wie werde ich stark."

14. "Ist der Kulturfilm ein 'krankes Kind'?," *General-Anzeiger* (Bonn), 4 November 1954.

15. Thome, "Für fünfzig Pfennig die ganze Welt."

16. Tautz, "Die zweite Mannheimer Kultur- und Dokumentarfilmwoche," 35.

17. LAB, "Filmgesellschaften, January 1949, Alt, W–Z," letter from Alf Zengerling to Berlin Senate, 31 May 1951.

18. Even during the Nazi period, state support for feature-length documentaries had dwindled since Goebbels saw no possibility for healthy profits. He threw his support behind the short *Kulturfilm*, which he could require as mandatory viewing in cinemas before the featured film. See Oertel, "Schicksal des Großkulturfilmes"; BayHStA, MK51818, Willi Cronauer, "Vormerkung zum Schreiben v. Herrn von Oerthel," 24 February 1949; and Kurt Joachim Fischer, "Der leidige Ärger mit dem deutschen Kulturfilm," *Kulturarbeit* 3 (1958): 51–52.

19. "Der Kulturfilm muß die Filmkultur hüten," *Mannheimer Morgen*, 17 May 1955, p. 4.

20. Kracauer, *From Caligari to Hitler*, 143; Töteberg, "Wie werde ich stark," 66–67.

21. Thome, "Für fünfzig Pfennig die ganze Welt."

22. Fischer, "Der leidige Ärger mit dem deutschen Kulturfilm," 52.

23. Between 1951 and 1960, the Cultural Ministry of North Rhine West-phalia dispensed a total of 4 million marks in awards to films deemed worthy. West German short films were eligible for the awards regardless of their state of origin. In addition, the federal government funded an annual film prize that was awarded to *Kulturfilme* and feature films. In 1956 the federal government initi-ated awards specifically for quality German *Kulturfilme*. Under this program in 1959, for example, 37 financial awards totaling 520,000 marks were bestowed. The average award was 10,000 marks for a short black-and-white film and 15,000 marks for a color film, with an additional 5,000 marks awarded to a film that appeared to promise international quality. See Hilmar Hoffmann, "Eine Chronik des Kultur- und Dokumentarfilms," *Filmforum* 9, no. 5 (May 1960). See also Hübinger, "Die Mannheimer Kultur- und Dokumentarfilmwoche."

24. "Nachtschicht für den Film," *Ruhr-Nachrichten* (Essen), 26 October 1956.

25. Quoted in Fischer, "Mannheim wird wohl nur ein Beispiel bleiben," 93. See also Hübinger, "Die Mannheimer Kultur- und Dokumentarfilmwoche," 21.

26. H. C. Opfermann, "Der Kulturfilm und sein Publikum," *Filmforum* 4, no. 8 (May 1955).

27. Fischer, "Mannheim wird wohl nur ein Beispiel bleiben," 93. Helga Haf-tendorn confirms that this was also the response of German audiences in the commercial cinemas in the town she studied. She found absolutely no popular interest in German *Kulturfilme*, even among schoolteachers. See Haftendorn, "Zusammensetzung und Verhalten des Filmtheaterpublikums in der Mittel-stadt," 20.

28. Fischer, "Mannheim wird wohl nur ein Beispiel bleiben," 94.

29. Andritzky, "1951–1961: Die Mannheimer Filmwoche"; Hübinger, "Die Mannheimer Kultur- und Dokumentarfilmwoche," 20–22.

30. In 1959, for example, 187 journalists, 204 filmmakers, 143 film club representatives, and 57 official government representatives attended the Mann-heim festival to watch films from 44 countries.

31. BayHStA, MK51782, letter from Ministerialrat Donndorf, Kultusmini-sterium of Baden-Württemberg, to Dr. Keim, Bayerisches Staatsministerium für Unterricht und Kultus, 27 December 1960.

32. In 1957 Oberhausen's Hilmar Hoffmann shifted his festival's dates from the autumn to the spring, placing the two festivals in direct competition for participants, a move that certainly worked to Mannheim's disadvantage. See

Kurt Joachim Fischer, "Gilt die Festivalneuordnung auch für Mannheim?," *Rhein-Neckar Revue* 10 (1970): 11; Bestand: Filmwoche #28, Stadtarchiv, Mannheim, correspondence of K. J. Fischer regarding his negotiations with Hilmar Hoffmann over the dates of the Oberhausen festival; and "Komprimiß wahrt Mannheims Interessen," *Allgemeine Zeitung*, 31 October 1957.

33. Holloway, *O Is for Oberhausen*, 16.

34. See Schlüpmann, " 'Das Leben ist viel zu kurz,' " 72–73.

35. Ibid., 73.

36. Enno Patalas, interview by author, Munich, 4 August 1987. Patalas mentioned in this interview that no one attended the festival to see German *Kulturfilme*. As with the film club screenings, audiences went to Oberhausen to see foreign films.

37. See Bettecken, "25 Jahre Wandlungen des Kurzfilms," 124–28.

38. Schlüpmann, " 'Das Leben ist viel zu kurz,' " 73–74; Holloway, *O Is for Oberhausen*, 19–22; Bettecken, "25 Jahre Wandlungen des Kurzfilms," 126–29.

39. The festival in Mannheim, in contrast, was marked by the conservative politics of Mayor Retschke. The event relied on federal funds, and therefore each year's program was required to be previewed in Bonn. Enno Patalas, interview by author, Munich, 4 August 1987. See also Holloway, *O Is for Oberhausen*, 20, and Schlüpmann, " 'Das Leben ist viel zu kurz,' " 74–75.

40. Ungureit, "Filmpolitik in der Bundesrepublik," 9.

41. Enno Patalas, interview by author, Munich, 4 August 1987.

42. Hilmar Hoffmann, "Die IV. Westdeutschen Kulturfilmtage in Oberhausen," *Kulturarbeit* 3 (1958): 50.

43. Holloway, *O Is for Oberhausen*, 19.

44. See " 'Roter Mond' über Oberhausen," *Der Abend* (Berlin), 3 December 1957; "Kulturfilm: Weg zum Nachbarn," *Handelsblatt*, 22 February 1958; and "Unter unserer Würde," *Berliner Zeitung* (East Berlin), 12 February 1958.

45. Schlüpmann, " 'Das Leben ist viel zu kurz,' " 74–75; Holloway, *O Is for Oberhausen*, 17–23.

46. " 'Roter Mond' über Oberhausen."

47. Schlüpmann, " 'Das Leben ist viel zu kurz,' " 75.

48. Holloway, *O Is for Oberhausen*, 20.

49. Quoted in Koch, *Die Bedeutung des "Oberhausensers Manifestes,"* 69.

50. The description of *Brutalität in Stein* is based upon Eric Rentschler's talk entitled "The Bread of the Early Years: Film, Politics, and History," delivered at the Symposium on the Work of Alexander Kluge, City University of New York Graduate Center, 28 October 1988. The published version is Rentschler, "Remembering Not to Forget." See also "Der Kurzfilm als Talentprobe," *Süddeutsche Zeitung*, 19 February 1961; "Kommt die deutsche Neue Welle?," *Rheinische Post*, 11 February 1961; and Günter Seuren, "Zu den VII. West-

deutschen Kurzfilmtagen in Oberhausen," *Deutsche Zeitung* (Stuttgart), 15 February 1961.

51. Program description from the 1961 West German Short Film Festival, quoted in Koch, *Die Bedeutung des "Oberhauseners Manifestes,"* 75. See also ibid., 74–82.

52. Organizers of the Mannheim and Oberhausen festivals excised the term "Kulturfilm" from their events' titles in order avoid association with the UFA-style product. The new, improved equivalent was termed "Kurzfilm" or short film. See Seuren, "Zu den VII. Westdeutschen Kurzfilmtagen in Oberhausen."

53. Edgar Reitz recalled that some of the Oberhausen rebels had not yet made a film at the time of the manifesto and that a few had not even aspired to becoming filmmakers. See Dawson, "A Labyrinth of Subsidies"; Jung, "Das Kino der frühen Jahre"; and Koch, *Die Bedeutung des "Oberhauseners Manifestes."*

54. Knight, *Women and the New German Cinema,* 1–11.

55. See the short biography section in Müller, *Film in der Bundesrepublik Deutschland,* 128.

56. Quoted in Koch, *Die Bedeutung des "Oberhauseners Manifestes,"* 68.

57. Quoted in Koch, *Die Bedeutung des "Oberhauseners Manifestes,"* 70. Reitz also noted, in an interview with Jan Dawson in 1978, that Kluge's attempt to politicize the proceedings provoked dissension in the group, a reaction that underscores the fact that there was no shared political (or artistic) vision. See Dawson, "A Labyrinth of Subsidies," 103.

58. Quoted in Koch, *Die Bedeutung des "Oberhauseners Manifestes,"* 53.

59. They also knew the limited rewards of self-help. In April 1959 in Munich, Haro Senft and Ferdinand Khittl called for the creation of DOC 59, an organization to "support artistic efforts on behalf of film." The aims of DOC 59 resembled those of the film clubs founded a decade before: to support and lobby for culturally and artistically valuable films, to facilitate discussion on film matters, to sponsor public lectures and discussions, and to maintain contact with international film associations. In contrast to the clubs, however, the organization resolved to finance short film projects out of its own funds. DOC 59 was a notable group effort that set the stage for the Oberhausen Manifesto, but it had no material base to sustain its ambitions to foster film production. Most of the founding members of DOC 59 went on to sign the Oberhausen Manifesto three years later. One notable exception was Enno Patalas. See Jung, "Das Kino der frühen Jahre," 327.

60. Ibid., 322, 329; Patalas, "Die Chance," 146–50.

61. Rentschler, "Germany," 234. On Hans Abich and his philosophy regarding the reconstruction of postwar film, see Susan Fuhrmann, "Noch immer nach Hugenberg riechend: Hans Abich über die Anfänge im Westen," in Bock and Töteberg, *Das Ufa-Buch,* 474–75.

62. The description of *nicht mehr fliehen* is from Günter Specovius's review in *Die Zeit*, 9 February 1956, reprinted in Hoffmann and Schobert, *Zwischen Gestern und Morgen*, 378; and DIFF, microfiche film review, Enno Patalas, "Die Filmkunst gegen ihre Verehrer in Schutz genommen," typescript. See also Jung, "Das Kino der frühen Jahre," 318–19, and Koch, *Die Bedeutung des "Oberhauseners Manifestes,"* 56–57.

63. Koch, *Die Bedeutung des "Oberhauseners Manifestes,"* 86–87.

64. Ibid. These were for best young director, best actress (for Vera Tschechow), best filmography, and best music; in addition, the film received second prize for best feature film.

65. See Patalas, "Die Chance," 147–49.

66. Jung, "Das Kino der frühen Jahre," 330–31.

67. In 1962 Alexander Kluge outlined the basic assumptions underlying their quest for an alternative film culture:

West German Film is in a crisis: its intellectual content was never more lacking, but today its economic status is equally threatened. This is happening at a time when in France and Italy, in Poland and Czechoslovakia . . . film has assumed a new artistic and political importance. Films like Italy's *Salvatore Giullano* . . . or *Ashes and Diamonds* from Poland, indicate that film has been able to interact with literary and other art forms as well as political consciousness. . . . It is . . . crucial that we

1. free film from its intellectual isolation in the Federal Republic,

2. militate against the dictates of a strictly commercial orientation operative in the film industry today,

3. allow for conditions which make film aware of its public responsibility, and consequently . . . seek appropriate themes: film should embrace social documentation, political questions, educational concerns, and filmic innovations, matters all but impossible under the conditions that have governed film production.

See Kluge, "What Do the 'Oberhauseners' Want?," reprinted in Rentschler, *West German Filmmakers on Film*, 10–12.

68. Pflaum and Prinzler, *Film in der Bundesrepublik Deutschland*, 110–11.

69. Sandford, *New German Cinema*, 20–22.

70. Ibid., 13.

71. Elsaesser, *New German Cinema*, 3.

72. Kluge noted that the Oberhauseners had to seek their own distribution channels, separate from those used by commercial films. See Kluge, "What Do the 'Oberhauseners' Want?," reprinted in Rentschler, *West German Filmmakers on Film*.

CHAPTER EIGHT

1. In the first year, the Berlin film festival received a subsidy of 40,000 marks from the Berlin Senate, a loan of approximately 20,000 marks from UFA reserves, and 35,000 marks from U.S. occupation officials, for a total of 95,000 marks. This was a small sum in comparison to the budgets of the film festivals at Cannes and Venice, which have been calculated as, respectively, the equivalent of 250,000 marks and 2.5 million marks. See LAB, IFB File, 1951, vom 6. Juni bis 17. Juni 1951, draft, Alfred Bauer, "Abschlußbericht über die Internationalen Filmfestspiele Berlin 1951." See also LAB, Filmfestspiele/Festwochen, 1956–58, "Bericht über die Internationalen Filmfestspiele Berlin gemäß Senatsbeschluß Nr. 1830/56 vom 12. April 1956."

2. Rossellini's *Germania anno zero* and Wilder's *Berlin Affair* were set in the ruins of the city and portrayed the material and spiritual devastation of the war.

3. The smaller festivals at Mannheim and Oberhausen received recognition as "B" fests, due in part to emphasis on documentary-style films.

4. See LAB, IFB File, 1953, "Vertrauliches Protokoll über die vierte Sitzung des Organisationskomitees der III. Internationalen Filmfestspiele Berlin 1953," 9 May 1953. For a short biographical sketch of Bauer, see Jacobsen, *Berlinale*, 14.

5. Alfred Bauer, "Entstehung und Entwicklung der Internationalen Filmfestspiele Berlin: Rückblick auf das erste Vierteljahrhundert des Wettbewerbs (1951–1976)," typescript, in the library of the Stiftung Deutsche Kinemathek, Berlin. See also Henseleit, *Die Internationalen Filmfestspiele Berlin*, 2.

6. LBS, IFB File, Horst Müting, "Berlin zwischen heute und morgen," *Der neue Film* (June 1951): 1.

7. Memo from the Berlin Senate, Wi IV H/65, to the Abgeordnetenhaus, "Bericht über Berlin als Filmstadt," April 1965, in the library of the Deutsche Film und Fernsehen Akademie, Berlin.

8. LAB, Beratender Ausschuß, Neuordnung der Filmwirtschaft, UFA Angelegenheiten vom 1.5.1951–30.4.1952, "Expose zum Brief an den Regierenden Bürgermeister," from the Verband der Filmschaffenden, e.V., 21 April 1952.

9. LAB, IFB File, 1951, vom 6. Juni bis 17. Juni 1951, letter from Oscar Martay, U.S. Information Services Branch, HICOG, to Stadtrat May, Magistrat, Groß Berlin, Abteilung Volksbildung, 5 December 1950.

10. The idea for the Berlin film festival is variously credited to Oscar Martay, Alfred Bauer, and Berlin journalist Manfred Barthel. Martay is cited as the festival's originator in a contemporary report from the office of the Berlin senator of popular education (*Senator für Volksbildung*), while Germans Bauer and Barthel are named in a more recent pamphlet issued by the festival office. The German film industry's identification of the festival as a U.S. project sug-

gests that Martay may well have been the initiator. See LAB, Filmfestspiele/ Festwochen, 1956–58, "Bericht über die Internationalen Filmfestspiele Berlin gemäß Senatsbeschluß Nr. 1830/56 vom 12. April 1956"; LAB, IFB File, 1951, vom 6. Juni bis 17. Juni 1951, letter from Fritz Podehl, FSK, to Herr Baensch, Berlin Senate, Abteilung Volksbildung, 28 February 1951. See also Henseleit, *Die Internationalen Filmfestspiele Berlin*; Borgelt, *Filmstadt Berlin*, 71–72; and Jacobsen, *Berlinale*, 11–14.

11. LAB, IFB File, 1951, vom 6. Juni bis 17. Juni 1951, copy of letter from Filmreferat, Berlin, to Arbeitsausschußes der Internationalen Filmfestspiele Berlin 1951, 30 December 1950.

12. Rosenberg, *Spreading the American Dream*, 99–100.

13. LAB, IFB File, 1951, vom 6. Juni bis 17. Juni 1951, Februar 1952, letter from Filmreferat, Berlin, to Stadtrat May, 14 October 1950, letter from May to Oscar Martay, 1 December 1950, and letter from Martay to May, 5 December 1950.

14. LAB, IFB File, 1951, vom 6. Juni bis 17. Juni 1951, letter from Oscar Martay, U.S. Information Services Branch, HICOG, to Stadtrat May, Magistrat, Groß Berlin, Abteilung Volksbildung, 5 December 1950.

15. Borgelt, *Filmstadt Berlin*, 38. Between 1946 and 1955, approximately 100 films were made in the Babelsberg and Johannisthal studios in East Berlin, compared to the approximately 150 films produced in West Berlin's Spandau and Tempelhof studios.

16. Wiesbaden, Munich, and Cologne had film festivals planned for the summer and fall of 1951. See LAB, IFB File, 1951, vom 6. Juni bis 17. Juni 1951, letter from Oscar Martay, U.S. Information Services Branch, HICOG, to Stadtrat May, Magistrat, Groß Berlin, Abteilung Volksbildung, 5 December 1950.

17. See Rosenberg, *Spreading the American Dream*, 202–28, for a discussion of the official promotion of U.S. culture for political purposes.

18. LAB, IFB File, 1951, vom 6. Juni bis 17. Juni 1951, letter from Oscar Martay, U.S. Information Services Branch, HICOG, to Stadtrat May, Magistrat, Groß Berlin, Abteilung Volksbildung, 5 December 1950.

19. LAB, IFB File, 1951, Bauer, "Abschlußbericht über die Internationalen Filmfestspiele Berlin 1951," 1.

20. LAB, IFB File, 1953, "Protokoll über die dritte Sitzung des Organisationskomitees der III. Internationalen Filmfestspiele Berlin 1953," 30 March 1953.

21. Ibid. Mass events not only served propaganda goals but were important for bringing money into the festival's chronically exhausted coffers.

22. Ibid. See also Borgelt, *Filmstadt Berlin*, 72.

23. The plan was voted down in the end due to the film's adult rating as well as the objections of theater owners that such a screening would snatch money from their pockets. Albers, however, was recruited for personal appearances at

the festival screenings in border theaters in later years. LAB, IFB File, 1952, "Protokoll über die fünfte ordentliche Sitzung des Arbeitsausschusses der II. Internationalen Filmfestspiele Berlin 1952," 4 June 1952.

24. LAB, IFB File, 1952, "Protokoll über die erste ordentliche Sitzung des Arbeitsausschusses der II. Internationalen Filmfestspiele Berlin," 15 February 1952.

25. In 1952 screenings were held at the Metro-Palast and Corso theaters. LAB, IFB File, 1952, "Protokoll über die vierte Sitzung des Arbeitsausschusses der II. Internationalen Filmfestspiele Berlin 1952," 23 May 1952; LBS, IFB File, Horst Müting, "Berlin zwischen heute und morgen," 1.

26. LAB, IFB File, 1952, "Protokoll über die erste ordentliche Sitzung des Arbeitsausschusses der II. Internationalen Filmfestspiele Berlin," 15 February 1952.

27. Ibid. After considering the objections of industry members regarding the special screenings in Neukölln and Wedding, Senator Tiburtius maintained that it was "a political necessity to extend the film festival to the working-class districts" of the city. Such screenings continued throughout the 1950s. Industry members, nonetheless, were able to persuade U.S. officials to alter their open-air program for East Berliners at the Potsdamerplatz. Although an evening of feature films was planned, U.S. officials switched to *Kulturfilme* after a German Film Theater Owners' Association representative protested the screening of feature films—which had not yet been fully exploited at the box office—to an unpaying audience of 20,000. Economic arguments could still, apparently, make an impression. LAB, IFB File, 1953, "Protokoll über die dritte Sitzung des Organisationskomitees der III. Internationalen Filmfestspiele Berlin 1953," 30 March 1953.

28. On the recruitment of film stars for the *Randtheater* screenings, see LBS, IFB File, "Schlußbericht: V. Internationalen Filmfestspiele Berlin 1955."

29. Borgelt, *Filmstadt Berlin*, 39. See also newspaper clippings on the Berlin festival at the LBS.

30. By the second year—when the official jury was eliminated and the public's vote determined the awards—the festival organizers drastically broadened the categories for competition and simplified the trophies. Inscribed plaques were awarded to the three feature films acclaimed by the public vote. In 1955 awards were also presented to the best short films. See "Die Preise der Berliner Festspiele" and "So wählte das Publikum!," *Filmblätter*, 22 June 1951, p. 506; LAB, IFB File, 1952, "II. Internationalen Filmfestspiele Berlin, 12.–25. Juni 1952, Richtlinien." See also LBS, IFB File, "Schlußbericht—V. Internationalen Filmfestspiele Berlin 1955," 5. For a list of the 1951 jury members, see Jacobsen, *Berlinale*, 22. For a list of winning films, see Marquardt, *Internationale Filmfestspiele Berlin*, and Jacobsen, *Berlinale*.

31. In 1957 the FIAPF had twenty-one members: Argentina, Austria, Bel-

gium, Britain, Denmark, Egypt, the Federal Republic of Germany, Finland, France, Holland, Israel, Italy, Japan, Mexico, Pakistan, Portugal, Spain, Sweden, Switzerland, Turkey, and the United States. See LAB, IFB File, 1953, "Protokoll über die erste Sitzung des Organisationskomitees der III. Internationalen Filmfestspiele Berlin 1953," 10 January 1953, 2.

32. The first year of the festival, Bauer had issued invitations to individual film production companies in the Western democracies. Producers from twenty nations participated, including Australia, Austria, Canada, Denmark, England, the Federal Republic of Germany, Ireland, Mexico, the Netherlands, Spain, Sweden, Switzerland, Turkey, the United States, and Yugoslavia. France and Italy also participated "unofficially" since producers in those countries were allowed to participate only in those fests recognized by the FIAPF. See LAB, IFB File, 1951, Bauer, "Abschlußbericht über die Internationalen Filmfestspiele Berlin 1951," 1–2; and LAB, IFB File, 1952, handwritten notes appended to letter from Renato Gualino, president, FIAPF, to festival office, 13 July 1951. See also Henseleit, *Die Internationalen Filmfestspiele Berlin*, 1, and Marquardt, *Internationale Filmfestspiele Berlin*.

33. LAB, IFB File, 1953, "Protokoll über die erste Sitzung des Organisationskomitees der III. Internationalen Filmfestspiele Berlin 1953," 10 January 1953.

34. The success of the Italian and French film industries in protecting the special status of Venice and Cannes as "A" festivals was attributable to their dominant position in the FIAPF. The organization had offices in two European cities, Rome and Paris, and was presided over by either an Italian or French industry member throughout the 1950s.

35. Receiving this designation was considered an accomplishment. In 1953, for example, twelve countries applied for a "B" rating for their festivals, but only Berlin and Locarno were successful in their bids. See LAB, IFB File, 1953, "Protokoll über die erste Sitzung des Organisationskomitees der III. Internationalen Filmfestspiele Berlin 1953," 10 January 1953.

36. LAB, IFB File, 1952, "Protokoll über die dritte ordentliche Sitzung des Arbeitsausschusses der II. Internationalen Filmfestspiele Berlin 1952," 9 May 1952; LAB, IFB File, 1953, "Protokoll über die vierte Sitzung des Organisationskomitees der III. Internationalen Filmfestspiele Berlin 1953," 9 May 1953.

37. LAB, IFB File, 1951, letter from H. B. Baum, Verband deutscher Filmproduzenten, e.V., to Magistrat, Groß Berlin, 19 March 1951. See also LAB, Rep. #14, Acc. 2323, #153–55, Fritz Podehl, "Beitrag zur Klärung der Produktionskrise des deutschen Films," typescript, n.d.

38. Johannes Semler, *Die deutsche Spielfilm-Produktion* (Munich, March 1956), appendix 9. See also LAB, Rep. #14, Acc. 2323, #153–55, Podehl, "Beitrag," 3. Podehl compared this state of affairs with that of 1932, when 132 German films were produced and only 81 were imported for screening.

39. LAB, IFB File, 1951, letter from H. B. Baum, Verband deutscher Filmproduzenten, e.V., to Magistrat, Groß Berlin, 8 March 1951.

40. LAB, IFB File, 1951, vom 6. Juni bis 17. Juni 1951, letter from Fritz Podehl, FSK, to Herr Baensch, Berlin Senate, Abteilung Volksbildung, 28 February 1951.

41. LAB, IFB File, 1952, letter from Fritz Podehl to Joachim Tiburtius, 8 August 1951, and letter from Baum to Tiburtius, 6 September 1951. See also LAB, Beratender Ausschuß, Neuordnung der Filmwirtschaft, UFA Angelegenheiten vom 1.5.1951–30.4.1952, "Expose zum Brief an den Regierenden Bürgermeister," from the Verband der Filmschaffenden, e.V., 21 April 1952.

42. LAB, IFB File, 1952, form letter from Alfred Bauer to German film production companies, 21 April 1952. See also LAB, IFB File, 1952, "Protokoll über die dritte ordentliche Sitzung des Arbeitsausschusses der II. Internationalen Filmfestspiele Berlin," 9 May 1952, pp. 6–7.

43. LAB, IFB File, Rep. #14, Acc. 2323, #153–55, "Schlußbericht—II. Internationalen Filmfestspiele Berlin 1952," 3–4.

44. At an organizational meeting in 1952, a representative from the theater association complained that industry members were not being included in the decision-making process for the festival. No doubt this contributed to industry ambivalence regarding the festival. Industry members generally abjured involvement through 1954, a fact that various members of the festival's organizing committee bemoaned regularly. By 1954 Alfred Bauer complained that the German film industry's indifference to the festival "endangered the prestige of Germany . . . and set a bad example." Moreover, he suggested that all producers and distributors whose films were made with the help of federal or state *Bürgschaften* be compelled to offer them for screening at the festival. By the mid-1950s, there was a marked improvement in industry response. LAB, IFB File, 1952, "Protokoll über die dritte ordentliche Sitzung des Arbeitsausschusses der II. Internationalen Filmfestspiele Berlin," 9 May 1952. See also LAB, IFB File, 1952, 1953, "Schlußbericht—II. Internationalen Filmfestspiele Berlin 1952," "Protokoll über die erste Sitzung des Organisationskomitees der III. Internationalen Filmfestspiele Berlin," 10 January 1953, and "Protokoll über die vierte Sitzung des Organisationskomitees der III. Internationalen Filmfestspiele Berlin," 9 May 1953; and LBS, IFB File, "Schlußbericht der IV. Internationalen Filmfestspiele Berlin 18.–29. Juni 1954."

45. Fritz Podehl, head of the FSK, presided over the first year's jury. In addition, Johannes Eckardt, president of the Association of German Film Clubs, was a regular member of the jury between 1951 and 1965. See "Mitglied der Auswahlgremium," in *Deutscher Filmpreis*, 146–47. See also "Ein deutscher 'Oskar,'" *Die neue Zeitung* (Munich), 20 May 1951.

46. See *Deutscher Filmpreis* for a list of winning films.

47. Elsaessar, *New German Cinema*, 20.

48. The films exhibited at the 1954 festival were *Das Berliner Schloß, Sowjetische Zone, 1953/54*, filmed by a refugee from an eastern area of the old German Reich, and *Lebensnahe Kunst*, a DEFA *Kulturfilm* on the Dresden Art Exhibit of 1953. See LBS, IFB File, "Schlußbericht der IV. Internationalen Filmfestspiele Berlin 18.–29. Juni 1954"; LAB, IFB File, 1953, "Protokoll über die dritte Sitzung des Organisationskomitees der III. Internationalen Filmfestspiele Berlin 1953," 30 March 1953, p. 10; and LAB, IFB File, 1952, "Schlußbericht—II. Internationalen Filmfestspiele Berlin 1952," 3.

49. The federal government had quietly been making financial contributions to the festival since its inception but was listed publicly as a cosponsor for the first time in 1955, although its support had been increasing over the two preceding years. The Berlin Senate had requested a greater financial commitment from the federal government in the spring of 1953; the decision of the federal minister of greater German matters to comply was made in early 1954. The festival was suffering from serious financial problems at this time, and Senator Tiburtius warned that it would not be able to continue without generous support from the federal government. To emphasize the urgency of the situation, Tiburtius, in a letter to Jakob Kaiser, federal minister of greater German matters, mentioned rumors that East Berlin was organizing a competing film festival for the coming year. See LAB, Filmfestspiele/Festwochen, 1956–58, "Bericht über die Internationalen Filmfestspiele Berlin gemäß Senatsbeschluß Nr. 1830/56 vom 12. April 1956," 2–3; and LAB, IFB File, 1955, letter from Tiburtius to Kaiser, 1 November 1954. See also LBS, IFB File, "III. Internationalen Filmfestspiele Berlin 18.–28. Juni 1953, Schlußbericht," and "Schlußbericht der IV. Internationalen Filmfestspiele Berlin 18.–29. Juni 1954."

50. LAB, IFB File, 1955, transcription of letter from Secretary Schindel for Dr. Schwarz, Export-Union der deutschen Filmindustrie, e.V., to Alfred Bauer, 12 November 1954. See also LAB, IFB File, 1955, "Kurzprotokoll der 1. Sitzung des Beirates der V. Internationalen Filmfestspiele," 6 April 1955.

51. LBS, IFB File, Friedrich Luft, " 'Herrliche Zeiten' lorbeergeschmückt," *Die neue Zeitung* (Munich), 17 June 1951.

52. In 1956, for example, the Foreign Office protested the plan to screen Resnais's documentary on the Nazi death camps, *Night and Fog*, in a special showing at the festival. Senator Tiburtius urged the federal representatives on the festival Planning Committee to use their influence to disarm Foreign Office objections. LAB, IFB File, Filmfestspiele/Festwoche, 1956–58, "Protokoll der 4. Sitzung des Beirates der (VI.) Internationalen Filmfestspiele Berlin," 25 May 1956. See also chapter 6.

53. LAB, IFB File, 1957, Will Wehling, "Was wird aus der Berlinale?," *Die Welt*, 16 February 1957.

54. See chapter 7.

55. Journalists and critics nonetheless exhibited a marked cultural Eurocen-

trism in this "apolitical" discussion of film quality. The well-known film critic Ludwig Thome, for example, urged the inclusion of Eastern European and Soviet films by excoriating the quality of film products included in the festival competition from the budding national cinemas of developing countries:

> As a friend of film, and someone knowledgeable about what the East has to offer in the way of cinematography, one regrets the absence of the Soviets, but also of the Poles, Hungary, and so on. A Soviet classic such as . . . Kosinzew's *Don Quixote* . . . , an example of the outstanding Polish school as represented by the directors Wanda Jakubowska and Alexander Ford, a Hungarian documentary film by accomplished artists such as Agoston Kollanyi or Dr. Istvan Homoki-Nagy—we won't make any secret of the fact that we would rather see th[ese] than a third-class strip from Egypt, or 400 or even 4,000 meters of artistically underdeveloped celluloid from South Africa or the Far East.

See LBS, IFB File, Ludwig Thome, " 'Berlinale' ohne Sowjets: Politisch belastete Filmfestspiele/Ungelöste Probleme," *Hannoversche Presse*, 21 June 1957.

56. The output of communist propaganda was believed to be on the increase in most of the world. Soviet friendship societies were appearing in many Western democracies; the Soviet Union successfully negotiated contracts for film coproductions with France and Italy and organized a week of Soviet film in Vienna. See U.S. Information Agency, *Communist Propaganda*, 3–135. For the response of major U.S. film interests, see Warner Brothers Papers, Mudd Library, Princeton University, Princeton, New Jersey, 1408–16533, MPEA confidential memo #600, 8 August 1957.

57. The festival at Karlovy Vary was not, in the end, scheduled to compete with the Berlinale. See "Termine," *Die Welt*, 1 February 1957.

58. Caught between the need to protect the festival's reputation and ward off a putative communist cultural offensive, Bonn officials were faced with the dilemma of how to include the films of developing countries, and keep them tied to the Western cultural sphere, while maintaining adequate standards of quality. A suggestion was made to screen films deemed substandard outside of the regular competition. But the concern was raised that such action could be interpreted as imperious in nature. A satisfactory solution was never agreed upon. See LAB, IFB File, Sitzungen, "Protokollnotizen—Sitzung des Filmfestspielbeirates am 29.1.1960," and "Protokollnotizen—Betr: 9. Sitzung des Internationalen Filmfestspiele Berlin-Beirates am 19. Juli 1960."

59. LAB, Filmfestspiele/Festwochen, 1956–58, draft of memo, "Zu beiliegender Pressenotiz 'Roter Mond über Oberhausen,' " 5 December 1957.

60. Bauer suggested that the invitation for the 1959 festival be issued by the Berlin Senate. Senator Tiburtius, however, rejected the idea, commenting that "if we did that, another explanation [for their refusal to participate] would be

sent." See LAB, IFB File, Sitzungen, "Protokollnotizen—Sitzung Internationalen Filmfestspiele Berlin-Beirat," 30 May 1959. The first Soviet feature film to be shown in competition at the Berlinale (*Toboj I Bes Tebja* [*With and Without You*], directed by Rodion Nachapetov) was screened in 1974, after Willi Brandt had initiated his *Ostpolitik*. The following year, a Soviet representative sat on the international jury in Berlin, and East Germany submitted its first official entry, Frank Beyer's *Jakob der Lügner* (*Jakob the Liar*). Eastern European films did, however, periodically appear on the program after 1966, the year the federal elections in West Germany resulted in a "Grand Coalition" between the Christian Democrats and Social Democrats. A few Czechoslovakian and Yugoslavian films were shown prior to 1970; in 1969 the Berlinale sponsored a Week of Young Yugoslav Films and a special program devoted to Yugoslavian short films. The same year, a Pole sat on the international jury.

61. The Corso cinema on the eastern border sold tickets to East Germans for a mere Ostmark, and East Germans could purchase tickets to the regular festival screenings at an exchange rate of 1:1. The West German government, in effect, subsidized the visits of Germans from the East. LAB, IFB File, Sitzungen, 18.5.57–24.5.62, "Niederschrift über die 4. Sitzung des Beirates der Internationalen Filmfestspiele Berlin," 12 June 1957.

62. LAB, IFB File, 1953, "Protokoll über die vierte Sitzung des Organisationskomitees der III. Internationalen Filmfestspiele Berlin 1953," 9 May 1953. See also LAB, IFB File, Sitzungen, 18.5.57–24.5.62, "Niederschrift über die 4. Sitzung des Beirates der Internationalen Filmfestspiele Berlin," 12 June 1957.

63. LAB, IFB File, 1956, 22.6.56–3.7.56, letter from J. Albitz, Heinrich-Zille-Gesellschaft, e.V., which owned the Filmbühne am Steinplatz, to Senat für Volksbildung, 22 June 1956.

64. Memo from the Berlin Senate, Wi IV H/65, to the Abgeordnetenhaus, "Bericht über Berlin als Filmstadt," April 1965, in the library of the Deutsche Film und Fernsehen Akademie, Berlin.

65. LAB, Filmfestspiele/Festwoche, 1956–58, "Protokoll der 4. Sitzung des Beirates der (VI.) Internationalen Filmfestspiele Berlin," 25 May 1956.

CONCLUSION

1. This distinction had at least a twenty-five-year history. In the interwar years, U.S. mass culture was considered by European intellectuals to be more "modern" than European. See de Grazia, "Mass Culture and Sovereignty," 57.

2. Maase, *Bravo Amerika*, chaps. 5–7, esp. 177–91.

3. Victoria de Grazia has noted the distinction between U.S. cinema organization, which "stood for major economies of scale, capital-intensive technologies, and standardization," and the "European tradition[, which] was identified

with decentralized artisan-atelier shops[,] . . . was associated with theatrical and dramatic conventions . . . [and] . . . rested on a commercial network mediated by intellectuals." See de Grazia, "Mass Culture and Sovereignty," 61.

4. See, for example, Rentschler, "How American Is It?," 603–19, and Elsaesser, *New German Cinema*, 2.

5. Even in this age of television and video, when Germans spend only an average of three hours a year at the movies, ninety of those minutes are devoted to U.S. films and only twenty minutes to their native product. See Elsaesser, *New German Cinema*, 37.

6. Enno Patalas, interview by author, Munich, 4 August 1987.

BIBLIOGRAPHY

PRIMARY SOURCES

Akten des Bayerischen Staatsministeriums für Unterricht und Kultus,
    Bayerisches Hauptstaatsarchiv, Munich
Akten des Bürgermeisters und Rats, Stadtarchiv, Munich
Bestand: Filmwoche, 1951–85, Stadtarchiv, Mannheim
Filmarchiv, Deutsches Institut für Filmkunde, Frankfurt
    Press clippings files and microfiche
Papers of the Office of the Military Government for Germany, United States,
    Information Control Division (later Information Services Division),
    National Archives and Records Service, Suitland, Maryland
    Papers of the Director's Office
    Papers of the Motion Picture Branch
Erich Pommer Collection, University of Southern California Cinema Library,
    Los Angeles
Presse-Archiv, Landesbildstelle Berlin
Presse Archiv Sammlung der Bayerischen Staatsregierung, Munich
Schriftgutarchiv, Stiftung Deutsche Kinemathek, Berlin
Papers of the Senator für Wissenschaft und Kunst, Rep. #14, Landesarchiv
    Berlin
Warner Brothers Papers, Mudd Library, Princeton University, Princeton, N.J.

JOURNALS

Evangelischer Film-Beobachter
Filmblätter
Filmdienst
Film-Echo
film 56
Filmforum
Film-Korrespondenz
Filmkritik
Internationale Film Revue
Jugend-Film-Fernsehen
Kirche und Film
Kulturarbeit

Mannheimer Hefte
Der neue Film
Rundfunk und Fernsehen
Der Spiegel
Süddeutsche Zeitung

SECONDARY SOURCES

Abel, Richard. *French Cinema: The First Wave, 1915–1929*. Princeton: Princeton University Press, 1984.

Abelshauser, Werner. *Die langen fünfziger Jahre: Wirtschaft und Gesellschaft der Bundesrepublik Deutschland, 1949–1966*. Düsseldorf: Schwann, 1987.

Abrams, Lynn. *Workers' Culture in Imperial Germany: Leisure and Recreation in the Rhineland and Westphalia*. London: Routledge, 1992.

Albrecht, Gerd. *Nationalsozialistische Filmpolitik: Eine soziologische Untersuchung über die Spielfilme des Dritten Reiches*. Stuttgart: Ferdinand Enke Verlag, 1969.

Allen, Jeanne. "The Film Viewer as Consumer." *Quarterly Review of Film Studies* 5, no. 4 (Fall 1980): 481–99.

Anderson, Mark M., ed. "Special Issue on Siegfried Kracauer." *New German Critique* 54 (Fall 1991).

Applegate, Celia. *A Nation of Provincials: The German Idea of Heimat*. Berkeley: University of California Press, 1990.

Arbeitsgemeinschaft der deutschen Jugendfilmclubs und -gruppen im Verband der deutschen Film-Clubs, e.V. *Zur Entwicklung der Filmerziehung in den deutschen Jugendfilmclubs*. Hamburg: Alsterdruck, 1967.

Arbeitsgemeinschaft "Wir alle." *Generation ohne Sicherheit*. Wiesbaden, 1951.

Bamberger, Stefan. *Christentum und Film*. Aschaffenburg: Paul Pattloch Verlag, 1968.

Baranowski, Shelley. "Consent and Dissent: The Confessing Church and Conservative Opposition to National Socialism." *Journal of Modern History* 59 (March 1987): 53–78.

Baranski, Zygmunt G., and Robert Lumley, eds. *Culture and Conflict in Postwar Italy: Essays on Mass and Popular Culture*. New York: St. Martin's Press, 1990.

Bartov, Omer. *Hitler's Army: Soldiers, Nazis, and War in the Third Reich*. New York: Oxford University Press, 1992.

Bathrick, David. "Max Schmeling on the Canvas: Boxing as an Icon of Weimar Culture." *New German Critique* 51 (Fall 1990): 113–36.

Bathrick, David, Thomas Elsaesser, and Miriam Hansen, eds. "Special Issue on Weimar Film Theory." *New German Critique* 40 (Winter 1987).

Baumert, Gerhard. *Deutsche Familien nach dem Kriege*. Darmstadt: Eduard Roether Verlag, 1954.

——. *Jugend der Nachkriegszeit: Lebensverhältnisse und Reaktionsweisen*. Darmstadt: Eduard Roether Verlag, 1952.

Benz, Wolfgang, ed. *Die Bundesrepublik Deutschland*. Vol. 2, *Gesellschaft*. Frankfurt: Fischer Taschenbuch Verlag, 1985.

Berger, Jürgen. "Bürgen heißt zahlen—und manchmal auch zensieren: Die Filmbürgschaften des Bundes, 1950–1955." In *Zwischen Gestern und Morgen: Westdeutscher Nachkriegsfilm, 1946–1962*, edited by Hilmar Hoffmann and Walter Schobert, 80–97. Frankfurt: Deutsches Filmmuseum, 1989.

Berghahn, Volker. *The Americanisation of West German Industry, 1945–1972*. New York: Cambridge University Press, 1986.

Bessen, Ursula. *Trümmer und Träume: Nachkriegszeit und fünfziger Jahre auf Zelluloid. Deutsche Spielfilme als Zeugnisse ihrer Zeit. Eine Dokumentation*. Bochum: Studienverlag Dr. N. Brockmeyer, 1989.

Bettecken, Wilhelm. "25 Jahre Wandlungen des Kurzfilms." In *Sprache des Kurzfilms: Beispiel—25 Jahre Westdeutsche Kurzfilmtage Oberhausen*, edited by Johannes Horstmann, 124–45. Munich: Verlag Ferdinand Schöningh, 1981.

Blessing, Werner K. " 'Deutschland in Not, wir im Glauben . . .': Kirche und Kirchenvolk in einer katholischen Region, 1933–1949." In *Von Stalingrad zur Währungsreform: Zur Sozialgeschichte des Umbruchs in Deutschland*, 3d ed., Quellen und Darstellungen zur Zeitgeschichte, Institut für Zeitgeschichte, vol. 26, edited by Martin Broszat, Klaus-Dietmar Henke, and Hans Woller, 3–111. Munich: R. Oldenbourg Verlag, 1990.

Bliersbach, Gerhard. *So grün war die Heide . . . : Thema—Film: Die gar nicht so heile Welt im Nachkriegsfilm*. Weinheim: Beltz Verlag, 1985. Reprint, Weinheim: Psychologie Heute Taschenbuch, 1989.

Bock, Hans-Michael, and Michael Töteberg, eds. *Das Ufa-Buch: Kunst und Krisen, Stars und Regisseure, Wirtschaft und Politik*. Frankfurt: Zweitausendeins, 1992.

Borgelt, Hans. *Filmstadt Berlin*. Berlin: Nicolaische Verlagsbuchhandlung, 1979.

Boyens, Armin. "Die Kirchenpolitik der amerikanischen Besatzungsmacht in Deutschland von 1944 bis 1946." In *Kirchen in der Nachkriegszeit*, edited by Armin Boyens et al., 7–57. Göttingen: Vandenhoeck & Ruprecht, 1979.

Boyens, Armin, et al., eds. *Kirchen in der Nachkriegszeit*. Göttingen: Vandenhoeck & Ruprecht, 1979.

Braun, Hans. "Demographische Umschichtungen im deutschen Katholizismus nach 1945." In *Kirche und Katholizismus, 1945–1949*, edited by Anton Rauscher, 9–25. Munich: Verlag Ferdinand Schöningh, 1977.

Bredow, Wilfried von, and Rolf Zurek, eds. *Film und Gesellschaft in Deutschland: Dokumente und Materialien.* Hamburg: Hoffmann und Campe Verlag, 1975.

Broszat, Martin, ed. *Zäsuren nach 1945: Essays zur Periodisierung der deutschen Nachkriegsgeschichte.* Schriftenreihe der Vierteljahrshefte für Zeitgeschichte, vol. 61. Munich: R. Oldenbourg Verlag, 1990.

Broszat, Martin, Klaus-Dietmar Henke, and Hans Woller, eds. *Von Stalingrad zur Währungsreform: Zur Sozialgeschichte des Umbruchs in Deutschland.* 3d ed. Quellen und Darstellungen zur Zeitgeschichte, Institut für Zeitgeschichte, vol. 26. Munich: R. Oldenbourg Verlag, 1990.

Brubaker, Rogers. *Citizenship and Nationhood in France and Germany.* Cambridge: Harvard University Press, 1992.

Bucher, Willi, and Klaus Pohl. *Schock und Schöpfung: Jugendästhetik im 20. Jahrhundert.* Darmstadt: Hermann Luchterhand Verlag, 1986.

Bühler, Karl-Werner. *Die Kirchen und die Massenmedien: Intentionen und Institutionen konfessioneller Kulturpolitik in Rundfunk, Fernsehen, Film und Presse nach 1945.* Hamburg: Furche Verlag, 1968.

Byg, Barton. "Generational Conflict and Historical Continuity in GDR Film." In *Framing the Past: The Historiography of German Cinema and Television,* edited by Bruce A. Murray and Christopher J. Wickham, 197–219. Carbondale: Southern Illinois University Press, 1992.

Cadars, Pierre, and Francis Courtade. *Geschichte des Films im Dritten Reich.* Munich: Carl Hanser Verlag, 1975.

Carter, Erica. "Alice in Consumer Wonderland: West German Case Studies in Gender and Consumer Culture." In *Gender and Generation,* edited by Angela McRobbie and Mica Nava, 185–214. New York: Macmillan, 1984.

Chamberlin, Brewster S. *Kultur auf Trümmern: Berliner Berichte der amerikanischen Information Control Section Juli–Dezember 1945.* Schriftenreihe der Vierteljahrshefte für Zeitgeschichte, no. 39. Stuttgart: Deutsche Verlags-Anstalt, 1979.

Coates, Paul. *The Gorgon's Gaze: German Cinema, Expressionism, and the Image of Horror.* New York: Cambridge University Press, 1991.

Cohan, Steven, and Ina Rae Hark, eds. *Screening the Male: Exploring Masculinities in Hollywood Cinema.* New York: Routledge, 1993.

Confino, Alon. "The Nation as a Local Metaphor: Heimat, National Memory, and the German Empire, 1871–1918." *History and Memory* 5, no. 1 (1993): 42–86.

Connor, Ian. "The Churches and the Refugee Problem in Bavaria, 1945–1949." *Journal of Contemporary History* 20 (1985): 399–421.

Corrigan, Timothy. *New German Film: The Displaced Image*. Austin: University of Texas Press, 1983.

Cramer, Heinz von. "Wer zahlt—darf tanzen: Versuch einer kritischen Biographie des deutschen Films." In *Bestandsaufnahme: Eine deutsche Bilanz 1962*, edited by Hans Werner Richter, 517–42. Munich: Verlag Kurt Desch, 1962.

Culbert, David. "American Film Policy in the Re-education of Germany after 1945." In *The Political Re-education of Germany and Her Allies after World War II*, edited by Nicholas Pronay and Keith Wilson, 173–202. London: Croom Helm, 1985.

Dawson, Jan. "A Labyrinth of Subsidies: The Origins of the New German Cinema." *Sight and Sound* 50, no. 2 (Spring 1981): 102–7.

De Grazia, Victoria. "Mass Culture and Sovereignty: The American Challenge to European Cinemas, 1920–1960." *Journal of Modern History* 61 (March 1989): 53–87.

De Hadeln, Moritz. "Special Tribute: Berlin International Film Festival—Thirty-five Years of Dedication to Film." In *International Film Guide 1985*, 347–56. London: Tantivy Press, 1985.

Deutscher Filmpreis, 1951–1980. Edited by Manfred Hohnstock and Alfons Bettermann. Bonn: Bundes Innenministerium, 1980.

Diehl, James M. *The Thanks of the Fatherland: German Veterans after the Second World War*. Chapel Hill: University of North Carolina Press, 1993.

Doderer, Klaus, ed. *Zwischen Trümmern und Wohlstand: Literatur der Jugend, 1945–1960*. Weinheim: Beltz Verlag, 1988.

Doherty, Thomas. *Teenagers and Teenpics: The Juvenilization of American Movies in the 1950s*. Boston: Unwin Hyman, 1988.

Dokumentation: XXV Internationale Filmwoche Mannheim 1976. Edited by Klaus Hofmann et al. Mannheim: Internationale Filmwoche Mannheim, 1976.

Dokumentation: 30 Jahre Internationale Filmwoche Mannheim, 1951–1981. Edited by Klaus Hofmann et al. Mannheim: Internationale Filmwoche Mannheim, 1981.

Dost, Michael, Florian Hopf, and Alexander Kluge. *Filmwirtschaft in der Bundesrepublik Deutschland und in Europa: Götterdämmerung in Raten*. Munich: Carl Hanser Verlag, 1973.

Drewniak, Boguslaw. *Der deutsche Film, 1938–1945: Ein Gesamtüberblick*. Düsseldorf: Droste Verlag, 1987.

Dyer, Richard. "Entertainment and Utopia." In *Movies and Methods*, vol. 2, edited by Bill Nichols, 220–32. Berkeley: University of California Press, 1985.

———. "Less and More Than Women and Men: Lesbian and Gay Cinema in Weimar Germany." *New German Critique* 51 (Fall 1990): 5–60.

———. *Now You See It: Studies on Lesbian and Gay Film*. New York: Routledge, 1990.

Eisenführ, Julieanne. "Die Sünderin: Geschichte und Analyse eines Kinoskandals." Master's thesis, Universität Osnabrück, 1982.

Eisner, Lotte. *The Haunted Screen*. Berkeley: University of California Press, 1973.

Eksteins, Modris. "War, Memory, and Politics: The Fate of the Film *All Quiet on the Western Front*." *Central European History* 13, no. 1 (1980): 60–82.

Elkins, Thomas Henry, and Burkhard Hofmeister. *Berlin: The Spatial Structure of a Divided City*. New York: Methuen, 1988.

Elsaesser, Thomas. *New German Cinema: A History*. New Brunswick, N.J.: Rutgers University Press, 1989.

Erens, Patricia, ed. *Issues in Feminist Film Criticism*. Bloomington: Indiana University Press, 1990.

Ermarth, Michael, ed. *America and the Shaping of German Society, 1945– 1955*. Providence: Berg, 1993.

Feldmann, Erich, and Walter Hagemann, eds. *Der Film als Beeinflüßungsmittel: Vorträge und Berichte der 2. Jahrestagung der Deutschen Gesellschaft für Filmwissenschaft*. Emsdetten: Verlag Lechte, 1955.

Filmstudien: Beiträge des Filmseminars im Institut für Publizistik an der Universität Muenster. 3 vols. Edited by Walter Hagemann. Emsdetten: Verlag Lechte, 1952, 1954, 1957.

Film und Kirche: Die wichtigsten Referate der Schwalbacher Tagung, 21.–25. Juni 1950. Munich: Verlag des Evangelischen Presseverbandes für Bayern, 1950.

Fischer, Kurt J. "Die Krise des deutschen Films: Wirtschaftliche Tatsache und Möglichkeiten." *Politische Meinung* 10 (1957): 49–62.

Ford, Charles. *Der Film und der Glaube*. Translated by Pierre Pascal. Nuremberg: Glock & Lutz, 1955.

Forster, Karl. "Entwicklungslinien in den Beziehungen von Kirche und Staat, 1949–1963." In *Kirche und Staat in der Bundesrepublik, 1949–1963*, edited by Anton Rauscher, 41–68. Munich: Verlag Ferdinand Schöningh, 1979.

Franklin, James. *New German Cinema: From Oberhausen to Hamburg*. Boston: Twayne Publishers, 1983.

Frei, Norbert. "Wie modern war der Nationalsozialismus?" *Geschichte und Gesellschaft* 19 (1993): 367–87.

Freier, Anna-Elisabeth, and Annette Kuhn, eds. *Frauen in der Geschichte*. Vol. 5, *"Das Schicksal Deutschlands liegt in der Hand seiner Frauen"—Frauen in der deutschen Nachkriegszeit*. Düsseldorf: Schwann, 1984.

Freud, Sigmund. "The Psycho-Analytic View of Psychogenic Disturbance of Vision (1910)." In *The Standard Edition of the Complete Psychological*

Works of Sigmund Freud, vol. 11, edited by James Strachey, 211–18. London: Hogarth Press, 1964.

Frevert, Ute. *Women in German History: From Bourgeois Emancipation to Sexual Liberation.* Translated by Stuart McKinnon-Evans. New York: Berg, 1988.

Frieden, Sandra, et al., eds. *Gender and German Cinema: Feminist Interventions.* Vol. 1, *Gender and Representation in New German Cinema.* Vol. 2, *German Film History/German History on Film.* Providence: Berg, 1993.

Friedrich, Thomas. *Berlin between the Wars.* New York: Vendome Press, 1991.

Frundt, Bodo, and Bernd Lepel. *Traüme unter Goldenen Palmen: Der deutsche Film auf dem Internationalen Filmfestival in Cannes.* Ebersberg: Edition Achteinhalb, Lothar Just, 1987.

Gießler, Dieter. "Filmzensur im Nachkriegsdeutschland." Ph.D. dissertation, Universität Osnabrück, 1986.

Gilbert, James. *A Cycle of Outrage: America's Reaction to the Juvenile Delinquent in the 1950s.* New York: Oxford University Press, 1986.

Gimbel, John. *The American Occupation of Germany: Politics and the Military, 1945–1949.* Stanford: Stanford University Press, 1968.

Gledhill, Christine, ed. *Home Is Where the Heart Is: Studies in Melodrama and the Woman's Film.* London: British Film Institute, 1987.

Golsan, Richard J. *Fascism, Aesthetics, and Culture.* Hanover, N.H.: University Press of New England, 1992.

Greschat, Martin. "Kirche und Öffentlichkeit in der deutschen Nachkriegszeit (1945–1949)." In *Kirchen in der Nachkriegszeit,* edited by Anton Rauscher, 100–124. Munich: Verlag Ferdinand Schöningh, 1977.

Grossmann, Atina. "*Girlkultur* or Thoroughly Rationalized Female: A New Woman in Weimar Germany?" In *Women in Culture and Politics: A Century of Change,* edited by Judith Friedlander et al., 62–80. Bloomington: Indiana University Press, 1986.

———. "The New Woman and the Rationalization of Sexuality in Weimar Germany." In *Powers of Desire: The Politics of Sexuality,* edited by Ann Snitow, Christine Stansell, and Sharon Thompson, 153–71. New York: Monthly Review Press, 1983.

———. " 'Satisfaction Is Domestic Happiness': Mass Working-Class Sex Reform Organizations in the Weimar Republic." In *Towards the Holocaust: The Social and Economic Collapse of the Weimar Republic,* edited by Michael N. Dobkowski and Isidor Wallimann, 265–93. Westport, Conn.: Greenwood Press, 1983.

Guback, Thomas. *The International Film Industry: Western Europe and America since 1945.* Bloomington: Indiana University Press, 1969.

———. "Shaping the Film Business in Postwar Germany: The Role of the U.S.

Film Industry and the U.S. State." In *The Hollywood Film Industry*, edited by Paul Kerr, 245–75. New York: Routledge, 1986.

Gundle, Stephen. "From Neo-Realism to *Luci Rosse*: Cinema, Politics, Society, 1945–1985." In *Culture and Conflict in Postwar Italy: Essays on Mass and Popular Culture*, edited by Zygmunt G. Baranski and Robert Lumley, 195–224. New York: St. Martin's Press, 1990.

Hack, Lothar. "Filmzensur in der Bundesrepublik: I. Das gefährliche Zelluloid; II. Die Gouvernante; III. Die Schweigepflicht." *Frankfurter Hefte* 19, nos. 10, 11, 12 (October–December 1964): 705–16, 785–92, 849–58.

Haftendorn, Helga. "Zusammensetzung und Verhalten des Filmtheaterpublikums in der Mittelstadt." In *Filmstudien: Beiträge des Filmseminars im Institut für Publizistik an der Universität Muenster*, edited by Walter Hagemann, 3:13–25. Emsdetten: Verlag Lechte, 1957.

Hake, Sabine. "Chaplin Reception in Weimar Germany." *New German Critique* 51 (Fall 1990): 87–111.

———. *The Cinema's Third Machine: Writing on Film in Germany, 1907–1933*. Lincoln: University of Nebraska Press, 1993.

———. "New German Cinema." *Monatshefte* 82, no. 3 (1990): 267–75.

Hansen, Miriam. "Decentric Perspectives: Kracauer's Early Writings on Film and Mass Culture." *New German Critique* 54 (Fall 1991): 47–76.

———. "Early Silent Cinema: Whose Public Sphere?" *New German Critique* 29 (Spring/Summer 1983): 147–84.

Hardt, Ursula. "Erich Pommer: Film Producer for Germany." Ph.D. dissertation, University of Iowa, 1989.

Hartenian, Larry. "The Role of Media in Democratizing Germany: United States Occupation Policy, 1945–1949." *Central European Studies* 20, no. 2 (June 1987): 145–90.

Hartlieb, Horst von. "Grundgesetz, Filmzensur, und Selbstkontrolle." In *Archiv für Urheber-, Film-, Funk-, und Theaterrecht*, Schriftenreihe der UFITA, 15:29–89.

Haß, Kurt. *Jugend unterm Schicksal: Lebensberichte junger Deutscher, 1946–1949*. Hamburg: Christian Wegner Verlag, 1950.

Heerman, Wilhelm. "Die Entwicklung der deutschen Filmwirtschaft von 1945 bis 1955." Master's thesis, Universität Osnabrück, 1983.

Heller, Reinhold. "Confronting Contradictions: Artists and Their Institutions in Wilhelmine and Weimar Germany." In *Art in Germany, 1909–1936: From Expressionism to Resistance*, edited by Reinhold Heller, 17–24. Munich: Prestel Verlag, 1990.

Helmreich, Ernst Christian. *The German Churches under Hitler: Background, Struggle, and Epilogue*. Detroit: Wayne State University Press, 1979.

Helt, Richard, and Marie E. Helt. *West German Cinema since 1945: A Reference Handbook*. Metuchen, N.J.: Scarecrow Press, 1987.

Hembus, Joe. *Der deutsche Film kann gar nicht besser sein: Ein Pamphlet von gestern—Eine Abrechnung von heute.* Introduction by Laurens Straub. Munich: Rogner & Bernhard, 1981.

Henseleit, Felix, ed. *Die Internationalen Filmfestspiele Berlin von 1951–1974 im Zeitraffer.* Berlin: Internationale Filmfestspiele Berlin, 1975.

Hermand, Jost. "All Power to the Women: Nazi Concepts of Matriarchy." *Journal of Contemporary History* 19, no. 4 (1984): 649–67.

Higonnet, Margaret Randolph, et al., eds. *Behind the Lines: Gender and the Two World Wars.* New Haven: Yale University Press, 1987.

Hiller, Jim, ed. *Cahiers du Cinema: The 1950s—Neo-Realism, Hollywood, New Wave.* Cambridge: Harvard University Press, 1985.

Hobsbawm, Eric. "Introduction: Inventing Traditions." In *The Invention of Tradition,* edited by Eric Hobsbawm and T. Ranger, 1–14. New York: Cambridge University Press, 1988.

Hoenisch, Michael. "Film as an Instrument of the U.S. Reeducation Program in Germany after 1945 and the Example of 'Todesmühlen.'" *Englisch-Amerikanische Studien* 1/2 (1982): 196–210.

Hoerning, Erika M. "Frauen als Kriegsbeute: Der Zwei-Fronten-Krieg. Beispiele aus Berlin." In *"Wir kriegen jetzt andere Zeiten"—Auf der Suche nach der Erfahrung des Volkes in nachfaschistischen Ländern: Lebensgeschichte und Sozialkultur im Ruhrgebiet 1930 bis 1960,* vol. 3, edited by Lutz Niethammer and Alexander von Plato. Berlin: Verlag J. H. W. Dietz Nachf., 1985.

Hoffmann, Hilmar. *"Und die Fahne führt uns in die Ewigkeit": Propaganda im NS-Film.* Frankfurt: Fischer Taschenbuch Verlag, 1988.

Hoffmann, Hilmar, and Walter Schobert, eds. *Zwischen Gestern und Morgen: Westdeutscher Nachkriegsfilm, 1946–1962.* Frankfurt: Deutsches Filmmuseum, 1989.

Höfig, Willi. *Der deutsche Heimatfilm, 1947–1960.* Stuttgart: Ferdinand Enke Verlag, 1973.

Holloway, Ronald. *O Is for Oberhausen: Weg zum Nachbarn.* Oberhausen: Verlag Karl Maria Laufen, 1979.

Horak, Jan-Christopher. *Fluchtpunkt Hollywood: Eine Dokumentation zur Filmemigration nach 1933.* 2d ed. Münster: MAKS Publikationen, 1986.

Horkheimer, Max, and Theodor W. Adorno. "The Culture Industry: Enlightenment as Mass Deception." In *Dialectic of Enlightenment,* translated by John Cumming, 120–67. New York: Continuum, 1991.

Horn, Wolfgang. *Kulturpolitik in Düsseldorf: Situation und Neubeginn nach 1945.* Opladen: Leske und Budrich, 1981.

Hübinger, Paul Egon. "Die Mannheimer Kultur- und Dokumentarfilmwoche aus der Sicht des Bundes." *Mannheimer Hefte* 1 (1958): 20–22.

Hudemann, Rainer. "Anfänge der Wiedergutmachung: Französische

Besatzungszone, 1945–1950." *Geschichte und Gesellschaft* 13 (1987): 181–216.

Hull, David Stewart. *Film in the Third Reich: A Study of the German Cinema, 1933–1945*. Berkeley: University of California Press, 1969.

Huyssen, Andreas. "Mass Culture as Woman: Modernism's Other." In *Studies in Entertainment: Critical Approaches to Mass Culture*, edited by Tania Modleski, 188–207. Bloomington: Indiana University Press, 1986.

Jacobsen, Wolfgang. *Berlinale: Internationale Filmfestspiele Berlin*. Berlin: Argon and Stiftung Deutsche Kinemathek, 1990.

Jaeger, Klaus, and Helmut Regel. *Deutschland in Trümmern: Filmdokumente der Jahre 1945–1949*. Oberhausen: Verlag Karl Maria Laufen, 1976.

James, Harold. *A German Identity, 1770–1990*. New York: Routledge, 1989.

Jansen, Peter W., and Wolfram Schütte, eds. *Herzog/Kluge/Straub*. Reihe Hanser 217, Reihe Film 9. Munich: Carl Hanser Verlag, 1976.

Jarvie, Ian. *Hollywood's Overseas Campaign: The North Atlantic Movie Trade, 1920–1950*. New York: Cambridge University Press, 1992.

Joesten, Joachim. "The German Film Industry, 1945–1948." New Germany Reports, no. 3. Typescript. Great Barrington, Mass., 1948.

Joseph, Robert. "Our Film Program in Germany: How Far Was It a Success?" *Hollywood Quarterly* 2, no. 2 (January 1947): 122–30.

Jung, Fernand. "Das Kino der frühen Jahre: Herbert Vesely und die Filmavantgarde der Bundesrepublik." In *Zwischen Gestern und Morgen: Westdeutscher Nachkriegsfilm, 1946–1962*, edited by Hilmar Hoffmann and Walter Schobert, 318–37. Frankfurt: Deutsches Filmmuseum, 1989.

Kaes, Anton. "The Debate about Cinema: Charting a Controversy (1909–1929)." *New German Critique* 40 (Winter 1987): 7–33.

———. *From Hitler to Heimat: The Return of History as Film*. Cambridge: Harvard University Press, 1989.

———. "Mass Culture and Modernity: Notes Toward a Social History of Early American and German Cinema." In *America and the Germans: An Assessment of a Three-Hundred-Year History*, vol. 2, *The Relationship in the Twentieth Century*, edited by Frank Trommler and Joseph McVeigh, 317–31. Philadelphia: University of Pennysylvania Press, 1990.

———. "Silent Cinema." *Monatshefte* 82, no. 3 (1990): 246–56.

———, ed. *Kino-Debatte: Texte zum Verhältnis von Literatur und Film, 1910–1929*. Munich: Deutscher Taschenbuchverlag, 1978.

———. *Weimarer Republik: Manifeste und Dokumente zur deutschen Literatur, 1918–1933*. Stuttgart: J. B. Metzlersche Verlagsbuchhandlung und Carl Ernst Poeschel Verlag, 1983.

Kater, Michael. *Different Drummers: Jazz in the Culture of Nazi Germany*. New York: Oxford University Press, 1992.

——. "Forbidden Fruit: Jazz in the Third Reich." *American Historical Review* 94, no. 1 (February 1989): 11–43.

Keilhacker, Martin, and Margarethe Keilhacker. *Jugend und Spielfilme: Erlebnisweisen und Einflüsse.* Stuttgart: Ernst Klett Verlag, 1953.

Kershaw, Ian. *The Hitler Myth: Image and Reality in the Third Reich.* New York: Oxford University Press, 1987.

——. "How Effective Was Nazi Propaganda?" In *Nazi Propaganda: The Power and the Limitations,* edited by David Welch, 180–205. Totowa, N.J.: Barnes and Noble Books, 1983.

——. *Popular Opinion and Political Dissent in the Third Reich: Bavaria, 1933–1945.* New York: Oxford University Press, 1983.

Kirchhoff, Gerhard, ed. *Views of Berlin: From a Boston Symposium.* Boston: Birkhaeuser, 1989.

Kleßmann, Christoph. *Die doppelte Staatsgründung: Deutsche Geschichte, 1945–1955.* Göttingen: Vandenhoeck & Ruprecht, 1982.

Knietzsch, Horst. *Wolfgang Staudte.* Berlin: Henschelverlag, 1966.

Knight, Julia. *Women and the New German Cinema.* New York: Verso, 1992.

Koch, Krischen. *Die Bedeutung des "Oberhauseners Manifestes" für die Filmentwicklung in der Bundesrepublik Deutschland.* Frankfurt: Peter Lang Verlag, 1985.

König, E., and W. E. Hintz, eds. *10 Jahre Berliner Filmclub, 1949–1959.* Berlin: Graphische Gesellschaft Grünewald, 1959.

Korte, Helmut, ed. *Film und Realität in der Weimarer Republik.* Munich: Carl Hanser Verlag, 1978.

Kracauer, Siegfried. "Cult of Distraction: On Berlin's Picture Palaces." Translated by Thomas Y. Levin. *New German Critique* 40 (Winter 1987): 91–96.

——. *From Caligari to Hitler: A Psychological History of the German Film.* Princeton: Princeton University Press, 1974.

Kramer, Alan. " 'Law-Abiding Germans'?: Social Disintegration, Crime, and the Reimposition of Order in Post-War Western Germany, 1945–1949." In *The German Underworld: Deviants and Outcasts in German History,* edited by Richard Evans, 238–61. London: Routledge, 1988.

Kreimeier, Klaus. *Kino und Filmindustrie in der BRD: Ideologieproduktion und Klassenwirklichkeit nach 1945.* Kronberg: Scriptor Verlag, 1973.

Kreuder, Thomas. "Ist die FSK verfassungswidrig?: Bereits 1958 beantwortet Johanne Noltenius diese Frage mit Ja." *Frauen und Film* 35 (October 1983): 78–87.

Kreuter, Wolfgang, and Joachim Oltmann. "Coca-Cola statt Apfelmost: Kalter Krieg und Amerikanisierung westdeutscher Lebensweise." *Englisch-Amerikanische Studien* 1 (March 1984): 22–35.

Krings, Hermann. *Was heißt wertvoll: Über Grundlagen und Maßstab der Filmbewertung.* 2d ed. Wiesbaden-Biebrich: Filmbewertungsstelle Wiesbaden, 1961.

Kroker, Arthur, and Marilouise Kroker, eds. *The Hysterical Male: New Feminist Theory.* New York: St. Martin's Press, 1991.

Krüger, Heinz-Hermann, ed. *"Die Elvis-Tolle, die hatte ich mir unauffällig wachsen lassen": Lebensgeschichte und jugendliche Alltagskultur in den fünfziger Jahren.* Opladen: Leske Verlag und Budrich, 1985.

Kuhn, Annette, ed. *Frauen in der deutschen Nachkriegszeit: Frauenpolitik, 1945–1949.* Vol. 2 of *Quellen und Materialien,* edited by Annette Kuhn. Düsseldorf: Pädagogischer Verlag Schwann-Bagel, 1986.

Kurowski, Ulrich, Michael Brandlmeier, and Andre Gerely. *Nicht mehr fliehen: Das Kino der Ära Adenauer.* Munich: Freunde des Münchner Filmmuseum, e.V., in Zusammanarbeit mit den Filmmuseum München, Abteilung Film, n.d.

——. "Was ist ein deutscher Film?" *Film-Korrespondenz* 11 (November 1973).

Labanyi, Peter. "Images of Fascism: Visualization and Aestheticization in the Third Reich." In *The Burden of German History, 1919–1945,* edited by M. Laffan, 151–77. London: Methuen, 1988.

Leiser, Erwin. *Nazi Cinema.* New York: Macmillan, 1974.

Lenman, Robin. "Mass Culture and the State in Germany, 1900–1926." In *Ideas into Politics: Aspects of European History, 1880–1950,* edited by R. J. Bullen, H. Pogge von Strandmann, and A. B. Polonsky, 51–59. Totowa, N.J.: Barnes and Noble Books, 1984.

Liebe, Ulrich. *Verehrt, verfolgt, vergessen: Schauspieler als Naziopfer.* Weinheim: Beltz Quadriga, 1992.

Loewenstein, Joseph, and Lynn Tatlock. "The Marshall Plan at the Movies: Marlene Dietrich and Her Incarnations." *German Quarterly* 65, nos. 3/4 (Summer/Fall 1992): 429–42.

Loth, Wilfried. "Soziale Bewegungen im Katholizismus des Kaiserreichs." *Geschichte und Gesellschaft* 17 (1991): 279–310.

Löwenthal, Richard. "Cultural Change and Generation Change in Postwar Western Germany." In *The Federal Republic of Germany and the United States: Changing Political, Social, and Economic Relations,* edited by James A. Cooney et al., 34–55. Boulder: Westview Press, 1984.

Lowry, Stephen. *Pathos und Politik: Ideologie in Spielfilmen des Nationalsozialismus.* Tübingen: Max Niemeyer Verlag, 1991.

Lyon, James K. "Bertolt Brecht's Hollywood Years: The Dramatist as Film Writer." *Oxford German Studies* 6 (1971/72): 145–74.

Maase, Kaspar. *Bravo Amerika: Erkundungen zur Jugendkultur der Bundesrepublik in den fünfziger Jahren.* Hamburg: Junius Verlag, 1992.

Malzahn, Manfred, ed. *Germany, 1945–1949: A Sourcebook*. New York: Routledge, 1991.

Marquardt, Axel, ed. *Internationale Filmfestspiele Berlin, 1951–1984: Filme, Namen, Zahlen*. Berlin: Internationale Filmfestspiele Berlin, [1985].

Mason, Tim. "Women in Germany, 1925–1940: Family, Welfare, and Work." *History Workshop* 1 (Spring 1976): 74–113; 2 (Fall 1976): 5–32.

Mayne, Judith. *Cinema and Spectatorship*. London: Routledge, 1993.

Merritt, Anna J., and Richard L. Merritt, eds. *Public Opinion in Occupied Germany*. Urbana: University of Illinois Press, 1970.

———. *Public Opinion in Semi-Sovereign Germany: The HICOG Surveys, 1949–1955*. Urbana: University of Illinois Press, 1980.

Meyer, Sibylle, and Eva Schulze. " 'Als wir wieder zusammen waren, ging der Krieg im Kleinen weiter': Frauen, Männer, und Familien im Berlin der vierziger Jahre." In *"Wir kriegen jetzt andere Zeiten"—Auf der Suche nach der Erfahrung des Volkes in nachfaschistischen Ländern: Lebensgeschichte und Sozialkultur im Ruhrgebiet 1930 bis 1960*, vol. 3, edited by Lutz Niethammerand Alexander von Plato. Berlin: Verlag J. H. W. Dietz Nachf., 1985.

———. *Von Liebe sprach damals keiner: Familienalltag in der Nachkriegszeit*. Munich: C. H. Beck Verlag, 1985.

———. *Wie wir das alles geschafft haben: Alleinstehende Frauen berichten über ihr Leben nach 1945*. Munich: C. H. Beck Verlag, 1985.

Mizejewski, Linda. *Divine Decadence: Fascism, Female Spectacle, and the Makings of Sally Bowles*. Princeton: Princeton University Press, 1992.

Moeller, Robert G. "The Homosexual Man Is a 'Man,' the Homosexual Woman Is a 'Woman': Sex, Society, and the Law in Postwar West Germany." *Journal of the History of Sexuality* 4, no. 3 (January 1994): 395–429.

———. *Protecting Motherhood: Women and the Family in the Politics of Postwar West Germany*. Berkeley: University of California Press, 1993.

———. "Protecting Mother's Work: From Production to Reproduction in Postwar West Germany." *Journal of Social History* 22, no. 3 (Spring 1989): 413–37.

———. "Reconstructing the Family in Reconstruction Germany: Women and Social Policy in the Federal Republic, 1949–1955." *Feminist Studies* 15, no. 1 (Spring 1989): 137–69.

Monaco, Paul. *Cinema and Society: France and Germany during the Twenties*. New York: Elsevier Scientific Publishing Company, 1976.

Mosse, George. "Two World Wars and the Myth of War Experience." *Journal of Contemporary History* 21 (1986): 491–513.

Mühl-Benninghaus, Wolfgang. "Verbotene Leinwand: Filmzensur." *Film und Fernsehen* 6 (1987): 46–52.

Muhlen, Norbert. "The Return of Goebbels's Filmmakers." *Commentary* 11, no. 3 (March 1951): 245–50.

Müller, Heinz, ed. *Film in der Bundesrepublik Deutschland*. Berlin: Henschelverlag, 1990.

Murray, Bruce A. *Film and the German Left in the Weimar Republic*. Austin: University of Texas Press, 1990.

———. "An Introduction to the Commercial Film Industry in Germany from 1895 to 1933." In *Film and Politics in the Weimar Republic*, edited by Thomas G. Plummer et al., 23–33. New York: Holmes and Meier, 1982.

Niethammer, Lutz. *Entnazifizierung in Bayern*. Frankfurt: S. Fischer, 1972.

Noltenius, Johanne. *Die Freiwillige Selbstkontrolle der Filmwirtschaft und das Zensurverbot des Grundgesetzes*. Göttingen: Verlag Otto Schwarz, 1958.

Oosterhuis, Harry, ed. *Homosexuality and Male Bonding in Pre-Nazi Germany: The Youth Movement, the Gay Movement, and Male Bonding before Hitler's Rise*. Binghamton, N.Y.: Harrington Park Press, 1991.

Opfermann, H. C. *Deutsche Filmkrise—Ihre Ursachen und ihre Überwindung*. N.p., n.d.

Orbanz, Eva, and Hans Helmut Prinzler, eds. *Staudte*. Edition Filme 6. Berlin: Volker Spiess, 1991.

Osterland, Martin. *Gesellschaftsbilder in Filmen: Eine soziologische Untersuchung des Filmangebots der Jahre 1949 bis 1964*. Stuttgart: Ferdinand Enke Verlag, 1970.

Padgett, Stephen, and Tony Burkett. *Political Parties and Elections in West Germany*. New York: St. Martin's Press, 1986.

Paech, Anna. "Schule der Zuschauer: Zur Geschichte der deutschen Film Club-Bewegung." In *Zwischen Gestern und Morgen: Westdeutscher Nachkriegsfilm, 1946–1962*, edited by Hilmar Hoffmann and Walter Schobert, 226–45. Frankfurt: Deutsches Filmmuseum, 1989.

Patalas, Enno. "Vom deutschen Nachkriegsfilm." In *Filmstudien: Beiträge des Filmseminars im Institut für Publizistik an der Universität Muenster*, vol. 1, edited by Walter Hagemann, 13–28. Emsdetten: Verlag Lechte, 1952.

Petley, Julian. *Capital and Culture: German Cinema, 1933–1945*. London: British Film Institute, 1979.

Petro, Patrice. *Joyless Streets: Women and Melodramatic Representation in Weimar Germany*. Princeton: Princeton University Press, 1989.

Petzke, Ingo. *Der deutsche Experimentalfilm der 6oer und 7oer Jahre*. Munich: Goethe Institut, 1990.

Peukert, Detlev J. K. *Inside Nazi Germany: Conformity, Opposition, and Racism in Everyday Life*. Translated by Richard Deveson. New Haven: Yale University Press, 1987.

———. "Youth in the Third Reich." In *Life in the Third Reich*, edited by Richard Bessel, 25–40. New York: Oxford University Press, 1987.

Pflaum, H. G., and H. H. Prinzler. *Film in der Bundesrepublik Deutschland*. Munich: Carl Hanser Verlag, 1979.

Pleyer, Peter. *Deutscher Nachkriegsfilm, 1946–1948*. Münster: Verlag C. J. Fahle, 1965.

Plummer, Thomas G., et al., eds. *Film and Politics in the Weimar Republic*. New York: Holmes and Meier, 1982.

Prinz, Friedrich, and Marita Krauss. *Trümmerleben: Texte, Dokumente, Bilder aus den Münchner Nachkriegsjahren*. Munich: Deutscher Taschenbuch Verlag, 1985.

Prinz, Michael, and Rainer Zitelmann, eds. *Nationalsozialismus und Modernisierung*. Darmstadt: Wissenschaftliche Buchgesellschaft, 1991.

Projektgruppe deutscher Heimatfilm. *Der deutsche Heimatfilm—Bildwelten und Weltbilder: Bilder, Texte, Analysen zu 70 Jahren deutscher Filmgeschichte*. Tübingen: Tübinger Vereinigung für Volkskunde, e.V., 1989.

Prokop, Dieter. *Soziologie des Films*. Neuwied: Hermann Luchterhand Verlag, 1970.

Pronay, Nicholas, and Keith Wilson. *The Political Re-education of Germany and Her Allies after World War II*. London: Croom Helm, 1985.

Pütz, Karl Heinz. "Business or Propaganda?: American Films and Germany, 1942–1946." *Englisch-Amerikanische Studien* 2/3 (1983): 394–415.

Rauscher, Anton, ed. *Kirche und Katholizismus, 1945–1949*. Munich: Verlag Ferdinand Schöningh, 1977.

———. *Kirche und Staat in der Bundesrepublik, 1949–1963*. Munich: Verlag Ferdinand Schöningh, 1979.

Regel, Helmut. "Der Film als Instrument alliierter Besatzungspolitik in Westdeutschland." In *Deutschland in Trümmern: Filmdokumente der Jahre 1945–1949*, edited by Klaus Jaeger and Helmut Regel, 39–50. Oberhausen: Verlag Karl Maria Laufen, 1976.

Rentschler, Eric. "The Elemental, the Ornamental, the Instrumental: *The Blue Light* and Nazi Film Aesthetics." In *The Other Perspective in Gender and Culture: Rewriting Women and the Symbolic*, edited by Juliet Flower MacCannell, 161–88. New York: Columbia University Press, 1990.

———. "German Feature Films, 1933–1945." *Monatshefte* 82, no. 3 (1990): 257–66.

———. "Germany: The Past That Would Not Go Away." In *World Cinema since 1945*, edited by William Luhr, 208–51. New York: Ungar Publishing Company, 1987.

———. "How American Is It?: The U.S. as Image and Imaginary in German Film." *German Quarterly* (Fall 1984): 603–19.

———. "Mountains and Modernity: Relocating the *Bergfilm*." *New German Critique* 51 (Fall 1990): 137–61.

——. "Remembering Not to Forget: A Retrospective Reading of Kluge's *Brutality in Stone.*" *New German Critique* 49 (Winter 1990): 23–41.

——. "The Triumph of Male Will: Münchhausen (1943)." *Film Quarterly* 43, no. 3 (Spring 1990): 15–23.

——. *West German Film in the Course of Time.* Redford Hills, N.Y.: Redgrave Publishing Company, 1984.

——, ed. *German Film and Literature: Adaptations and Transformations.* New York: Methuen, 1986.

——. *West German Filmmakers on Film: Visions and Voices.* New York: Holmes and Meier, 1988.

Ribbe, Wolfgang, ed. *Geschichte Berlins.* Vol. 2, *Von der Märzrevolution bis zur Gegenwart.* Munich: C. H. Beck Verlag, 1987.

Riess, Curt. *Das gibt's nur einmal: Das Buch des deutschen Films nach 1945.* Hamburg: Henri Nannen Verlag, 1958.

Roeber, Georg, and Gerhard Jacoby. *Handbuch der filmwirtschaftlichen Medienbereiche: Die wirtschaftlichen Erscheinungsformen des Films auf den Gebieten der Unterhaltung, der Werbung, der Bildung, und des Fernsehens.* Pullach: Verlag Dokumentation, 1973.

Rogoff, Irit, ed. *The Divided Heritage: Themes and Problems in German Modernism.* New York: Cambridge University Press, 1990.

Romani, Cinzia. *Tainted Goddesses: Female Film Stars of the Third Reich.* Translated by Robert Connolly. New York: Sarpedon Publishers, 1992.

Rosenberg, Emily S. *Spreading the American Dream: American Economic and Cultural Expansion, 1890–1945.* New York: Hill and Wang, 1982.

Roth, Wilhelm. *Dreißig Jahre Oberhausen: Eine Kritische Retrospektive.* Oberhausen: Verlag Karl Maria Laufen, 1984.

Ruge, Wolfgang. "Üb 'immer Treu' und Redlichkeit: Imperialismus und Film, 1900–1945." *Film und Fernsehen* 6 (1987): 25–28.

Ruhl, Klaus-Jörg, ed. *Deutschland 1945: Alltag zwischen Krieg und Frieden in Berichten, Dokumenten, und Bildern.* Darmstadt: Luchterhand, 1984.

——. *Frauen in der Nachkriegszeit, 1945–1963: Dokumente.* Munich: Deutscher Taschenbuch Verlag, 1988.

——. *"Mein Gott, was soll aus Deutschland werden?": Die Adenauer-Ära, 1949–1963.* Munich: Deutscher Taschenbuch Verlag, 1985.

Rupieper, Hermann-Josef. "Bringing Democracy to the Frauleins: Frauen als Zielgruppe der amerikanischen Demokratisierungspolitik in Deutschland, 1945–1952." *Geschichte und Gesellschaft* 17 (1991): 61–91.

Sandford, John. *The New German Cinema.* London: Oswald Wolff, 1980.

Saunders, Thomas J. "Comedy as Redemption: American Slapstick in Weimar Culture." *Journal of European Studies* 17 (1987): 253–77.

——. "History in the Making: Weimar Cinema and National Identity." In

Framing the Past: The Historiography of German Cinema and Television,
edited by Bruce A. Murray and Christopher J. Wickham, 42–67.
Carbondale: Southern Illinois University Press, 1992.

——. *Hollywood in Berlin: American Cinema and Weimar Germany.*
Berkeley: University of California Press, 1994.

——. "Politics, the Cinema, and Early Revisitations of War in Weimar
Germany." *Canadian Journal of History* 23 (April 1988): 25–48.

Schäfer, Hans Dieter. *Das gespaltene Bewußtsein: Über deutsche Kultur und
Lebenswirklichkeit, 1933–1945.* Munich: Carl Hanser Verlag, 1981.

Schlüpmann, Heide. " 'Das Leben ist viel zu kurz, um sich einen deutschen
Film anzusehen': Ein Gespräch mit Eva M. J. Schmid." *Frauen und Film* 35
(October 1983): 62–77.

Schmidt-Harzbach, Ingrid. "Eine Woche im April: Berlin 1945—
Vergewaltigung als Massenschicksal." *Feministische Studien* 2 (November
1984): 51–65.

Schmieding, Walther. *Kunst oder Kasse: Der Ärger mit dem deutschen Film.*
Hamburg: Rütten und Loening, 1961.

Schmitt, Heiner. *Kirche und Film: Kirchliche Filmarbeit in Deutschland von
ihren Anfängen bis 1945.* Schriften des Bundesarchivs, no. 26. Boppard am
Rhein: Harald Boldt Verlag, 1979.

Schnurre, Wolfdietrich. *Rettung des deutschen Films: Eine Streitschrift.*
Stuttgart: Deutsche Verlags-Anstalt, 1950.

Schörken, Rolf. "Jugendalltag im Dritten Reich: Die 'Normalität' in der
Diktatur." In *Geschichte im Alltag—Alltag in der Geschichte,* edited by
Klaus Bergmann and Rolf Schörken, 237–46. Düsseldorf: Pädagogischer
Verlag Schwann, 1982.

Schubert, Doris, ed. *Frauen in der deutschen Nachkriegszeit: Frauenarbeit,
1945–1949.* Vol. 1 of *Quellen und Materialien,* edited by Annette Kuhn.
Düsseldorf: Pädagogischer Verlag Schwann-Bagel, 1984.

Schulberg, Stuart. "The German Film: Comeback or Setback?" In *Quarterly of
Film, Radio, and Television* 8 (Summer 1954): 400–404.

Schulte-Sasse, Jochen. "Toward a 'Culture' for the Masses: The Socio-
Psychological Function of Popular Literature in Germany and the U.S.,
1880–1920." *New German Critique* 29 (Spring/Summer 1983): 85–105.

Schulte-Sasse, Linda. "Retrieving the City as *Heimat:* Berlin in Nazi Cinema."
In *Berlin: Culture and Metropolis,* edited by C. W. Haxthausen and H.
Suhr, 166–86. Minneapolis: University of Minnesota Press, 1990.

Schwab-Felisch, Hans. "Die Affäre Harlan." *Der Monat* 3, no. 28 (January
1951): 414–22.

Seidl, Claudius. *Der deutsche Film der fünfziger Jahre.* Munich: Wilhelm
Heyne Verlag, 1987.

Silberman, Marc. "Semper fidelis: Staudte's *The Subject*." In *German Film and Literature: Adaptations and Transformations*, edited by Eric Rentschler, 146–60. New York: Methuen, 1986.

Silverman, Kaja. "Historical Trauma and Male Subjectivity." In *Psychoanalysis and Cinema*, edited by E. Ann Kaplan, 110–27. New York: Routledge, 1990.

Sixteen Encyclicals of His Holiness Pope Pius XI. Washington, D.C.: National Catholic Welfare Conference, n.d.

Sorlin, Pierre. *European Cinemas, European Societies, 1939–1990*. London: Routledge, 1991.

Spielmann, Yvonne. *Eine Pfütze in bezug aufs Mehr: Avantgarde*. Frankfurt: Peter Lang Verlag, 1991.

Spiker, Jürgen. *Film und Kapital: Der Weg der deutschen Filmwirtschaft zum nationalsozialistischen Einheitskonzern*. Berlin: Spiess, 1975.

Spotts, Frederic. *The Churches and Politics in Germany*. Middletown, Conn.: Wesleyan University Press, 1973.

Spreng, Eberhard. "Propaganda als Unterhaltung?: Drei Regisseure des deutschen Films, 1929–1945." In *Projekt: Spurensicherung—Alltag und Widerstand im Berlin der 30er Jahre*. Berlin: Elefanten Press, 1983.

Stacey, Jackie. *Star Gazing: Hollywood Cinema and Female Spectatorship*. New York: Routledge, 1994.

Stark, Gary D. "Cinema, Society, and the State: Policing the Film Industry in Imperial Germany." In *Essays in Culture and Society in Modern Germany*, edited by Gary D. Stark and B. K. Lackner, 122–66. College Station: Texas A & M University Press, 1982.

Stettner, Herbert. *Kino in der Stadt: Eine Frankfurter Chronik*. Frankfurt: Eichborn Verlag, 1984.

Tautz, Eberhard. "Die zweite Mannheimer Kultur- und Dokumentarfilmwoche." *Mannheimer Hefte* 2 (1953): 35–36.

Tent, James F. *Mission on the Rhine: Reeducation and Denazification in American Occupied Germany*. Chicago: Chicago University Press, 1982.

Theis, Wolfgang. " 'Anders als du und ich' (§175)/'Different from You and Me' (§175)." In *Vergessene Zukunft/Forgotten Future*, edited by Christian Philipp Müller, 56–75. Munich: Kunstverein München and Edition Atelier, 1992.

Thelan, David. "Memory and American History." *Journal of American History* 75, no. 4 (March 1989): 1117–29.

Theweleit, Klaus. *Male Fantasies*. Vol. 1, *Women, Floods, Bodies, History*. Translated by S. Conway, E. Carter, and C. Turner; foreword by Barbara Ehrenreich. Minneapolis: University of Minnesota Press, 1987.

Thiel, Reinold E. "Obrigkeitszensur und Gruppenzensur." *Filmkritik* 2 (February 1964): 67–72.

Thierfelder, Jörg. "Die Kirchenpolitik der vier Besatzungsmächte und die evangelische Kirche nach der Kapitulation 1945." *Geschichte und Gesellschaft* 18 (1992): 5–21.

Thompson, Kristin. *Exporting Entertainment: America in the World Market, 1907–1934.* London: British Film Institute, 1985.

Tröger, Annemarie. "Between Rape and Prostitution: Survival Strategies and Chances of Emancipation for Berlin Women after World War II." Translated by Joan Reutershan. In *Women in Culture and Politics: A Century of Change,* edited by Judith Friedlander et al., 97–117. Bloomington: Indiana University Press, 1986.

Trommler, Frank. "Working-Class Culture and Modern Mass Culture before World War I." *New German Critique* 29 (Spring/Summer 1983): 57–70.

Trommler, Frank, and Joseph McVeigh, eds. *America and the Germans: An Assessment of a Three-Hundred-Year History.* Vol. 2, *The Relationship in the Twentieth Century.* Philadelphia: University of Pennsylvania Press, 1990.

Trumpener, Katie. "Theory, History, and German Film." *Monatshefte* 82, no. 3 (1990): 294–306.

Turner, Henry Ashby, Jr. *The Two Germanies since 1945.* New Haven: Yale University Press, 1987.

Turner, Ian D. *Reconstruction in Post-War Germany: British Occupation Policy and the Western Zones, 1945–1955.* New York: Berg, 1989.

Ungureit, Heinz. "Filmpolitik in der Bundesrepublik." *Filmkritik* 1 (January 1964): 9–16.

Usborne, Cornelie. "The Christian Churches and the Regulation of Sexuality in Weimar Germany." In *Disciplines of Faith: Studies in Religion, Politics, and Patriarchy,* edited by J. Obelkevich, L. Roper, and R. Samuel. London: Routledge & Kegan Paul, 1987.

———. *The Politics of the Body in Weimar Germany: Women's Reproductive Rights and Duties.* Ann Arbor: University of Michigan Press, 1992.

U.S. Information Agency. *Communist Propaganda: A Fact Book, 1957–1958.* Washington, D.C., 1958.

Verband der Film- und Fernsehschaffenden der Deutschen Democratischen Republik. "Berlin: Dossier einer Großstadt." Special issue of *Film und Fernsehen* 6 (June 1987).

Vogel, Angela. "Familie." In *Die Bundesrepublik Deutschland,* vol. 2, *Gesellschaft,* edited by Wolfgang Benz, 98–126. Frankfurt: Fischer Taschenbuch Verlag, 1985.

Voigt, Hans-Gunter. "Markttag am Wittenbergplatz: Dokumentarfilme der zwanziger Jahre." *Film und Fernsehen* 6 (1987): 21–24.

Vollnhals, Clemens. "Die Evangelische Kirche zwischen Traditionswahrung und Neuorientierung." In *Von Stalingrad zur Währungsreform: Zur*

Sozialgeschichte des Umbruchs in Deutschland, 3d ed., Quellen und Darstellungen zur Zeitgeschichte, Institut für Zeitgeschichte, vol. 26, edited by Martin Broszat, Klaus-Dietmar Henke, and Hans Woller, 113–67. Munich: R. Oldenbourg Verlag, 1990.

Wagnleitner, Reinhold. "The Irony of American Culture Abroad: Austria and the Cold War." In *Recasting America: Culture and Politics in the Age of Cold War,* edited by Larry May, 285–301. Chicago: University of Chicago Press, 1989.

Weiss, Andrea. *Vampires and Violets: Lesbians in Film.* New York: Penguin Books, 1993.

Welch, David. "A Medium for the Masses: Ufa and Imperial German Film Propaganda during the First World War." *Historical Journal of Film, Radio, and Television* 6, no. 1 (1986): 85–91.

———. *Propaganda and the German Cinema, 1933–1945.* New York: Oxford University Press, 1983.

———, ed. *Nazi Propaganda: The Power and the Limitations.* Totowa, N.J.: Barnes and Noble Books, 1983.

Westdeutscher Kurzfilmtagen. *Dreißig Jahre Oberhausen: Eine kritische Retrospektive.* Oberhausen: Verlag Karl Maria Laufen, 1984.

Westermann, Bärbel. *Nationale Identität im Spielfilm der fünfziger Jahre.* New York: Peter Lang, 1990.

Wexman, Virginia Wright. *Creating the Couple: Love, Marriage, and Hollywood Performance.* Princeton: Princeton University Press, 1993.

Whalen, Robert Weldon. *Bitter Wounds: German Victims of the Great War, 1914–1939.* Ithaca, N.Y.: Cornell University Press, 1984.

Willenbacher, Barbara. "Zerrüttung und Bewährung der Nachkriegs-Familie." In *Von Stalingrad zur Währungsreform: Zur Sozialegeschichte des Umbruchs in Deutschland,* 3d ed., Quellen und Darstellungen zur Zeitgeschichte, Institut für Zeitgeschichte, vol. 26, edited by Martin Broszat, Klaus-Dietmar Henke, and Hans Woller, 595–618. Munich: R. Oldenbourg Verlag, 1990.

Willett, Ralf. *The Americanization of Germany, 1945–1949.* London: Routledge, 1989.

Willis, F. Roy. *The French in Germany, 1945–1949.* Stanford: Stanford University Press, 1962.

Winkler, Andrea. "Starkult auf germanisch: Goebbels und Hitler hielten sich an die Rezepte Hollywoods." *Medium* 18, no. 3 (July–September 1988): 27–30.

Witte, Karsten. "Visual Pleasure Inhibited: Aspects of the German Revue Film." *New German Critique* 24/25 (Fall/Winter 1981/82): 238–63.

Wolf, Steffen. *Filmförderung oder Zensur?: Von "Der dritte Mann" bis "Otto—der Film." Gedanken zum Film, zur Filmbewertung, und zur*

Filmförderung. 35. Jahre Filmbewertungsstelle Wiesbaden (FBW), 1951–1986. Ebersberg: Edition Achteinhalb, Lothar Just, 1986.

Wollenberg, H. H. *Fifty Years of German Film.* London: Falcon Press, 1948. Reprint, New York: Arno Press and New York Times, 1972.

Woller, Hans. *Gesellschaft und Politik in der amerikanischen Besatzungszone: Die Region Ansbach und Fürth.* Munich: R. Oldenbourg Verlag, 1986.

Zinnecker, Jürgen. *Jugendkultur, 1940–1985.* Opladen: Leske und Budrich, 1987.

INDEX